Wha... ...u'd like
to have...

A large ... ...urch, followed
by home, ...y club reception where
everyone is ...ed?

A formal, semiformal or informal church or
chapel wedding, followed by a small home or club
reception to which only the families and intimate
friends are invited?

A small wedding in a church, club or home to
which only a few friends and the two families are
asked, followed by a reception which includes all
your friends?

A garden, home or club wedding which includes a reception for everyone?

A small chapel wedding without a reception
where the bridal couple receive friends in the
foyer of the church or chapel?

A military wedding (usually formal) at the
chapel on the Army Post or Navy Base, followed
by a large reception at home or at the officers'
club on the Post?

The purpose of this book is to help you fulfill
your heart's desire, plan *your wedding* without
having a nervous breakdown or spending next
year's income, and above all have a good time in
the busy weeks ahead. Here's a design for spinning that special day into a cherished memory so
wonderful that even your grandchildren will want
to hear about it over and over again. Moreover
the book is so completely informative on all points
of wedding procedure that you will want to keep
it in your library for reference when you are invited to somebody else's wedding!

Your Wedding

YOUR
WEDDING

How To Plan and Enjoy It

NEW AND
REVISED EDITION

By

MARJORIE
BINFORD
WOODS

Illustrated by
JEAN BAKER

THE BOBBS-MERRILL COMPANY • INC.

Indianapolis   *Publishers*   New York

Dedicated to *You*—Today's Bride
with the wish
that *your wedding* will graciously follow
the time-honored dignities
and fine traditions of the past . . .
yet be as individual
and precious in expression
as your own romantic love.

TABLE OF CONTENTS

CHAPTER I

FROM THIS DAY FORTH

19-23

THE GRACIOUS WAY IS THE CORRECT WAY	20
HAPPY IS THE BRIDE WHO BEGINS AT THE BEGINNING	21
It's a Family Occasion	21
It's the Bridegroom's Wedding Too	22
Budget Your Time, Money, Energy	22

CHAPTER II

A TOKEN AND A PLEDGE

24-33

HOW SHALL I ANNOUNCE MY ENGAGEMENT?	24
WHEN SHALL I MAKE THE ANNOUNCEMENT?	24
HOW ABOUT AN ANNOUNCEMENT PARTY?	26
ANY QUESTIONS?	27
When Parents Are Divorced	28
Broken Engagements	28
PRENUPTIAL PARTIES	29
WHO SHOULD GIVE SHOWERS?	29
KINDS OF SHOWERS	30
ENTERTAINING FOR YOUR BRIDESMAIDS	31
IS THERE TO BE A BACHELOR'S DINNER?	32
THE BRIDAL DINNER	32
THE MEETING OF THE CLAN	33

CHAPTER III

RULES TO HONOR AND OBEY

34-52

TIME TO GET READY	34
BRIDE'S WORKING SCHEDULE	36
First of All	36
Next in Order	37
Necessary Reminders	38
Check List for Last Week	39
WHAT TYPE OF WEDDING FOR YOU?	41
CERTAIN THINGS YOU CAN'T GET AWAY FROM	42
Responsibilities of the Bride's Family	42
Responsibilities of the Bridegroom	43
GET YOUR CALENDAR IN HAND	43
WHAT TIME SHOULD IT BE?	44
WHAT SORT OF RECEPTION SHOULD FOLLOW?	45
SPECIAL TIPS TO MEMBERS OF BOTH FAMILIES	46
The Bride's Family	46
Mother's Responsibilities	46
Dear Old Dad	47
The Groom's Family	48
HOW A WISE BRIDE LED HER MAN *Straight* TO THE ALTAR	49
REMINDERS FOR THE BRIDEGROOM	50
SPECIAL QUESTIONS AND ANSWERS	52

CHAPTER IV

CONSIDER YOUR WORLDLY GOODS

53-84

MEASURE YOUR POCKETBOOK	53
WHAT ABOUT THE MAN IN YOUR LIFE?	54
RENTAL DEPARTMENTS OFFER A SOLUTION	55
THE SEMIFORMAL DRESS	56
INFORMAL DRESS	57

Table of Contents ix

GETTING DOWN TO BRASS TACKS 58
IS IT TO BE A FORMAL CHURCH WEDDING? 59
GET IN STRIDE 61
MAKE NOTES AS YOU GO ALONG 63
DETAILS TO BE NOTED 64
   Arrival at the Church 64
   Preliminaries to the Ceremony 66
   Procedure for Leaving the Church 68
THE FORMAL HOME WEDDING 68
   Keep a Home Atmosphere 69
   What About Music? 71
   No Recessional 72
THE CLUB OR HOTEL WEDDING 73
WHAT TO WEAR FOR A FORMAL DAYTIME WEDDING 74
WHAT TO WEAR FOR A FORMAL EVENING WEDDING 75
SEMIFORMAL WEDDING 76
WHAT TO WEAR FOR A SEMIFORMAL DAYTIME WEDDING 79
WHAT TO WEAR FOR A SEMIFORMAL EVENING WEDDING 80
THE INFORMAL WEDDING 81
WHAT TO WEAR FOR AN INFORMAL DAYTIME OR
   EVENING WEDDING 83
CHECK LIST FOR ANY TYPE OF WEDDING 84

CHAPTER V

THE HONOUR OF YOUR PRESENCE IS REQUESTED

85-109

MAKING UP YOUR LISTS 86
WHO ISSUES THE INVITATIONS? 87
FORM OF INVITATION 87
WORDING OF INVITATION 88
RECEPTION CARDS 89
TYPICAL INVITATION FORMS 90
   Church Admission Cards 92
   Pew Cards 92
   Invitation to a Club Wedding 93

Announcements   93
   Typical Announcement Form   94
   "At Home" Cards   94
Addressing Invitations or Announcements   95
Attendants Receive Invitations   96
Special Courtesy to Groom's Family   96
Should Minister and Wife Receive an
   Engraved Invitation?   97
When to Mail   97
Special Invitations and Announcements   98
   When Parents Are Divorced   98
   If the Bride's Mother Has Remarried   99
   When the Bride's Mother Is Widowed   100
   When a Bride Is Being Sponsored by Other than Parents 101
   If It's Altar Trip Number Two   102
Double Weddings   103
Special Announcements   105
   For Divorcees   105
Military Weddings   106
When Wedding Invitations Must Be Recalled   108

CHAPTER VI

IN THE PRESENCE OF THIS COMPANY

110-119

How Many Bridesmaids?   110
Maid and Matron of Honor   111
Junior Bridesmaids   112
Flower Girls   113
Ring Bearer   113
Ushers   114
Who Is to Give You Away?   115
The Best Man   116
Case History of a Best Man Who Enjoyed Himself   117

CHAPTER VII

THE VOW AND COVENANT

120-130

THE MILITARY WEDDING	120
MEN'S DRESS REGULATIONS	121
RECEPTION PROTOCOL AND REMINDERS	122
THE GARDEN WEDDING	123
Any Mood You Choose	123
THE DOUBLE WEDDING	125
IF IT IS ALTAR TRIP NUMBER TWO	126
IF THE BRIDE'S PARENTS ARE DIVORCED	127
THE OLDER BRIDE	128
THE CIVIL CEREMONY	129
IS IT EVER PERMISSIBLE?	130

CHAPTER VIII

IN HOLY WEDLOCK

131-150

ANY CHURCH FEES?	131
CHURCH REGULATIONS TO HONOR	132
FAVORED HOURS FOR PROTESTANT WEDDINGS	132
NO SPECIAL RESTRICTIONS FOR WEDDING PARTY	133
MARRIAGE OF DIVORCED PERSONS	133
THE MARRIAGE CEREMONY	133
THE PROTESTANT EPISCOPAL SERVICE	134
THE QUAKER WEDDING	138
THE ROMAN CATHOLIC WEDDING	139
Time of Marriage	140
Special Rulings	141
Usual Place of Marriage	141
Procedure at Altar	142

ORTHODOX CATHOLIC WEDDING 143
  Ceremonial Essentials 143
  Attendants' Duties 144
  Altar Procedure 144
SYMBOLIC LUTHERAN WEDDING CUSTOMS 145
THE ORTHODOX JEWISH WEDDING 146
  Customary Head Coverings 147
  The Wedding Canopy Used in Traditional Ceremonies 148
  The Wine-Cup Ceremony 148
SPECIAL QUESTIONS AND ANSWERS 150

CHAPTER IX

TO BE REMEMBERED AS LONG AS YOU BOTH SHALL LIVE

151-177

WHAT SUITS YOU? 151
COLORS AND FABRICS 153
HARMONY IS THE THING 155
WHAT LENGTH TRAIN? 155
YOUR WEDDING VEIL 156
HEADDRESSES 158
WHAT COLOR HOSE? 159
SHOES 159
WILL YOU NEED GLOVES? 160
WEDDING COSTUME 160
IT'S TIME TO OUTFIT YOUR ATTENDANTS! 161
SPRING AND SUMMER WEDDINGS 163
FALL AND WINTER WEDDINGS 164
CHRISTMAS WEDDING SUGGESTIONS 165
DOUBLE-WEDDING SUGGESTIONS 166
AS TO FABRICS 168
BRIDESMAIDS' HEADDRESSES 168
GLOVES AND SHOES FOR BRIDESMAIDS 169
  Note 170

THE MOTHERS' COSTUMES 170
  For a Morning Wedding 171
  For an Afternoon Wedding 171
  Evening 172
  Informal Weddings 172
KEEP THE RECORD CLEAR 172
SENDING WEDDING ANNOUNCEMENT TO NEWSPAPERS 173
TYPICAL WEDDING ANNOUNCEMENT 174
YOUR WEDDING PHOTOGRAPHS 177

CHAPTER X

TO HAVE AND TO HOLD

178-190

GIFTS . . . COMING AND GOING 178
FROM THE BRIDEGROOM TO HIS ATTENDANTS 179
WHEN TO PRESENT THE ATTENDANTS' GIFTS 179
GIFTS TO OTHER FRIENDS WHO SERVE AT YOUR WEDDING .. 179
FROM THE BRIDE TO THE GROOM AND VICE VERSA 180
DON'T HESITATE TO SPEAK UP ON THE
    WEDDING-GIFT SUBJECT 180
YOUR SILVER PATTERN 181
MATCH YOUR CHINA, SILVER AND CRYSTAL 182
GET ORGANIZED BEFORE GIFTS START ARRIVING 183
DISPLAY OF GIFTS 184
CARDS LEFT ON? 185
WRITING YOUR THANK-YOU NOTES 186
WHEN A GIFT HAS TO BE RETURNED 188
SPECIAL QUESTIONS AND ANSWERS 189

CHAPTER XI

STRAINS OF LOHENGRIN

191-197

PRELIMINARY MUSIC 191
INCIDENTAL ORGAN MUSIC 191

Introduction 192
Processional 192
Recessional 192
During the Ceremony 192
ARE YOU HAVING A VOCALIST? 193
MUSIC FOR HOME WEDDING 195
MUSIC FOR THE PROCESSION 195
DURING THE CEREMONY 196
WILL THERE BE A CHOIR? 196
RECEPTION MUSIC 196

CHAPTER XII

ROSE PETALS IN YOUR PATHWAY

198-210

CHURCH DECORATIONS 198
FOR A SPRINGTIME WEDDING 199
IS IT TO BE A SUMMERTIME CEREMONY? 200
FOR AN AUTUMN WEDDING 202
A WINTER WEDDING 203
FLOWERS FOR A HOME WEDDING 204
A GARDEN WEDDING 205
FLOWERS FOR THE BRIDE'S TABLE 206
YOUR BRIDAL BOUQUET 206
CORSAGES FOR INFORMAL WEDDINGS 208
BRIDESMAIDS' BOUQUETS 209

CHAPTER XIII

MEMORIES TO CHERISH

211-231

RECEIVING LINE 212
A WEDDING BREAKFAST OR SUPPER 214

High Tea for the Afternoon Wedding 214
The Bride's Cake 214
If It's a Military Wedding 216
Cutting the Cake 216
Bridal-Table Seating Arrangements 218
At a Large Breakfast or Supper 219
Appointments for the Bridal Table 220
Catering Service 221
What to Drink? 222
A Toast to the Bride 223
A Borrowed European Custom 224
Menu Suggestions 225
   Wedding Breakfast 225
   Sit-Down Breakfast Suggestions 226
   Buffet Breakfast 226
   Afternoon Reception 227
   Evening Supper 227
Throwing Your Bouquet 227
Saying Your Farewells 228
Romance Is Its Own Reward 229
Check List for Any Reception 230

CHAPTER XIV

THE HAPPY WAY

232-241

For Wedding Guests 232
You Are Invited to a Wedding! 232
Typical Form for Formal Acceptance 233
Typical Formal Reply Sending Regrets 233
Replies to Informal Invitations 234
Upon Receipt of a Wedding Announcement 234
It's Time to Send a Wedding Gift 235

SHOWER GIFTS 236
WHAT TO WEAR TO A WEDDING 236
ARRIVING AT A CHURCH WEDDING 237
GUEST INFORMATION FOR A HOME OR CLUB WEDDING 238
RECEIVING LINE PROCEDURE 239
DINING-ROOM ETIQUETTE 240
SPECIAL NICETIES 240

CHAPTER XV

FOR BETTER OR WORSE

242-257

PLAY YOUR PART 242
WHO IS TO TAKE CHARGE? 242
WHO SHOULD ATTEND THE WEDDING REHEARSAL? 243
WHAT STEP WILL THE WEDDING PARTY USE? 244
PROCEDURE FOR CHURCH WEDDING 245
HOME OR CLUB WEDDING 249
INSTRUCTIONS TO THE USHERS 250
  Things Every Usher Should Know 250
BEST MAN 252
MAID OF HONOR 253
PROCEDURE AT CATHOLIC WEDDING 253
PROCEDURE FOR DOUBLE WEDDING 254
MILITARY WEDDING 255
  Recessional 256

CHAPTER XVI

"I PLIGHT THEE MY TROTH"

258-260

YOUR WEDDING DAY 258

Your Wedding

CHAPTER I

From This Day Forth

THIS IS A BOOK ON HOW TO PLAN YOUR WEDDING WITHOUT
having a nervous breakdown or spending next year's income.

It is a guide on how to have a good time in the midst of
wedding welter; how to satisfy your romantic soul and be as
sentimental as you always swore you wouldn't be.

Once, when you were young and blasé about life, you probably disclaimed any interest in all the fuss and feathers of a
wedding. Why couldn't two people simply run around the
corner to the Justice of the Peace and be married—without
involving anyone else?

. . . But that was before you fell in love.

Now you are probably looking longingly at church aisles
and wondering if all the frightening things the etiquette
books say can be true.

If your Timid Soul is quaking and quivering over the wedding question, perish the thought here and now that stuffy

pomposity must go hand in hand with a real wedding. There
are no hidebound rules that need keep you tossing in a sleep-
less bed or necessitate melting grandma's silver service to
meet expenses.

Wedding etiquette in the deep-rooted traditional sense has
remained steadfast to inherited dignities and customs. As today's bride you'll wear "something old, something new, something borrowed, something blue," just as your mother and
grandmother did before you; you'll walk to the altar in slow
measured tread; you'll choose a bride's cake filled with good
luck tokens and toss your bridal bouquet in customary manner to the next bride-to-be.

But beyond the fundamental formalities founded upon
tradition, convenience, good manners and sentiment which
you will follow, you can write your own ticket and use as
much originality as you choose, whether it's an informal home
ceremony or a big church wedding.

It has been discovered by practical experience that the gracious and natural way of conducting a wedding is the correct
way. You can't double time your steps up the aisleway, nor
chant your vows to a swoon tune. But as long as you carry
out dignity and charm in all corresponding details, it isn't so
much what you do in your wedding as the way you do it.

It has been proved too (and you'd better sit up and take
notice) that some of the most beautiful weddings and those
which linger longest in everyone's memory are the most un-
pretentious affairs. They may have been carried out for a
mere song but with such an effective background of intelli-
gent planning and with such ingenious touches that they seem
to have been created by heaven itself.

It is not just the picture your wedding presents to your guests that makes it worth while. More important is what it does for you and your bridegroom. A couple misses something very meaningful if this most momentous event doesn't reflect romance, religious solemnity and beauty of atmosphere.

So remember . . . it isn't just *a wedding* you are having— but *your wedding!* As individual and precious as your love. So wonderful even your grandchildren will want to hear about it over and over again.

HAPPY IS THE BRIDE WHO BEGINS AT THE BEGINNING

The beginning is your attitude.

Right now you are giddy with hearts and flowers. Life is utterly super-delicious.

The trick is to keep it that way.

Just being a prospective bride puts you on a sort of pedestal, out of the realm of humdrum things. Your family is ready to give you the moon if they can reach it; your friends and relatives are standing by to help celebrate your heyday.

It's a once-in-a-lifetime period (with all patents pending). Do make the most of it.

Ever since you were a babe in arms your mother has been conjuring up dreams of you on your wedding day. Don't let her down now. Be your gayest, happiest self. Go into close family conferences and make your plans together.

Try to avoid hurting the sensibilities of the people you care most about. Listen to their ideas with both your heart and mind. You may think them old-fashioned, but then . . . isn't marriage?

Share your thrills and happiness with everyone who cares. Give a smile to salespeople . . . soft answers to the seamstress who sits at your feet pinning up your wedding gown.

Etiquette, actually, is only a formal word for courtesy, based on kindness. You don't have to know all the rules of etiquette to show consideration and thoughtfulness to others. But when you do recognize the value of both good manners and accepted social custom you can gracefully take any situation in your stride while charting happy wedding plans.

Don't treat the bridegroom as the forgotten man. He plays a part in this event too, remember, even though he is helpless to do much about it. He may balk at the idea of a wedding at first, but he'll enjoy showing you off when he gets into the spirit of the debacle. Consult him along the way and he'll be less bewildered.

Make up your mind to take the little disappointments in your stride (some are bound to come) . . . along with your share of blissful thrills.

Discourage your friends from filling *all* your prenuptial days and nights with showers and parties. Leave some time to yourself to relax the last few weeks. (Suggest some after-honeymoon parties if your calendar begins to take on the semblance of a railway schedule.)

If you budget your time, your money and your energy you won't lose your sweet serenity because of muddle-mad lists, aching feet and that befuddled "where-do-I-go-from-here" feeling.

"Marriages may be made in heaven," your mother will

sigh and say, "but the practical fact still remains that they are performed here on earth."

Right she is! And this book has been designed to deal firmly with wedding complications and the necessary details without skipping a single heartbeat. (This goes for your mother's heart too.)

The "What to do first, second, third, et cetera department" is set up for you on the following pages. Don't try to absorb all the information in one sitting. Study it as diligently as you studied your college textbooks. Simplify to your heart's content, if you must . . . but whatever you do, have fun!

CHAPTER II

A Token and Pledge

HOW SHALL I ANNOUNCE MY ENGAGEMENT?

DON'T DEPEND ON THE GRAPEVINE ROUTE AND DON'T SEND out engraved announcements.

Scatter the tidings by note to close friends and relatives. Then tell the rest of the breathless world of your engagement by formal announcement in local newspapers, both yours and the bridegroom's. The simple way of proclaiming the news is the smartest way.

Your family should sponsor this announcement and the task of sending the information to the society editors falls to your mother. The item should be a mere statement of fact, typed in double space, with release date clearly marked, and your telephone number listed for verification. The customary deadline for Sunday editions is early in the week, so be sure to check if you wish a week-end announcement.

Order glossy prints from the photographic studio if your picture is to appear with the notice. Mark name and address on back of photos for identification.

WHEN SHALL I MAKE THE ANNOUNCEMENT?

You may make your announcement three or four months before the wedding and withhold the wedding date until later. Or you may want to announce a definite wedding date, if one has been set.

Your enraptured friends will appreciate it more if they have a breathing spell for planning your prenuptial parties. It will also give you a leisurely period for spinning your marriage plans—and a definite date to work toward.

Don't announce your engagement farther ahead than a year (life is too uncertain) or less than six weeks before the wedding date, if you can manage it.

As a guide for your announcement notice to the papers, follow one of these forms:

Mr. and Mrs. William Graham Brown announce the engagement of their daughter, Nancy Ann, to Mr. Paul Allen Tucker, son of Mr. and Mrs. George Marvin Tucker. No date has been set for the wedding.

Or:

The engagement has been announced of Miss Nancy Ann Brown, daughter of Mr. and Mrs. William Graham Brown, to Mr. Paul Allen Tucker, son of Mr. and Mrs. George Marvin Tucker. The wedding will take place in the spring.

Or you may announce the definite time and place of the wedding in either form. If the society editors wish more details in announcement, you may include facts on schooling and club memberships, along with information on your fiancé's business affiliation.

When in doubt be as brief as possible and model your announcement after those used in your own community papers.

How About an Announcement Party?

We have our tongue in our cheek on the announcement party subject. Nine out of ten girls skip it. But, go ahead, if you must have your bit of fanfare. Surprises *are* fun!

The party is your family's responsibility, of course, although now and then an intimate friend of the bride may step in and do the honors.

It may be a tea or a luncheon just for the girls, with your mother as hostess. (Don't forget your prospective mama-in-law.) Or a cocktail party, or a dance.

Rehearse your dad or big brother on an announcement speech in your and the bridegroom's behalf. A phonograph recording might be made beforehand—then played at the propitious moment, just for novelty. In a more traditional manner, you might have gay little boutonnieres (tagged with the two names) heaped artistically in a shallow basket, to be given to each guest as a surprise favor.

There are a great variety of ways to make your party announcement but guard against straining to be clever or coy. Place cards at a dinner party or luncheon might be facsimiles of a newspaper clipping proclaiming the news, or you might have initialed candy mints or petits fours as a teatime triumph. What about having match booklets coupling your first names or novelty brick ice cream with frozen names in contrasting colors?

Make it festive if you wish, but do soft-pedal too much emphasis on the cupid theme.

ANY QUESTIONS?

Q. Should the modern swain ask the girl's father for her hand, as in days gone by?

A. It's much more likely that today's couple will go together to the bride's family to break the news casually. However, that serious talk between father and future son-in-law should take place sometime before things go too far.

Q. What is the bridegroom's parents' duty toward the bride?

A. Etiquette or no etiquette, the bride-elect naturally expects to be welcomed by her future in-laws. If they live at a distance they write to her at once to extend their felicitations, and usually invite her to visit them. If they live near by, the fiancé's mother and probably his sisters call upon the bride and her mother. If they are socially inclined they may wish to give a tea or a dinner in her honor. At least some gesture of hospitality is expected—a family dinner or Sunday-night supper which includes the bride's parents as well.

When Parents Are Divorced

Q. How should an announcement be made when parents are divorced?

A. If the bride-to-be is living with her divorced mother, the announcement is made in the mother's name. If her mother has married again she may, if everyone so desires, send out the announcement in the name of the stepfather as well. It may read:

"Mr. and Mrs. Clifford Berg announce the engagement of her daughter, Mary Stewart White, to . . . etc."

The same rule applies if the girl is living with her father.

Broken Engagements

Q. What is the procedure when an engagement is broken?

A. If the engagement has been formally announced in the papers a notice should be sent immediately to the same papers. The notice usually takes this form:

The engagement of Miss Nancy Ann Brown and Mr. Paul Allen Tucker has been terminated by mutual consent.

The engagement ring and all presents should be returned at once. If wedding invitations have been issued, engraved cards should be sent to everyone who has received an invitation. (See page 86.) If there is not sufficient time for engraved cards, members of the bride's family may recall the invitations verbally, by personal note, telegram or telephone.

In the tragic instance of a fiancé's death prior to the wedding, presents are always returned by thoughtful members of the bride's family.

PRENUPTIAL PARTIES

The prenuptial festivities that go hand in hand with a wedding are all part of the fun.

Borrow any pretty excuse you please for entertaining your bridal party and those who drop by to see your wedding gifts and trousseau trappings, but do discourage your friends from booking a marathon of showers and parties for you. An excessive number wears everyone out—*you* included.

WHO SHOULD GIVE SHOWERS?

Your friends may entertain with shower parties in your honor, but the bridegroom's immediate family or yours should never give a shower.

If the families wish to book a gala event or two which includes both of you for an evening get-together, or as a feminine affair, such parties should have no gift-strings attached.

Do act surprised at your showers, even though you may have known long beforehand exactly what was coming.

Be sure to follow up each party with a sincere thank-you note to the hostess, and individual notes to gift donors some time before the wedding.

KINDS OF SHOWERS

The setting for a shower may be almost anything—a breakfast, luncheon, dinner or afternoon tea for ladies only. Or it may be a cocktail party, dance, supper or evening party where the bridegroom and his friends are included.

If you are asked to specify the kinds of showers you would like, you may mention with perfect propriety any of your

personal choices. They may include anything from linen, kitchen, bar and bathroom showers, to boudoir, notions or cupboard delicacies.

An "idea shower" is a novelty with no drain on the purse strings. The shower hostess provides a leather-bound loose-leaf notebook with the bride's name inscribed on the cover. The guests then contribute to the book by filling the pages with favorite household tricks, coveted recipes and helpful ideas to start her on the right track as a homemaker.

There are book showers and magazine subscription showers appropriate for couples who are avid readers; a library shower with rare secondhand volumes by old masters, to serve as a substantial cornerstone for a future collection.

A wine or liqueur shower for both bride and groom might be appreciated, if your fiancé wishes to stock up for later entertaining.

Shower invitations may be issued by informally written notes or by telephone, telegram or by trick invitations devised by a clever hostess.

Your mother, and the bridegroom's mother, are often invited to your shower parties, but as honor guests they are not asked to contribute to the shower fund (if one pitch-in gift is given) or to bring individual gifts.

ENTERTAINING FOR YOUR BRIDESMAIDS

A farewell luncheon for your bridal party is a traditional part of the festivities of a big formal wedding. It is sometimes called "the spinster luncheon" (or dinner) and should take place a few days before the wedding. You may give your presents to the attendants at this party if you wish, or you may present them at the bridal dinner, or at an informal ceremony at your home.

Invitations usually are issued by word of mouth or by an informal note and the occasion may be as festive in décor as you want to make it. Often there's a bride's cake of lady pink with pink icing and sentimental fortunes for everyone.

This party may be given even though the wedding is not to be formal. Or you may entertain your attendants more simply at an afternoon tea or trousseau affair where they can have a peep at your new wardrobe.

Is There to Be a Bachelor's Dinner?

John Groom has a perfect right to round up his friends and attendants for a farewell party, too, if he wishes. Many bridegrooms omit the bachelor's dinner nowadays because of the added expense, but it's a personal matter.

The dinner usually takes place at a club or in the private dining room of a hotel. Music is often provided, the guests invited informally by the groom, and the gifts to the ushers and best man presented at their places at table.

Though tradition has it that this dinner is a veritable carousal, this is rarely the case today. It is wise, however to schedule the dinner to take place several nights before the wedding, so that there may be more free time for the bride and groom as the wedding time nears.

The age-honored glass-breaking ceremony is the high light of the bachelor's dinner according to custom. In this sentimental rite the bridegroom, toward the end of the dinner, rises and holds his champagne-filled glass high as he says, "To the bride!" Every man rises, drinks the toast standing, then breaks the delicate stem of the wine glass. The idea of so destroying the glasses is that these particular wine glasses may never be used for "a less honorable purpose."

The Bridal Dinner

The bridal dinner is given by the bride's parents in honor of the bridal couple. The invitation list includes all members of the wedding party, the bridegroom's parents, the minister and his wife (if they are well known to the host and hostess) and any out-of-town relatives of the bride and groom who have come on for the wedding.

If the dinner is formal it should be in the nature of a seated affair with floral decorations and place cards. (See bridal table chart for seating arrangements, page 219.)

If the wedding is less formal it may be a buffet dinner or an after-rehearsal supper party, where the wedding attendants receive their gifts from the bride and the groom.

Guests are invited by the bride's mother for any type of bridal dinner. The invitations may be by word of mouth or by personal note.

The party may be held in the bride's family home, or at a club or hotel and is customarily planned to take place the night before the wedding, with the rehearsal following.

THE MEETING OF THE CLAN

Sometime before the wedding the thoughtful bride will want to arrange an occasion where uncles, aunts, cousins, grandparents and old friends of both families have an opportunity to meet and get acquainted. A Sunday-afternoon tea, or Sunday-night supper would be an appropriate time, perhaps, and it should be a jolly, informal affair.

CHAPTER III

Rules to Honor and Obey

"HOW MUCH TIME SHOULD I HAVE TO PLAN MY WEDDING?"
Everyone asks this question. The answer is up to you and
your calendar.

Many a lovely wedding has been planned and carried out
in a few short weeks without causing nervous collapse or
family bankruptcy. So it *can* be done if you're geared for
speed and have a firm resolve to do or die.

But actually it's like the great oaks and little acorns adage.
You'll enjoy it more if you can start with the little things and
give them time to grow. It will add to your resources and
subtract from your liabilities in the long run.

You'll have more time to shop and so avoid the disappoint-
ment of hasty selections. You can be more deliberate in your
plans and so have fewer mistakes to charge up to inexperi-
ence in the final summing up. Remember, too, that perfection of detail and the happy air of ease really come from
careful preparation and advance concentration.

If your family is new at wedding preparations, you'll all
welcome a bride's time schedule to keep you moving steadily
in the right direction. It's simple to follow if you are good
at knowing your own mind and have fitted the kind of wedding you want to the time you have for getting ready.

Begin planning three months ahead if possible and build
a framework of budgets to cover "Wedding Expenses," "Re-

ception Expenses," "Trousseau Expenses." Then add another budget for "Extras."

Fortify yourself with a notebook for your own notes. Sharpen your pencil and follow the schedule step by step, noting down your decisions, and checking off the things accomplished. This chapter is your working guide and should be used constantly to check on your progress.

We recommend that you make each decision in the order in which the steps are presented here. Study each chapter to which you are referred and choose your own plan. Then go on to the next step.

To give you a graphic idea . . . here's the way to work.

Are you ready to decide on the type of wedding you'll have? Then turn to page 41 and study up on the various kinds of weddings there are. Get all the wise family heads together and come to some agreement on the first important question. Then set your date. Now turn back to the Bride's Working Schedule and check that off as settled. Proceed to the next reminder and follow through the entire chart up to the very last day.

Of course you'll probably run clear through this book first. But don't say we didn't warn you if you attempt to take all the chapters in one gulp. After you have reviewed the whole job of wedding preparation, calm down and go at the schedule week by week. That's the purpose of it—to keep you steadily moving on a well-organized plan.

BRIDE'S WORKING SCHEDULE

First of All

Go into a family huddle and decide on:

1. Type of wedding (page 41): Formal, Semiformal, Informal, Military.
2. Date and time (page 43).
3. Minister and organist. (Engage them now; you will have to consult them before the date and time can be considered final.)
4. Start work on invitation lists (page 86).
5. Type of reception, breakfast, or what have you. (Get estimates on catering and music.)

Choose your bridal attendants:

1. Your maid of honor, bridesmaids, flower girl, etc. (pages 110-114).
2. The bridegroom's best man (page 116) and ushers (page 114).

Use these references for your specific type of wedding:

Formal church wedding (page 59).

Formal home or club wedding (page 68).

Semiformal church or home wedding (page 76).

Garden wedding (page 123).

Informal wedding (page 81).

Wedding reception (page 45).

Begin shopping for trousseau, linens and household items.

Next in Order

Complete your guest lists and order:

1. Wedding invitations (page 87).
2. Announcements (page 93).
3. Note paper for handwritten notes if it's an informal or semiformal wedding (page 88).
4. Thank-you note paper (page 88).

This is a good time for showers and parties. (Don't let your friends book a long list of showers for you. Too many tire everyone out and are too great a financial drain for your circle of intimates.) (Page 29.)

Start addressing wedding invitations (page 87).

It's time to tell your friends your chosen patterns (page 30).

Shop for:

1. Wedding gown, veil, etc. (pages 74, 155, 163).
2. Bridesmaids' costumes (pages 74, 161, 163).
3. Your mother's gown (pages 75, 170).

Continue trousseau shopping.

Decide on gifts for your attendants (pages 31, 170, 178).

Necessary Reminders

Confer with florist and order flowers (page 198).

Mail formal wedding invitations three weeks from the date. If invitations are to be handwritten, mail them two or three weeks ahead.

Have wedding-gown fittings and bridesmaids' fittings. Get samples of all dresses (page 172).

Decide on musical selections for wedding (page 191).

Arrange for display of gifts (page 184).

Acknowledge each gift the day that it arrives (page 186).

Do you need a permanent?

Complete reception arrangements (page 45).

Order the bride's cake and wedding-cake boxes if you are having them (page 214).

Have bridal photograph taken at last wedding-gown fitting. Arrange for photographer to take wedding pictures at the reception (pages 60, 177).

Study rehearsal procedure for best altar effects (pages 63, 243).

Arrange for either:

1. Bridesmaids' luncheon four or five days before the wedding (page 31).
2. Or bridal dinner before or after rehearsal the night before the wedding. (See chart on page 218.)

Make plans for billeting out-of-town guests.

See proofs of your wedding pictures. Order glossy prints for the newspapers.

If it's a formal wedding, decide whether to dress at home

or at the church. Arrange for your bridal consultant, or someone, to help you dress and start you down the aisle.

Check List for Last Week

6 days before: Check to see if all trousseau purchases have arrived. Right sizes? Any additions?

Keep up to date with your thank-you notes.

Eat regularly all week.

Rest between times when you aren't receiving gifts and the many friends who are sure to be dropping in from now on.

5 days before: Are you having a bridesmaids' luncheon (page 31)? Everything ready? Have someone dependable around all the time with a car to run errands.

Don't stray off the path of note-writing.

Check and double check delivery instructions for all wedding clothes.

Confirm the wedding date with caterer, florist, etc.

4 days before: Do you have your wedding pictures?

Have ready all the wedding information for the newspapers (page 173).

Are the gifts rolling in? Don't forget to say "thank you" immediately.

Have you invited family friends to come in for tea and to see your gifts? It's a nice idea.

3 days before: Send wedding information to society editors (page 173).

Relax, if possible.

Have going-away clothes pressed and ready.

Any out-of-town guests due today? See that they are met.

2 days before: Check on final wedding details.

Review rehearsal procedure (page 242).

Is everything all set for the bridal dinner tomorrow night? Place cards written? Your dress pressed?

1 day before: Getting shivers of excitement? Take it easy! Have your hair done. Get a manicure, and make it a pale and demure shade of polish. See that bridesmaids have the same.

How about writing a few thank-you notes?

Better review the wedding gifts so you'll know their donors.

Pack all but last-minute things. Go to bridal dinner and rehearsal.

Your Wedding Day: This is *it*. Have breakfast in bed, can't you? Stay out of the way of caterers and their kitchen crew. Check on the florist as he decorates for the reception. Write some notes to keep your mind off the Big Moment.

Be leisurely about your dressing but be ready in plenty of time. Be moderate on the make-up. Depend on that *someone* who is to zip you up to arrange your train and veil as you start down the aisle.

If it isn't fun, what is it?

Best luck!

WHAT TYPE OF WEDDING FOR YOU?

This exciting decision really depends on your own heart's desires, the size of your budget, the size of your families (yours and the bridegroom's) and the number of relatives and guests you'll want to include.

It's bound to be *one* of these:

1. The large formal wedding in a church, followed by home, hotel or country-club reception where everyone is invited.

2. The formal, semiformal or informal church or chapel wedding, followed by a small home or club reception to which only the families and intimate friends are invited.

3. The small wedding in a church, club or home to which only a few friends and the two families are asked, followed by a reception which includes all your friends.

4. The garden, home or club wedding which includes reception for everyone.

5. The small chapel wedding without reception where bridal couple receive friends in foyer of the church or chapel.

6. The military wedding (usually formal) at the chapel on the Army Post or Navy Base, followed by a large reception at home or at the officers' club on the Post.

Which shall it be? (See wedding dress charts, pages 74-81.)

CERTAIN THINGS YOU CAN'T GET AWAY FROM

Before you start romancing about your wedding let's have a look at the obligations which belong to you and your family and those which belong to the bridegroom.

Responsibilities of the Bride's Family

1. The bride's trousseau.
2. The wedding ensemble. (Gown, veil, etc.)
3. The wedding invitations.
4. All wedding decorations, for ceremony and reception.
5. The bridesmaids' bouquets (or the bridegroom *may* pay for these if he wishes).
6. The bridesmaids' gifts.

    Gifts to musicians and other helpers who are friends.
8. Bride's gift to the groom (optional).
9. The church expenses, except clergyman's fee—these include:

    aisle canvas (necessary for formal wedding)

    canopy (expensive, and necessary for only the most formal type of wedding)

    music

    tip to church sexton
10. Bridal dinner or bridesmaids' luncheon if you wish to entertain for your attendants.
11. Housing of out-of-town bridal attendants and special guests.
12. Transportation of bridal party to and from church.

13. The wedding breakfast or reception.

14. Wedding gifts to the bride from all members of the immediate family.

Responsibilities of the Bridegroom

1. The wedding ring.

2. The marriage license.*

3. The bride's bouquet, boutonnieres for the men and corsages for both mothers and grandmothers.

4. Gifts for the bride, best man and ushers aside from the matching ties and gloves presented to men of the wedding party in formal wedding.

5. The bachelor dinner (if he wants to give one).

6. The clergyman's fee. (Ten dollars is the usual fee for people of moderate means—but the larger the wedding, and wedding budget, the larger the fee.)

7. The wedding trip.

GET YOUR CALENDAR IN HAND

Now, let's consider the date for this important step of yours and decide on the time of day for the ceremony.

June, of course, is traditionally the bride's month but statistics show that April, May and October also are coming into their own as chosen months for many fashionable weddings.

---

* The bridegroom is responsible for ferreting out all legal information on marriage necessary to know, in locale where couple plans to be married; length of waiting period, proper certification, physical examination, etc.

Marriage-license bureaus are busy every day of the year issuing the necessary documents, so it is purely a matter of your own personal taste and convenience.

Individual ministers are guided by their own preferences in the matter of dates, however, so consult your clergyman before you make your actual decision.

Saturday afternoons and evenings are the most popular of all days in the week because of convenience to business people. But if you want to choose Wednesday at four, or some other time that suits you, don't be influenced by what anyone else has done.

WHAT TIME SHOULD IT BE?

Most fashionable Catholic weddings, celebrated with a Nuptial High Mass, take place at noon. If you want Low Mass said, ten o'clock is a timely hour. If yours is an informal service to be held early in the morning, set the time for eight or nine. If it is to be the simplest of Catholic ceremonies celebrated in the church, without Mass, it may take place in the afternoon.

The most favored hours for Protestant ceremonies are at four or four-thirty in the afternoon and twelve or twelve-thirty for the morning wedding. Three-thirty is a nice hour if you are following the service with a simple teatime reception.

Easterners frown on the formal evening wedding, but it's a very popular time in the South because of the extreme daytime heat. The Middle West and Far West favor it largely because it offers an easy answer to the formal dress problem.

The invariable hours for the evening ceremony are eight, eight-thirty and nine o'clock.

You may make your own rules and set your own time, unfettered by tradition, if you are having an informal affair. Your own convenience is the main thing to consider.

WHAT SORT OF RECEPTION SHOULD FOLLOW?

The high-noon wedding is apt to cost more than the mid-afternoon, since the wedding breakfast which follows usually calls for a luncheon menu.

Weddings held late in the afternoon are generally followed by a reception supper, similar in bill of fare to the breakfast.

The reception following the three-thirty or four o'clock ceremony entails less expense if you limit refreshments to teatime food.

If you are budget-conscious, weigh all these pros and cons before you set the hour. This bit of forethought will help make your wedding add up to exactly what you want in the grand total.

The degree of formality carried out in your wedding ceremony should be matched by the reception. A party of formal type should follow the formal church ceremony. A less formal function is in mood with the semiformal or informal ceremony.

Formality in entertaining does not mean fussiness or pomposity, however. It means carrying out correctness and charm and doing it with a flair.

SPECIAL TIPS TO MEMBERS OF BOTH FAMILIES

The Bride's Family

Family conferences on wedding issues are essential, with every member having a finger in the pie. Father, with his open checkbook, presides as the head of the house, and Mother with her check list is chairman of the arrangements committee, directing her corps of working aides in masterful fashion.

It's a time to delegate as many duties as possible to willing friends and relatives who wish to share in the excitement of wedding preparations. Bridesmaids may help in the addressing of invitations and announcements, if penmanship is passable. There's appointment-making, gift-listing, phone-answering, billeting and meeting of out-of-town guests that may wisely be turned over to trusted friends and so leave the family free for other duties.

Mother's Responsibilities

As soon as wedding plans have been formed, the *bride's mother* should advise the bridegroom's mother of details, so that the latter may select her gown and make necessary plans.

She will work on the guest list with the bride and confer with the bridegroom's mother on his family's lists.

She will consult with the caterer, get estimates from florists, engage the photographer, assist in shopping, help with the gift display—check and double check everything!

It is the mother's responsibility to see that there are cars to take the wedding party to and from church, to see that arrangements are made for housing out-of-town bridal attendants.

If the reception is not being held at the bride's home, it is the mother's duty, if she can so arrange it, to entertain with a tea or luncheon, sometime before the wedding, so that friends may view the gifts.

If the bride's mother is a widow, she will act as both host and hostess, taking over a father's usual duties. She may, if she wishes, give her daughter in marriage by stepping forward from her pew, or merely rising in her place and answering "I do," when the minister asks, "Who giveth this woman to be married to this man?"

Dear Old Dad

The bride's father comes into his own as the official host at his daughter's wedding.

He necessarily must conform to the conventional dress decreed for the type of wedding chosen. If he doesn't own the correct attire he should rent or borrow it. Otherwise the bride must change her plans and key her wedding to his wardrobe.

As head of the house, Father generally foots most of the bills for the wedding. For instance, there are floral decorations, bridesmaids' flowers, the musicians (the church sets the organist's fee and it may run anywhere from ten to thirty dollars), the sexton's fee or tip which is in accordance with the elaborateness of the wedding (five to ten dollars is usually ample).

Is there to be a special traffic policeman? If so, Dad will want to fork over at least ten or fifteen dollars in his behalf.

All the reception expenses are his responsibility—as are trousseau clothes, if the bride has no nest egg of her own for such a purpose.

The bride and her father drive alone to the church, with a chauffeur or friend at the wheel. She is escorted up the aisle by him (on his right arm) and given in marriage at the altar.

He acts as host at the reception. He may or may not stand in the receiving line, but he remains throughout the reception until the last guests have been bidden good-by.

Don't forget that the right family attitude calls for pitching in joyfully on wedding plans, for such an attitude goes a long way toward making a calm, well-poised, *happy* bride at the altar!

The Groom's Family

"Look pleasant, please—and conform to the wedding plans set forth by the bride's family." That's the principal rule for the bridegroom's family to follow in wedding procedure.

As honor guests at their son's wedding the parents stand in the receiving line to meet all guests. They are dressed to conform with the rest of the wedding party.

The bridegroom's family customarily gives the bride some very special present, traditionally a silver service.

At the bidding of the bride's mother, the groom's mother

should comply promptly with her request for making up the invitation and announcement list. She is obliged to welcome the bride-to-be into the family as soon as she hears the good news.

If the families live in the same city, the groom's family should call upon the bride's family and welcome the bride to their home. If the bride lives in another city, a note of welcome is due her from the bridegroom's mother.

A reception or party of introduction is an appreciated gesture before the wedding (or following), if the bride is not known to friends of the groom's family. It is only courtesy that the bride's family be included by invitation to such an affair.

How a Wise Bride Led Her Man *Straight* to the Altar

Joan was decidedly Daché . . . and even smarter than her hat.

She knew something about men in general and more about Bill in particular.

She knew he was shy about formal parties. (He looked stunning in tails.)

She knew he was the one man for her. (Their marriage was a mere three months away.)

She knew that like most men he was utterly vague on the subject of weddings. (He was to be a principal in one of the biggest in June.)

Most of all Joan knew that Bill would have to be managed if things were to go off as she'd planned.

Gradually, by dint of reminders and schedules and notes on the cuff, he learned about weddings from her.

It may give you an insight into the pre-ceremony maneuvers to see Bill's "list" and know that he lived up to Joan's reminders to the very last one.

Here it is (just as Joan planned it and as *you* can too, for your own partner-to-be).

REMINDERS FOR THE BRIDEGROOM

Bring to light that little red memorandum book with all your old addresses. Hold a session with a telephone book, Alumni Directory and your business telephone list. Who knows the names and addresses of all your relatives? Tabulate full names and addresses of guests to be invited to the wedding. Put your family to work on this job. Decide which guests are to come to the reception.

Make notes (to be given to the ushers later) on where to seat Aunt Carrie from Albany, the Boss and your most valued friends.

Don't you think George is a "natural" for best man? He's dependable and a good bolsterer of spirits. (And besides, he is the apple of the maid of honor's eye.)

Follow your own hunches in selecting your ushers. But don't forget you want them to wear uniform ties and gloves. Which of the trappings do you want to supply? And what about gifts . . . would they like sets of gold belt buckles and matching tie clasps? Or, how about sets of studs and cuff links?

George is green-eyed over your cowhide luggage. If he turns out to be the best man, why not something personal like that? Buy his ascot and gloves for the wedding to match yours.

Just as a hint—you asked for it—remember the pearl beads Ray gave Alice as a wedding gift? Twenty-five dollars is tops, remember, for my gift.

I'm not the only one who has a trousseau. What about your clothes? You won't need more than two new suits, will you? And a few pairs of slacks for the country.

Please don't get delusions of grandeur when you plan our wedding trip. But don't forget the tickets.

Better make a date with me to get our marriage license. What about taking me to lunch afterward?

If you really want to have a stag dinner, get an estimate from the club. (Since we're having the bridal dinner, it isn't necessary, you know.) Better stage it at least three days before the wedding. No hangovers permitted on the big day!

Our mothers should rate handsome corsages, don't you think? But consult me before you order. I'll give you a tip or two on my own bridal bouquet at that time. Order boutonnieres at the same time.

Trade in one of your ten-spots for a brand new bill as the minister's fee. It should be enclosed in an envelope before the best man presents it.

At the rehearsal, appoint a head usher to keep the others in tow.

Check up on your supply of collar buttons before the last hectic minute. Dress and arrive for the wedding a half hour early.

I'll promise not to smear you with lipstick if you'll remember to kiss me at the altar.

Let's not be so wrapped up in our own plans that we dash away on our honeymoon without telling our parents good-by.

Remind me that we want to send telegrams to our families back home the day after the wedding.

Don't forget your wife when we get to the hotel! "Mr. and Mrs." is the way you sign the register.

SPECIAL QUESTIONS AND ANSWERS

WHAT TYPE OF WEDDING IS APPROPRIATE

. . . when one of the families is in mourning?

If there has been a death in either the bride's or the bridegroom's immediate family within a period of less than ten months, a large ultra-formal wedding should not be considered. If the bride is so disposed, however, there is no reason why she cannot have a smallish wedding in the formal mood either in church or at home six months after a death has occurred.

*. . . when a girl in moderate circumstances
marries a wealthy man?*

The bride's family should plan a wedding that is in complete accord with the family's circumstances, and financial aid should never be accepted from the groom or his family. The groom's mother may give a large reception for the bridal pair if she wishes, but not on the wedding day.

CHAPTER IV

Consider Your Worldly Goods

THIS "GETTING MARRIED" BUSINESS, THRILLING THOUGH IT may be, is bound to cost something. Whether it's money from your piggy bank or the National Savings and Trust, it should be budgeted and allocated to stretch as far as it will.

You'll add peace of mind to that special day, and to days that are to follow, if you accurately measure your pocket-book and make your plans to fit it.

Remember that there are varying degrees of formality for both a wedding and reception. You as the bride will set the pace by your choice of a bridal costume and the extent of your wedding invitation list.

If it's to be *Lohengrin* and a long-trained wedding gown . . . if your invitation list reaches from here to there, including everyone from the bridegroom's fourth cousin to your long-lost kindergarten friends, then don't be misled. That's a big formal wedding and should be carried out with all traditional "musts" and corresponding fanfare. (In small communities three hundred guests may comprise an all-inclusive list of both families' friends and relatives and mean a big formal wedding; while in larger cities a really formal affair is just as likely to run into thousands on the guest list. But the same basic rules for a formal wedding may apply all the way through.)

If your wedding gown is less formal and your guest

list held down to the families and a limited number of friends then you'll voluntarily strike an in-between, semi-formal mood.

It is *your* wedding, don't forget. Not to be done for effect. Nor to keep up with the Joneses. But to express you, your own desires and inclinations, and to be in accordance with the type of life you are going to lead.

If your parents' scale of living is simple, don't make yourselves conspicuous by putting on a super de luxe affair that will pull at the family purse strings and subject you to deserved criticism. Plan something simple and in good taste . . . in accordance with what you can comfortably afford.

WHAT ABOUT THE MAN IN YOUR LIFE?

Before you jump to the conclusion that you must have a big formal wedding, consider the bridegroom, his attendants and their financial status. *Your* bridal costume sets the mood

for your wedding and the men in the bridal party MUST follow suit. There can be no compromise on this.

You may have your heart set on rustling down the church aisle in a slipper-satin gown with long flowing train, six lovely bridesmaids and all the trimmings . . . but what about your fiancé, his attendants and your father?

Are they prepared to meet your mood in cutaways and striped trousers for the formal daytime wedding or tail coats and full dress for evening? If it's a military wedding, will your service man and the ushers be prepared to wear full-dress uniforms?

The men principals at a formal wedding are found sadly wanting when they appear in double-breasted business suits to serve as props for the bride and her bridal party who are bedecked in long formal gowns. There are some communities where such inconsistency may be accepted without a raise of the eyebrows, but it is definitely unsuitable. Unless you knowingly wish to throw propriety to the four winds don't be guilty of this breach of what is considered the best taste. The change to a less formal wedding can give you almost everything you have set your heart on and make the clothes problem much simpler for the men in your "train."

RENTAL DEPARTMENTS OFFER A SOLUTION

Department stores and men's furnishing shops in every city are equipped to meet this problem in their rental departments. Few young men, particularly in the Middle West, have occasion to wear morning clothes except when they participate in a wedding.

The renting of such attire may not have occurred to you before—but the necessity for uniformity among men on such occasions has resulted in the establishing of this custom in many localities. It is a simple matter for them to have their clothes fitted and sent out for the event, to be returned a day or two after the wedding. Since the rental charge is far less than the cost of buying the complete outfit, it is a practical and inexpensive method of meeting a required situation and should not be looked upon with disfavor.

In many instances the bridegroom invests in his own formal wedding paraphernalia but his ushers and best man take advantage of this wedding service. And no one is the wiser.

THE SEMIFORMAL DRESS

Because many a male has hesitated at the prospect of wearing such unaccustomed daytime apparel, practicality has joined hands with tradition. The result is what we choose to call the semiformal mood for the wedding keynote.

It solves the problem for the girls who strive to please their men with informality but who themselves wish to step into that magic circle of real-for-sure *Brides*.

Wedding-dress manufacturers made it all possible when they introduced (by popular demand) the short-trained and trainless wedding gowns. With either style you may wear a short wedding veil and all the beloved accouterments.

If the wedding is in the daytime, the men wear their own black or Oxford-gray business coats (as substitutes for cutaways) with striped trousers, and four-in-hand ties in place of the formal ascots. If it's summertime they may wear white linen or Palm Beach suits, or dark-blue or gray jackets with white flannel trousers.

Dinner jackets (or tuxedos) are worn instead of tails and white ties for the semiformal evening wedding after six. (See dress chart, page 80.)

This in-between type of wedding may have especial charm and sweet simplicity so . . . dry your tears if the men's dress problem is your complication, and happily settle on this compromise.

INFORMAL DRESS

There are practically no problems at all facing you (in the matter of the men's apparel, that is) if you are to be an informal bride.

During normal weather conditions the groom may wear either a plain dark-blue or Oxford-gray business suit and his best man would conform. For summer or summer country weddings, white linens or Palm Beach suits are always appropriate.

Whatever your choice, mark it down in your notebook (or merely stamp it on your brain) that the co-ordination of your entire wedding hinges on this question of clothes consistency . . . and that uniformity on the part of the men of the bridal party is one of the most important points in attaining the effect we're striving for.

Now talk it all over with the groom and take stock together before you plunge! (See dress chart, page 81.)

GETTING DOWN TO BRASS TACKS

By now you have made up your mind on a thing or two. So let's capitalize on every factor that's offered for *your* type of wedding.

If you live in a small town, where you are surrounded by a multitude of friends and relatives who can hardly wait for *the day,* go ahead and plan that church wedding you've pinned your hopes on. If your home is too small to accommodate them all for a big reception, couldn't you receive them under the big elm tree in your side yard? Why not set your bridal table in the orchard and make it a very chatty reception with guests mingling together for hours?

If you have a handkerchief-size apartment where only the two families and the bridal party can wedge in for a cozy little reception, choose for the wedding ceremony a church that is large enough for all your friends. Pause after the recessional to greet them in the back of the church. It's a friendly and charming custom when the reception is limited to "families only."

Maybe you have star dust in your eyes and only a hundred dollars in your purse. Well, come out of the moonbeams and make the most of it. Perhaps you can wear your grandmother's wedding gown and carry out the charm of an old-fashioned wedding. Dispense with bridesmaids, if you have two or three nieces or cousins to precede you down the aisle as flower girls dressed in Kate Greenaway style. Invite only your dearest friends and relatives by intimate note and make it a simple home wedding with unusual touches.

Put your ingenuity to work on your own specific problems. Single out the data that covers *your* kind of wedding, follow through with the fundamentals as a framework . . . then use as much originality as you please.

Is It to Be a Formal Church Wedding?

If so, that doesn't mean it should be stiff or pompous. The word "formal" *is* rather misleading. "Traditional" is more apt, as it applies to the procedure and dress regulations which are customarily accepted. For even formality has varying degrees.

If your social position, the size of your church and the state of your pocketbook warrant, your wedding may well be a large and elaborate affair with *all* the trimmings. . . . Canopies to the curb, confetti on the sidewalk, envelopes within envelopes, white gloves, liveried doormen and *you* as the star in a whoosh of veiling and a long-trained wedding gown.

It's a memory you'll cherish forever . . . the pictorial beauty of a performance perfect. The ultra-formal wedding!

Or again, it may be quite simple in its appointments, completely without trumpet flourish, with only a small gathering of the clan at the church—yet carried out in formal tempo throughout.

There are certain MUSTS for any type of formal church wedding:

1. You must wear a formal wedding gown with a train. (It may be the usual three-yard length or longer.)

2. The men in the wedding party must wear formal attire.

3. You must send engraved wedding invitations and reception cards. (If it's a very large wedding you will send such enclosures as "Behind the ribbons" and entrance cards to the church.)

4. You must have an aisle canvas. (You should have aisle ribbons and pew decorations.)

5. You will need the services of a professional florist.

6. You must have a caterer of some sort to relieve your mother of reception responsibilities.

7. You may or may not want a church canopy. (This is desirable in case of rain, if the church entrance is not protected.) Carpeted outside steps are customary. Do you want a doorman?

8. Your family should entertain with a formal bridal dinner before the wedding. (Preferably the night before, with rehearsal following.)

9. You must have a maid of honor to attend you. You will probably want to have bridesmaids as well.

10. You must have ushers. (One for every twenty-five to fifty guests is considered adequate in a large wedding.)

11. The bridegroom must have a best man.

12. You should be given in marriage, by your father, if possible, or an uncle or close family friend.

13. You should have a formal receiving line to greet guests at the reception.

14. You must have a bride's cake. You should have individual boxes for the wedding (or groom's) cake if it is quite formal.

15. You should have instrumental music at the reception.

16. You should have photographs taken of the bridal

party. Candid shots during the reception are a happy solution.

17. You should throw your bridal bouquet at the reception, as you leave to dress for going away.

18. Real or artificial rose petals or rice should be distributed in individual packages to guests at going-away time. No sneaking out the back way as you leave for your honeymoon! You and your bridegroom must run the gantlet of rice-throwing, confetti and old shoes as you pass the guest line in leaving the house.

GET IN STRIDE

Any kind of party takes some organizing . . . so don't let a few formal "musts" frighten you out of your original plans if a formal church wedding it is to be!

The sooner you lay the foundations for your wedding structure, the faster and more firmly you'll be able to build toward its final conclusion.

Now let's see about further details.

If you plan to be married in your own church, in most cases there is no charge. If you have selected a church where you or your family are not members, there usually is a fee. Not all churches will allow nonparishioners to be married in them, so better check on church rules before you blunder.

The bride usually chooses the church in which she wishes to be married, but it may be the bridegroom's church, just as well.

You and your fiancé should call on the minister well in advance of the wedding. It's not only a courtesy but a canon-

law requirement in the Roman, Greek Catholic and Episcopal Churches.

Besides your own minister chosen to officiate, you may also have an assisting clergyman in attendance at the altar if you wish. This is often done when a family friend or relative is a minister in another city, but it is necessary to arrange this in advance with the minister of the church where the wedding will be held.

The church organist generally has a set fee for church weddings. If you engage the choir or a church vocalist, handle the proceedings as you would any business proposition and engage all the musicians for the rehearsal, as well as for the wedding, on terms confirmed in advance.

Perhaps you have some special friend whom you've always counted on to sing or play at your wedding. Talk this over with your minister to see if your plans conform with his particular standards. Plan to give the musician friend a gift if there is no regular fee for his services (see page 179).

MAKE NOTES AS YOU GO ALONG

Check on the seating capacity of the church. Do not add more people to your invitation list than there is room to accommodate.

Take into consideration the amount of space that is available at the altar. Is there plenty of room for all your bridesmaids to show off to advantage? As we have said, a formal wedding presents opportunity for pretty pageantry. Make use of this fact as you plan it, step by step.

Visit your church and make a study of the physical effects.

Note the color of walls, the shades used in the seat cushions, the predominating color tones in the stained-glass windows, the woodwork and the altar embellishments. If the background colors are extremely vivid and varied—or neutral and dull—be sure to jot down this information in your notebook. It will be important when it comes time to choose your wedding colors.

Then observe the lighting facilities—daylight, electric light or candlelight. Does the church glow with flattering shadows as the afternoon sun wanes? Is the hour which you have tentatively set for the ceremony exactly right to take full advantage of this dramatic touch? Is the altar lighted by rich and beautiful transept windows that cast a soft warmth over the chancel at noontime? Take all of these things into consideration now while you are forming your plans and there is still time to change.

Look for a principal point of interest, a focal point, around which the church has been built.

If the architecture is modern, without the ornamentation of deeply colored glass windows, note this fact and plan the details of your wedding accordingly. It would be out of place to key your wedding to an old-fashioned theme in such a setting.

If your church is a small and simple structure, don't plan an elaborate processional but keep your wedding simple.

Snow-white pillars, lavish gold decoration and blue-canopied ceilings, often found in the churches of early American setting, inspire dreams of a colonial wedding realistically come true.

Make a point of looking up the sexton while you are taking notes at the church. You can confer with him on important details such as fire laws, bell ringing, the aisle canvas, stair carpet and such. He will know the church's rules on permitting candlelight weddings, if that happens to be part of your plan. Get his name and telephone number. You may need him later.

Is a prayer bench used in this particular church? If it is supplied by the church, you will be saved an item of expense at the florist's. See if candelabra are available for wedding services. The sexton will know. Your florist will supply them and also the tapers, if the church does not have them.

DETAILS TO BE NOTED

Arrival at the Church

The ushers should arrive one hour before the ceremony and take their places at each inner door leading from the vestibule, as directed by the head usher. Guest lists should be distributed by the head usher to selected ushers. If flowers are delivered to the church the sexton should see that all male members of the wedding party receive their boutonnieres. (See page 114 for ushers' specific duties.)

The bridegroom and the best man should arrive together at the church a half hour before the ceremony, receive their boutonnieres and go directly to the vestry. The best man takes the bridegroom's hat and coat (and his own) to the vestibule preceding the ceremony and leaves them in care of the sexton. (See page 116 for detailed duties of best man.)

The bridesmaids and other bridal attendants should arrive together at least ten minutes before the appointed time of the ceremony and retire to rooms which adjoin the vestibule to await the bride and her father who will follow immediately in the next car. In cases where the bride and her attendants dress at the church, they should all assemble in the vestibule of the church three or four minutes before the signal for the wedding march is given. The bride's father then joins the wedding party there. (See page 110 for bridal attendants' duties.)

The bridegroom's family usually arrives at the church about eight or ten minutes before time for the ceremony.

Is there a suitable place at the church for you and your attendants to dress for the wedding?

Lucky *you* if there is. Your wedding ensemble and bridesmaids' costumes can be sent on hangers directly to the church from the store. They should be delivered early on the day of your wedding and cared for by the sexton in the dressing rooms provided for this purpose. Someone should check their delivery and spread a clean white sheet on the dressing-room floor. Then everything will be in readiness for you and the bridesmaids to saunter in at least two hours before the ceremony and dress in perfect leisure—with never a fear of a wrinkle as you walk down the aisle. You can arrange to have on hand your make-up expert, your hairdresser, the bridal consultant (or whoever is to help you dress) and everything in hand to make you gorgeous.

The bride's mother goes to the church with other members of her family in time for the mother to be escorted to her place of honor one minute before the wedding march begins.

Preliminaries to the Ceremony

The introductory music begins about a half hour before the ceremony. Vocal solos or choral services should be scheduled to take place during the last few minutes before ceremony time, after most of the guests have arrived and are seated.

Candles should be lighted by the sexton before guests arrive unless a traditional candlelighting service is to be performed.

Reserved pews for special guests usually number from ten to twenty, depending on the size of the church, and pew cards are presented by guests to the ushers at the door.

The bridegroom's mother, about five minutes before time for the ceremony, is escorted to her place in the first pew on the right side. The bridegroom's father follows a pace behind and takes his place in the pew beside her. Both leave outer wraps with the sexton in the vestibule, but the mothers wear their hats (or appropriate head coverings) and gloves throughout the ceremony.

The bride's mother is escorted to her place in the first pew on the left about one minute before the ceremony begins. No one is seated by an usher after she takes her place. When guests arrive after the ceremony starts they should go directly to the gallery and seat themselves or remain in the rear of the church.

If aisle ribbons are used, two ushers walk to the front of the church, where ribbons are attached on the front pews, and draw them over the tops of the pews, all the way to the back of the church.

If the aisle canvas has not already been tacked down by the florist, it should be attended to by the ushers. As soon as the pair of ushers drawing the ribbons has returned to the back of the church, another pair of ushers should go to the front of the church and draw the canvas along the aisle. It will have been folded, accordian fashion, so that it unfolds easily as the ushers walk back along the aisle, holding the outside corner of the canvas strip and drawing it behind them as they go.

The wedding march signal should be given to the organist by the sexton when the procession is ready to start.

If the congregation stands during a wedding ceremony in your church, all guests follow the lead of the bride's and groom's families and rise at the first note of the wedding march. They remain standing until the minister indicates that everyone be seated.

Altar Arrangement (see chart, page 247).

Processional (see chart, page 246).

Recessional (see chart, page 248).

Procedure for Leaving the Church

The bride's car (the same one in which she arrived with her father at the church) should await her and the bridegroom at the curb. It is the first car to leave the church.

Next come the cars filled with bridesmaids and the best man; third, the parents of the bride; and fourth, the parents of the groom, followed by the cars occupied by immediate families of both the bride and the groom, the clergyman, ushers and other guests.

THE FORMAL HOME WEDDING

If it is to be a home wedding, the plan can be flavored with much intimate charm and sentiment . . . yet still be keyed to the formal symbols.

There's the wide winding stairway (down which you will come so effectively) railed with the bannister where you used to go tumbling and sliding. There's the big spacious living room (your vows will be spoken there) . . . filled with all your endearing memories of gay family gatherings.

There's something sort of nostalgic about it all—and terribly, terribly thrilling.

Now step back and take a look around. (We must be practical, you know.)

Is there plenty of space for everyone you want to invite?

Can the French doors be opened and the screened porch used?

Will you wear ice-blue to match the blue of the ceiling? Ideas will come burgeoning right and left when you once begin.

Look back on page 59 at the list of MUSTS for the formal church wedding. The same measuring stick is used, the same rules apply, except that—

You Can Eliminate:

A canopy (unless it's extreme weather and you want to go luxurious).

Separate cards, "Behind the ribbons" and entrance cards.

A professional florist if your garden (or your neighbor's) is overflowing with flowers, and someone in the family has a special knack for decorating.

You'll send the same sort of formal invitations, wear a wedding gown, a train and decide for yourself whether ushers are necessary.

A special point to consider is your caterer. You will need somebody *capable* to lift this responsibility off your mother's shoulders and send her cares fading into oblivion. If you can afford a professional caterer, you'll find it well worth the money.

Keep a Home Atmosphere

The charm of a house wedding is that it is *your* home and reflects that sort of an atmosphere.

Your mother may stand near the door to receive wedding guests as they arrive, if she wishes. Or if she prefers to remain with you and your attendants until just before the ceremony, she may delegate a close friend or relative to this duty, and later personally greet everyone in the receiving line. She should take her place in the front row, to the left of the altar, just before time for the ceremony to start. In a home wedding, your mother, as the hostess, usually does not wear hat or gloves. The bridegroom's family are shown to their places in the front row, at right of the altar, when they arrive for the wedding.

Unless it is necessary to accommodate all the guests you want, don't move out all the furniture and give it the appearance of a rented ballroom. Leave the davenports, a few occasional chairs and tables (they can be moved back against the wall) and don't do away with all the lamps.

Remove the small objects and any of the pictures which interfere with your decorative effects.

Guests at a home wedding usually stand during the ceremony. A fairly large room can accommodate fifty or sixty people comfortably and if there are other rooms adjoining with wide doorways, it makes a convenient arrangement.

When the clergyman arrives for the wedding, he should be escorted to a room which has been reserved for him, the groom and the best man.

Your fireplace in the living room, a large bay or picture window, any of these will provide a suitable background for the ceremony. Make certain that you select the setting which serves as a central point for everyone. No wedding guest wants to be crowded out of seeing the ceremonial proceedings.

It is not unusual in a home wedding to omit an altar arrangement and have, instead, a prie-dieu against a background of greenery and flowers. Kneeling benches may be borrowed from a church, a florist or a church supply house. An altar may be easily improvised, however, by covering a small table with a square of fine white silk, linen or lace. Or you may wish to borrow a real altar frontal from your church.

If you can arrange it, the altar should be so situated that the bridegroom and his attendant may come from a door on the right. This eliminates the awkwardness of crossing in front of the altar as they take their places on the right side.

Make a study of the color scheme and background of your home as to walls, curtains, carpets and lighting effects. Search out harmonious blends as a setting for your bridesmaids and make the whole artistic and unusual. You'll find there's more to work with than you'd dreamed of if you concentrate on your all-too-familiar surroundings.

If your curtains don't contribute to the effect you're striving for, take them down and decorate the shades with garlands of flowers . . . or replace them with new ones that will turn the trick.

Plan, right now, where guests will leave their wraps. A maid or a house man should be in attendance to direct each man and woman respectively.

If your house has a handsome social room, have the guests directed there and your wedding gifts on display. Or consult your parents about moving to a guest room so that the presents may be set out in the master bedroom.

What About Music?

If you want a background of organ music for your formal wedding at home—and nothing is more appropriate—don't despair, for here's a cue.

The rental department of almost every large music store is equipped with desk-sized electric organs, and the rental charge isn't at all prohibitive. You can get a professional organist (perhaps from the same music company) for a reasonable fee.

Or perhaps you know someone in your town who personally owns an electric organ which could be transported for your rehearsal and the wedding day. The owner, no doubt, is a musician and could be engaged for the occasion.

If not organ music, you might have a harpist or a string trio with piano accompaniment.

A small choir of young boys, or of feminine voices, chanting the wedding march to organ or piano accompaniment offers a beautiful and impressive variation to the usual instrumental solo.

The wedding procession for a formal home wedding follows in the same order as the church wedding procession.

No Recessional

At the close of the ceremony, the groom kisses the bride, the minister congratulates the bridegroom and gives felicitations to the bride, then withdraws. The couple then turns to receive greetings from both sets of parents after which a receiving group is formed in front of the altar.

Your floral decorations may be exquisite, yet simple and not overabundant. If you are depending on a professional florist to carry out some of your own inspired ideas, arrange for him to visit your home and submit sketches and estimates.

You'll find a few decorating suggestions in a later chapter that may give you some clues on what to do.

THE CLUB OR HOTEL WEDDING

A club or hotel wedding is treated in much the same manner as a home wedding. It may lack the personal background but it can be very dignified and lovely in its appointments.

It means that you put many of your contingent problems into the hands of experts—which is often a welcome plan. Clubs and hotels usually do not charge for the rooms used if they are commissioned to do the catering.

Meet with the maître d'hôtel and engage the ballroom or other rooms suitable for the ceremony and reception. Consult your florist and go with him to the prospective scene of the wedding to discuss decorations.

Get estimates on everything and confirm your orders in writing.

See about your music, approve the reception menu and go about making your plans just as outlined for a formal home wedding.

Your mother may receive the guests as they arrive, then take her proper place in front of the improvised altar on the left side of the room. Other members of the family who are not in the bridal party mingle with the guests before the ceremony, as do the parents and immediate family of the groom.

The place you select for the ceremony depends on the shape of the room and the convenience of the occasion. (Follow details for home wedding as outlined on page 68.) If no aisleway is marked off, the ushers should see to it that an aisle space is indicated just before ceremony time. Or the aisleway could be formed by having four or six of your friends (two or three on each side) carry ropes of greenery and flowers which could be stretched to form a pathway to the altar.

Your father may give you in marriage, as in any service. If you prefer to have only a short distance to walk to the altar you may enter from a doorway at the left of the altar, preceded by your attendants if there are to be any.

In a simpler ceremony you may choose to greet your own guests and step up to the altar naturally and easily, with the bridegroom at your side.

What to Wear for a Formal Daytime Wedding

Bride: Wedding gown with train, long or short veil. Long gloves if sleeves are short. Material subject to season, with satin traditional favorite. White, antique or pastel shade. Shoes to match gown. Flesh tone hose. Bridal bouquet or white prayer book. Real jewelry in good taste.

Bridal Attendants: Formal-length gowns, customarily matching in style. Colors selected by bride. Gloves usual if sleeves are short. Matching or contrasting accessories. Bouquets. Maid or matron of honor; may match or contrast in style and color.

Bridegroom: Cutaway coat, striped trousers, silk top hat. Formal gray or beige waistcoat (white piqué in summer). Gloves to match waistcoat, four-in-hand or Ascot tie, spats optional. Patent or black calf oxfords, black hose. Boutonniere of lilies of the valley or white carnation.

Best Man, Ushers, Fathers: The same as groom. Boutonnieres differ from the groom's. When groom wears lilies of the valley, best man and bride's father wear gardenias; ushers and groom's father carnations.

Mothers: Dresses, formal length, in flattering colors; black is not appropriate. Chic hats and smart accessories. Corsages.

Women Guests: Afternoon dresses or costume suits of street length. Hats and accessories to match or contrast.

Men Guests: Men wear formal afternoon clothes like the ushers or Oxford jackets.

WHAT TO WEAR FOR A FORMAL EVENING WEDDING

Bride: Same costume as formal daytime wedding. Conservative décolletage. With short sleeves use opera-length gloves. Long veil (a yard longer than train) is more formal than short veil. Bridal bouquet or white prayer book. Diamond or pearl jewelry.

Attendants: Conservative evening dresses or dinner gowns. Long gloves. Jacket type dresses are practical for reception dancing. Headdresses. Bouquets. Accessories to match or contrast. Maid or matron of honor: same degree of formality as bridesmaids, matching or contrasting in style and color.

Groom: Full evening dress. Black or midnight-blue full dress suit. High silk or opera hat. White waistcoat, white bow tie, stiff bosom shirt, wing collar, white kid gloves. White or black pearl studs. Patent leather pumps, black hose. Boutonniere same as formal daytime.

Best Man, Ushers, Fathers: Full evening dress the same as groom. Boutonnieres same as formal daytime wedding.

Mothers and Women Guests: Formal evening gowns with opera-length gloves in white or to match costume. Accessories in keeping. Head coverings required in many churches. Real jewelry. Mothers: conservative flowers.

Men Guests: Full evening dress as ushers.

SEMIFORMAL WEDDING

Your wedding, in semiformal tempo, may be as exquisite, and rapturous, and intimate, and all the other adjectives, as you want to make it.

It should strike a happy medium, in dress and procedure, between the highly formal and the very casual types. It offers you more opportunity for variation than the formal wedding.

Your list of MUSTS is cut down considerably. As a romantic realist you will forgo the opulence of a trumpet-flourishing wedding, but you will walk up the church aisle in the legendary beauty of bridal tradition—as the most serene of brides in a flurry of white.

As you already know, you may choose a wedding gown of floor length that is wearable for other occasions later without alteration. You may wear a veil and all the other bridal bib-and-tucker of tradition, and carry a truly, truly wedding bouquet, a dainty sheath of blossoms or a prayer book on which is an orchid or floral spray—whatever is in keeping with the simplicity of your gown.

You won't have to goad the bridegroom, and indirectly his attendants, into wing collars, cutaways and top hats. (Was that the echo of a relieved sigh we heard?) Most young chaps have striped trousers and Oxford-gray or blue coats, don't they? Or dinner jackets, if it's an evening affair? For summertime, they may don white suits or white flannel trousers and blue coats. See dress charts.

Of course you may have attendants (try to limit them to three or four at the most) in festive gowns but not too formal.

You may skip the aisle canvas if you are to be *sans* train. And by all means, don't even consider a canopy or any of the ultra touches if semiformality and simplicity are the theme.

The semiformal wedding may be held in a church or chapel, at your home or club. It may even be a garden wedding.

Make your floral decorations beautiful in their simplicity. Let candlelight dance through the foliaged shadows if it's to be late afternoon or evening. Use evergreen branches for background against snow-white, gleaming gowns for an all-white wedding in midwinter, colorful arrangements of garden flowers in the summer. Call in a florist, if you must, but use discernment in whatever you plan.

If you are thirtyish, or your marriage is a second venture into matrimony, wear a dinner gown of pastel or jewel tones with matching hat, and add an extra zest with richly shaded flowers.

Send engraved invitations (the small, less formal kind) if your guest list totals more than fifty, or send them even for a smaller wedding if expense isn't an item.

If only a very few close friends and relatives are to be privileged to come, then invite them orally or by handwritten notes which your mother may write. If you wish to assist her, that's also permissible.

Issue the invitations (either kind) about three weeks before the wedding.

Your mother might say, when she telephones to guests, "Helen and Steve are planning to be married on the sixth of June in Graceland Chapel. It is to be a small wedding at half past four. We do want you to be there, and also to come to our apartment following the wedding for a cup of tea and some wedding cake. I hope you can be with us."

To other friends and relatives who may live out of town, she might write something like this:

Dear Ellen:

Helen and Steve are to be married at half past four on Saturday, the sixth of June, in Graceland Chapel, here in Huntington. It will be a small intimate wedding with a little reception following at our apartment. You know how much we want you to be with us on that day.

Affectionately yours,

Catherine

What to Wear for a Semiformal Daytime Wedding

Bride: Short-trained or trainless gown of white or pastel shade. Finger-tip veil or veilless headdress. Shoes to match. Bridal bouquet or white prayer book. Conservative jewelry.

Attendants: Formal-length gowns, customarily matching in style. Colors selected by bride. Long gloves or mitts optional. Matching or contrasting accessories. Bouquets. Maid or matron of honor: may match or contrast in style and color.

Bridegroom: Oxford jacket, striped trousers, matching vest or light gray double-breasted vest, stiff collar, white shirt, four-in-hand or bow tie, gloves optional. Lily-of-the-valley boutonniere. Summer: white linen suit or light flannels with dark jacket. Dark business suit may be worn if Oxford jacket not available.

Best Man, Ushers, Fathers: All men of party follow suit with groom. See formal wedding dress chart for boutonnieres.

Mothers: Formal-length gowns or street length may be worn with suitable corsages.

Women Guests: Street-length dresses or costume suits appropriate. Chic hats and matching accessories.

Men Guests: Oxford jackets and striped trousers or dark business suits. Summer: white linen suits or light flannels and dark coats.

WHAT TO WEAR FOR A SEMIFORMAL EVENING WEDDING

Bride: Short-trained or trainless wedding gown of white or pastel shade. Finger-tip veil or veilless headdress. Shoes to match. Bridal bouquet or white prayer book. Jewelry in good taste.

Attendants: Formal-length gowns, matching or contrasting in color, same style for bridesmaids. Colors selected by bride. Long gloves or mitts optional. Matching or contrasting accessories. Bouquets. Maid or matron of honor: formal-length gown matching or contrasting in style and color to bridesmaids. Bouquet.

Bridegroom: Tuxedo and black tie is accepted for semiformal evening wear in most communities. Black patent or calf oxfords, black hose. Lily-of-the-valley or gardenia boutonniere. Summer: light tuxedo coat, black trousers; all-white suit or light flannel with dark jacket.

Best Man, Ushers, Fathers: All men of the wedding party follow suit with groom. Best man wears gardenia and ushers wear carnations as boutonnieres.

Mothers: Dinner dresses or conservative evening gowns with head coverings and corsages.

Women Guests: Dinner dresses suitable if invited to reception following ceremony. Street-length costumes if invited to church only.

Men Guests: Tuxedos usual for all seasons except summer. Light tuxedo coat and black trousers or all-white suit for summer.

You may have wedding announcements engraved for your many friends who will not be present at the wedding. This is not obligatory, but we hope you can manage it.

THE INFORMAL WEDDING

You may be one of those couples who prefer to be married strictly without fuss. You don't want to slide down a rope ladder and be a runaway bride. You want to wear your going-away costume or an afternoon dress and have another couple "stand up" with you at the altar. Yet you want the simplest of ceremonies in the presence of a mere handful of people.

Perhaps it's a spur-of-the-moment occasion with no time to get ready for a big wedding.

You can still make it memorable and impressive in a chapel, at home, in your garden or at your club.

Decide on all the fundamentals and—if possible—at least two weeks before the date you and your mother should call the guests and write notes to out-of-town relatives.

Hold yourselves down to one attendant each. Walk to the altar beside your maid of honor, for moral support, if you choose.

Have some sort of music if you can possibly arrange it. All the masterpieces in wedding music are available on phonograph records. Had you thought of that?

Keep the decorations simple with greenery and a few flowers at the altar to blend with the color scheme of your clothes. Autumn leaves could be arched over the altar if it's a fall marriage. Evergreens and holly are festive for the Christmas season, informal garden flowers in soft colors for summer.

If it's a church wedding, dispense with aisle decorations or pew markings. Don't march down a long aisle, if only a few seats in the church are to be occupied. Enter from the side door at the left of the altar *with* your maid of honor or following her. The bridegroom and the best man will come from the vestry door on the right in the usual manner.

Stop at the back of the church and greet your guests before dashing away, if there is to be no get-together afterward.

If there's to be a breakfast or a small reception, don't plan anything sumptuous but make it very informal and gay. It might be a buffet or a simple tea at your family's home with your wedding cake as the main attraction. Or you could engage a small private dining room in a hotel or restaurant for the gathering.

This is the easiest sort of wedding to have if you don't mind forgoing some of the traditional touches. It may still have true dignity and beauty which are always essential to any sort of wedding.

Here are a few ideas to start you thinking along your own lines:

1. Wear a creamy-white sheer wool dress with matching hat if it's wintertime and you want to live up to some of the

bridal traditions. Exchange vows before the burning fireplace.

2. If you are wearing your traveling costume in a fall or winter church wedding, carry a tiny fur muff adorned with a single orchid.

3. Have a late afternoon ceremony in the shadow of the Christmas-tree lights during the holiday season. Add a touch of mistletoe or holly to your shoulder corsage as a festive innovation.

4. If it's springtime or summer, top your costume with a lighthearted hat made entirely of white flowers draped with a white face-veil and have your corsage made of the real flowers to match. You might choose a shaded porch or the cool shelter of a great spreading tree in the back yard as the scene of the ceremony.

WHAT TO WEAR FOR AN INFORMAL DAYTIME OR EVENING WEDDING

Bride: Dinner-type dress of floor length, or afternoon dress or going-away suit. Veilless headdress or hat. Harmonizing accessories. Corsage or small bouquet. Conservative jewelry.

Attendants: Usually one or two attendants only. Dresses same length as bride wears. Corsages or small bouquets. Suitable accessories.

Bridegroom: Dark-gray or blue business suit, white shirt, stiff collar and four-in-hand or bow tie. Boutonniere: maroon carnation. Summer: light trousers, dark jacket or all-white suit.

Best Man, Ushers, Fathers: All men wear business suits, following lead of the bridegroom. Carnation boutonnieres.

Mothers and Women Guests: Informal dresses or suits, street length. Hats and conservative jewelry. Mothers may wear corsages.

Men Guests: All wear business suits for informal weddings.

CHECK LIST FOR ANY TYPE OF WEDDING

1. Check on church or room capacity. Do not invite more guests than can be comfortably accommodated.

2. Consider the amount of space available at the altar before you decide on the exact number of attendants.

3. Observe the lighting facilities by daylight, electric light or candlelight; then take advantage of the best time of day for flattering shadows, direct sunrays across the aisleway, glowing warmth cast by transept windows or colorful draperies, to give dramatic effect.

4. If it's a church wedding, go into a session with the church sexton. Note his name and telephone number for future reference.

5. Locate a suitable place at the church where you and your attendants may dress for the wedding.

6. Go into a huddle with your florist to chart decoration plans. Get estimates in writing.

7. Check on the preliminary music and add your own special favorites.

8. Confer with the minister on all arrangements. Remember to schedule the rehearsal.

9. Engage your caterer. See him later for details.

THE HONOUR
OF YOUR PRESENCE
IS REQUESTED

CHAPTER V

ENGRAVED INVITATIONS ARE AS MUCH A PART OF WEDDING tradition as the bridal veil itself.

Even though yours is to be an informal occasion, if *other* than close friends and relatives are going to be there, you will want to send out the formal kind.

It's logical that you (or your mother) wouldn't wish to telephone or send informal notes to a large group of casual friends or mere acquaintances—as you would do in the case of a very small wedding.

Forms are rigid as engraved invitations go, so there is little chance of going astray in their selection. The size and type of engraving may vary, but the general make-up and the wording remain *status in quo*.

Announcements and invitations should always be engraved to be correct, and the quality of paper should be of the best.

There is a near-engraving process on the market which

85

is much less expensive than real engraving but it is not advisable to resort to a facsimile method unless you are forced to cut corners drastically.

MAKING UP YOUR LISTS

Both families (yours and the bridegroom's) contribute to the invitation list and the time to start working on them is at once.

It is one thing, above all, that shouldn't be done haphazardly.

Consult your old address books. Start on a neighborhood list, your school list, a club list, a relative list, Christmas-card lists and a friend list. Then get the same tabulation from the groom's family.

If your wedding is in church and your reception at home, it is wise to make two separate lists—one for those who are to receive invitations to the wedding only, another for those who are to be included in the reception.

When you do your final pruning try not to cut down too rigidly. Everyone loves to see a wedding and to dance at one. It's a gracious custom in a large formal wedding to include old friends of the family who knew you when you were a child, servants of long standing, your seamstress and all those to whom your wedding has special sentimental significance.

Guests invited only to the church are under no obligations to send gifts, you know, if there is to be a reception. But an invitation to the wedding reception automatically calls for a present.

WHO ISSUES THE INVITATIONS?

Your parents should issue the invitations and announcements, even though you are not living at home. If your parents are not living, your aunt and uncle or nearest relatives may sponsor your wedding. A close friend or guardian may issue them, if it seems feasible. An older bride and groom often send their own announcements.

FORM OF INVITATION

There is a variety in paper sizes and colorings, with enclosure cards to correspond. You may have snow-white opaque paper, ivory, cream-laid or thin parchment paper in oyster-white.

The large, folded square is usually associated with the formal wedding and the smaller size with the less formal one.

"Shaded Roman" and "English Script" are among the most popular engraving styles. There are also "London Script," "Solid Roman," "Norman Trinity Text" and others. Any reliable engraver knows what is correct and will have a wide selection for you to see.

The invitation or announcement proper occupies only the first page, leaving the others blank.

Two envelopes are used, the inside one to enclose the invitation or announcement and the accompanying cards; the outside one for addressing and to protect the enclosure.

When you order from the engraver it's a good plan to request that the envelopes be sent out ahead of the invitations or announcements so that you can have them addressed and ready.

Order your thank-you note paper while you are at the engravers. You may use white "informals" (those folded white cards with your name engraved on the outside), or small folded sheets of white stationery or anything that is currently in vogue. Check your invitation lists for the number you will need. Have your stationery monogrammed, if you wish, with your maiden initials for notes to be sent before the wedding. Obviously, your married monogram should never be used until after your name has been changed. Colored note paper is smart for writing your shower gift thank-you expressions, but white is in better taste for wedding-gift notes.

If your wedding is to be small and you plan to send handwritten notes, select good quality white linen stationery in small folded sheets.

WORDING OF INVITATION

1. "Request the honour of your presence" is generally the accepted form to use for church wedding invitations. The word honour, you'll notice, is spelled with a "u."

2. "Request the pleasure of your company" is used for a home, club or hotel wedding since invitations include the reception following the ceremony.

3. First names should be written in full as initials do not identify sufficiently. Nicknames are never used.

4. Don't abbreviate titles, other than Mr., Mrs., and Dr. Junior should be spelled in full if space permits.

5. When invitations or announcements are issued by anyone other than the parents of the bride, or her bachelor

brother or unmarried sister (who all bear the same last name), the bride's full name should be used.

6. The name of the bride should be prefixed by "Miss" if the invitations are issued by someone who is not related to the bride. If it is a second marriage for a young woman, her parents may send the invitations or announcements without the prefix "Mrs."—but will use her married name. See page 102.

7. The street address may be engraved under the name of the church but it usually is not necessary.

8. "Daylight-saving time" may be engraved after the time of day on an invitation to avoid confusion.

9. Either the date line or the hour line should indicate whether the ceremony is to take place in the morning, afternoon or evening if the hour selected is one that would be confusing.

10. When the wedding takes places at noon, the hour may be designated as follows:

> "at high noon"
> "at twelve o'clock"
> "at twelve o'clock noon"

RECEPTION CARDS

Reception cards are enclosed in the same envelope with the wedding invitation.

It has become essential to ask for a reply on the reception card. The most commonly used forms are:

> Please respond.
> R.S.V.P.
> The favour of a reply is requested.
> Please send response to (address).

R.S.V.P. address should always be included on reception cards.

"Breakfast" is the word customarily used for the reception after the ceremony if it is before one o'clock in the afternoon.

"Reception" is the correct wording for the party after the ceremony if it is after one o'clock in the afternoon.

TYPICAL INVITATION FORMS

CHURCH WEDDING

Mr. and Mrs. George Clinton Ward
request the honour of your presence
at the marriage of their daughter
Margaret Ann
to
Mr. Thomas Lothrop Denny
on Thursday, the sixth of October
at four o'clock
Wesley Memorial Chapel
Brookline, Massachusetts

Reception card to accompany invitation:

> *Mr. and Mrs. George Clinton Ward*
> *request the pleasure of your company*
> *on Thursday, the sixth of October*
> *at half after four o'clock*
> *Forty-eight West Drive*

R.S.V.P.

Or the reception card may take this simplified form:

> *Reception*
> *immediately following the ceremony*
> *Forty-eight West Drive*

Please Respond

If you are inviting a limited number of persons to the wedding ceremony and wish to have a large reception you may use the following form, engraved on regulation size wedding paper:

> *Mr. and Mrs. George Clinton Ward*
> *request the pleasure of your company*
> *at the marriage reception of their daughter*
> *Margaret Ann*
> *and*
> *Mr. Thomas Lothrop Denny*
> *on Thursday, the sixth of October*
> *at half after four o'clock*
> *Forty-eight West Drive*
> *Brookline, Massachusetts*
> *The favour of a reply is requested*

The conjunction "and" couples the names of the bride and groom-to-be. The time given is one half hour after that set for the ceremony.

To those invited to both the ceremony and reception to follow, a small card of invitation to the ceremony should be enclosed with the invitation to the reception, for example:

Ceremony
at four o'clock
Wesley Memorial Chapel

CHURCH ADMISSION CARDS

Occasionally at a large wedding cards of admittance to the church may be necessary. They usually take this form:

Please present this card at
The Wesley Memorial Chapel
Thursday, the sixth of October

PEW CARDS

Cards to reserved pews are sometimes enclosed, also, for very large church weddings.

They may be thus engraved:

Please present this to an usher
Pew No. ——
on Thursday, the sixth of October

Or, the bride's mother may use her own calling card, writing in ink the number of the pew, in the upper left-hand corner; or she may write "Within the ribbons," which means the holder is seated in a reserved space marked off with ribbons.

INVITATION TO A CLUB WEDDING

Mr. and Mrs. John Charles Marshall
request the pleasure of your company
at the marriage of their niece
Rosemary Ellen Hinkle
to
Lieutenant Edward Lee Vance
United States Navy
Wednesday, the fourth of June
at twelve o'clock noon
The Meridian Club
Evanston, Illinois

R.S.V.P.
Ten Twelve Eastdale Avenue, Evanston

This invitation is extended by the aunt and uncle of the bride, therefore the bride's surname must be given.

The same wording is used in the home wedding invitation, i.e., "request the pleasure of your company," as it is considered the most cordial bidding in every instance where a reception follows the ceremony in home, club or hotel.

ANNOUNCEMENTS

There are three choices for the opening of the announcement of your wedding:
"announce the marriage of"
"have the honour to announce"
"have the honour of announcing"

The date and year as well as the city in which the ceremony is held should be given. This holds true even after an elopement, regardless of the time that has elapsed between the marriage and the announcement.

The year and the date are always spelled out.

Although the announcements are usually issued in the name of the bride's parents, it is also permissible to issue them in the names of the bride and groom.

TYPICAL ANNOUNCEMENT FORM

Mr. and Mrs. Gordon Charles Stuart
announce the marriage of their daughter
Unison Jane
to
Mr. Dale William Deebe
on Saturday, the ninth of February
Nineteen hundred and fifty
at Tabernacle Christian Church
Chicago, Illinois

Automobile direction cards are often engraved or printed and enclosed with the invitations to a country wedding.

"AT HOME" CARDS

Engraved "At Home" cards, such as the following, are often enclosed with announcements:

At Home
after the first of August
Thirteen hundred Elm Street
Evanston, Illinois

"At Home" cards have the advantage of informing out-of-town friends of your whereabouts. When they are not used, it is advisable for both the bride and the bridegroom to drop personal notes to those with whom they wish to keep in touch, telling their news and giving a return address.

ADDRESSING INVITATIONS OR ANNOUNCEMENTS

After your lists are complete, arrange them in alphabetical order to avoid confusion in checking.

If your own family is to attend to the addressing of the invitations, enlist the aid of those who have decorative handwriting. One member of the group might be responsible for addressing all those from A to G, another from G to P and so on. Give everybody plenty of elbow space, good pens, black ink and firm tables on which to write. The groom might like to participate in this chore if he has a steady hand.

If life is too complicated to take on this responsibility at home, stationers will refer you to a professional secretary who will relieve you of addressing, stamping and mailing your invitations. There is a charge for this service, of course.

All invitations must be sent out at one time. The invitations and enclosures are inserted in the inside envelope, which has no glue on the flap. The tissue squares which accompany the folded sheets eliminate the possibility of ink smears and should remain as the engraver has placed them.

The inner envelope should be addressed, "Mr. and Mrs., etc.," *only the last name without address.* If it is necessary to include an entire family with one invitation, the "and family" may be added on the inside envelope but *never on the outside envelope.*

You'll show greater courtesy if each individual member of a family (with the exception of "Mr. and Mrs.") receives a separate invitation or announcement. In the case of families with several small children an invitation may bear all their names, such as, "Mary, Jean, Jack and Fred Kingan," or you may say "The Misses Kingan" on one invitation and "The Messrs. Kingan" on another and enclose these envelopes in the outer envelope addressed to the parents.

The outside envelope bears both the name and address, with names of streets and names of states spelled in full. No abbreviations should appear on the envelope except "Mr." and "Mrs." and "Dr."

ATTENDANTS RECEIVE INVITATIONS

Each member of the wedding party should receive an engraved invitation, sent at the time all other invitations are mailed.

SPECIAL COURTESY TO GROOM'S FAMILY

As soon as the invitations are off the press, why not send a batch of three or four unsealed invitations on to the bridegroom's family so that they may see them and have them as keepsakes? Your mother might enclose a little note to the bridegroom's mother, saying something like this: "Your list of invitations is ready to be sent out on such-and-such a date and we wanted you to share in the thrill of seeing them right away . . . etc."

To all other members of the bridegroom's family living at

their home (perhaps a grandmother or an aunt) personally addressed invitations should be sent at the regular mailing time.

SHOULD MINISTER AND WIFE RECEIVE AN ENGRAVED INVITATION?

Usually the minister and his wife are sent an engraved invitation to the reception at the time all invitations are mailed. However, if there is a hesitancy in not wishing to obligate the clergyman's family for a wedding gift, an informal invitation may be issued by word of mouth to the minister and his wife by the bride's mother or by the bride herself.

WHEN TO MAIL

Invitations should be mailed three weeks in advance of the ceremony; if yours is to be a very large formal wedding you may mail them four weeks in advance.

Announcements should be mailed immediately after the ceremony, on the same day if possible. Send them only to those who were not invited to the wedding.

SPECIAL INVITATIONS AND ANNOUNCEMENTS

WHEN PARENTS ARE DIVORCED

Here's where the most gracious way of coping with a situation is the correct way. And where sensitive feelings must be handled with care.

If the bride lives with her mother who has not remarried, the following invitation is customary, using the mother's maiden and married names, never her former husband's Christian name:

Mrs. Wilson Wood
requests the honour of your presence
at the marriage of her daughter
Alice Jean

In the case of friendly divorce where neither parent has remarried and both expect to participate in the wedding, the bride's father and mother may be tempted to send out invitations which bear both their names as wedding sponsors, i.e., "Mrs. Wilson Wood and Mr. James Lawton Wood request the honour . . . etc."

This is *not* considered good taste, however, among discerning persons and belongs only in the "raised eyebrow department."

IF THE BRIDE'S MOTHER HAS REMARRIED

Any one of the following invitation forms is correct.

The mother alone may issue the invitation to the wedding ceremony:

Mrs. George Barton Steele
requests the honour of your presence
at the marriage of her daughter
Alice Jean Wood
to

Or, the bride's stepfather may join his wife in sponsoring the wedding, using either of the following forms:

Mr. and Mrs. George Steele
request the honour of your presence
at the marriage of Mrs. Steele's daughter
Alice Jean Wood
to

If the bride's father is more or less out of the picture:

Mr. and Mrs. George Steele
request the honour of your presence
at the marriage of their *daughter*
Alice Jean Wood
to

Although the wedding invitation may be issued in the name of one parent alone, the reception invitation *must* be issued in the name of the couple who are giving the party. For instance, the bride's father alone may "request the honour of your presence at the marriage of his daughter." *But,* if he has remarried, he and his wife sponsor the reception and send out reception cards in both names. In the event the bride's mother has remarried, the same rule holds true for the inclusion of her husband.

Giving the bride's surname in the case of divorced and remarried parents clarifies the relationship and is customary, though not obligatory.

WHEN THE BRIDE'S MOTHER IS WIDOWED

Unless the bride's widowed mother has remarried, the wedding invitation is issued in the following form:

Mrs. Arthur Oliver Burton
requests the honour of your presence
at the marriage of her daughter
Gloria Ann
to

A widower substitutes the expression "his daughter."

When the bride's mother has remarried the relationship between the bride and her stepfather is clarified thus:

Mr. and Mrs. James Claridge Mason
request the honour of your presence
at the marriage of Mrs. Mason's daughter
Gloria Ann Burton
to

If the bride has been adopted by her stepfather or is very close to him, the following form is correct:

Mr. and Mrs. James Claridge Mason
request the honour of your presence
at the marriage of their daughter
Gloria Ann Burton
to

WHEN A BRIDE IS BEING SPONSORED BY OTHER THAN PARENTS

The bride's surname should be given when invitations are extended by other than parents. The words "his sister," "her sister" or "their niece" are substituted for the phrase "their daughter."

If the bride is being sponsored by close friends, the invitation should carry the bride's full name, prefaced by "Miss."

Mr. and Mrs. Paul Thomas Hale
request the honour of your presence
at the marriage of
Miss Constance Caroline Stevens
to

When a couple has no wedding sponsor, they may correctly send out their own invitations worded as follows:

The honour of your presence
is requested at the marriage of
Miss Gertrude Jennifer
to
Mr. Benjamin Foster Decker
on Friday, the fourth of May
at four-thirty o'clock
First Presbyterian Church
Evanston, Illinois

IF IT'S ALTAR TRIP NUMBER TWO

The bride's parents should issue invitations for the second wedding of a widowed daughter just as in the first wedding. Following is the usual form:

Mr. and Mrs. Hamilton Trenton Burns
request the honour of your presence
at the marriage of their daughter
Mary Lou Burford
to

The invitation for a divorced bride reads:

Mr. and Mrs. Hamilton Trenton Burns
request the honour of your presence
at the marriage of their daughter
Mary Burns Burford
to

The prefix "Mrs." is never used before the bride's name unless she and the bridegroom are issuing the invitations themselves as in the case of the widow who has no one to sponsor her wedding:

The honour of your presence is requested
at the marriage of
Mrs. Harold White Aiken
to
Mr. John Patton Rusk

The following reception card may be enclosed with the above invitation:

The pleasure of your company is requested
Thursday the twentieth of June
at five o'clock
The Town Club
Los Angeles, California

R.S.V.P.
33 Dalton Place

DOUBLE WEDDINGS

A formal invitation to a double wedding of sisters is as follows:

Mr. and Mrs. John Dexter Randolph
request the pleasure of your company
at the marriage of their daughters
Jenny Lou
to
Dr. James Frances Taylor
and
Helen Frances
to
Mr. Burton Kenneth Lowell
on the evening of Saturday, June first
at eight o'clock
Eight hundred and nine North High Street
Richmond, Virginia

When the brides in a double wedding are not sisters, regular separate invitations may be sent by each family, or they may unite to send the following type invitation:

Mr. and Mrs. Joseph Axton Lee
and
Mr. and Mrs. Floyd Murton Brown
request the honour of your presence
at the marriage of their daughters
Helen Hinckle Lee
to
Mr. Gerald Allen Burkett
and
Dorothy Elizabeth Brown
to
Mr. Reginald Fenton West

SPECIAL ANNOUNCEMENTS

FOR DIVORCEES

The older bride who has been divorced may wish to send out her own announcements, along with her new husband. The form is as follows:

> *Mrs. Stafford Williams*
> *and*
> *Mr. Clifford Aaron Whyte*
> *announce their marriage*
> *on Wednesday, the first of June*
> *etc.*

The divorcee uses her maiden name combined with the surname of her first husband. She should never address herself as Mrs. George Williams, for instance, since her former husband may have married again.

If the divorced bride is still young, her parents should send out the wedding announcements as follows:

> *Mr. and Mrs. Burton Quincy Freeman*
> *have the honour to announce*
> *the marriage of their daughter*
> *Margaret Freeman Brice*
> *to*
> *Mr. Jack Deeley Ford*
> *on Saturday, the fifth of August*
> *one thousand nine hundred and fifty*
> *Washington, D. C.*

A young widow's announcements would follow the example above, carrying her first husband's name (omitting her maiden name) if she wishes. The older widow, sending her own announcements, may use her husband's given name, i.e.:

Mrs. Harry Waldon Anderson
and
Mr. James Townsend Knight
announce their marriage

MILITARY WEDDINGS

The use of service titles is the only distinguishing difference between civilian and military types of formal invitations and announcements.

The groom's title (or the bride's, if she is a member of the armed services) precedes his name only if he is an officer holding the rank of captain or higher, in the Army or Marine Corps, or a senior-grade lieutenant or higher, in the Navy.

It is more or less traditional for noncommissioned officers, privates in the Army and Marine Corps and petty officers and nonrated men in the Navy, to use "Mr." before the groom's name with the branch or corps name following on the next line, i.e., "Infantry United States Army" or "Supply Corps, United States Navy." Military men sometimes prefer the omission of the "Mr." before the name, in which case the following is correct:

Louis Tompkins Price
Second Lieutenant, Infantry, United States Army

or

Walter Wilkins Bryden
Supply Corps, United States Navy

Junior officers usually prefer the omission of the "Mr." before their names, as follows:

Claude Ruskin Wright
Ensign, United States Navy

When the groom is a member of the Reserve Corps in active service, the correct wording on invitations or announcements would be "Army of the United States" or "United States Naval Reserve," in place of "United States Army" or "United States Navy." The preceding rules apply as to titles, etc.

If the groom is a student in a Reserve Army Officers' School, the title "Cadet" is properly used under his name and with his branch.

A formal invitation to the wedding of an Army daughter whose prospective bridegroom is in the service would read:

Colonel and Mrs. Frank Carraway Morrison
request the honour of your presence
at the marriage of their daughter
Winifred Mary
to
Commander George Custis Worthington
United States Navy

Or, if the groom is a junior officer:

to
George Custis Worthington
Lieutenant, United States Navy

If the groom is an officer or enlisted man in the Marine Corps, the same rules apply as in the case of Army personnel with the designation "United States Marine Corps" instead of "United States Army."

WHEN WEDDING INVITATIONS MUST BE RECALLED

If it is necessary to postpone or cancel a formal wedding and there is sufficient time, engraved cards, enclosed in one envelope only, may be sent to everyone who received an invitation.

Typical form for recalling invitations with reason for cancellation given:

Mr. and Mrs. Herbert O'Dair Gifford
regret that owing to illness in the family
the invitations to their daughter's wedding
on Saturday, October fifteenth
must be recalled

If not wishing to state reason for recalling invitations:

Mr. and Mrs. Herbert O'Dair Gifford
regret that they must recall
the invitations to their daughter's wedding
on Saturday, October fifteenth

In case there is not sufficient time for having engraved cards made, members of the bride's family may recall the invitations verbally by personal note, telegram or telephone.

If the wedding is definitely cancelled and time permits, the bride's parents should send out an engraved card following this form:

Mr. and Mrs. Herbert O'Dair Gifford
announce that the marriage of their daughter
Frances Kay
to
Mr. Glen Morton Plessing
will not take place

In such circumstances wedding gifts must be returned to the senders.

CHAPTER VI

In the Presence of This Company

IT'S ONLY NATURAL THAT YOU WILL WANT TO GATHER YOUR dearest friends and members of your family about you on the great day, as wedding attendants. There'll be much to share that you'll all remember romantically so long as you all shall live. Give some serious thought as to whose *presence* is important to you on this momentous occasion.

"This company" will not only lend you moral support but will be highly useful and very decorative.

How many attendants you have depends on how many you want, on the size of your wedding and the place it is to be held.

In making up your personal list use some discretion. Don't ask girls who can't afford to buy their own wedding trappings, for it is always customary for wedding attendants to buy their own outfits and pretty things have a way of running into money. Do try to be as considerate as possible, however, in your clothes selections, and help them choose something that will look as well dancing to Lombardo in days to come as it does marching to Lohengrin on the wedding day.

HOW MANY BRIDESMAIDS?

There are no cut-and-dried rules on the number you should choose. You may be married in the largest church in your town, with hundreds of guests, and yet have no bridesmaids —only a maid of honor to hold your bouquet and straighten your train as you leave the altar. Bridesmaids, like ladies in waiting, furnish the colorful backdrop to your wedding picture, so the prettier the girls, the lovelier the wedding.

Regardless of the dozen or so college chums you airily invited to be in your wedding when it was a remote subject, don't have more than eight. It always seems a bit theatrical to have a chorus looking like the Rockettes at Music Hall precede you down the aisle. For a simple wedding you'll want fewer bridesmaids.

You may have one, two, four, six or eight. If you decide on an uneven number you might have three bridesmaids. They will make an effective scene walking single file, followed by the maid of honor. Or you might have five, with the shortest girl leading, alone, followed by the other bridesmaids walking in pairs.

Consider yourself fortunate if the girls in your wedding party are all near the same height so that they will make a lovely and "balanced" picture at the altar.

You will want your most intimate friends to attend you, but don't forget about the groom's sisters, if he has any. Whether the attendants are married or not makes no difference.

MAID AND MATRON OF HONOR

Why not have both a maid and a matron of honor if you are planning a big wedding? Your married sister is the logical matron, and your unmarried sister or best friend might serve as maid.

It's going a little strong to have two matrons of honor or two maids of honor, but it may be done in a large wedding.

Your maid or matron of honor is indispensable to you at the altar. She adjusts your veil and train, she holds your bouquet during the ceremony and lifts back your face veil at

the close of the ceremony. She is one of the two witnesses to sign the marriage certificate. She may help you dress for the wedding; she will see to it that the bridesmaids are ready on time and will serve as your lady in waiting in all details.

JUNIOR BRIDESMAIDS

Is your little sister too young to be a bridesmaid . . . yet too tall to act as flower girl? By all means use her as junior bridesmaid in your wedding.

A girl of that in-between age (from a tall ten to sixteen) may lead the procession as junior bridesmaid with the bridesmaids following singly or in twos. She wears a long gown similar in style to the bridesmaids and perhaps corresponding in color to the maid or matron of honor's.

Her bouquet is of the same type as the other attendants but proportionately smaller.

FLOWER GIRLS

You may have two little flower girls in long, flowing skirts trip down the aisle scattering rose petals in your pathway. They should be about the same size and between the ages of four and eight to be effective. Tiny tots too young to understand what is going on are likely to play games at the altar and steal the bride's show.

Little sisters of either the bride or groom may serve as flower girls, but have anyone you want. There may be one only or you may have more. They often carry Colonial bouquets or old-fashioned nosegays instead of a French basket of rose petals. Dresses may match the bridesmaids' in color, or they may be entrancing little Kate Greenaway gowns with matching bonnets. A flower girl may simply wear a pretty party dress, short length. Her shoes may be ballet slippers, white or pastel kid Mary Janes.

RING BEARER

Few brides have ring bearers any more. However, if there is a little round-eyed boy of four or five in your family let him take part in this pageant of yours.

He should wear a white linen suit or a little-boy dark suit and white blouse (never knickers or miniature Tuxedos or tails). He might carry a satin cushion with the ring tied on to insure its safe journey to the altar. A token ring is sometimes tucked into a calla lily which the ring bearer carries instead of the pillow. It is risky to entrust the real ring to a ring bearer unless special precautions are taken.

As to his place in the processional, he may go down the aisle with the flower girl or alone, preceding you and your father.

A ring bearer may also be a little girl, you know, and dressed much the same as a flower girl. Children look most effective when quite simply dressed.

USHERS

The size of your wedding determines the number of ushers whom you'll ask to serve in the wedding. It would be ridiculous to have ten or twelve ushers at a small wedding with only a handful of guests. One usher for every twenty-five or fifty guests is considered adequate.

It is not necessary to have exactly the same number of ushers as there are bridesmaids but the wedding party is in better balance when there is somewhere near the same number.

A large church wedding requires quite a number of ushers: at least two or more for every hundred guests invited. In a house wedding ushers are more honorary than active. It's a good idea though to have two who will escort each of the mothers to their respective places just before the ceremony. Also, they are helpful in seeing that very old or distinguished friends are personally taken to the reception line after the ceremony.

A garden wedding may have one, two or more ushers, or you may decide on none.

When there are a number of ushers, the bridegroom usually selects one as head usher to direct the others.

They should all be dressed as nearly alike as possible. This is not only for the sake of uniformity, but it also makes them readily distinguishable from other guests.

At a formal wedding the ushers generally wear boutonnieres of white carnations with their formal clothes. Red carnations or blue bachelor buttons go well with the informal mood, if they tie in with the general color scheme.

The ushers should arrive at the church at least an hour before the ceremony so that they may escort early arrivals to their seats. Their duties extend on into the reception . . . but we'll see that they get their final instructions when it's nearer time for the wedding (page 250).

WHO IS TO GIVE YOU AWAY?

Your father is the logical one to give you away and he will escort you down the aisle on his right arm. If not your

father, then your uncle, brother or nearest and dearest relative.

This escort of yours is considered a member of the bridal party and should follow the dictates of the bridegroom in the matter of dress. He may use his own discretion in the selection of neckwear, but generally conforms in all other details. (See dress chart, page 55.) At the altar he stands just behind and a little to the left of the bride until the question is asked, "Who giveth this woman to be married to this man?" He then answers, "I do,"* and takes his place in the first pew on the left of the middle aisle, beside the bride's mother.

If you should wish your mother to give you away in the absence of your father, you will walk up the aisle alone. She will merely stand in her place in the front left pew, and at the proper time during the ceremony will murmur, "I do," in answer to the minister's inquiry.

THE BEST MAN

The best man may be a brother of the groom, a cousin or an intimate friend. Or he may be the groom's father. He should wear the same attire as the groom at a formal wedding with only a difference of boutonniere. (Usually he wears a white gardenia or carnation and the bridegroom wears a sprig of lily of the valley.)

The best man's official position is a cross between valet, trained nurse and general manager . . . and he is the hardest-working member of the wedding crew as you will soon see.

---

* One devoted father of a bride recently thrilled the wedding guests by unexpectedly answering the minister's question with, "Her mother and I."

CASE HISTORY OF A BEST MAN WHO ENJOYED HIMSELF TO THE LAST DROP

In the world of best men, Jerry rated high.

He had a natural knack for bolstering bridegrooms and prided himself on never having dropped a ring.

He could cope with situations and always remained in a state of unruffled calm. Just a veritable tower of strength on whom quaking bridegrooms could lean.

As he surveyed his good friend Tom dressing for the wedding, he took his duties in his stride. He mastered a recalcitrant wing collar and assumed his role of valet.

He had been Tom's constant companion since the bridegroom had arrived from his home out of town. He had seen to it that his formal clothes were pressed for the wedding and had personally brushed his top hat till it shone. He had packed for him that morning and had stowed his honeymoon luggage safely away in the car.

Now Tom wandered over to the hotel window, dazedly watching the world go by. Jerry adroitly brought him back to the present with flattering words about being so "lucky in love." He answered the hotel telephone when it rang like a warning signal and assured the inquirer that yes, they would be on time at the church. The bridegroom was doing as well as could be expected and he was lending all *his* moral support.

Skillfully he tied Tom's ascot and administered the necessary last-minute touches.

He consulted his watch, called a cab to be sure that one

would be waiting and virtually propelled Tom out the door.

They arrived at the church with a half hour's leeway and went directly to the vestry by the side door. The boutonnieres were on the desk waiting to be pinned on their coat lapels.

Jerry extracted a brand-new bill from Tom's wallet and slipped it into an envelope, to be given to the minister later . . . then he proceeded to take the bridegroom's hat and gloves around to the vestibule.

He saw that the guests were fast arriving and there were only a few more minutes to wait. Back in the vestry, he gave Tom a final going over and as the bridal march rolled out its first melodious notes, Tom was steered through the door with Jerry following after and—the wedding had begun!

"There goes another man from our college Bachelor's Club . . . and no more Tom-and-Jerry sessions for us!" he mourned to himself as he produced the ring at just the right minute and listened while Tom earnestly plighted his troth to the lovely creature on his left.

He stood by as prompter as Tom tenderly kissed the bride. Then he joined the maid of honor and followed the bridal couple in the recessional.

"So far, so good," Jerry breathed as the wedding party left for the reception and he dashed back to the vestry to give the minister his fee and pick up his own hat, gloves and stick.

While the reception was getting under way at the bride's home he went out to check on the baggage, just to make sure. He saw to it that Tom's traveling clothes were awaiting him in the guest-room closet where he had hung them earlier in the day.

Everything was going as he had planned (he could perform the ritual in his sleep) . . . so he joined the bridal party in time to drink a champagne toast to the bride and nibble on some cake.

Then back again to the guest room with Tom, to assist him into his going-away clothes and maneuver him around as he made his last adieus.

At last, through a shower of rose petals, the bridal couple made a safe honeymoon get-away.

Proudly Jerry pulled out of his pocket a typewritten list headed "Duties of a best man." Every item had been duly checked off . . . another scalp added to his belt.

But now that his role was ended, he no longer felt so cocksure. Suddenly he made a beeline for the punch bowl for a bit of needed bolstering. A bad reaction was setting in and he was as nervous as a bridegroom.

CHAPTER VII

The Vow and Covenant

THE MILITARY WEDDING

YOU WILL PARADE UNDER THE SHINING BLADES OF YOUR service man's ushers and the men will be in uniform. That, in brief, is the outstanding difference between the civilian and military ceremonies.

You will follow the same suggested pattern of the formal church wedding if that is the type you have chosen. The basic structure remains the same as in any other wedding.

It is classified as "military" when the groom is a member of the armed services and chooses ushers from among his military friends only. The best man may or may not be a civilian. If he is a civilian, he and the bride's father (or whoever gives her in marriage) should wear formal attire. (See chart, page 75.) The main variation in ritual is that after the completion of the ceremony the ushers draw their sabers and frame the arch under which you and the bridegroom pass in the recessional.

If the bridegroom is a West Point graduate or a Naval Academy man, he presents his bride with a miniature of his own class ring, set either with a smaller stone similar to his, or a diamond. This, according to military custom, is her engagement ring.

If you are an Army or Navy daughter, steeped in the customs of the service, you doubtless will want to have all the fanfare of a true military wedding.

If you live with your parents on a post you probably will wish to have the Army chaplain (or Navy, if you live on a Navy base) officiate at the wedding. All garrison officers and their wives are usually invited to both the ceremony and reception.

If you are not an Army daughter and the wedding is not held on the post, you should see to it that the groom's post commander and his commanding officer are invited with their wives.

Likewise, in a Navy wedding which is not held on a naval base, it is customary to invite the groom's commanding officer, his executive officer and the head of his department.

MEN'S DRESS REGULATIONS

In a very formal wedding during peacetime, both Army and Navy personnel may wear dress uniforms—Army blues in winter, dress Army whites in summer, and the same for Navy men. During a period of war and national emergency, however, officers after graduation are not required to include formal dress uniforms, so may wear olive drab for Army, and regulation Navy blues for a Navy wedding. All military members wear side arms and leave their caps in the vestibule. No boutonnieres are worn with uniforms.

The entire wedding party should conform to formal or informal dress, according to the mood set by the uniforms. Civilian guests wear formal daytime or evening dress at formal military weddings, business suits for informal weddings.

In both Army and Navy weddings medal ribbons may be worn with the regulation uniforms. Large medals are worn with dress uniforms. Miniature medals are worn with undress uniforms, on the left lapel.

For feminine attire in formal, semiformal and informal ceremonies see charts, pages 75-84.

Decorations: Usually the bride and groom stand under the national and regimental colors or unit standard arranged with the decorations at the altar. These flags may be crossed or stand separately. White flowers may be used at the altar, as well as aisle-post decorations for formal weddings.

The wedding procession differs very little from any civilian ceremony procession, but the recessional is distinctly its own. (See pages 255-257 for specific details.)

RECEPTION PROTOCOL AND REMINDERS

The bride and groom together cut the bride's cake with saber or sword. After the wedding party is seated at the bridal table, if it's a sit-down affair, other guests are seated according to military rank.

The arch of swords or sabers is for commissioned officers only.

There is no rule prompting anyone to have a strictly military wedding merely because the bridegroom happens to be in the service.

Reserve officers do not have military weddings unless they are on active duty.

For information on invitations to military weddings see page 106; for detailed information on reception following military service see page 216.

THE GARDEN WEDDING

An exchange of vows under clear blue skies. How perfect!

The only drawback is that the skies cannot always be counted on to be clear blue and no one ever heard of a bride carrying an umbrella down the aisle.

The only thing to do is to plan two altars instead of one. One for the garden and the other for indoors in case of rain. Since your house will be in order anyway it will require very little trouble to move the kneeling bench and altar arrangement of flowers inside if the weather is threatening. The important point is to be prepared.

Any Mood You Choose

A garden wedding may be strictly formal, semiformal or informal. It all depends on the type of clothes you wear.

If you choose a wedding gown with long train, with the men in formal attire, follow the rules set down for the formal house wedding.

If the bridegroom and his attendants want to wear white linen suits or white flannel trousers and dark coats, wear a simpler wedding gown of floor length and make it semiformal.

If you want to wear a street-length dress of white or light pastel of the informal sort, the men may wear light summer clothes. There is much latitude offered in such a wedding.

An aisle canvas should outline the way to the altar for the formal wedding. You may have it for the semiformal wedding if you wish.

In these days of vitamin treatment for flowers, a host of plants may be transplanted while they are in bloom . . . to glorify your garden if you need them. And trellises may be arranged and planted with trailing vines.

For the less elaborate affair, the smooth green lawn will serve as a setting for the sort of wedding everyone enjoys.

A clump of bushes, a niche in a garden wall, a columned summer house or the shade of a lovely big tree will serve as a beautiful background for the ceremony.

Look about the garden and decide on a spot for the altar. Try to arrange it so that guests may view the ceremony without facing the sun if possible.

Add the charm of color—pedestals of flowers or garlands of green outlining the aisle pathway . . . your bridal party in frothy frocks as debonair as a summer breeze.

Place the punch bowl and table under the rose arbor, or arrange to have buffet service in the summer house. Serve your wedding repast at small tables under a marquee in another part of the garden, if the occasion is to be that elaborate. Or have guests proceed to the porch or a shaded terrace for light refreshments which they can take standing up.

THE DOUBLE WEDDING

A double wedding ceremony with its sweet sentiment and beautiful pageantry offers twice as much opportunity for developing your ideas as a single wedding.

It may be carried out in formal, semiformal or informal mood. However you wish it. The brides may be sisters or very close friends. Each has her own wedding party group who precede her to the altar.

Harmony of color and style in the matter of clothes is important, but the brides do not have to be dressed exactly alike, nor do their respective attendants.

If the brides are sisters, the older one is given in marriage by her father and precedes the younger bride to the altar. The second bride may be escorted by her brother, uncle or near relative.

If there is an unusually wide aisle both sisters may be escorted by their father, one on each arm.

If the brides are friends, instead of sisters, each father gives his own daughter in marriage.

Be sure to select a church with ample altar space (if it's to be a church wedding) before you arrange for a large number of attendants. In one double wedding of note, the brides, who were sisters, served as maid and matron of honor to each other. This arrangement lessened the size of the wedding party, yet furnished the required number of witnesses and was doubly impressive.

You'll find details on double-wedding invitations and church procedure, in other chapters (pages 103 and 254).

If It Is Altar Trip Number Two

If this is your second entrance into marriage there's no reason why you should have to sneak surreptitiously away from family and friends for a bleak civil ceremony. Naturally you will not plan a large pompous cathedral wedding, but hearts in love are ever young and sentimental, so why not make it a memorable occasion of sweet simplicity, dignity and tradition—"to be remembered as long as you both shall live!"

Wouldn't you like to wear a lovely pastel or deep-toned dinner gown with a stunning little hat . . . and follow the rules for the semiformal wedding? Or maybe you'll want to wear your going-away suit with orchids pinned to your muff or an afternoon dress with a corsage at your belt. You can be a pretty, pretty bride and still not wear white, you know.

Even though you may have been married very young and soon widowed, even though you may feel that you were cheated out of having a big fancy wedding—don't consider white for a second wedding. A long flowing veil is equally bad taste if you have been married before.

In every other respect, however, you may follow many of the tenets and traditions of a semiformal or informal wedding (page 102). Your family may send out engraved invitations, just as in a first marriage. More often guests are invited orally or by informal notes. Or you may have your parents send out announcements only.

Your father may give you away, even though he may have done so in your first wedding. You may be married in a church, chapel or at home or club. Your decorations follow the same style suggested for any informal wedding, as does the time of your wedding.

Your groom will have a best man, and may have ushers if occasion demands. You may have a maid or matron of honor but don't have a great number of bridesmaids. You don't have to have *any*. If you are a widow, you may wish to have your own daughter as flower girl or maid of honor with you in the wedding.

If it is the groom's second marriage and the bride's first, the wedding plans may be of a more formal nature and still remain in good taste. It is unlikely, however, that a bride will want to celebrate with too much fanfare. Good common sense, local custom and the dictates of your church will all come in good stead.

If the Bride's Parents Are Divorced

Here's where the most gracious way of coping with a situation is the correct way. And where sensitive feelings must be carefully considered.

It is perfectly permissible for a bride to be given in marriage by her divorced father if she so desires, even though her mother with whom she lives has married again. The invitations should be issued by the mother only. But the reception cards will be in the name of the mother and her second husband, since he will act as host for the reception. (See invitations, page 100.)

The bride's father is unlikely to go to the reception, but again he may, accompanied by his second wife, if there is a friendly feeling existing between the two families.

After the bride's father (in these circumstances) has given her in marriage at the altar, he retires by a side aisle into a rear pew.

On the other hand, if the bride is not close to her own father, she may be given in marriage by her stepfather, an uncle or whomever she chooses.

Invitations or announcements may be sent in both the mother and stepfather's name if the stepfather is to sponsor the bride through her entire wedding. The invitations may even read "request the honour of your presence at the marriage of *their* daughter," if the bride's own father is out of the picture.

If the bride-to-be lives with her father, he should sponsor her marriage. Whether or not her mother attends the wedding is a matter to be settled individually.

The Older Bride

If the older bride, who has always dreamed of a white wedding, is youthful enough in appearance and not too mature in age, she may sidestep censure among her friends by settling for a wedding in the semiformal mood, rather than playing the lead in a large formal church wedding with pageantry as a premium.

She may select a white wedding gown of traditional style with short train or trainless, and carry out all conforming details. If she wishes she may wear a mass of white flowers in her hair in place of a finger-tip veil and feel less conspicuous as she trips to the altar.

White is a bridal right for any first-time bride, but age and appearance should all be taken into consideration before decking oneself out in full wedding regalia.

A large reception is in perfect order following a church ceremony. The bride may be given in marriage by her father and be attended by both maid of honor and bridesmaids. Junior bridesmaids or flower girls make lovely attendants for the older bride, but the number in the wedding party should be held down to reasonableness in any case.

THE CIVIL CEREMONY

If, for your own special reasons, you and your bridegroom wish to evade all wedding fanfare, you may go quietly to a county clerk or a judge or the justice of the peace to exchange your vows.

Either a suit or short dress is customary for wearing to the courthouse or the justice of the peace's office or home. When you are married at the home of a judge, however, you may wear a long dress and be attended by a maid or matron of honor if you so wish.

In any circumstances you may have a reception or wedding breakfast for any number of friends following this kind of quiet ceremony.

Is It Ever Permissible?

Q. Is it ever permissible in an informal wedding to hold the ceremony in the new home of the bridal couple?

A. If there is no alternative but a county clerk's unromantic office, by all means don't hesitate to create an atmosphere of charm as a wedding background even though it may be only a handkerchief-sized apartment to which you resort. It is an irregularity in the world of wedding etiquette, but one that is understandable to your friends. However, make certain in such circumstances that your mother or a close relative is present to sponsor the occasion and act as hostess at the wedding and reception.

CHAPTER VIII

In Holy Wedlock

WHATEVER YOUR RELIGIOUS FAITH, THERE ARE CERTAIN FAC-tors to respect and consider before making your complete wedding plans.

You will not want to plan a large church wedding, for instance, during Lent or Holy Week. Lutheran and Episcopalian clergymen, as well as many others, will not solemnize a marriage service on a solemn holy day such as Christmas or Easter or any day of abstinence. Others object to Sunday weddings, largely because of the heavy church duties of that day.

ANY CHURCH FEES?

It is well to bear in mind that there often is a very sizable fee for holding a wedding in a large city church due to the expense of the lighting, heating and other janitorial services. Some churches require, in addition, a nominal sum for office fees, rehearsal charges and other "extras." Financial rates for church musicians are usually established by the church if regular organist and choir members are used.

If the church supplies canopy, carpet, candles, et cetera, there is an additional fee.

131

CHURCH REGULATIONS TO HONOR

An orthodox musical service is followed in a great number of churches. Many have a ruling that all wedding music, vocal and instrumental, must be approved by the choir director. It is usually permissible to bring a soloist from outside the church, and when a fee is paid it is in accordance with the musician's professional rate. Soft music may be played throughout the ceremony in most churches, but during prayers the organist must remain silent.

In many churches it is mandatory that the congregation rise and remain standing during the wedding ceremony. Your minister will advise you on this important point so that your family and the groom's may take the lead for guests seated in the pews behind them.

The bridal kiss at the close of the ceremony is not permitted in some churches. It is a matter of personal choice at any time.

Suitable head coverings for bridal party members and feminine guests is required in most churches.

FAVORED HOURS FOR PROTESTANT WEDDINGS

The most favored hours for Protestant weddings of a formal character are high noon (twelve o'clock), four o'clock in the afternoon and eight o'clock in the evening.

When the wedding is small and informal the ceremony may take place in the minister's study, his home, in the church parlors or in the chapel at any time convenient to the clergyman.

No Special Restrictions for Wedding Party

Members of the bridal party are not required to belong to the same church or to any church.

Ministers usually wish to have at least two other persons besides the bridal pair present for the ceremony even though the marriage takes place in a state which requires no witnesses to the wedding.

Marriage of Divorced Persons

Most Protestant churches recognize divorce and will permit remarriages to take place in the church edifice provided the couple are Christians. There are certain strictures employed in some churches, however, which may justly cause a minister to refuse to marry certain divorced couples. This should be discussed confidentially with your clergyman early in the wedding planning.

The Marriage Ceremony

The modern marriage service consists of three parts: (a) the betrothal; (b) exchange of vows; (c) the benediction. The ring ceremony is usually the most solemn part of the service, coming directly after the mutual promises of fidelity and love.

A beautiful ring ceremony symbolizing the perfect circle of married life is one that is used by many Protestant ministers. It is made up of the following steps:

1. The best man gives the ring to the groom
2. The groom gives it to the bride
3. The bride in turn gives it to the minister
4. The minister hands it again to the groom
5. The groom places it on the ring finger of the bride, saying (after the minister), "This ring I give thee in token and pledge of our constant faith and abiding love."

When a double ring ceremony is used, your minister will instruct you fully before the ceremony as to procedure.

THE PROTESTANT EPISCOPAL SERVICE

Many Protestant churches other than the Episcopal Church use the Episcopal wedding ceremony, which is as follows:

Dearly beloved, we are gathered together here in the sight of God, and in the face of this company, to join together this Man and this Woman in holy Matrimony; which is an honourable estate, instituted of God, signifying unto us the mystical union that is betwixt Christ and his Church: which holy estate Christ adorned and beautified with his presence and first miracle that he wrought in Cana of Galilee, and is commended of Saint Paul to be honourable among all men: and therefore is not by any to be entered into unadvisedly or lightly; but reverently, discreetly, advisedly, soberly, and in the fear of God. Into this holy estate these two persons present come now to be joined. If any man can show just cause, why they may not lawfully be joined together, let him now speak, or else hereafter for ever hold his peace.

And also speaking unto the Persons who are to be married, he shall say,

I require and charge you both, as ye will answer at the dreadful day of judgment when the secrets of all hearts shall be disclosed, that if either of you know any impediment, why ye may not be lawfully joined together in Matrimony, ye do now confess it. For be ye well assured, that if any persons are joined together otherwise than as God's Word doth allow, their marriage is not lawful.

The Minister if he shall have reason to doubt of the lawfulness of the proposed Marriage, may demand sufficient surety for his indemnification: but if no impediment shall be alleged, or suspected, the Minister shall say to the Man,

N. wilt thou have this Woman to thy wedded wife, to live together after God's ordinance in the holy estate of Matrimony? Wilt thou love her, comfort her, honour, and keep her in sickness and in health; and, forsaking all others, keep thee only unto her, so long as ye both shall live?

The Man shall answer,

I will.

Then shall the Minister say unto the Woman,

N. wilt thou have this Man to thy wedded husband, to live together after God's ordinance in the holy estate of Matrimony? Wilt thou love him, comfort him, honour, and keep him in sickness and in health; and, forsaking all others, keep thee only unto him, so long as ye both shall live?

The Woman shall answer,
I will.
Then shall the Minister say,
Who giveth this Woman to be married to this Man?
*Then shall they give their troth to each other in this man-
ner. The Minister, receiving the Woman at her father's or
friend's hands, shall cause the Man with his right hand to
take the Woman by her right hand, and to say after him as
followeth.*
I N. take thee N. to my wedded Wife, to have and to hold
from this day forward, for better for worse, for richer for
poorer, in sickness and in health, to love and to cherish, till
death us do part, according to God's holy ordinance; and
thereto I plight thee my troth.
*Then shall they loose their hands; and the Woman with
her right hand taking the Man by his right hand, shall likewise say after the Minister,*
I N. take thee N. to my wedded Husband, to have and to
hold from this day forward, for better for worse, for richer
for poorer, in sickness and in health, to love and to cherish,
till death us do part, according to God's holy ordinance; and
thereto I give thee my troth.
*Then shall they again loose their hands; and the Man shall
give unto the Woman a Ring on this wise: the Minister taking the Ring shall deliver it unto the Man, to put it upon the
fourth finger of the Woman's left hand. And the Man holding the Ring there, and taught by the Minister, shall say,*
With this Ring I thee wed: In the Name of the Father,
and of the Son, and of the Holy Ghost. Amen.
*And, before delivering the Ring to the Man, the Minister
may say as followeth.*
Bless, O Lord, this Ring, that he who gives it and she who
wears it may abide in thy peace, and continue in thy favour,
unto their life's end; through Jesus Christ our Lord. Amen.
*Then, the Man leaving the Ring upon the fourth finger of
the Woman's left hand, the Minister shall say,*

Let us pray.

Then shall the Minister and the People, still standing, say the Lord's Prayer. . . .

Then shall the Minister add,

O eternal God, Creator and Preserver of all mankind, Giver of all spiritual grace, the Author of everlasting life; Send thy blessing upon these thy servants, this man and this woman, whom we bless in thy Name; that they, living faithfully together, may surely perform and keep the vow and covenant betwixt them made, (whereof this Ring given and received is a token and pledge,) and may ever remain in perfect love and peace together, and live according to thy laws; through Jesus Christ our Lord. Amen.

The Minister may add one or both of the following prayers.

O Almighty God, Creator of mankind, who only art the well-spring of life; Bestow upon these thy servants, if it be thy will, the gift and heritage of children; and grant that they may see their children brought up in thy faith and fear, to the honour and glory of thy Name; through Jesus Christ our Lord. Amen.

O God, who hast so consecrated the state of Matrimony that in it is represented the spiritual marriage and unity betwixt Christ and his Church; Look mercifully upon these thy servants, that they may love, honour, and cherish each other, and so live together in faithfulness and patience, in wisdom and true godliness, that their home may be a haven of blessing and of peace; through the same Jesus Christ our Lord, who liveth and reigneth with thee and the Holy Spirit ever, one God, world without end. Amen.

Then shall the Minister join their right hands together, and say,

Those whom God hath joined together let no man put asunder.

Then shall the Minister speak unto the company.

Forasmuch as *N.* and *N.* have consented together in holy wedlock, and have witnessed the same before God and this company, and thereto have given and pledged their troth, each to the other, and have declared the same by giving and receiving a Ring, and by joining hands; I pronounce that they are Man and Wife, In the Name of the Father, and of the Son, and of the Holy Ghost. Amen.

The Man and Wife kneeling, the Minister shall add this Blessing.

God the Father, God the Son, God the Holy Ghost, bless, preserve, and keep you; the Lord mercifully with his favour look upon you, and fill you with all spiritual benediction and grace; that ye may so live together in this life, that in the world to come ye may have life everlasting. Amen.

The so-called High or Anglo-Catholic branch of the Church has a nuptial mass for wedding couples. The nuptial mass, which follows almost the same ritual as the Roman Catholic, is celebrated after the regular Episcopal ceremony.

Marriage of divorced persons in the Episcopal Church is permitted only by special dispensation. You should confer with your clergyman on this matter.

THE QUAKER WEDDING

Simplicity is the keynote of the Quaker ceremony throughout. When it is carried out in traditional manner, the wedding party members enter without music and take places in seats at the head of the aisle facing the guests. Because the Friends' Church has no clergy, the bride and groom marry each other by themselves, in the presence of the Committee which has oversight of the marriage. The signing of the marriage certificate takes place in the presence of witnesses and is read by a member appointed by the Meeting.

A couple's proposal for marriage in the Friends Meeting House must be laid before the Meeting at least two months before the appointed wedding date. The suitability of the marriage and the clearness of the parties to enter such a contract is investigated by a designated committee and reported to the Meeting before a marriage date is set.

A Friend may marry a non-Friend in the Meeting House and nonmembers of the Friends Church are also welcomed by the Meeting for exchange of vows.

The marriage ceremony itself which is repeated by the bridal couple is very brief, i.e., "In the presence of the Lord, and these our friends, I take thee (name of bride or groom) to be my ("wife" or "husband" as applicable); promising with Divine assistance, to be unto thee a loving and faithful ("wife" or "husband") as long as we both shall live."

The bride may walk to the altar on her father's arm, but he does not give her away. The attendants usually seat themselves in the Facing Seats—with all ushers on one side and all bridesmaids on the other. If the bride so chooses, however, it may be an alternating arrangement.

THE ROMAN CATHOLIC WEDDING

A nuptial Mass customarily follows the actual marriage ceremony in a Roman Catholic wedding. The solemn High Mass is the most formal ceremonial of the church.

In large and elaborate marriage ceremonies, guests are usually provided with small Mass books which give instructions as to proper procedure for standing, kneeling and sitting. Whether Roman Catholics or not, all guests should observe the customs of the Church out of courtesy.

Marriage is one of the Sacraments of the Church. The important symbolic actions in the present Roman Rite are: joining of the right hands of the bride and groom at one point in the service; the Solemn Blessing by the priest and the giving of the ring by the groom to the bride, the latter a very ancient pre-Christian symbol of faithfulness adopted by the Church.

Time of Marriage

Most fashionable Catholic weddings take place at High Mass, which must be held before noon, or at high noon (twelve o'clock), followed by a wedding breakfast. Less formal weddings may take place at eight or nine o'clock in the morning with Low Mass celebrated. (This service is chanted by the priest without the liturgical music of the choir in High Mass.)

Weddings without Mass may take place in the afternoon. Five o'clock is the favorite hour for this type of wedding. Such ceremonies in this country rarely occur after sundown.

Nuptial High Mass is celebrated in the Lenten season only with special permission, although Roman Catholics may be married formally during Lent if they wish.

A Roman Catholic wedding may take place on Sunday, but it must be before six o'clock in the evening.

Special Rulings

A nuptial blessing is only received at a first marriage, never at the marriage of widowed persons.

The marriage of divorced persons is not allowed in the Roman Catholic Church unless a canonical annulment of the previous marriage has been granted. This is a very important matter to be taken up with your priest.

A mixed marriage never takes place in a Protestant Church unless by special dispensation granted by the bishop. The officiant in such a case must necessarily be a Roman Catholic priest. Mixed marriages do take place in a club, hotel or house, but again only by special dispensation and only with a Roman Catholic priest officiating.

If the non-Catholic member of the couple proves he is a baptized Christian it facilitates the dispensation for a mixed marriage.

Usual Place of Marriage

The marriage usually takes place in the parish church of the bride. If this is not the parish where the couple was baptized, they must furnish a copy of their baptismal certificate or the testimony of an eyewitness.

A priest, to officiate outside of his parish church, must have the permission of the parish rector. Brothers, uncles or clerical relatives are customarily allowed to officiate.

Procedure at Altar

When the bride is married in traditional bridal array at a formal wedding, she usually wears a face veil which is thrown back or lightly detached after the wedding service. This duty is performed by her maid of honor, who also helps the bride with her wedding-dress train and her flowers.

The procession and recessional follow the usual wedding order, but the father or guardian of the bride does not give her in marriage, but joins her mother the moment he has left her at the chancel steps.

In a very formal ceremony all of the wedding party go into the sanctuary, bridesmaids and ushers pairing off on either side. During the wedding ceremony, the best man and maid of honor join at the chancel steps and follow the wedding party. The bridal pair then enter the sanctuary and move forward together to meet the priest.

During Mass special seats in the sanctuary or in the choir stalls are usually assigned the wedding party. They remain kneeling throughout except when they stand for the Gospel. The bride and groom, who have been provided with a special chair and prie-dieu for each of them, sit and kneel before the raised altar.

If a church rules that the wedding party is prohibited from the sanctuary during Mass, the members should be assigned special pews near the front of the church.

Only the bride and groom receive communion.

All feminine guests and wedding attendants are required to wear a head covering of some sort.

At the rehearsal non-Roman Catholics will be taught when and how to genuflect in unison for the service.

Each Roman Catholic Church has its own rules of decoration. However, most chancel decorations are allowed, as are aisle-post decorations. The altar is always simply dressed with liturgical candles and flowers in altar vases.

ORTHODOX CATHOLIC WEDDING

Filled with pageantry and ostentatious love of color and ornamentation, the Greek Orthodox Church in America has retained the principal features of its Byzantine origin which made the weddings in Bulgaria, Armenia, Greece and principally in prerevolutionary Russia, a thing of gorgeous beauty.

The wedding rites are intricate beyond those of the Roman Catholic Church with which it differs sharply at many points.

Ceremonial Essentials

The ceremony itself takes thirty-five minutes. A ten-minute betrothal service takes place before the iconostasis or altar screen, followed by a twenty-five-minute marriage service observed at the altar steps.

The chief points in the ceremony which differ from other religious ceremonies are: the hands of the bride and groom literally are bound together; their heads are crowned; the phrases are repeated three times; they march around the priestly table; and lastly come the nuptial kiss and priestly blessing.

After the Gospel is read in the marriage service, a cup of wine is shared by the bride and groom.

Attendants' Duties

The maid of honor and the best man have more complex duties in this service than is customary in other services. They are called the *koumbari* in the Greek Church and receive the bride's and groom's rings after the priest has blessed them and slipped them on for the first time. The maid and best man then exchange the rings between the bride and groom three times, signifying the Trinity.

During the marriage service, the priest links the hands of the bride and groom and sings, "The Hand of God Descends." He then places a wreath of waxy flowers and ribbons on the head of each of the bridal pair. The *koumbari* again step forward and turn the wreaths around three times.

Altar Procedure

The usual Protestant processional is the order of the Greek Church. Just before the ceremony begins at the altar, however, the best man leads the groom to the subaltar or table where the ceremony is performed.

The bride enters on the arm of her father, and he stands next to her at the altar, giving her in marriage, then retires to join the bride's mother.

Originally the members of a congregation stood throughout the ceremony. Most Greek churches in America, however, provide benches where guests may sit, standing only for the most sacred moments.

Choir music, without accompaniment by a musical instrument, is customary in an Orthodox Catholic wedding. "Lohengrin" sung with Greek devotional words is impressive. Or you may have the old Byzantine chants, traditional in the Greek Church.

Following the recessional, friends of the family customarily gather on the church steps and distribute among the guests Jordan almonds festively wrapped.

Both the bride and groom are not required to be members of the Orthodox Catholic Church as long as one is, and both have been baptized Christians.

No Orthodox Catholic wedding can take place during Lent or the Feast of the Blessed Virgin Mary, August first to fifteenth. Weddings of this faith must take place sometime in the afternoon.

It is customary, even in this country, for the Orthodox Catholic bride to wear her wedding ring on the third finger of the right hand. No such wedding is considered complete without a feast and dancing, and the festivities usually take place in a hotel or a rented hall.

SYMBOLIC LUTHERAN WEDDING CUSTOMS

Lutherans, whether they be Swedish, Norwegian, German, Italian or Spanish (all these branches exist), follow the wedding ceremony prescribed by Luther himself five hundred years or more ago.

In the time of Luther the act of giving in marriage was performed "before the church," that is, at the church doors, with the ring ceremony following in the church proper before the altar.

In all essentials the order remains the same except that the service now appears in one part, performed before the chancel rail. Where a platform extends in front of the altar the groom proceeds to the center of the platform with the best man and then walks by himself to meet his bride. They both proceed to the altar alone a few steps in advance of the wedding party, then kneel and receive the blessing.

If the pastor (as he is commonly called in the Lutheran church) gives the customary ten-minute address before the ceremony, chairs are provided for the bridal party.

The church bells are rung when the bridal party arrives and continue until they have entered the *narthex* or vestibule.

The tossing of rice or confetti at the church door is frowned on as a heathenish custom. The kiss between the bride and groom is considered bad taste also.

THE ORTHODOX JEWISH WEDDING

Centuries of tradition form the background for the orthodox Jewish wedding, and many of these beautiful ancient rites may be revived and utilized in the modern wedding ceremony.

Large formal weddings are more often held in hotels, clubs or banquet halls rather than in a synagogue, probably because Jewish weddings from the earliest times have been accompanied by feasts and dancing.

Smaller formal weddings often take place in the chapel of a synagogue or in the auditorium of a synagogue house.

Customary Head Coverings

In accordance with the Oriental tradition of covering the face of a woman, it is customary for the bride to wear a veil, even though she wears an informal street-length dress. She should wear long sleeves or long gloves if her dress has short sleeves. Her attendants should wear headdresses and their costumes should conform to the formality or informality of the bride's gown.

All men attendants and guests are required to wear head coverings whether the ceremony takes place in a synagogue, hotel, club or home. High silk hats are worn if the wedding is an elaborate one. When it is less formal all the men wear silk skull caps, which the bride's family usually supplies and presents to the men guests as they enter for the wedding. (These skull caps may be procured through your local Jewish bookstore or synagogue.)

Marriage is regarded as a religious sacrament wherever it takes place, and the head covering is worn during the ceremony and throughout the wedding feast which follows.

The families of the bridal couple are usually escorted to their reserved pews, closed off by white silken bands, before other guests are seated. The wedding procession is generally led by the groom, who enters accompanied by his father and mother, usually one on either side. The bride follows, also with her parents. This procedure may be modified so that the bride is led by her father and the groom by his mother. There is no formal giving-away of the bride by her father, nor does he take part in the ceremony, except as an escort.

The Wedding Canopy Used in Traditional Ceremonies

Traditionally no Jewish bride could be married unless she stood under the wedding canopy, or "Chuppah." The "Chuppah" of today is a richly ornamented silk or white satin canopy, supported by tall velvet-covered standards. It is owned by the synagogue or is the property of the rabbi and may be transported to the scene of the wedding if it is to be held outside the synagogue. This canopy is carried by the men of the wedding party, fathers of the nuptial couple, uncles, brothers, cousins and best friends.

In a simple wedding where only the immediate family is to be present, a praying shawl ("Talis") may be used instead of the large canopy. These shawls are generally the property of the male members of either family.

In a synagogue marriage the bridal pair faces toward the east (traditionally toward Jerusalem). The bride stands to the right of the groom, with the maid of honor on her right. The best man stands to the left of the groom and the other attendants stand outside the canopy in the usual order.

The Wine-Cup Ceremony

The wine-cup ceremony is considered by most rabbis as an integral part of the rite, though it is not obligatory. A small white-covered table bearing two cups of wine is used in this part of the ceremony. Following a blessing over the wine, the rabbi hands one of the wine cups to the groom. He sips from it and passes it in turn to the bride. At the conclusion of the wine ceremony the groom places the ring (usually a plain gold band) on the forefinger of the bride. After the ceremony she changes it to her "ring" or third finger, and may even replace it with a platinum or diamond band. She should never wear her engagement ring during the ceremony.

After a short address by the rabbi, the bride and groom drink from the second wine cup. The groom receives the glass from the rabbi, places it on the floor and crushes it with his heel.

This symbolic "shattering of the glass" by the groom is the final step in the ceremony. This quaint custom has many reputed sources. Some authorities say that it means that the marriage will last until the shattered pieces can be reunited. Others maintain that it is an ancient superstition that an evil presence must be placated by a gift of wine. The young girls in the wedding party often gather up a fragment of the glass as a "good luck piece," much in the same way that they carry home a piece of bride's cake to dream on.

The bride's family usually furnishes the wine and glasses, unless it is a small wedding in the rabbi's study in which case he furnishes both the wine and the glasses. Sherry or port wine is generally used and the receptacle which is shattered is of plain, thin glass. A picturesque note may be added to the ceremony by the use of the beautiful "Kiddish" or Sabbath-Eve wine cups, which in some families are handed down from generation to generation. They are usually richly chased silver or gold goblets, used only for the first wine-cup ceremony.

A marriage grace is said at the wedding reception. Otherwise, the occasion is similar to any other reception.

Jewish weddings never take place from sunset on Friday afternoon until sunset on Saturday or on Festival days.

SPECIAL QUESTIONS AND ANSWERS

What sort of a ceremony is customary . . .

. . . when a Catholic and non-Catholic marry?

After a special dispensation from the Church has been obtained for a mixed marriage of this sort, the couple usually is married in the rectory without benefit of music and with only a limited number of wedding guests and one attendant each.

No nuptial Mass can be said for the couple, no sacred vestment is worn by the priest, and no "Solemn Blessing" is read. Although the ring is given by the bridegroom to the bride as usual, it is not first blessed by the priest.

If there is a very special reason that seems to warrant it in the opinion of the Bishop of the Diocese, the ceremony may be authorized to take place in the bride's house, or sometimes in the Church itself, but this is not common custom.

. . . when a church does not recognize
a couple's right to marry?

A civil ceremony only is used in such cases. Very often when one member of the bridal pair has been divorced, when a Jew and a Gentile marry; when a Catholic and Protestant wish to marry and the latter does not adopt the faith of the former—a civil service must be used.

Americans marrying in foreign countries often are required to have both the civil and religious ceremonies.

CHAPTER IX

To Be Remembered As Long As You Both Shall Live

IT'S TIME TO CONCENTRATE ON *you* . . . AND THAT MO-
mentous wedding gown, all the attending costumes and the
general color schemes.

The gown you choose is like the flare that sets off the
complete fireworks. Upon its style and color depend the
bridesmaids' costumes, the flowers, the charm of the entire
picture.

If you've ever been really beautiful, or ever expect to be—
this should be the opportunity.

WHAT SUITS YOU?

Are you one of those who would love to wear ice-blue satin
with matching tulle veil studded with glistening crystal drops
and carry a sheaf of calla lilies tied with ice-blue tulle?

Or do you like traditional things and dream of wearing
candlelight slipper-satin with a sweetheart neckline, and
mists of tulle cascading from a tiara of orange blossoms?

Would you want to wear marquisette in a delicate blush
shade and array your bridesmaids in a deeper shell-pink?

Maybe you are blessed with a sleek figure that would take
to silk jersey in a trainless gown of snow white with a draped

151

cowl headdress. Would you be daring enough to wear a Hawaiian lei of white carnations set on your head and falling to form a necklace? Perhaps you'll toss all your preconceived notions into the blue . . . and wear a beautiful borrowed dress or a wedding gown descended in the family . . . or browse about antique shops for a breath-taking length of lace or embroidery to be made into a blossom-dotted stole.

You don't have to spend a king's ransom, rest assured of that. Brides are on a budget everywhere. You will be amazed at how a few yards of inexpensive fabric can float down the aisle in the guise of a perfect wedding gown.

Maybe you are the tomboy type who would be satisfied in a simple white piqué dress with classic princess lines, a Dutch-boy cap with veil winging back at the sides and an arm bouquet of white African daisies. Such an outfit could be bought for next to nothing . . . or it *could* be custom-made.

You are the main attraction in this show. Dress to your own type, choose a gown with flattering lines and put into it what you can well afford. Remember only that it should not be sleeveless or too décolleté.

COLORS AND FABRICS

It doesn't have to be stark white. There's candlelight (a glowing deep cream shade), bridal ivory, café au lait, egg-shell, ice-white and there are soft pastels of Madonna blue and blush-pink.

What is your most becoming color?

Most any style gown that strikes your fancy can be ordered in your color choice if you start in plenty of time.

Bridal shops everywhere offer a glorious selection of fabrics for all seasons.

Traditional satin is the perennial favorite, winter and summer. The stiffened, stand-alone kind, slipper, moiré, brocade and Duchess satin are all especially adaptable. Keep the gowns of these fabrics austerely plain and depend on lines for your effects.

A touch of heirloom lace worked into a Queen Anne collar or a yoke will add glamour to your satin gown. Seed pearls and self cordings are often used for trimming.

Net and marquisette are charmers among the sheer materials, very youthful and picturesque when fashioned in bouffant styles.

For an evening or late-afternoon wedding just such dresses

would be enchanting. The bride could wear billows of cloud-tinted pink net, her matching veil topped with the palest of pink camellias, and carry a bouquet of camellias outlined with green leaves. The attending bridesmaids could wear cloud-blue tulle skirted gowns with exciting accents of deep and light camellias for hair adornment. They might carry ropes or swinging balls of shiny green leaves pierced with camellia blossoms. This would be especially effective in a church lighted only by candles.

There is crisp taffeta (with variations of faille and seer-sucker) which is an all-year-round favorite; you may like chiffon for the soft flowing Grecian-line gowns; lace, delicately stiffened or in natural softness, is lovely for the bride with the height and figure to carry classic dignity; and silk jersey for the statuesque.

Sheer cottons in cobwebby dotted Swiss, organdy (plain or of all-over floral pattern) and point d'esprit all make appealing wedding gowns. Linens and piqués adapt themselves to the more tailored types.

Varieties of velvet are effective for fall and winter weddings. You might wear a candlelight shade (off-tone white), and have your attendants in varying shades of beige, shading from light to dark. For drama they could carry clusters of dahlias in bright hues of pink or red, or rusty pink chrysanthemums tied with brown velvet ribbons to match hats of the same color.

Many other novelty fabrics are dictated by fashion's mode every season. All we ask is that you use judgment in choosing a fabric and style that will become you and harmonize with the setting of your wedding.

HARMONY IS THE THING

Check back those notes of yours on your church or home background. (We told you they would be important!) Is there a modern feeling in the church architecture? If so you'll be wise to select a gown of streamlined style. Nothing is more stunning, really, than the close-fitted, "figure-revealing" lines.

Is your home of Colonial type? Then concentrate on the bouffant styles if you are the type to wear them.

White organdy made in shepherdess style is perfect in the garden. It might be made with huge pockets to be filled to overflowing with trailing blossoms, for a semiformal wedding.

Period gowns are always picturesque but everything must be consistent with them: the headdresses, bridesmaid's gowns, the floral bouquets and the wedding background.

One church wedding of splendor we'll long remember was reminiscent of medieval times, the bride in silver moiré, carrying a silver prayer book with a spray of orchids. The bridesmaids wore jewel tones of royal blue and ruby red, reflecting the colors in the stained glass windows. Wristlets of silver leaves and glistening mesh choir-boy caps emphasized the medieval note.

WHAT LENGTH TRAIN?

Trains on modern wedding gowns are as wide as a church aisle. They sweep the floor gracefully because of this extreme width, whether they are three or six yards long.

Naturally a six-yard train belongs in a stately cathedral, not in a tiny chapel or a small apartment. A happy medium for the average formal wedding is the three-yard train which comes on most of the wedding gowns. Trains can always be cut down to conform with your type of wedding, without destroying the grace and symmetry of the style. If you wish a train of extra length, specify this when you go to buy.

The bridal gowns for the semiformal wedding are fashioned exactly as other wedding gowns except that they are short-trained or trainless. Trainless skirts should sweep the floor a few inches in the back to be most graceful. The front hemline of all wedding gowns should merely escape the floor to the extent that there is no danger of your tripping as you go down the aisle.

If bridesmaids' gowns are to have slight trains, make sure that they are all altered to the same length. Speaking of alterations—this is one time in your life that you should be fussy about the fit of garments to be worn on parade. Even the most expensive gown can look like less than two cents if the skirt hikes or the blouse cups at the waistline. So be sure to check on everything at final fittings.

Your Wedding Veil

Veils are the fluff that dreams are made of. Into yours can be gathered all the romance that belongs to you on your wedding day.

1. Your veil may be either long or short and still be formal.

2. Long veils are not worn with trainless dresses—choose a shoulder, waist or finger-tip length.

3. A long veil should measure a half-yard longer than your dress train as it extends on the floor.

4. Veils are customarily fashioned of tulle, illusion or sheer marquisette.

If you are miniature in size, a full-length veil will make you appear taller. If you are quite tall, you may prefer a cape veil to cut your height, or a triple-tiered effect with the first length coming to the shoulders, the second to the elbows and the third falling just below the hipline.

The style of your wedding gown and the degree of formality in your wedding should be your guide in selecting your veil. A gown made with a full-length back panel calls for a full-length veil to enhance the sweeping lines of the dress. Finger-tip veils of circular styles are very popular, especially with young girls, as are shoulder-length veils for the less formal occasions.

If you are planning to wear a face veil (or blusher), your maid of honor should assist you at the altar in brushing it back from your face after the ceremony. It is worn back over the head for the remainder of the time.

Sheer veils in illusion and tulle are usually left unhemmed and may be trimmed off to any desired length. When you have your gown fitted, try your veil with it. Have the outer edges of your veil (if it is full-length) trimmed on the sides to follow the outline of your circular dress train (rounded instead of squared-off on the corners). Let it remain a half-yard longer than your dress, however.

Make a notation, while you think of it, to stock up on plenty of hairpins for your wedding. They are very useful for pinning your veil securely around your head so that there is no chance of its slipping.

HEADDRESSES

Whether yours is to be long or short, circular or straight, falling into extended points—it's the headdress of your veil that is important. It forms a frame for your face and should be perfectly suited to your face and coiffure.

Real flowers, or artificial ones, offer beguiling touches to the headdress.

You might wear a crown of tiny orange blossoms (crystallized ones if you haven't an accommodating friend in California who can ship fresh ones), then add shoulder-length flower streamers following your hairline on each side.

Or try daisies, gardenias, freesias or carnations clustered over each ear in muff fashion. Sprinkle your long veil with stephanotis or lily-of-the-valley clusters and repeat the cluster on top of your head. Top your tresses with a white Spanish comb from which hangs a lace-edged veil.

You might like a close-fitting tulle turban with tulips thrust through the twist in front for a look of sophistication ... or a pailletted veil falling straight and simply if you wear your hair pompadour.

If you have a scarf of real lace, wear it mantilla-fashion, anchored at the temple with a spray of blossoms. If it's only a small piece of heirloom lace, have it made into a Baby Stuart cap smooth over the head, or arrange it as a coronet to give you height. An off-the-face bonnet trimmed with the lace would tie in with a Colonial costume, or it could be medieval in feeling to wear with a gown of that period.

Perhaps you have a Venetian-lace baby cap which you

wore at your christening. Dramatize your costume by wearing it combined with white tulle or delicate blush shade to match your gown.

Ostrich feathers, plumed together to form a topknot for your veil, would be attractive. Seed pearls on a Juliet cap or worked into a coronet design are becoming to wear with lustrous satin.

Pillboxes, brimless caps, ruffled halos and a dozen and one other fashions that will set your heart spinning are all available for you to see and try with your wedding gown.

Whatever your choice, be sure it is devastatingly becoming and in harmony with your gown.

What Color Hose?

Select the very sheerest of pale beige, champagne or flesh-colored hose to wear with your wedding gown.

Shoes

Slippers of satin or crepe should exactly match the tone of your gown. White may be dyed to match your sample. Many of today's brides choose white satin boudoir slippers for tripping up the aisle; or if height is not an issue, why not wear white ballet shoes? Linen slippers may be worn with piqué and other cotton fabrics.

Pumps or opera styles in slippers that cover the foot as much as possible are in better taste than heelless and toeless sandals, just as even the formal evening gown—as we've reminded you—has sleeves and not a low décolletage.

Will You Need Gloves?

If your wedding is formal and the sleeves of your bridal gown are short, you should wear gloves to match. Doeskin or French suede is generally worn with satin and heavy fabrics, and they should be eighteen or twenty-button length. Short kid gloves are often chosen for less formal gowns of sheer fabrics, or you may have net or lace gloves or mitts made to match your dress.

The alteration department which took care of your dress will see to it that the third finger of the left hand glove (your ring finger) is ripped for the occasion so that it may be tucked into the hand of your glove during the ceremony. A few stitches will repair the damage later and your gloves will be as good as new.

In an informal wedding, when a street-length costume is worn with a hat, wear your right glove and carry the left. It eliminates fumbling at the altar when it comes time to slip the ring on the third finger, left hand!

Wedding Costume

(Lest you forget some of the little things)

Wedding gown	Handkerchief
Veil (or hat)	Shoes
Wrap (if weather is cold)	Hose
Slip or petticoat	Perfume
Foundation garment or lingerie	

Something old, something new, something borrowed,
something blue
—and a sixpence or silver coin in your shoe!

IT'S TIME TO OUTFIT YOUR ATTENDANTS!

Consider the little dramatic things like flower-sprinkled parasols, flirtatious little fans, becoming wide-brimmed straw hats caught under the chin with misty veils, and whooping big skirts—if it's a garden wedding.

Or if the girls are particularly young and it's a country atmosphere, choose petal-tinted sheer plain dimity with velvet ribbons; or flower-sprigged organdy with wide taffeta sashes and natural straw hats or organdy cartwheels. Then wear organdy yourself.

What about a jonquil-yellow spring wedding, with all the bridesmaids in yellow taffeta and the maid of honor in leaf-green?

Or your bridesmaids might wear moonstone-blue satin (a gray purple-blue). The maid or matron of honor could wear magnolia. All would carry apple blossoms and pussy willows. You could wear gardenia-white, and carry Madonna lilies.

Or make it a cherry-blossom wedding with your bridesmaids in pastel dimity with large butterfly bows tied in the back, little-girl fashion, carrying armfuls of cherry blossoms. What about setting the ceremony under blossoming peach trees or in a field of daisies and field flowers where a hay mower has mowed an aisle through the field leaving a strip for aisle, altar and guests? For such a wedding your maids might carry flowers of the field or sheaves of spring fruit blossoms. Dress them in white to match your cotton gown, tie moss-green sashes around their tiny waists and let them trail, with pale-pink petticoats showing as they walk up the aisle.

If it's fall and you want to wear cream antique satin, put your bridesmaids in copper-rust velvet with hats to match. Have them carry informal bouquets of yellow-gold gladioli, mounted like orchids. The maid or matron of honor would be dressed in a gold shade with brown and gold trim on her velvet hat. She would carry deep-rust chrysanthemums. The little flower girl could wear creamy yellow.

Before you go too far, consider the colors that are becoming to the various attendants. Can Betty wear yellow? Will orchid be right with Margaret's red hair?

These girls are buying their own dresses, don't forget. Be sure they are the right price for all the pocketbooks and for practical wear later. Headdresses of natural flowers or little circular veils to match each gown can be effectively concocted for a mere trifle if honest-to-goodness hats run into too much money.

As you plan, keep in mind the church or home background that is to form your setting. (There we go again . . . but we can't stress it *enough*.) If there is vivid color in altar screen and windows, settle on a neutral shade and accent the costumes with flowers in all the tones of the background. If your background shades are neutral, brighten up the picture with more dashing colors.

Here's a color chart to ponder over:

Spring and Summer Weddings

	GOWN	FLOWERS
Bride	Pale-blue satin	White lilac crown. Carries mass of white lilacs.
Maid of Honor	Pale-blue satin	Carries armful of lavender lilacs. Wears brimmed bonnet of pale-blue net caught at side with bunch of lilacs.
Bridesmaids	Pale-blue satin	Carry armful of lavender lilacs. Wear brimmed bonnets of pale-blue net caught at side with bunch of lilacs.
Bride	White	Carries creamy-white roses.
Maid of Honor	White	Carries American Beauty roses.
Bridesmaids	White	Carry a great rope of flowers woven into a brilliant stream of color.
Bride	White	Carries white lilies.
Maid of Honor	Flesh-pink	Carries rosy lilies bound with satin bands.
Bridesmaids	Flesh-pink	Carry rosy lilies bound with satin bands.
Bride	White	Carries African daisies.
Maid of Honor	Yellow	Carries African daisies.
Bridesmaids	Madonna-blue	Carry African daisies.
Bride	Delicate pink	Carries apple blossoms.
Maid of Honor	Leaf-green	Carries apple blossoms accented with green leaves.
Bridesmaids	Light-pink	Carry apple blossoms with green leaves.
Bride	White	Carries white bouvardia with white orchid.
Maid of Honor	Deep-aqua	Carries mixed bouquet with red geraniums for color splash.
Bridesmaids	Light-aqua	Carry mixed spring flowers with red geraniums
Bride	White	Carries roses with gardenia center.
Maid of Honor	Coral	Carries cabbage roses made of carnations dyed coral and turquoise.
Bridesmaids	Turquoise	Carry cabbage roses of same.
Flower Girl	Light-aqua	Carries small cabbage rose.
Bride	Creamy-white	Carries mixed bouquet of white spring flowers.
Maid of Honor	Vintage wine	Carries mimosa and wine snapdragons.
Bridesmaids	Straw color	Carry mimosa and wine snapdragons.
Bride	White	Carries white rambler roses.
Maid of Honor	Larkspur-blue	Carries rambler roses and blue larkspur.
Bridesmaids	Dusty-rose	Carry rambler rose and blue larkspur.

	GOWN	FLOWERS
Bride	Champagne	Carries long-stemmed cream roses.
Maid of Honor	Peach	Carries small compact bouquet of talisman roses with peach gladioli.
Bridesmaids	Appalachian-green	Carry small compact bouquets of talisman roses with peach gladioli.
Flower Girl	Light-toned peach	Carries small nosegay of roses.
Bride	White	Carries mixed spring blossoms in white. Tiny bouquets to match tucked in the folds of wedding veil.
Maid of Honor	Deep-rose	Carries fuchsia snapdragons, blue delphinium and pussy willows.
Bridesmaids	Moonstone-blue	Carry same as maid of honor.
Flower Girl	Light-blue	Carries French basket of rose petals.
Bride	White	Carries white violets with gardenia center.
Maid of Honor	Soft coral tone	Carries basket of purple violets and flowering quince.
Bridesmaids	Soft-gray	Carry baskets of purple violets and flowering quince.
Bride	Light-pink	Carries stephanotis and white orchids.
Maid of Honor	Matching pink	Wears bouvardia and tight blossoms made into lei which outlines the off-shoulder neckline. Carries small compact bouquet to match.
Bridesmaids	Matching pink	Wear bouvardia and tight blossoms made into leis which outline the off-shoulder necklines. Carry small compact bouquets to match.
Bride	White	Carries a tiny 1880 reticule starred with flowers instead of conventional bouquet.
Maid of Honor	Any pastel shade	Carries a Gainsborough hat tied with wide satin ribbons and filled with a garden of flowers.

Fall and Winter Weddings

	GOWN	FLOWERS
Bride	Off-white	Carries orchids.
Maid of Honor	Fuchsia	Carries sheaves of wheat with fuchsia and yellow asters.
Bridesmaids	Champagne	Carry sheaves of wheat with fuchsia and yellow asters.
Bride	Creamy satin	Carries creamy chrysanthemums.
Maid of Honor	Tone of beige	Carries bronze chrysanthemums.
Bridesmaids	Wear tones of beige deepening into toast tones	Carry bronze chrysanthemums.

	GOWN	FLOWERS
Bride	White	Carries star-shaped bouquet of white asters.
Maid of Honor	Amethyst	Carries star-shaped bouquet of orchid, pink and moonstone-blue asters.
Bridesmaids	Shell-pink	Carry same bouquets as maid of honor.
Bride	Azure-blue	Carries muff of pink roses with silvered leaves entwined.
Maid of Honor	Wine	Silvered leaves, wine roses and blue delphinium.
Bridesmaids	Deeper blue than bride	Silvered leaves, wine roses and blue delphinium.
Bride	Blush-pink	Carries Colonial bouquet of pink roses and blue forget-me-nots.
Maid of Honor	Blush-pink	Carries Colonial bouquet of pink roses and blue forget-me-nots.
Bridesmaids	Blush-pink	Carry Colonial bouquet of pink roses and blue forget-me-nots.
Bride	Candlelight shade	Carries an ivory-and-lace fan in lieu of flowers.
Maid of Honor	Copper-rose	Carries deep-toned dahlias with autumn foliage.
Bridesmaids	Sage-green	Carry same as maid of honor.
Bride	White	Carries sheaves of wheat painted gold.
Maid of Honor	White	Carries sheaves of wheat painted gold.
Bridesmaids	White	Carry sheaves of wheat painted gold.
Bride	White	Carries muff of white chrysanthemums.
Maid of Honor	Cocoa-brown	Carries yellow and dark rust chrysanthemums.
Bridesmaids	Yellow	Carry same flowers as maid of honor.
Bride	White	Carries spray of white chrysanthemums.
Maid of Honor	Gold	Carries sprays of rust-colored mums.
Bridesmaids	Jade-green	Carry same flowers as maid of honor, with yellow mums added to bouquet.

CHRISTMAS WEDDING SUGGESTIONS

	GOWN	FLOWERS
Bride	White	Carries poinsettias wired in cascade form or white ostrich-feather fan caught at the base with flaming poinsettia blossoms.

	GOWN	FLOWERS
Maid of Honor	White	Carries poinsettias wired in cascade form or white ostrich-feather fan caught at the base with flaming poinsettia blossoms.
Bridesmaids	White	Carry poinsettias wired in cascade form or white ostrich-feather fans caught at the base with flaming poinsettia blossoms.
Bride	White velveteen	Carries a muff made of sprays of silver-touched ivy.
Maid of Honor	Deep-green velveteen	Carries blazing red poinsettias.
Bridesmaids	Deep-green velveteen	Carry blazing red poinsettias.

DOUBLE-WEDDING SUGGESTIONS

MAID OF HONOR	BRIDESMAIDS	FLOWERS

I. In shaded colors (each bride to have five attendants):

First Bridal Party

Petal-pink	Two bridesmaids in light Madonna-blue	Armfuls of pink tulips for bridesmaids; purply-blue and pink for maid of honor
	Next two in deeper blue	

Second Bridal Party

Madonna-blue	Two bridesmaids in bonbon-pink	Deep-purple tulips for bridesmaids; pink and a few purply-blue tulips for maid of honor
	Next two in deeper pink	

II. In rainbow colors (each bride to have three attendants) :

First Bridal Party

Yellow	Bridesmaids in orchid	Soft-shaded snap-dragons with sprigs of delphinium

Second Bridal Party

Sky-blue	Bridesmaids in pale-fuchsia	Same flowers

III. Autumn wedding (each bride to have three attendants) :

First Bridal Party

Autumn-gold	Copper-rose	Autumn-toned asters with trailing ivy for bridesmaids; rose and purple asters with trailing ivy for maid of honor

Second Bridal Party

Sage-green	Amber	Deep-rose, yellow and purple asters with trailing ivy for bridesmaids; autumn tones for maid of honor

These suggestions may give you an idea or two toward working out your own color scheme.

Every bridesmaid's dress is not purchasable in every color, as you've already guessed. Don't set your head too definitely on the combinations until you go shopping. But it's better to have a few thoughts on the subject before you start. Many wedding gowns have bridesmaids' dresses to match and your problems will be simplified if the combination happens to strike you.

As to Fabrics

With a satin wedding gown your attendants may wear satin, satin and net combined, taffeta, chiffon, or crepe in the early spring. For summer they may also choose net or marquisette.

If you are wearing velvet, put your attendants in satin or velvet.

If organdy or some such cotton fabric is your selection, let them follow suit.

Various kinds of laces don't mix well. Your attendants would be wise to wear net if your gown is of lace.

Bridesmaids' Headdresses

First of all, their headdresses must conform in style to the type of gown each is wearing. They should go well with your own headdress and they should be as becoming as possible to all the girls.

Many of the frocks available in bridal shops come with especially designed hats or headdresses which are sold with the dresses.

Headdresses of natural flowers to match the bouquets are less costly than hats made to order. They can be charmingly arranged as topknots with ribbon streamers, as halos or bandeaus to be worn low on their curls in the back, as ear muffs, or countless other ways that you and a clever florist can devise.

Butterflies of organdy fastened jauntily in the hair are an unusual touch for a garden wedding.

Think about Juliet caps of satin strips or silver mesh sprinkled with tiny stars.

Coronets, or off-the-face bonnets of net, big floppy straw hats, or turbans wound around the head, all are ideas to consider.

GLOVES AND SHOES FOR BRIDESMAIDS

If you are wearing long gloves with a short-sleeved bridal gown, then it is important (in a formal wedding) to have your attendants also wear them. Colors to match their costumes are more effective than white. Often net mitts may be made up to match gowns of sheer fabrics, and velvet gloves are suitable for winter.

In less formal weddings, gloves for the bridesmaids and maid of honor are usually omitted.

Shoes should be dyed to match or contrast with gowns. Or all may wear silver or gold if it conforms with the costumes.

Note

Be sure your bridesmaids aren't planning to wear jangling bracelets with their wedding togs . . . or ill-assorted earrings and other jewelry. It's a happy solution to the jewelry problem if you present them with something suitable to wear for the occasion. See gifts, page 178.

THE MOTHERS' COSTUMES

Next to you and your bridal party on your wedding day, your mother is more important than anyone. As hostess and "ambassadress'" she should be dressed to express dignity and graciousness.

Many mothers leave their own dress problems until the eleventh hour and grab up anything in their wardrobes that will serve the purpose.

Don't let this happen at your house . . . for everyone will be looking at your mother and the groom's mother, and both should be gowned in harmony with your wedding colors. They will stand together in the receiving line and should complement each other in the shades they choose. The formality of the wedding, of course, will dictate 'the type of dress. Whatever it is, it should dovetail to personality and bespeak quiet assurance and poise. Remember, there no longer is "the matron's hat" or "the dowager's dress." What remains is the true expression of ageless designing for the mature woman— which bears out the creed that there are no dowagers, only beautiful women of every age.

For a Morning Wedding

If yours is to be a formal or semiformal morning wedding, street-length costumes with hats and gloves are in order for the mothers. Costume suits, comprised of dress and jacket or dress and coat, are appropriate, worn with furs. Floor-length gowns may be worn if the wedding is ultraformal. (See chart, page 76.)

For an Afternoon Wedding

For the semiformal or formal afternoon affair, floor length gowns of the dinner type, with long or short sleeves, are correct. Simple laces in soft, flattering shades are always stand-bys. Silk crepe, jersey, chiffon and velvet (for fall) are all very fitting to the occasion.

Cardinal principles to follow in selecting a dress are that it should be soft of hue (violent contrasts make the figure look heavy) and flawless in line. Pale shades such as muted blue, beige and gray are chic when worn with matching gloves.

The glowing purples, wines and rosy shades are splendid tonics for graying hair and bring a glow to the skin tones as well. Dull colors don't necessarily make one look thinner, only sadder.

Choose an outfit that will give a "pretty picture" look to the complete wedding pageant from color and style stand-points, then concentrate on handsome accessories.

The hat your mother selects for your wedding should be

dramatic and exciting. It should be the prima donna note to her costume and add zest to the whole wedding.

Her flowers should tone in appropriately with her gown and, to avoid breaking up the smooth line of the silhouette, they might well be worn as a bouquet pinned to her belt in place of the obvious shoulder spot. Or she might wear a bracelet of flowers around her long gloves. Orchids pinned to pocketbook or fur muff are smart. Flowers also stay fresh and show up beautifully pinned deep into the skins of a fur scarf.

Evening

A formal evening wedding may be more dressy. Formal gowns of metal cloth, velvet, crepe, jersey or lace, with matching boleros or jackets, are generally chosen by the mothers. In this type of gown each looks appropriately gowned, wearing jacket, hat and gloves, as she proceeds down the church aisle on the usher's arm. Later, at the formal reception, she is fittingly dressed after she removes her jacket and hat.

Informal Weddings

Street costumes are always worn for informal weddings.

KEEP THE RECORD CLEAR

After you have made all your clothes selections, be sure to ask for samples of all the gowns so that you may take them to the florist.

Also ask the bridal consultant, or the salespersons who sold the various costumes, to give you descriptions of the gowns, or make notes on them yourself in your notebook, now growing fuller day by day. You will need these notes when you send information for your wedding article to the newspapers.

SENDING WEDDING ANNOUNCEMENT TO NEWSPAPERS

Some society editors like to publish the announcement of a wedding-to-be several weeks in advance of the occasion, then follow up with the descriptive account immediately after the wedding has taken place.

In sending data to the papers, the same rules of good taste should be followed as in sending engagement announcements (page 85). Many papers have printed forms that may be filled in and returned to the society department. All proper names should be given in full, either complete first name or two initials. It's a wise idea to take notes as you go along to make sure you have full names of the minister, organist, soloist, etc., as a last-minute time-saver.

It is the bride's family's responsibility to see that the wedding notices are sent to the newspapers at the right time. All accounts should be typed, double spaced, and addressed in care of the Society Editor. A release date should be indicated at the top of the first page, with the bride's telephone number for verification.

The actual wedding story should never appear in the paper before the wedding takes place. If the wedding is held in the morning or at noon, the afternoon papers would carry

the notice first; or if the ceremony takes place in the evening, the morning papers would get the break.

TYPICAL WEDDING ANNOUNCEMENT

If there is to be a brief announcement story in advance of the wedding, such a news item might read:

The marriage of Miss Nancy Ann Claridge, daughter of Mr. and Mrs. Douglas Randolph Claridge of Irvington, and Mr. Lee Cayton Bell, son of Dr. and Mrs. Joseph Linden Bell of Chicago, Illinois, is to take place Thursday afternoon, the fifth of September, in Trinity Church. A reception will follow the ceremony at Spring Dale Country Club.

The bride's sister, Mrs. Donald Ross Kerrington of Boston, Massachusetts, will serve as matron of honor. The bridesmaids will be Miss Helen Thurman and Miss Betty Beale of Cleveland, Ohio, and Mrs. George Alden and Mrs. Wilbur T. Vanness of Irvington.

Martin Hale of Chicago, Illinois, will act as best man
and ushers will include William Wright, L. Roger
Chandler, Jaspar Ingle and Landon Carrington.

The wedding story which often includes a great deal
of detail, the decorations, costume descriptions, prominent
guests, etc., most likely will be requested by your local newspaper. Oftentimes the information is given on the telephone,
but for accuracy it is preferable that it be typed and sent to
the society editors.

Your own local papers will be your guide, so follow their
requests. Do have your information well organized before
attempting to give it out. Get the correct names of the flowers
from the florist; have your out-of-town guest list ready for
quotation, etc. When you wish to have your wedding picture included with the story you may send in a glossy print
of your wedding portrait, or the society editor may request
one. Do not be surprised, however, if the photograph does
not run at the time the article appears, for often there is not
sufficient space for running both and the picture appears
later. The photographer often services the newspapers with
glossies, free of charge, if his credit line is used. In some
towns the newspapers will send photographers to cover your
wedding. But whatever you do, do not permit any of them
to take a flash of any of the inside church scenes.

Be sure to keep clippings of your wedding account for
your book of memories which record that day of days.

The announcement of a very informal ceremony simply
states:

Miss Isabelle Black, daughter of Mr. and Mrs. Edward L. Black of Dayton, Ohio, was married to Mr. Roscoe Walton, son of Mr. and Mrs. Roy Donaldson Walton of Chattanooga, Tennessee, on Saturday afternoon, the twentieth of April, at the Wesley Heights Chapel, Dayton, Ohio.

A formal announcement of your marriage may be made by your parents if you have been married away from home in a very quiet ceremony, thus: "Mr. and Mrs. Walter Huntington announce the marriage of their daughter," etc.

When the bride's parents are divorced, if the bride's mother has remarried and wishes to include her former husband, the announcement in the newspapers should read, "The daughter of Mrs. Thaddeus Burns of this city and Mr. Jasper Chittenden of Baltimore, Maryland . . ."

If, for personal reasons, the bride's mother wishes to omit the name of her former husband, only her name would appear in the announcement, i.e., "daughter of Mrs. Thaddeus Burns of this city, etc."

The wedding account of a second marriage rarely includes many details, though the announcements follow the same form as for any first marriage, with names of parents given, etc. The prefix "Mrs." is customarily used for the bride, i.e., "The marriage of Mrs. Alice Lynn Blair and Mr. Felix Wharton Young took place . . . etc."

If the bride's mother (or the bridegroom's mother) is a widow, the following phrasing is customary, "the daughter of Mrs. Oliver Selden and the late Mr. Selden."

Your Wedding Photographs

You will doubtless want to have your posed formal wedding photographs made as soon as your bridal gown is ready. Pictures may be taken at the store where your dress was purchased if there are suitable facilities. When bridal departments are equipped with good photographic studios, the picture-taking operation is greatly simplified, for veil and gown are freshly pressed for the occasion and there is much less fuss and bother than when the bride goes to a photographic studio with all her wedding trappings.

If wedding photographs are taken at home, the simplest sort of background should be used. Often the photographer will provide a backdrop which is in contrast with your gown.

How about engaging a photographer to take candid shots of your wedding reception and "before" and "after" ceremony pictures! You'll want them for your scrapbook for sure.

CHAPTER X

To Have and To Hold

GIFTS . . . COMING AND GOING

ALTHOUGH YOU ARE ON THE RECEIVING END FOR MOST OF the gifts that are given during your prenuptial days there are a few tokens you yourself will wish to give as compliments of attention and devotion.

What to give your bridal attendants that will serve as a lasting symbol of appreciation may be answered by something personal such as strands of matched pearls, cameo lockets or jeweled clips as accessories to be worn with their wedding costumes. Or it may be monogrammed compacts, perfume atomizers, silver wedding ring trays or evening bags.

The larger and more elaborate the wedding the more valuable the gifts, though no bride should give such lavish gifts that they set a precedent difficult to live up to for future brides in the group.

Bridesmaids' gifts, customarily, are all alike. The maid or matron of honor may receive a more personalized present of slightly greater value than the bridesmaids' gifts.

Short, single-strand pearls, a pair of silver barrettes or a dainty bracelet all make appropriate gifts for little flower girls.

To ring bearers and train bearers you might give boxes of fine linen handkerchiefs, monogrammed or initialed.

FROM THE BRIDEGROOM TO HIS ATTENDANTS

The ushers' gifts should all be alike and may take the form of gold belt buckles, gold-mounted fountain pens, cuff links, cigarette cases or sterling silver money clips.

The best man usually rates a special gift. It may well be a piece of luggage, a case of rare liquor, a lined leather billfold or even a wrist watch.

At a formal daytime wedding the bridegroom may give his ushers their vests, ties, gloves and spats to make for uniformity.

WHEN TO PRESENT THE ATTENDANTS' GIFTS

Each gift should be appropriately boxed and wrapped with special wedding paper, ready to present to attendants at the bridesmaids' luncheon and the bachelor dinner respectively. They may be given at the bridal dinner the night before the wedding if there are no separate bride and bridegroom parties.

GIFTS TO OTHER FRIENDS WHO SERVE AT YOUR WEDDING

Friends who are engaged to play or sing at your wedding or reception may refuse to accept a fee. In such case gifts from you would be in order. They also should be presented at the bridal dinner.

It's a gracious gesture to send a corsage to any woman who

is taking part in your wedding, but this courtesy does not take the place of a more lasting personal gift.

Young girls who may have been asked to assist in the dining room at the reception should receive some sort of small remembrance in behalf of their services.

FROM THE BRIDE TO THE GROOM AND VICE VERSA

There's nothing obligatory about the gift-giving custom between bride and groom but it's usual in the large formal wedding.

What you choose to give each other is a personal matter but gifts should have a sentimental keepsake quality. (Never articles of clothing, however.)

Often the bridegroom presents his bride with an heirloom brooch, lovely matched pearls, a bracelet or jeweled watch. You, in turn, may give him a dated and monogrammed watch, gold cuff links, matched luggage or a handsome wallet with his name plate. You'll know what he wants!

DON'T HESITATE TO SPEAK UP ON THE WEDDING-GIFT SUBJECT

When eager-to-please gift givers beg you to tell them what you want for a wedding present, don't evade the issue with a careless "Oh, just anything."

How much better to say frankly that your china and crystal are still incomplete or that you need an electric toaster or a card table (if you do) than to be forced to exchange un-wantables for them later.

Consider the giver's financial status and don't suggest gifts beyond his means. Give out ideas on your color schemes and hints on things you'd really adore.

There are bound to be some "white elephants" and your friends dread that. So for everybody's sake give them some helpful tips on the subject.

Make a comprehensive list of what you need for your new home and refer to it often.

What about an electric percolator, a pair of boudoir lamps, a kitchen clock, a knocker for the front door? Include all the necessaries and whatever luxuries you can't live without.

Most stores have gift-preference lists which you may fill out and leave with them. This is a service to questioning friends who may consult the store when gift shopping and are advised which patterns you have chosen and which pieces have not yet been ordered.

YOUR SILVER PATTERN

A bride's sterling silver flatware is traditionally the nicest gift from her family. But plenty of families can't give wedding and silver, too. You and your family are the best judges of that.

But that shouldn't keep you from selecting your pattern. If you can manage to start with only the few pieces to make place settings for two, your friends will probably add to it.

Because your silver will be one of your most prized possessions, to last a lifetime, you want to choose your pattern with the utmost care.

You may go in for the classic or the consciously streamlined modern. Keep in mind the type of home you will have and the kind of entertaining that suits you.

Don't decide on it hurriedly. Ponder over all the available patterns in your price line. Take your fiancé along with you to make your final decision. (You'll want to keep your husband as long as you do your silver, remember.)

If you plan to have your silver monogrammed, sift down your choices to a pattern that lends itself to the type of monogram you like. There are many shapes and styles in monograms varying from long, narrow diamond shapes to flourishing Old English letters in scroll design. The beauty of your monogram depends on how well the initials lend themselves to the pattern.

MATCH YOUR CHINA, SILVER AND CRYSTAL

Play the game of matchmaking when you go on your shopping spree for prospective gifts. Your silver, china and crystal should all go together.

Salespeople in the respective departments will gladly assemble complete place settings for you to see if you are in doubt as to the co-ordination of certain patterns.

Naturally you won't want to match them *exactly.* But choose the same *type* of patterns—a floral motif, something with simple classic lines, or more ornate patterns provided they go well together.

The stores will register your choices, and your friends will be grateful for the chance to learn what will be most pleasing to you. You can then tell people who ask you what you want where you have recorded your tastes, and stores will see that gifts are not duplicated.

GET ORGANIZED BEFORE GIFTS START ARRIVING

It's an altogether exciting world—like Christmas every day —when those white-tissued, beribboned packages start drifting in. It's likely to turn into an inundation before it's over and we warn you that chaos undoubtedly will set in unless you get a firm grip on a pencil and a Gift Record Book and get organized beforehand.

1. Check to see that you have an adequate supply of thank-you note paper and stamps. It's better to have an over-supply than to run short at the last hectic moment. Arrange a special place for them and see that they are kept in their place when not in use.

2. Get a Gift Record Book with numbered stickers. (These may be purchased at any stationery department.) As each gift arrives enter the number of the gift, the name of the donor, date and description on the gift list pages. Be accurate about this and it will save you many a headache.

3. Acknowledge each gift the day it arrives if at all possible. Set aside a certain hour each day to do this.

4. Arrange a suitable place for your gifts. (It is quite proper to display them at your wedding reception if you have room.)

DISPLAY OF GIFTS

Remove all the large pieces of furniture from the room which you have chosen for the display of your gifts.

If card tables aren't adequate why not try trestle tables? They can be rented, or possibly borrowed from the church basement, and arranged like counters around the side of the room and down the center.

Most etiquette books say to cover the tables with plain white damask cloths but with all the exciting materials on the market it seems a little tame to use plain white linen. (And who has that many matching banquet cloths, anyway?)

Several yards of inexpensive material in soft peach or powder-blue to blend with the color scheme of the room would be much more artistic. You can use the material later for bedroom curtains. There are sheer fabrics, glazed ones, metallics, dull materials and shimmering ones. . . . You can concoct your own trimmings.

Instead of massing all your silver together, all your glass on another table and your china on another, play storekeeper and use some skill in the display. Save some of your larger gift boxes to use as steps for gifts on your table tops to show some of your loveliest things to best advantage.

Your shower gifts may be arranged all together on one table, or mixed in with other gifts, just as you wish.

Be sure to take out a temporary floater insurance policy for your gifts while they are on display. During the reception you may want to engage a plain-clothes detective to guard the gifts if there are many costly ones.

CARDS LEFT ON?

Most people of discernment agree that donors' cards should be removed from the gifts when they are displayed. It is actually a matter which you and your family may decide, however, for there is no reason as far as propriety goes why cards shouldn't be left with the gifts. Everyone will want to know who gave you this and that . . . so someone in the family should be responsible for giving out this information.

Don't display your checks (if you are lucky enough to re-

ceive some) but you may mention them and their donors.
"Uncle Arthur sent us a check," you may say . . . and add,
"for our bedroom furniture," or whatever.

WRITING YOUR THANK-YOU NOTES

This is the part you dread, isn't it? Well, it may tax the
gray matter a bit to dash off a dozen or so notes a day, but
after all it's the least you can do—just look what you are
getting.

Don't hold back your enthusiasm because you think it
sounds schoolgirlish. Most people love exuberance, especially when it's over something they selected for you.

Don't forget to write thank-you notes for your shower gifts
and a note of appreciation to your party hostesses. Since
many of your closest friends will probably give you more than
one shower gift, wait until near your wedding date (after
all the parties are over) and write thank-you notes to include all the shower presents each has given you. In this
instance you don't need to mention them by name, if there
is quite a list, but write a general "thank-you" for everything.

Although the wedding gifts belong to you, the bride, try
to include the bridegroom in your letter of thanks.

When wedding gifts are sent by a married couple, direct
your note to the wife. You may mention her husband, if
you choose, but usually "you" is understood to mean "you
both."

Refer to the gift specifically when you write the donors. If
you are in a quandary as to what it is, speak of it as "your
silver piece" (or china, glass, or whatever it is).

Help yourself to a few ideas to get started:

Dear Mrs. Warner:

The cocktail shaker is a beauty and it was the nicest idea to have Jim's initials put on it. He calls it *his* gift and displays it on all occasions!

The only thing lacking is that coveted collection of Mr. Warner's special bar recipes, but we're hoping to inveigle a few of his specials soon.

Jim sends you a delighted "thank you" for *his* gift and I'm just as pleased and grateful as he is.

We'll be expecting you as our first real party guests.

Most sincerely,

Jean Barton

Dear Mrs. Cushing:

What dears you were to select such a lovely lamp for our new home. It not only fits into our blue and white color scheme beautifully, but it pleases the practical housewife side of my nature because of its washable shade. I'll try always to keep it as gleaming white as it is now.

Jim joins me in hoping that you will be among the first to come see us when we return the middle of October.

Affectionately,

Jean Barton

Dear Miss Edith:

To think that you should have taken time out of your busy life to make this marvelous needlepoint for me! I can't tell you how very much both Jim and I appreciate your sweet thoughtfulness—and thank you!

We're looking forward to seeing you on our wedding day.

Most sincerely,

Jean

Marilyn—you dear:

Now you will *have* to come up soon and see our etchings and us.

How did you know that Jim and I both were yearning for those particular contemporary ones for either side of the living-room windows? Nothing could have pleased us more and we love you for it.

Do come to tea next Wednesday afternoon and see my gifts.

Till then,

Jean

Dear Mrs. Carewe:

Ever since I was a little girl I have adored quaint little objects of art. Now, to have that precious white circus horse with its brilliant trappings for my very own in our new home is really a thrill.

Jim thinks it is one of the cleverest decorative pieces he has ever seen—so, you see, we are both proud owners.

Bring Mr. Carewe and come visit us, and the new pet, at our apartment very soon.

Most sincerely,

Jean Barton

WHEN A GIFT HAS TO BE RETURNED

Dear Mrs. James:

You were so kind to send us those lovely demitasse spoons and we do appreciate your thought of us. I want to tell you, though, what happened and I hope you'll approve.

We discovered that we had two dozen demitasse spoons and only six demitasse cups and saucers. So we took the liberty of exchanging your gift for another half-dozen matching cups and saucers in our china pattern. Now, our service for after-dinner coffee is complete and we are delighted.

Jim and I send our sincere thanks to you and Mr. James and hope that you will come soon to see us.

Most sincerely,

Jean Barton Smith

Unless you know that someone has spent a great deal of time and effort in selecting a certain wedding gift, it is perfectly correct to exchange a present if you feel so inclined. Gift donors expect you to take back a gift if it is duplicated. Let your good taste be your guide, however, and don't do a mass exchange.

When a wedding is definitely called off, all gifts must be returned by the bride's family. If the wedding is merely postponed an announcement is sent to guests and the presents are not returned (see page 108).

SPECIAL QUESTIONS AND ANSWERS

Q. Are printed "thank-you" cards ever permissible?

A. Printed "thank-yous" are never permissible, but sometimes in a rush of gifts, engraved cards acknowledging the receipt of the present may be sent out with the promise of a personal note to follow. This is one way of reassuring gift senders that their presents arrived safely, if it is impossible to make acknowledgment immediately. Stationers and jewelers carry samples of these forms, but it is not advisable to resort to this method unless unavoidable.

It goes without saying that you should follow up with personal thank-you notes as soon as possible.

Q. How should acknowledgment be made when a wedding gift is sent from a large group of fellow employees in an office?

A. When individual names are listed on the gift card a personal note should be written to each contributor. An all-inclusive note may be sent to the office, addressed to the leader of the group, if a general "From Your Office" card is the only one enclosed with gift. If the gift is in the form of a check or a gift certificate, it is well to make mention in your thank-you note of what you intend to buy for your home as a lasting remembrance from this group of friends.

CHAPTER XI

Strains of Lohengrin

WHEN THE ORGAN BEGINS ITS WHISPERED NOTE YOU'LL PROB-
ably be too excited to know what it's playing. But all the
other victims of love's old sweet song will be there to drink
in the full measure of its enchantment. So choose the musical
selections for your wedding carefully to keep harmony and
beauty hovering over the atmosphere.

PRELIMINARY MUSIC

The incidental music, which will begin about a half-hour
before the ceremony, should be of classical type. Selections
from any of the old masters, such as Mendelssohn, Wagner,
Brahms and Schubert, are always appropriate to the occasion.

INCIDENTAL ORGAN MUSIC

Following is a program of incidental music for a formal
church wedding as suggested in *The Cokesbury Marriage*

191

Manual. It's your privilege as a bride, however, to consult with your organist and make your selections together.

Introduction

"Allegro" and "Pastorale" from
   "1st Symphony".......................*Guilmant*
"Fugue" from "Toccata and Fugue in C".........*Bach*
"Prelude in G Major"........................*Bach*
"Festival March"...........................*A. Foote*
"Grand Triumphal Chorus"..............*Guilmant*
"Ave Maria Lourdes"
   Traditional music arranged by *Pietro Yon*
"Adagio in A Minor".........................*Bach*
"Panis Angelicus"...........................*Franck*
"Choral in G Minor".........................*Bach*
"March Pontificale" ....*De la Tombelle*

Processional

"Bridal Chorus" from "Lohengrin"..........*Wagner*

Recessional

Recessional from "Midsummer Night's
   Dream"...........................*Mendelssohn*

During the Ceremony

(if you wish soft organ music in accompaniment)
"Oh Promise Me"........................*De Koven*
"Meditation" from "Thais"................*Massenet*
"Wedding Song".........*H. Ware* (arr. *J. H. Rogers*)
"Liebestraum" ....*Liszt*

ARE YOU HAVING A VOCALIST?

Such favorites as "At Dawning," "I Love You Truly" and "Ah! Sweet Mystery of Life" seem to be invariable as vocal music. It will be a welcome innovation, however, if you or the bridegroom have a significant poem that can be sung to special music, or an appropriate hymn that you both treasure. Here are a few vocal selections as suggestions:

"I Follow Thee Also"......................*J. S. Bach*
(from the St. John Passion)
"My Heart Ever Faithful".................*J. S. Bach*
(from the Pentecost Cantata)
"Be Thou Contented" ....*J. S. Bach*
"Entreat Me Not to Leave Thee"........*C. F. Gounod*

Many churches have a ruling that all wedding music, vocal and instrumental, must be approved by their choir directors.

You'd better check this with your organist before you make your final selections.

Don't plan to have more than two (or three, at the most) vocal selections. This musical program should be scheduled to take place after most of the guests have arrived and are seated. You might time the last song to take place just before the wedding march, while the mothers are being escorted to their places.

Be sure to have the vocalist go through his or her part of the program at your rehearsal so that it may be clocked to the minute.

The chants of the *Missa pro Sponsa et Sponsa* are available for solo and choral use as incidental nuptial music:*

Introit: The God of Israel *(Deus Israel)*, from Tobit 7-8
Gradual: Thy wife *(Uxor tua)*, from Psalm 128
Verse: The Lord Send thee Help, from Psalm 20 (mode viii)
Verse: The Lord that made Heaven, from Psalm 134 (mode iv)
Tract: Behold, that thus, from Psalm 128 (mode viii)
Offertory: I trusted in thee, from Psalm 31 (mode ii)

One or more stanzas of the following hymns make excellent solos or choir numbers. In some cases the tunes will serve admirably as simple processional and recessional music.

"O perfect love," Barnby
"The voice that breathed o'er Eden" (tune: St. Alphege, Gauntlett)
"O Father, all creating" (tune: Ellacombe)
"O blest the house" (tune: Retreat, Hastings)
"Let me be thine forever" (tune: *Ich dank dir, lieber Herre*)
"Jesus, thou joy of loving hearts" (tune: *Christe Redemptor*, mode i)

A touch that would add drama to a large formal church wedding has been suggested by a talented church organist. He proposes that a feminine choir of ten members, dressed in white choir robes, march slowly down the aisle preceding the bridal party, softly chanting the *Lohengrin* "Bridal Chorus."

---

* Choral music also from *The Cokesbury Marriage Manual*.

They would enter by twos from the back of the church and proceed to the choir loft where they would continue to chant as the procession formed at the altar. Isn't it a lovely idea?

MUSIC FOR HOME WEDDING

If you are having an electric organ, a string organ, a string trio (two violins and a cello) or a harp and trio (two violins and a cello) or a harp and violin, the preliminary music might include such selections as:

"Spring Song" .... *Mendelssohn*
"Toujours L'Amour"...................... *Friml*
"Dreams" .... *Schumann*
"Aria of Nicolanta" from "Lakme," played by cello
"Song of Songs"................. *Rimsky-Korsakov*
                 (for voice)
March .... *Svendsen*

Give your instructions in writing to the organist or musicians who are to play at your wedding. It will help prevent any misunderstandings.

MUSIC FOR THE PROCESSION

The "Wedding March" from the third act of *Lohengrin* usually is chosen for the processional, followed by Mendelssohn's "Wedding March" for the recessional. These selections are not at all compulsory, however, if you prefer some variations. But it *is* important that the music you select have a satisfactory rhythm and timing for walking down the aisle.

The organist will serve as your guide and will set the pace for the wedding party at your rehearsal.

DURING THE CEREMONY

If you wish to have soft organ music played during the ceremony, here are some suggested selections:

"Oh Promise Me".......................*De Koven*
"Meditation" from "Thais"...............*Massenet*
"The Old Refrain".......................*Kreisler*
"Liebestraum" ....*Liszt*

WILL THERE BE A CHOIR?

An adult choir or a boy's choir may be engaged to sing before the ceremony. The selections you choose may include appropriate anthems or hymns which are adapted to the solemnity of the occasion. Confer with your organist or choir director for suggestions on these special musical arrangements.

RECEPTION MUSIC

Your party music should be gay and light and may include popular tunes of a sentimental vein.

If an orchestra is to play for dancing, the current musical hits, of course, will fill the program.

If you've had to scratch reception music off the list, appoint someone to look after the phonograph and furnish a musical background with recordings.

Here's a tip or two on suitable selections:

"Valse Bluette".............................*Drigo*
"Melody in F"........................*Rubinstein*
"Kiss Me Again"...................*Victor Herbert*
"Lullaby"................................*Brahms*
"The Swan".........................*Saint-Saëns*
"Chanson Bohémienne".....................*Boldi*

If it's a military wedding, strains of "Army Blue," "Anchors Aweigh"—or whatever is appropriate for the branch of the service—rightfully claims a place in the musical program.

CHAPTER XII

Rose Petals in Your Pathway

DECORATING FOR YOUR WEDDING IS A DIRECT CHALLENGE TO your imagination. A handful of blossoms against a background of green can work wonders if you add a dash of ingenuity. So *do* lend your inspiration and ideas, even if you are having a florist take over. It will be much more fun to have a part in it.

CHURCH DECORATIONS

Connive with your decorator for something unusual if you are having a big formal church wedding.

You'll doubtless want to have a banking of greenery as a foundation for your floral decorations at the altar. But don't have a few stiff palms and ferns set up and let it go at that. If the wedding is in a church where there is a choir loft directly back of the chancel, get an estimate on massing it with tall symmetrical evergreens for a winter wedding. Or use a latticework intertwined with fernery and flowers as the background for your pastel colors in springtime.

Plan on flowers that are in season if you wish to hold down your expenses. Meet your florist at the church for a consultation and take into consideration the interior layout and architectural style of the church before you go too far.

FOR A SPRINGTIME WEDDING

A bower of delicate blossoms, such as apple blossoms, peachtree branches or flowering dogwood can turn a chapel into a breath-taking fairyland at small cost.

In a larger church, masses of blossoms might be arranged on either side of the altar in place of the more customary palms, and with charming effect.

Quince, plum or wild cherry blossoms spilling over from tall altar vases and tied at pew ends are happy ideas for effective arrangement.

Or you might daringly combine Easter lilies and yellow forsythia branches if yellow is one of the bridal colors. Easter lilies combine beautifully with shiny lemon leaves in altar bouquets and for aisle-post decoration.

Lilacs in lavish bunches lend themselves exquisitely to springtime weddings. Potted tulips or jonquils (which you may rent and so be saved the expense of buying outright) would be lovely interspersed with potted ferns as a mass decoration on either side of the chancel.

White flowers are traditional for altar embellishment, but maybe you've noticed that gay and brightly colored blooms have added the right touch to many a wedding which otherwise would have been somber in note.

Just picture in your mind's eye mimosa trees in tubs, sprinkling their feathery yellow beauty throughout a church from chancel to window ledges. There are numerous varieties of mimosa ranging from short spiky trees to the fuller cloudlike delicate varieties which may be mixed together with effectiveness.

Short-stemmed flowers massed in low bunches might be used as chancel decoration in a small church. Try fragrant lilies of the valley mixed with white violets, baby's breath and maidenhair fern as pew bouquets and prie-dieu decorations. Long trailing bows of white tulle tied to the bouquets give an airy, ethereal effect.

Candles are important if it's to be a late afternoon or evening ceremony. There are tall single standards, those of cathedral type or the many-branched candelabra. Aisle-post candles are entrancing when an all-out candlelight wedding is planned. And don't forget to mass small flickering candles on low window sills wherever available, and match them with tall tapers mixed with greenery at the altar.

At one formal wedding, long talked about, electric chandeliers were filled with burning candles in place of light bulbs, and the soft glowing light flickered from side walls and high-hanging center chandeliers alike.

Tall white tapers are customary in decorations unless you are carrying out the delicacy of blush-pink or light-blue in your bridal array.

Have a look at the pedestals, urns, vases and baskets which are available at the church and the florist's for the flowers you choose. Select the most decorative ones that will add grace and beauty to the scene.

Is It to Be a Summertime Ceremony?

Roses and the June bride go together as naturally as a cake and its frosting. Creamy-white roses are old-fashioned favorites though there are many shades ranging from snow-white to deep cream. Dainty arrangements of sweetheart roses interspersed with forget-me-nots and baby's breath are appealing for both bride and bridesmaids. Rambler roses wound about pillars, or aisle arches, give an unusual touch, as does an altar screen laced with greenery and dotted with aromatic roses in artistic bunches.

Peonies, snapdragons, snowballs and spirea are all dramatic flowers when used in large bouquets for altar and pew-end decoration.

Ropes of mixed summer flowers may be stretched in bright pattern along the aisle in place of the usual white ribbons. The same flowers, in small bunches, could be tied to pews as markers and used in clusters at the chancel.

Night-blooming stock and white larkspur are appropriate for chancel decorating as are white albion lilies. Great masses of field daisies filling the chancel and echoed throughout the church in smaller motifs create a memorable wedding effect with greenery punctuating the flowers' laciness.

At one formal church wedding where the bride wore an old-fashioned blue gown, the altar and pews were decorated in Madonna color scheme with blue and white delphinium and gladioli fashioned in Colonial bouquet style with lace doily bases. The same arrangement in miniature was carried out in the flowers worn by the bride and her maids.

Great clouds of baby's breath filling the chancel and surrounding the kneeling bench may be balanced with bouvardia and larkspur to create an ethereal effect.

When a large church is used for a small wedding it may be attractively decorated to resemble a chapel by screening off the back section with latticework, flowers and greenery. Birch branches or rambler roses on a trellis make a pretty screenway also, though this is likely to be an expensive process if church proportions are tremendous.

FOR AN AUTUMN WEDDING

Combine sheaves of wheat with rich-toned chrysanthemums for handsome decoration. Use branches of autumn foliage for cutting down the size of a church. Spear yellow mums with branches of red-leafed oak for daring effects.

Autumn with its bright foliage presents striking possibilities for color at the altar and throughout the church.

Imagine a chancel radiant with autumn leaves, lighted by glowing candles in tall candelabra, wound with trailing leaves, asters and mums. Then have the bridal attendants carry candles entwined with flowers and leaves—and be prepared for a breathless hush as guests drink in the beauty.

Dahlias in deep hues provide a beauteous background for

rich jewel-toned gowns. Bundles of grains—rye, barley, oats —mixed with white asters present an effective autumn aspect when used for allover decoration.

Spider "mums" and shaggy-petaled fujis are in season from the first of September until Christmastime and may be had in orchid tones, bronze, white and yellow. Mixed with croton leaves they are most unusual for bouquets as well as for altar decoration.

A WINTER WEDDING

Roses are the bride's best stand-by for winter wedding decorating, and many unusual effects may be achieved with the use of winter greens as background arrangements.

Picture a forest of fir trees around the altar, ropes of greenery swagging certain sections of the pews and entwining white church columns; then set off by an altar banking of red, red roses. If white is a more suitable motif for your wedding, try white roses for banking the altar or in vases artistically placed.

During the holiday season white or red poinsettias may be found most effective with evergreen or holly background. Christmas trees sprayed with silver star dust or turquoise-tinted will create a fairyland picturesqueness as will silver-sprayed box hedges.

A formal wedding of more elaborate plan might include decorations of small symmetrical orange-bearing trees. Growing in tubs the full-fruited trees might be arranged in stately rows down the aisleway and around the altar. Alternating with the sun-kissed fruit, small flowering orange trees might be used for dramatic variety. With this arrangement no added flowers would be necessary for altar or pew decoration.

Had you thought of a winter wedding in complete candlelight, with tapers of all sizes flickering from all sides of the church?

Azaleas in potted form may be found at most florists along toward the end of winter. Gorgeous in their hugeness, they might be used along the aisleway and at the altar for breathtaking beauty.

Church decorations should never be so ostentatious that they steal attention from the wedding party or transform a church completely. They should always be in keeping and in matching color scheme with your wedding.

FLOWERS FOR A HOME WEDDING

The altar may be banked with greenery and flanked on each side with flowers in vases, with candelabra in the background. Or you might use tall white pillars holding vases of flowers and trailing ivy to outline an improvised altar.

Pedestals, baskets or tall containers overflowing with blossoms are often used to indicate the aisle along which the bridal party enters. White satin ribbons are rarely used for home or club weddings any more.

You might have your bridesmaids carry a rope of greenery, with flowers tucked in here and there, to form the aisleway. In this case you'll dispense with other floral markers.

The stairway and hall banisters may be festooned with

greenery and flowers, and the house throughout simply decorated with vases of mixed flowers.

If only the reception is to take place in your home, the background for the receiving line is your main concern.

One such wedding reception was planned so that the end of the living room served as the background for the receiving line, instead of the fireplace. The setting was decorative with drapings of transparent white and silver cloth between two pillars of white. These were festooned with ropes of flowers extending from the center of the drape to each side. Tall French windows were also decorated with flower ropes, and directly over the bride and groom in the receiving bower hung an old English "kissing hoop" wound with myrtle, the flower of love.

If you'll be satisfied with something less ornate, then decorate the fireplace mantel with greenery and a plateau of flowers to extend all the way across. Have lighted candles in holders at each end if the hour is suitable—there is a special dignity and charm in the soft glow of candlelight.

Or let your receiving line background be unadorned and mark the spot only with tall pedestals or baskets of flowers at each end.

A GARDEN WEDDING

You'll want to keep the decorations for a garden wedding as natural as possible. A little white gate wired with flowers can lead to the altar proper. Or you may have shepherdess crooks, tied with nosegays, fastened upright in the ground as an outline for the aisleway on either side. Or try tall white pedestals holding arrangements of garden flowers.

FLOWERS FOR THE BRIDE'S TABLE

Keep the dining-room flowers in bridal white, unless you are keying your wedding to certain pastel tones. Lilies of the valley in silver or crystal baskets of miniature size, or white lilacs clustered in low, spreading bowls are always in keeping with the wedding theme. Sweetheart roses, delicately tinged camellias and light-blue delphinium are dainty additions if color you must have.

Maidenhair fern, smilax, croton leaves or lemon leaves are often used as a decorative edging for the bride's cake. Or it may be arranged with gardenias or white carnations—any flowers you wish.

Plateaus of medium-tall flowers are sure to create a lovely effect on a table where candles gleam in silver holders on each side.

For your place cards at the bride's table, tie each one with a tiny silver bell and a miniature nosegay, if you want to add an extra dash.

Guest tables, for a sit-down breakfast or supper, may be decorated with small bowls of flowers in pastel shades or with crystal brandy goblets adorned with one single full blossom.

YOUR BRIDAL BOUQUET

Yes, the bridegroom buys it, that's true. But you should have an active part in its planning so you'll know your flowers will conform to the wedding motif.

If you are having a mass of flowers at the altar, you'll want your bouquet and the attendants' to be something simple and attractively styled. A spray of butterfly orchids, of lilies of the valley or lilacs, attached to your prayer book . . . or cabbage roses in graduated sizes on one long stem. That's the trick!

If, however, your background is all greenery, carry an armful of blossoms or a cascade bouquet of flowers delicately falling all the way to the hemline of your gown. But don't let it hide you or your dress.

There are so many exciting arrangements. Don't be satisfied to accept just anything if you want to create a little extra stir.

There are fans covered with flowers, muffs of flowers, wired garlands of gladioli or large-blossomed flowers, basket arrangements, and silvered leaves trailing from a spray bouquet. Flowers can be frosted with something sparkling to make a lovely Christmaslike glitter in a palely lighted church.

Shower bouquets are the favorites of traditional brides. The smartest bouquets now use ribbons only for binding the stems. Round, compact styles are quaint; Colonial bouquets are for the old-fashioned weddings; tall graceful lilies suit the tall stately bride . . . now, what for you?

Bouquets made of all one type of flower are very smart. But if you wish to have your going-away corsage (or an orchid) centered in your bouquet, to be slipped out before you toss your flowers to your bridesmaids, it can be done.

Most bouquets are made on a handle or cuff which slips over your arm. This arrangement will make yours easy to carry and to transfer to your maid of honor.

Lilies of the valley have always been known as the bride's flowers and seem to typify romance. Orchids are coveted by many brides, with the "canhamiana" the most popular specimen sparkling white with deep orchid throat. Then there's stephanotis, the waxy, star-shaped flower which looks very much like an orange blossom; and velvety white roses, sweet peas, narcissi, white violets—just take your choice.

What about carrying a large cluster of white freesia set in the middle of enormous bows of soft white maline?

Talk it all over with your florist, get his ideas *and his estimates.* You don't want to bankrupt the bridegroom before you marry him, that's sure.

CORSAGES FOR INFORMAL WEDDINGS

Shoulder corsages are most generally worn with informal dress. But if it suits your costume you may wear a wristlet of tiny asters or small blossomed flowers . . . or if you are wearing a fall shade of afternoon dress, try carrying a few single stalks of long-stemmed chrysanthemums. Informal bouquets of summer flowers or little nosegays have come into fashion to be carried with sheer light-colored clothes.

Orchids of rare species and colors combine beautifully with more tailored street costumes and are lovely with furs. Rubrum lilies offer a dash of bright hue for dark-colored things. Camellia foliage combined with carnations make a pretty bouquet; and often variegated foliages can be put to use without the benefit of blossoms, when in the hands of an ingenious florist.

If you have a yen for all white flowers in your corsage (they will look more bride-ish), you might like lilies of the valley with a gardenia center, or all white violets. White roses and white pansies are velvety. But choose something you adore.

Pin the stems of the corsage flowers downward, just as they grow naturally, and you can enjoy their fragrance more.

BRIDESMAIDS' BOUQUETS

When you settled on those lovely gowns for the attendants, couldn't you just picture them as a background for the flowers?

You probably thought then and there, Roses and anemones will set them off to perfection. . . . Or maybe: Sweet peas will carry out the color blends best. But whatever you've decided on, we've only a little word to add. Don't let the size of the bouquets overpower the girls or cover up their dresses. Tremendously large bouquets simply are not smart.

The flowers may be in sprays or in round and formal bouquets. They may be in a cascade or Colonial in arrangement.

They may be flower muffs, nosegays adorning artistic little fans, ropes or garlands, flower-covered parasols, armfuls of blossoms or baskets spilling over with vibrant color.

For a morning wedding, how would you like your attendants to carry prayer books with trailing ivy, or a simple arrangement of blossoms framed with begonia leaves sprayed around the edges with star dust?

Are you familiar with "glamellias?" They are gladioli which have been artistically wired, blossom by blossom, to resemble camellias. Made up in variegated array they will be conversation pieces that add exciting color touches to your wedding.

Would you prefer to have your girls carry the same kind of flowers you are going to have? For instance, you might carry white peonies, your bridesmaids pink peonies and your maid of honor might carry lavender shades.

Take the samples of all dress materials to the florist with you to work out color effects. If you are having a period wedding, by all means have your florist arrange to see the gowns so that the bouquets will fit into the picture perfectly.

Check with your florist on all other details, such as:

> Prayer bench
> Candelabra
> Tapers
> Canvas
> Canopy
> Corsage for organist (if she is a special friend)

CHAPTER XIII

Memories to Cherish

YOUR WEDDING RECEPTION IS *really* A PARTY, AND SHOULD be a heavenly affair whether it's under the old peach tree or atop a skyscraper hotel.

Your home is the logical place to entertain. It's practical because your gifts will be there on display, your going-away clothes will be waiting in your own room for you to step into them . . . and sentimentally speaking, it's home-sweet-home.

If your home is too small for a large reception, how about your aunt's big house or the home of your mother's best friend? There is always someone who would be overjoyed to fill her house with flowers and play hostess to such a joyous gathering . . . with your family footing the bills, of course.

A town or country club or a hotel ballroom offer the next

best solutions, though they lack the personal background and may add to your expenses.

For a small wedding you might invite your friends to your new apartment after the ceremony, to drink a toast and wish you happiness.

RECEIVING LINE

The receiving line doesn't necessarily have to be stiff and formal, but can be formed in group arrangement to greet friends as they arrive from the church. The bride and groom usually receive on the side of the room opposite the entrance. But that's for you to decide. Choose the most effective and convenient background and decorate it as you will.

Your mother will be first in line to receive, with the bridegroom's mother next, then the bridegroom's father. This arrangement gives your mother an opportunity to present the bridegroom's parents to all the guests. Next comes your father, then the bride, the bridegroom, the maid of honor and the bridesmaids, all in a row. (It is optional whether or not your father stands in line. If he'd prefer, he may roam around among the guests.)

The ushers and best man have no place in the receiving line, but make themselves as useful as possible. Often the head usher (or any selected usher) acts as announcer asking the names of the guests as they appear in the receiving line and presenting each, in turn, to the bride's mother. She always introduces the guests to the groom's parents, who pass the name down the line to the bride and groom.

You, the bride, still in full wedding costume, may continue to hold your bouquet in your left hand as you stand in the receiving line. Or you may place it carefully aside.

If long gloves are part of your formal costume you need not remove them until time to go into the dining room. (The same rule follows for all feminine members of the wedding party.) The mothers, if wearing hats, will leave them on throughout the reception.

All men of the wedding party will remove their gloves and leave them with their coats upon arrival at the reception, even though they have worn them during the ceremony. According to social custom, no gentleman shakes hands with a lady while wearing gloves.

As the bride, you will present the bridegroom to anyone he does not know. He will likewise introduce his relatives or friends to you, unless the guest is a much older woman, in which case he will present you to her.

As guests pass through the line you should acknowledge the wedding gift each person has sent, even though thank-you notes are mandatory as well.

Conversations should be fairly brief if the line is long. You'll have time later to talk it all over with your closest friends.

A Wedding Breakfast or Supper

1. It may be a general sit-down breakfast or supper where all the guests are seated at small tables and served with a luncheon in courses.

2. Or you may have a stand-up affair where the guests serve themselves from a long buffet table while the bridal party only is seated at the bridal table.

3. It may take the form of a stand-up affair served buffet-style to everyone, with no special table for the bridal party.

High Tea for the Afternoon Wedding

High tea is the usual thing for the afternoon reception. It may be served with guests either standing or seated, depending upon the menu.

Most frequently it is a stand-up reception with the punch bowl as the main attraction for the younger crowd.

The Bride's Cake

The bride's cake should be the gala attraction of the entire occasion. It may be a fabulous spun-sugar bouquet piled tier upon tier and topped with a pair of graceful white doves, an ornate wedding bell or any special decoration you want to dream up. It may be a single-tiered confection, formed in the shape of a wedding ring, or a huge orchid. It may even be two wedding-bell cakes, side by side, with calla lilies rearing their delicate heads from between them.

Modern pastry chefs are as clever as *couturiers* in designing and concocting masterpieces, so save up a few greenbacks to invest in a cake that's a wonder of wonders. You won't be sorry.

Do you know the real difference between the bride's cake and the wedding cake? There seems to be a great deal of confusion about which is which.

The bride's cake is the confection we've been discussing, which is cut and eaten at the wedding. And often it's the only cake in view.

The wedding cake is traditionally the groom's cake. It is a dark fruit cake which guests are given as mementos to take home and dream on . . . and it usually is cut in advance.

It is customary for the wedding cake to be sliced and packed in small white or silver boxes, tied with ribbon, which are placed at each cover of the table for a seated breakfast or reception. If you have a buffet affair, the boxes are stacked on silver platters and left on the main table, or put on a table near the door so that each departing guest may help himself.

You may buy the boxes already filled at your confectioner's and be saved the bother of doing it at home if time is at a premium.

If you are having a simple wedding and want to forgo this expense, be sure to have squares of waxed paper or white cocktail napkins available for the romantic guests who want to carry a few bride's cake crumbs away with them.

Here's a way that the bride's cake and the groom's cake could be combined into one. The top tier of the bride's white cake (frosted and decorated just like the other tiers) could conceal a tin box tightly sealed and filled with wedding fruit cake. The lower tiers of the bride's cake would be cut and served at the reception and the tin box saved to open in celebration of your first wedding anniversary. Wouldn't it be novel, and fun?

IF IT'S A MILITARY WEDDING

It's a lovely idea to have the bride's cake baked in the shape of the bridegroom's corps insignia. An impressive white castle as a reproduction of the Engineer Corps insignia, for instance, would be thrilling.

The bride, assisted by the bridegroom, cuts the cake with his sword. She makes only the initial cut (the first piece) and is supposed to make a wish.

Usually, according to Army custom, there is a toast to the bride, welcoming her into the Army. Following this, the best man and the ushers draw their sabers together at the commands "Draw" and "Saber" and cross them to form an arch over the bride's head. The glasses are held in the left hand and the toast is generally concluded with "How!"

Don't get so enthralled with this colorful performance (if *you* are the military bride) that you forget and drink a toast to yourself. You should remain seated like a little lady.

CUTTING THE CAKE

A silver cake knife, festive with a white satin or tulle bow, is provided for cutting the bride's cake.

In an afternoon reception, where the cake is not reserved for the dessert course, you will want to cut it as soon as all your guests have been received. The bridegroom and your attendants will go to the dining room with you and everyone will gather round.

You should cut the first slice of cake (from the bottom tier) and divide it with the bridegroom . . . as evidence that you are willing to share with him now and forever. Usually a servant or caterer's assistant then takes over the cutting and serving of the remainder of the cake. Or, at a buffet, the guests may cut it themselves or you may appoint a friend to take on this task.

If your dining-room space is limited and few people can be accommodated, it would be an ingenious touch to have the cake carried to you in the living room where the guests are assembled. Everyone loves to have a peep at this part of the festivities, so try to plan it so no one will be cheated out of a view.

If the reception is to be a large one, you might arrange with your photographer to have a spotlight play on the buffet table as you and the bridegroom cut the cake. It could then be turned upon your bridesmaids, and your mother and the in-laws as they receive their slices of cake.

The cake may be garlanded with maidenhair fern and flowers and arranged as a centerpiece on the bride's table, the buffet table or a serving table.

BRIDAL-TABLE SEATING ARRANGEMENTS

If your reception or breakfast includes only a few guests, you will all be seated at one table. (Unless it is buffet-style, of course.) You will want to use place cards for everyone and the seating plan follows:

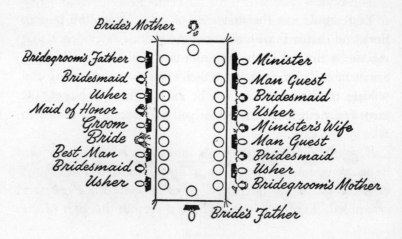

This same arrangement is suggested for your bridal dinner preceding the rehearsal. It is not necessary on this occasion to include the minister and his wife, unless they are close personal friends. As at any formal dinner, husbands and wives are separated at the table. If you are planning an informal, buffet rehearsal dinner before or after rehearsal, dispense with the place-card idea.

AT A LARGE BREAKFAST OR SUPPER

The wedding party will be seated at a separate table if the reception is quite large. Your mother and father, the bridegroom's parents, the minister and his wife, and close relatives should be seated at another table, and your guests will sit where they like at other small tables. If the tables are supplied by your caterer, they will probably be the small round kind like the tables in French restaurants. Or you may use card tables supplied by friends and neighbors.

The bride's cake will form the centerpiece for your table, to be ready at hand when the time comes to cut it. If your bridal attendants are married, their husbands and wives should be invited to the reception but are not seated at the bridal table unless they are members of the bridal party.

Here is a chart to use as a guide in arranging your place cards for the bridal-party table:

Usher Bridesmaid Usher Bridesmaid Usher Bridesmaid Best Man Bride Groom Maid of Honor Usher Bridesmaid Usher Bridesmaid Usher Bridesmaid

Appointments for the Bridal Table

There is glorious opportunity for real artistry in the decorations and appointments of the bridal table. The same ideas would apply for the buffet table, if you are not seating guests at the reception or breakfast.

Plan your table around the color scheme of the entire wedding, if you want a departure from white. But do it delicately.

You might let the cloth reflect the shimmering white of your gown. The table could be high-lighted with gold-banded white china and that lovely gold-colored flat service . . . to match your new wedding ring. Then for your introduction of color, let the ice-blue and dusty-pink (or any pastel shades) of the attendants' gowns be faintly echoed among the white blossoms in a gold bowl as the centerpiece.

Why not make a special cloth for the occasion? Sheer white organdy over white or pale-pink satin. Or an old-fashioned eyelet-embroidery cover, with ruffles at the bottom to accent the Victorian theme. Keep it all white or run pastel baby-ribbon through the eyelets below the edge of the table. If you want something really sumptuous for a formal affair, use shining silver lamé for the cloth with appointments of silver and gleaming crystal.

Tablecloths like these are fairly simple to make and their effect is well worth the effort. You simply sew together (or have hemstitched) three lengths of material to fit your specifications. Measure the table itself and its height from the floor. Select a fabric that is wide enough to cover the table top so that seams will not show on the flat surface. Fifty-four-inch material is usually ample. The seams should come at the edge of the table, and the cloths should have a drop on all sides of twelve to eighteen inches.

Arrange for your bridesmaids to place their bouquets on the buffet (or some suitable place) as a decoration during the refreshment hour. For a small wedding they might even be placed on the bridal table as a centerpiece if you don't wish to provide other flowers.

All these touches can be created without going overboard on expense, and the spirit of the party will rise higher because of the decorative festiveness.

CATERING SERVICE

If you'll settle for nothing short of five courses served in a marquee on the lawn, an outdoor dance floor and a legion of servants, you'll have to consider yourself on your own.

We're dealing principally with brides who can't afford to give carte blanche to the most expensive and lavish of caterers.

Our main concern is that your mother should be completely free of kitchen responsibilities during the entire reception. She shouldn't be forced to keep one eye fixed fearfully on the pantry door as she stands in the receiving line greeting her guests.

Whatever your circumstances, you should be able to lean on someone for reception details who is not a regular member of your household.

Every town of any size has a reliable wedding caterer or

cateress who is in the medium-price bracket. He or she will move in with the china, glassware and linens if you wish, and certainly several trained helpers.

Most such people charge a flat sum for supplying the service. If you have enough dishes of your own, you can eliminate this item of expense. The cost of the food and waiters is added and depends on your choice of menu. You can get exact estimates and know where you stand when you engage the caterer.

If the catering service isn't practical, there's the woman who comes to serve at dinner parties in your neighborhood. She could take over the serving end with the assistance of another regular or two.

Her duties, after the menu is planned, are to check in advance your supply of linen, glasses, silver and china. (You can borrow or rent the extras you need.) She should outline the duties of the kitchen help and get everything organized.

You'd better work out in advance a system by which used dishes can be stacked quickly and put out of the way. Couldn't your built-in cabinets be cleared for this purpose, or dishes be piled on trays and put on the back porch temporarily? Don't plan for any dishwashing while the party is in process unless you have ample kitchen space.

WHAT TO DRINK?

Champagne is the classic wedding beverage. Just to hear the corks pop is exhilarating in itself. There are excellent domestic brands that are less expensive than imports served in other years. If you are having a raft of people, you may have to compromise on a punch of some sort. White wine or a rum punch is often used. A fruit punch, ice-cold and not too sweet, is delicious and of course less disastrous if it is a hot, thirsty day.

Put the punch bowl on a table all its own, out of the line of regular traffic to the buffet table. The punch bowl itself may be formed of colored ice (no, it won't melt too fast) or you can fill a crystal bowl with a huge cake of ice and decorate it with a great bunch of frosted grapes hanging over the side.

A Toast to the Bride

After the cake is cut and the drinks served, the best man usually proposes a toast. He may say, simply, as he stands and raises his glass, "Here's health and happiness to the loveliest of brides."

All in the group, except the bride, then rise, raise their glasses and drink the toast. If the toast is dedicated to both bride and groom, both remain seated. Then the groom replies with thanks for them both.

Other members of the wedding party, and the bride's and groom's fathers may, in turn, propose a toast to the bridal pair and it may well be a gay spontaneous interlude in reception festivities. Anyone wittily inspired to propose an original and personalized wish—in keeping with the dignity of the occasion—may do so, but long-winded speeches are definitely out of order on such an occasion.

Following are some simple suggestions on the subject of wedding toasts:

"To the health of the bride and groom—and may they always be as joyous as this wine and as constant as these good wishes, which are eternal."

> "Here's orchids to the bride,
> Champagne to the groom,
> Happiness to their union
> And a lifelong honeymoon."

If there are congratulatory telegrams from absent friends or members of the family, they may be read at this time by whoever is acting as impromptu toastmaster.

A BORROWED EUROPEAN CUSTOM

For adding charm and romance to the occasion the revival of an old French custom—the *coupe de mariage*—will delight the heart of any bride.

The custom, as it is practiced in France, centers around a two-handled silver cup of delicate shape upon which are engraved the names of the bride and the groom and the place and date of the wedding ceremony. This small cup may be bought at any good jeweler's, and handed on to future generations for use at their weddings, as is traditional in France.

The cup, filled with wine, is presented to the bridal couple and each drinks in turn to seal their troth to a secure, happy and endless marriage, while all the guests gather around to witness the sentimental ceremony.

The cup may be given place of honor near the cake, on a little pedestal wreathed with flowers and greenery. The best man may officiate at the ceremony, calling for the guests' attention before the bridal pair shares the cup.

MENU SUGGESTIONS

Even though your guests may have an eye on the food as well as on your wedding gown, don't serve too much. The spirit of the party is the main thing and sustenance secondary. Be satisfied to make it tempting to look at *and* *good*.

Wedding Breakfast

Climates and seasons should influence you in deciding on your breakfast or supper menus. A wedding in Virginia, for instance, conjures up thoughts of juicy, succulent ham, while out-of-town guests at a New Orleans breakfast will be delighted to find French or Creole dishes.

Chicken is popular everywhere, at any time. Caterers admit that nothing more appropriate has been devised for wedding fare. So, if chicken it is to be, make it a proud, tempting dish. Cooked in white wine with a clove of garlic, then added to sautéed mushrooms and cream sauce, and served in paste puff patties, it is perfect for a stand-up buffet. The good old patty shell does simplify matters for everyone!

Try chicken paprika or chicken in pieces with lemon and sour cream. Substitute fresh green salad for the usual green peas; or baked zucchini, broccoli or wild rice.

For dessert, ice cream is the wedding favorite. Or an ice (but not if the weather is scorching, as it melts rapidly), and always the delicious rich bride's cake. Then a demitasse, black and steaming.

Sit-Down Breakfast Suggestions

Grapefruit cups
Chicken salad (or chicken patties)
Lattice potatoes
Hot biscuits and marmalade

Mint ice cream   Bride's cake
Bonbons   Demitasse

Vichysoisse
Creamed sweetbreads and mushrooms
Avocado salad

Melba toast   Chocolate parfait
Bride's cake
Mints   Demitasse

Consommé Royale
Baby guinea hen with juniper sauce
Broccoli
Small French rolls
Ice cream with spun sugar
Bride's cake
Mints   Demitasse

Buffet Breakfast

Smorgasbord

Sliced smoked turkey   Mousse of chicken
Tomato aspic salad   Celery   Olives
Croissantés
Vanilla ice cream with brandied cherry sauce
Bride's cake
Coffee   Mints

Afternoon Reception

Assorted tea sandwiches
Lobster salad
Champagne punch
Bride's cake
Coffee and tea for those
who don't take punch

Ice cream in molds
Bride's cake
Nuts, mints and bonbons
Coffee and tea

Evening Supper

Fresh fruit supreme
Green turtle soup
Broiled spring chicken   Parisienne potatoes
Green peas
Endive salad   Cheese straws
Orange-water ice
Bride's cake
Chocolate-covered mints
Demitasse

THROWING YOUR BOUQUET

Linger as long as you can with your guests after the refreshments. Then throw your wedding train over your arm, gather up your bridal bouquet and let some of your attendants spread the word around that you are on your way to change. If your bouquet is centered with a going-away corsage, your

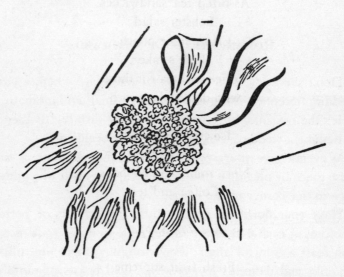

maid of honor should see that it is extracted and placed with your traveling clothes. Throw your bouquet as you start to go upstairs, and may the next bride win!

SAYING YOUR FAREWELLS

It's never the gracious thing to "run out" on your guests, even though the cellar window may appear tempting as a secret escape from prankish friends. Whether it's a highly formal wedding or an intimate gathering, you should face the rice and rose petals and leave on your honeymoon by "the front way."

Whatever you do, don't dash off without saying good-by to your family and your new in-laws. Send for them to come to your dressing room and make your adieus in private.

ROMANCE IS ITS OWN REWARD

Don't shy away from sentimental traditions, whether your wedding reception is big and formal or small and intimate.

It's the romantic little touches that pay such big dividends in making a wedding and reception truly beautiful.

Why not give your springtime wedding reception a surprise touch by placing a pair of chirping love birds in a gilded cage in one corner of the room?

Have your florist set up gay little flower carts of potted blossoms at each end of the bridal table to make your reception feast a colorful affair. For springtime there are tulips, jonquils, and daffodils in gay array. Fall boasts of rambler roses in full bloom, small button mums and asters in tawny hues.

While you're about it don't forget festoons for the bridal car. Have your florist tie a festive bow and a sprig of myrtle to the radiator cap of the car. Or a beflowered horseshoe for good luck. All the other wedding cars in the formal procession may also be decorated if you wish.

As a final family gesture, your doting mama might send you and your bridegroom off in the honeymoon car well fortified with the makings of an intimate wedding feast. Tucked away in a surprise wicker hamper there could be a bottle of champagne (with opener and glasses), tasty hors d'oeuvres, salted nuts, mints and generous slices of bride's cake, plus its decoration, for memory's sake.

CHECK LIST FOR ANY RECEPTION

1. Consider the convenience to guests of wedding reception place, parking facilities, and the size of place in relation to number of guests expected.

2. Remember that the reception is the real fillip of the momentous occasion—and plan it with gaiety in mind.

3. Arrange reception acceptances and regrets in separate files so that the number of guests to prepare for is easily ascertained.

4. Don't forget to inform your caterer of the approximate number of guests expected, at least two days before wedding.

5. Decide in advance of reception just how you wish receiving line made up (whether the bride's father will stand in line or mix with guests) then inform the bride's parents, etc.

6. If you are going to have an announcer at the head of the receiving line, arrange for him in plenty of time.

7. Be sure to have a suitable knife for cutting the cake.

8. Be sure to remain in the receiving line until all guests have been greeted.

9. Make certain that the minister and his wife are provided with transportation to the reception, and that they are assigned places at the parents' table if you are having one.

10. When the orchestra breaks into the opening waltz it is time to dance your first dance with your new husband.

11. Remind your bridegroom that he should be ready to respond to the best man's toasts.

12. Have your maid of honor remove your corsage from the bridal bouquet and place it with your going-away clothes, lest you forget it.

13. Make a ceremony of tossing your bouquet, while everyone gathers round.

14. Stay as happy as you are!

CHAPTER XIV

The Happy Way

FOR WEDDING GUESTS

THERE ARE CERTAIN TRADITIONS AND CUSTOMS WHICH THE guest at a wedding will wish to observe, along with the natural niceties and courtesies that make up the everyday social graces. When in doubt as to the correct procedure to follow in wedding rules and rites, let consideration and kindness, tempered with good common sense, lead the way— and you'll rarely go astray on etiquette problems.

YOU ARE INVITED TO A WEDDING!

The postman has just put into your hands an exciting white vellum square. It's an engraved invitation to a friend's church wedding with a formal reception card enclosed.

You prepare to answer it in formal style, posthaste, even though the reception invitation does not request a response in so many words. It could have said "R.S.V.P.," "Please Respond," or "The favour of a reply is requested." But even though not indicated on this invitation you know your wedding etiquette well enough to realize that a formal response is expected in all circumstances when a wedding invitation includes a reception invitation.

If the invitation includes the wedding ceremony only, no formal note of acceptance or regret is necessary, unless a pew

232

card is enclosed. In this case, a formal acknowledgment is made, out of deference to the bride's family. An invitation to a home, club or hotel wedding which requests "the pleasure of your company" also requires a formal response.

You'll write your formal response to the invitation in your best-tailored handwriting, in the third person, on fine white double-sheet note paper. Space it according to the engraved form and follow the same wording, although it is not necessary to repeat every word of the invitation. (Do not use "informals" or tinted note paper.)

The date and time are repeated to show that they have been correctly noted, but the names of the bride and bridegroom are not repeated.

TYPICAL FORM FOR FORMAL ACCEPTANCE

Mr. and Mrs. Robert Karen Clemson
accept with pleasure
Mr. and Mrs. Donald Lockridge Hogate's
kind invitation
to the wedding reception of their daughter
on Saturday, the twentieth of June
at half after four o'clock
Fifty-four Park Avenue

TYPICAL FORMAL REPLY SENDING REGRETS

Mr. and Mrs. Van Leer Justice
regret that they are unable to accept
Mr. and Mrs. Donald Lockridge Hogate's
kind invitation for
the wedding reception of their daughter
on Saturday, the twentieth of June

REPLIES TO INFORMAL INVITATIONS

Invitations by handwritten notes should be acknowledged in the same intimate style and addressed to the sender of the invitation.

Dear Frances:

Dick and I are delighted to be asked to Janet's wedding on the twelfth of August at Graylyn Chapel. We are planning to be there—and to the reception following to wish the happy couple all the joy in the world.

Affectionately,

Rosemary

An informal note of regret should give the reason for not being able to attend the wedding. For instance:

Dear Frances:

Bob and I regret so much that we will be away on the twelfth of August, for we have looked forward greatly to this wedding "in the family."

We have reservations on a London-bound plane next Monday and won't return for six weeks.

Please express every good wish to Janet and Jack from us. We hope to see them immediately upon our return.

Affectionately,

Rosemary

UPON RECEIPT OF A WEDDING ANNOUNCEMENT

You should sit right down and write personal notes to both the bride's family and the bridal couple if you wish to do the courteous thing when you receive a formal wedding announcement. Neither a gift nor a formal acknowledgment is required of an announcement, so writing a personal greeting is little enough to do in return for being remembered by the bride or her groom.

IT'S TIME TO SEND A WEDDING GIFT

When you receive an invitation to a wedding reception following a church ceremony, or to a home, club or hotel wedding, it is obligatory that you send a gift. (If invited only to the wedding ceremony in a large church affair, you are under no obligation to send a gift.)

Send the wedding gift to the bride at her home as soon as possible after receiving the invitation. Enclose your personal engraved card and have the gift-wrapped present sent from the store where it was purchased.

If you are married and have no "Mr. and Mrs." visiting cards handy it is perfectly permissible to write "Mr. and" in front of Mrs. X. If you feel so disposed, you may write a personal wish for happiness to the bridal pair at the top of the card, though this is not usual unless the guest is a most intimate friend of the bride.

Often a business acquaintance of the bride's father, or of the bridegroom, wishes to send a wedding gift to the bride even though she (the bride) has never met the donor. The card, in such an instance, usually includes, for propriety's sake, the name of both the businessman and his wife.

In making your gift selection it is advisable either to confer with the bride or someone in her family as to her wants and needs; or to seek the assistance of the bridal consultant who has her gift preference list. Most altar-bound misses list their silver, china and glass patterns at their leading local stores so that guests may easily obtain such information.

Thoughtful friends do not mark occasional silver articles like candelabra, trays, bowls and odd pieces of flat silver, because of the possibility of duplicates.

When a present is not sent until after the wedding because of unavoidable circumstances, a note should be enclosed, or sent separately, explaining the reason for delay.

SHOWER GIFTS

Unlike wedding gifts, shower remembrances are usually given in person to the bride at partytime.

In some communities shower gifts often take the place of wedding gifts. In other communities wedding presents are sent in accordance with the conventions of etiquette regardless of how many showers a guest may have attended. The customs of one's own community should serve as the guide.

WHAT TO WEAR TO A WEDDING

Choose a costume that flatters *you* but does not eclipse the bride! Dress in keeping with the formality of the occasion, but do not overdress. (See charts, pages 75-84.)

Hats (or suitable headdresses) and gloves are appropriate for feminine guests at any sort of wedding. Gloves and wraps usually are not removed during the ceremony.

According to tradition black gloves have long been banned

for wedding wear, but nowadays, fashion dictates black as indispensable in accessories. Hence, if black gloves are the necessary addition to your costume, have no hesitancy in wearing them.

ARRIVING AT A CHURCH WEDDING

Your arrival as a guest at a church wedding should be scheduled for at least a half-hour before ceremony time. If it's quite a large affair you would do well to make your appearance three quarters of an hour ahead of time.

Guests with reserved seat space should arrive about fifteen minutes before the ceremony. None should be later than five minutes before the hour scheduled, if possible to so arrange it.

When guests do arrive late they should go directly to the gallery and seat themselves, or remain in the rear of the church during the ceremony.

Upon entering the church you will be met at the aisle entrance by an usher who will ask (if no pew card is presented to him) whether you are a friend of the bride or the groom.

If one is a friend of both the bride and groom he or she should so indicate and the usher then places guest in the best unoccupied place, either on the bride's side (the left side of the church) or the groom's side (the right side).

A woman guest takes the proffered arm of the usher and is escorted up the aisle. If she is attended by a man, he walks behind them. A low-voiced conversation may take place between the ushers and guests as they proceed along the aisle.

Feminine guests customarily keep outer wraps, hats and gloves on throughout the ceremony. Men carry their hats up the church aisle and follow the usual procedure customary in church.

Guests should conform as nearly as possible to church rules, as observed by its members, when attending weddings in churches foreign to their own faith. They should take their tips on procedure from the families in the front pews, but should not try to carry out church rituals with which they are not familiar.

Though there may be no aisle ribbons to restrain the guests from rising and taking leave after the recessional, it is only common courtesy that all should remain in their respective pews until the ushers have escorted the two bridal families to the rear of the church. This includes grandmothers, aunts and all family relatives seated in front pews.

GUEST INFORMATION FOR A HOME OR CLUB WEDDING

Ten to twenty minutes before the ceremony hour is the correct arrival time for guests at a home or club wedding.

The right side of the room, facing the altar is for the groom's friends and relatives; the left side for the bride's, just as in a church wedding.

Guests should take their places on either side and remain standing during the entire proceedings, unless chairs are provided for special persons not able to stand for such a length of time.

Women guests do not remove their hats or gloves. The latter are left on until refreshment time.

Guests may chat with those about them until the triumphal note of the wedding march sounds . . . then all should be hushed silence.

RECEIVING LINE PROCEDURE

As guests pass along the receiving line, shaking hands with everyone, pleasant and brief remarks about the wedding are in order. A bride is wished happiness, and a groom is congratulated.

It's a time-honored custom that relatives and intimate friends are privileged to kiss both the bride and the groom on their wedding occasion.

When the bride thanks her friends for their gifts, as each passes along the receiving line, gracious acknowledgment of the thanks should be made, but no long dissertations or explanations about the gifts should be made by the guest. "I'm so happy you like it," or a brief explanation, "I didn't have it monogrammed so that you may exchange it if there is a duplication!"—will suffice.

DINING-ROOM ETIQUETTE

If the reception is in the form of a large seated breakfast or supper, guests who are not seated at honor tables with place cards may seat themselves wherever they like.

At a stand-up type of party they are served, or serve themselves at a buffet and move about as they choose. As soon as the bride and groom enter the dining room to cut the cake everyone gathers around to watch.

After leaving the dining room or the receiving line, guests usually go to see the wedding gifts if they are on display in another part of the house.

After the bride has thrown her bridal bouquet guests assemble in the hallway or outside the house to await the honeymoon get-away.

Guests should take their leave soon after the bridal couple has made an exit, unless invited to stay for special festivities to follow. In the strict sense of the word, farewells are not necessary at a wedding party but complimentary words about the wedding and the bridal pair are always appreciated by the bride's family, and are fitting as a guest's responsibility to the party.

SPECIAL NICETIES

If the wedding reception is scheduled to be over at an early evening hour, it is a thoughtful gesture for relatives or close friends of the bride's family to plan an intimate little dinner or gathering of some sort in honor of the bride's family, so that the evening may not suffer an untimely letdown. Wedding aftermaths may be as gala as the receptions themselves, and will fill in the gap for the bridegroom's family and all visiting bridal party members who linger on.

CHAPTER XV

For Better or Worse

PLAY YOUR PART

IT'S BOUND TO BE "FOR BETTER" IF YOU SPURN THOSE WORN-
out superstitions and take part in your own rehearsal. The
idea of an understudy playing the part of the bride while
she looks on is passé in most communities and has nothing
to do with etiquette.

If you want your wedding to reach the peak of perfection,
don't leave this important role to anyone else, but *rehearse*
with the rest of the wedding party.

WHO IS TO TAKE CHARGE?

Perhaps you've arranged with your bridal consultant to be
at the church (or your home) for the rehearsal. If so, she
will aid you in corralling everyone and putting each in his
place. If not, the clergyman and the organist may be depended on to take charge of details.

There's always an unquenchable spirit of fun at the wedding rehearsal (a cover-up for last-minute nervousness, no
doubt) but it shouldn't be too frolicsome. See to it that
everyone understands his responsibilities and knows exactly
what to do.

Regardless of who is to be in charge of your rehearsal,

work out your own ideas with your mother beforehand. Know the procedure you wish to follow and talk it over with your clergyman to be sure that it conforms with his regulations.

Maybe you are eager to carry out something unusual in arrangement. If your church should happen to have a balcony leading down into the chancel, why not come down the stairs from the balcony, following your bridal party, instead of down the center aisle? It would be beautiful in effect and add an individual touch to your wedding that would be long remembered.

Or if there is no center aisle, have the ushers walk down the right aisle, just before you and your attendants come down the left aisle.

You have been working toward this ceremonial climax—your wedding—for months. Give some thought to all these possibilities of pageantry which will dramatize the moment and make a beautiful wedding picture.

Who Should Attend the Wedding Rehearsal?

Every member of the wedding party, including the bride's father, of course.

The clergyman (or clergymen, if there are two) who will perform the ceremony.

The organist.

The vocalists who are to participate.

The bride's family and the groom's family usually are present for a preview and a back view of the performance.

If your rehearsal follows the bridal dinner, all the guests may be invited to witness the proceedings if you care to have them.

What Step Will the Wedding Party Use?

It is most important that the wedding party have uniformity and smoothness of motion as they proceed down the aisle.

For this reason, the traditional "skating" step, which tends to be jerky and wobbly, is on the way out. Some people still cling to its use but unless you are certain that all your attendants have mastered it and can execute it without losing their balance, insist on the more modern step.

This newly adopted version is nothing more than a slow natural walk, with no sliding of the foot. The weight is kept on the forward foot and you merely hesitate with the back foot before advancing in each normal step.

It should be done in rhythm with the music and should be fairly slow but not draggy. Try it out with the organist for the right tempo. Start everyone off on the left foot and see that they are all in step.

An equal distance must be kept between members of the bridal party as they walk down the aisle. The ushers should have at least the distance of two full steps between them. The bridesmaids and maid of honor should be about eight feet apart unless the church aisle is exceedingly long and you wish to space them farther apart. There should be about twelve feet between you and the maid of honor (or flower girl).

The procession usually goes down the aisle in the following order:

Ushers (usually walk in pairs, the shortest leading)

Bridesmaids (may walk singly, or in pairs, according to height)

Maid or matron of honor

Flower girl and ring bearer

Bride on her father's right arm

PROCEDURE FOR CHURCH WEDDING

The ushers, bridesmaids and all the bride's attendants and her father should take their places in the vestibule. The bridegroom and best man are with the clergyman in the vestry.

Immediately after the fanfare (the first two triumphant bars of the *Lohengrin* "Wedding March") the clergyman enters from the vestry door. The bridegroom and best man wait until he has reached his place in the chancel. Then the bridegroom enters from the vestry, followed by the best man. (They should not walk together.)

The bridegroom takes his position immediately in front of the first pew on the right, where his family is seated. He half turns so that he may see his bride as she comes down the aisle. The best man takes his place in line with the bridegroom and a pace to the right.

At the same time the bridegroom leaves the vestry, the ushers start their slow tread down the aisle from the back of the church. It is awkward to leave the bridegroom and best man waiting too long a time at the altar, if the church aisle is very long. The groom and best man should be in their respective positions only a few seconds before the ushers reach the chancel.

Following the ushers, the bridesmaids walk down the aisle; then the maid or matron of honor, who walks alone. If you are having both a maid and a matron of honor, they may be dressed alike and walk together, or their gowns may contrast if each walks alone. The one whose title is purely honorary precedes the actual witness, who will stand by you at the altar.

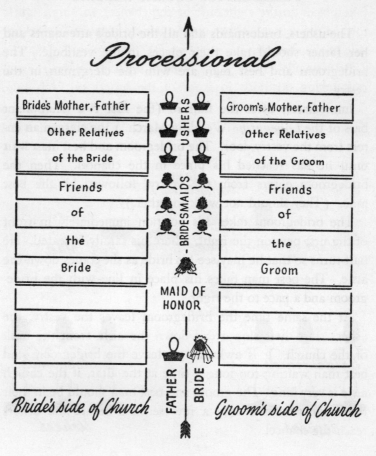

Processional

Bride's Mother, Father	USHERS	Groom's Mother, Father
Other Relatives		Other Relatives
of the Bride		of the Groom
Friends	BRIDESMAIDS	Friends
of		of
the		the
Bride	MAID OF HONOR	Groom

FATHER   BRIDE

Bride's side of Church   *Groom's side of Church*

The ring bearer (if you are having one) may walk alone, next, or he may accompany the flower girl, who directly precedes you on your father's right arm.

In a church which has no middle aisle, the bridal party should enter by the left aisle and leave by the right.

As each pair in the bridal procession reach the chancel rail, they separate. Ushers who are on the right side of the aisle take places on the right side of the chancel, turning slightly toward the center. Those on the left do likewise on the left side of the chancel.

Bridesmaids in the same fashion separate at the chancel rail, taking positions in front of the ushers on each side.

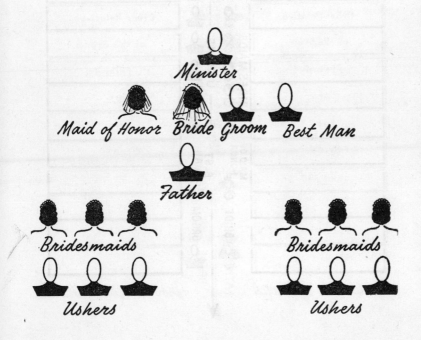

All attendants stand in oblique positions, half facing the congregation, with their eyes on the approaching bride.

The maid of honor stands opposite the best man. When the bride reaches the head of the aisle where the bridegroom is waiting, she releases her hand from her father's arm, takes a step ahead of her father and stands by the bridegroom on the left. The bride's father remains standing just behind and

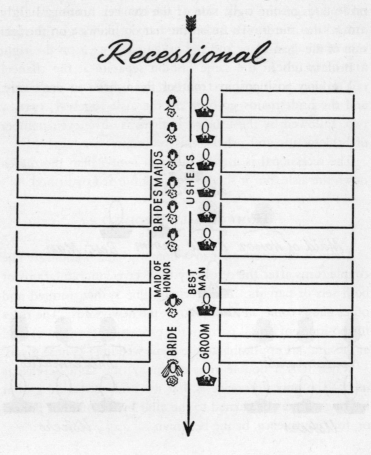

Recessional

a little to the left of the bride until he responds to the question, "Who giveth this woman to be married to this man?" He then answers, "I do," and takes his place in the first pew on the left of the middle aisle, beside the bride's mother.

The minister will instruct you in the service, according to his own preferences.

The recessional is the reverse of the processional. The bride and groom walk first (bride on her husband's right arm), then the flower girls, the maid of honor on the right arm of the best man, and the bridesmaids each on the right arm of an usher.

You may wish to have the best man retire to the vestry, and the bridesmaids go back up the aisle together, two by two, followed by the ushers. If there is an uneven number of bridesmaids and ushers, this procedure is advisable.

The recessional is a trifle faster in tempo than the march down the aisle, but it should not look hurried or rushed.

HOME OR CLUB WEDDING

There is no recessional in a home or club wedding. The couple turns after the ceremony to receive congratulations of both sets of parents. The receiving line is then formed and other guests come, in turn, to greet the newlyweds. The rules for positions of bridal party in the procession (see chart) and at the altar are applicable to the home wedding, as here given.

When it is a double ring ceremony, the same service is used. The only difference is that the bride gives the groom his ring. It may be carried to the altar by the maid of honor, or, for convenience, by the best man.

INSTRUCTIONS TO THE USHERS

If the bridegroom has followed his "Reminder" notes he will have appointed a head usher. Or he may have asked the best man to appoint one of them to manage the others.

Things Every Usher Should Know

The left side of the church is reserved for the relatives and friends of the bride. The right side is reserved for the groom's relatives and friends.

If the church has no center aisle, but has pews in the center, the dividing line extends down the middle of the center pew.

Ushers should arrive at the church one hour before the ceremony. If flowers are delivered to the church the sexton should see that the ushers receive their boutonnieres.

An usher, or ushers, should be delegated to stand at each inner doorway leading from the vestibule (or rooms where guests will enter).

Ushers should inquire about special pew cards issued to important guests. They should receive instructions as to seating arrangements for special relatives of each family.

An usher asks each lady who enters (if he doesn't know her), "Are you a friend of the bride or of the bridegroom?" He then offers her his right arm and escorts her to whichever side of the church she has specified. They may talk quietly as they proceed down the aisle.

A gentleman is never ushered to his seat. If he is with a lady, he walks a pace behind the usher and his companion.

The usher should pause for a moment at the end of the pew while guests whom he has escorted take their places. He should then return to the vestibule doorway to resume his duties.

About five minutes before time for the ceremony the bridegroom's mother is escorted to her place in the first pew on the right side. The bridegroom's father follows a pace behind and takes his place beside her.

About two minutes before the ceremony hour the bride's mother is escorted to her place in the first pew on the left. Special arrangements should be made at rehearsal to delegate certain ushers for the duties of escorting the mothers.

No one is seated by an usher after the bride's mother takes her place.

If aisle ribbons are used, two ushers walk to the front of the church, where ribbons are attached on the front pews, and draw them over the tops of the pews all the way to the back of the church.

The aisle canvas (if it has not already been tacked down by the florist) should be brought from the front of the church to the back by two other ushers as soon as the first two have returned from drawing the ribbons. The canvas will have been folded accordion fashion when made ready. Each usher holds the outside corner of the canvas strip and they walk back up the aisle drawing it behind them as they go.

The head usher should arrange for the sexton to give the signal to the organist when the procession is ready to start.

The ushers line up for the procession (in the vestibule) in front of the bride and her party.

Immediately after the recessional, as soon as the bridal

party has reached the back of the church, the usher who escorted the bride's mother to her place before the ceremony turns directly around and goes down the aisle to escort her back again. The bride's father follows behind.

As soon as they have reached the rear of the church the usher for the bridegroom's mother does likewise.

Immediately after both sets of parents have reached the rear of the church the two ushers who stretched the ribbons start from the back of the church to wind the ribbons. The guests then are free to leave the pews.

This completes the ushers' duties and they join the bridal party in the waiting cars to go on to the reception.

At the reception, the ushers (though not in the receiving line) may stand together at one side of the line to speak to guests.

They should mingle with the guests, see that everyone has an opportunity to speak to the bridal party and that no guest is neglected and everyone has a good time.

BEST MAN

The best man should be a constant moral support to the bridegroom. He helps him pack for his trip; he sees that his luggage is stowed in the car for the honeymoon; he helps him dress for the wedding.

He sees that the bridegroom arrives with him at the church a half-hour before the ceremony. He takes the bridegroom's hat, coat and stick to the vestibule and leaves them in care of the sexton, before the ceremony. He never takes part in the processional but may in the recessional. He pays the clergyman (the groom of course having provided the fee).

He carries the wedding ring to the altar (he may carry a duplicate in another pocket) and presents it at the right time.

He rushes back to the vestry after the ceremony, and collects his own hat, stick and gloves.

He calls the cars for the bridal party, proposes a toast to the bride at the reception, sees that everything is taken care of for a honeymoon get-away, and helps the bridegroom change into his traveling clothes.

MAID OF HONOR

The maid of honor will receive instructions from the minister as to the timing of her duties at the altar. She should take your bouquet early in the ceremony; assist you in putting back your face veil just before the bridegroom kisses you; return your flowers after the kiss, and arrange your train as you turn to go up the aisle in the recessional.

PROCEDURE AT CATHOLIC WEDDING

The processional and recessional, in a Catholic marriage ceremony, are customarily the same as in other weddings.

The bride's father escorts her down the aisle (on his right arm) to the chancel steps but does not give her away, as in the Protestant service. He then retires immediately to his place in the front left pew, to be seated beside the bride's mother.

In most instances, all members of the wedding party proceed up the chancel steps into the sanctuary for the ceremony. First, the ushers take their places in groups on either side, followed by the bridesmaids, who stand in front of the ushers.

The maid of honor and best man meet at the chancel steps and proceed together into the sanctuary. The bride takes the left arm of the bridegroom, as they meet at the chancel steps. They take their places in the sanctuary, standing directly before the altar.

After the marriage vows have been spoken the ushers and bridesmaids may retire to the front pews to remain during the Mass and until time for the recessional.

PROCEDURE FOR DOUBLE WEDDING

In a double wedding ceremony where the brides are sisters, this is the usual procedure:

All the ushers walk first, in pairs, followed by all the bridesmaids, walking two by two.

The older bride's maid or matron of honor directly precedes the older bride (unless there is a flower girl or a ring bearer who follows the maid of honor). The first bride is on the right arm of her father. The second maid or matron follows, and last in procession is the second bride who may be escorted by a brother, uncle or near relative (she takes his right arm).

At the altar the bridesmaids usually take their places in front of the ushers, as in any other wedding ceremony, and may form a semicircle on each side of the bridal pairs who stand facing the minister, one couple a little to the left, the other a little to the right.

If the brides are not sisters, each is preceded down the aisle by her own attendants and each father acts as escort to his own daughter.

At the altar, each father stands a step behind and a little to the left of the bride he has escorted down the aisle, and follows the same rules previously given for the single wedding procedure.

The ceremony itself is no different in procedure from the single wedding except that the first couple having taken their vows, this part of the service is repeated for the second couple.

In the recessional the bride who goes first in the procession is first in line with her bridegroom, followed by the second bridal pair. Then come the maids of honor with the best men, and the bridesmaids on the arms of the ushers according to the usual wedding order.

Considerable rehearsing is advisable in a double wedding of any size to insure the best arrangement at the altar.

MILITARY WEDDING

There may be some variations in the military wedding service, set by precedents observed on military reservations or by the customs of the particular church in which the ceremony is performed.

However, the following description of the ceremony may be considered "typical," as based on customs widely observed throughout the Army.

In the procession the ushers walk down the aisle two by two (never single file, as they *may* be permitted to do in a

civilian service). They are followed by the bridesmaids, maid
of honor, the bride and her father, as in any other wedding.

The groom, with his best man, enters from the vestry, taking an oblique position in front of the lectern. The bridal
party proceed down the aisle and divide at the chancel steps,
the ushers taking oblique positions, half facing the congregation, and the bridesmaids follow the same procedure, each
standing in front of an usher.

The maid of honor stands opposite the best man. The
bride and her father come down the aisle together and stand
in the center facing the Chaplain.

The maid of honor and the best man are on either side of
the bride and groom. The bridesmaids face each other, still
remaining on the lower level, and the ushers take their places
(facing each other) nearest the congregation, at the foot of
the chancel steps.

Recessional

At the close of the wedding ceremony, the ushers, remaining in their same positions, draw their swords at the com-
mand "Draw Sabers" (from one of the ushers). The bride
and groom pass under the arch, followed by the maid of
honor and the best man and then the bridesmaids by twos.
They proceed up the aisle while the ushers go out the side
door, hasten to the chapel steps and again form the arch of
swords for the bridal party to pass under as they leave the
chapel.

If you prefer, it is equally correct to have the ushers escort
the bridesmaids in the recessional, after the bride and groom

have passed under the arch. As is customary the bridegroom, best man and groomsmen each offers his right arm to bride, maid of honor and bridesmaids respectively, thus avoiding any entanglement of sabers and dresses and leaving his left hand free to carry his cap, which is held with the visor pointing left oblique.

CHAPTER XVI

"I Plight Thee My Troth"

LET'S SUPPOSE TODAY'S THE DAY.

You'll wake up in the morning with love in the air and a sparkle in your eyes.

You'll want to laugh and cry . . . and shout and whisper, all at the same time. You'll wonder if this is *you* . . . you who are going to be serene and calm, come what may. Then you'll tell yourself there's nothing to be panicky about. Mother may lose her gloves, the best man may drop the ring, and the ice cream may turn out to be soup. But you'll take it in your stride and count it all part of the fun.

If you're really smart, you'll linger on and have breakfast in bed. You'll look around and remember that there's really

nothing to do. Your going-away outfit is pressed and all ready with accessories near by. Your bags are packed except for the last-minute crushables. Your fingernail polish looks benignly pale and correct. And you remember with a start that now is a good time to transfer your engagement ring to your right hand till the ceremony is over and your wedding ring in place.

Then you'll check on your "list," with a smug little feeling that all those weeks' work is now paying dividends. The out-of-town guests have all been happily quartered. The traffic police are scheduled to be on duty at the church. The caterer has moved into the kitchen. You can hear the florist and his helpers in the rooms below.

You have something *old* (Mother's lace hankie), lots that's *new,* something *borrowed* (the bridegroom's mother's brooch), and a new satin garter that's *blue.* Then, there's a shiny dime to tuck in your shoe. Your new white wrap to wear over the wedding gown, orange-blossom perfume to spray on your hair, and your luggage keys in their secret hiding place just in case there are any pranksters about.

You'll start reviewing your gifts and their donors so you can say "Thank you" and *mean* it as your friends go through the receiving line.

You'll look back and see in kaleidoscopic review that an amazing number of things have been accomplished and that you *must* be a genius to have pulled together all the loose ends.

You'll think, with a start, that it will soon be time for music and people . . . and all you've been hoping for come true.

You know you'll be smiling and radiant as you walk down the aisle. You're sure that no one was ever so happy. And most of all, you know it's not *just* for today.

.THE END

Dependent Industrialization in Latin America

Rhys Owen Jenkins

The Praeger Special Studies program—
utilizing the most modern and efficient book
production techniques and a selective
worldwide distribution network—makes
available to the academic, government, and
business communities significant, timely
research in U.S. and international economic, social, and political development.

Dependent Industrialization in Latin America

The Automotive Industry in Argentina, Chile, and Mexico

PRAEGER SPECIAL STUDIES IN INTERNATIONAL ECONOMICS AND DEVELOPMENT

Praeger Publishers　New York　Washington　London

Library of Congress Cataloging in Publication Data

Jenkins, Rhys Owen, 1948-
    Dependent industrialization in Latin America.

    (Praeger special studies in international economics and
development)
    Includes bibliographical references and index.
    1. Automobile industry and trade—Argentine Republic.
2. Automobile industry and trade—Chile.   3. Automobile
industry and trade—Mexico.   4. International business enterprises.   I. Title.
HD9710.L32J45   338.4'7'6292098   76-25352
ISBN 0-275-23220-4

PRAEGER PUBLISHERS
111 Fourth Avenue, New York, N.Y. 10003, U.S.A.

Published in the United States of America in 1977
by Praeger Publishers, Inc.

To Ruth

Cuando sonó la trompeta, estuvo
todo preparado en la Tierra
y Jehová repartío el mundo
a Coca-Cola, Anaconda,
Ford Motor y otros entidades

When the trumpet sounds
All will have been made ready on earth
And Jehovah will divide the world
Among Coca-Cola, Anaconda,
Ford Motors and the others.

Pablo Neruda, Canto General

PREFACE

This study arose from a general concern with the problems of imperialism and underdevelopment, particularly as they affected Latin America. Many writers have contributed to our understanding of the operations of contemporary imperialism in Latin America at a theoretical level, but considerable empirical work still needs to be done to fill in the details of the mechanisms of imperialism. One fruitful approach to advance knowledge in this direction is the study of individual industries. The industry selected here, motor vehicles, is only one of many. Hopefully, in the future, similar studies will be undertaken.

The fieldwork on which this study is based was carried out during two separate visits to Latin America, the first of nine months in 1971-72, financed by the United Kingdom Social Science Research Council, and the second of three months in 1974, financed by the University of East Anglia. I am indebted to all the individuals and organizations, too numerous to mention, who assisted me during my visits to Latin America—officials of automotive companies, trade associations, and government agencies, as well as individual researchers. I am also grateful to Brian Van Arkadie, Charles Cooper, Chris Edwards, David Felix, D. G. Rhys, and Constantine Vaitsos, who read and commented on all or part of earlier versions of this study. My greatest intellectual debt is to Robin Murray, who supervised the doctoral thesis on which this study is based and who, despite many disagreements, provided me with the stimulus to complete the work. I am also indebted to the comrades of the Conference of Socialist Economists who first stimulated my interest in the theory of imperialism. Finally, I would like to thank the staff of the Institute of Development Studies at the University of Sussex library where much of this work was written.

CONTENTS

	Page
PREFACE	vii
LIST OF TABLES AND FIGURES	xii
LIST OF ABBREVIATIONS	xviii

Chapter

1 INTRODUCTION ... 1

    The Context of the Study ... 1
    The Industry as a Focus for Study ... 8
    The Choice of a Specific Industry ... 10
    Notes ... 12

2 THE INTERNATIONAL AUTOMOTIVE INDUSTRY ... 16

    The Automotive Industry Before World War II ... 16
    Concentration in the Postwar Period ... 19
    The Internationalization of the Automotive Industry ... 24
    The Present Structure of the World Automotive Industry ... 29
    The Causes of Concentration and Internationalization ... 30
    The Expansion of the Automotive Industry in the Underdeveloped Areas ... 38
    The Oil Crisis and Future Developments in the International Automotive Industry ... 43
    Conclusion ... 44
    Notes ... 44

3 THE SPREAD OF THE AUTOMOTIVE INDUSTRY TO LATIN AMERICA ... 48

    The Assembly Phase ... 48
    Government Policy and the Growth of the Latin American Automotive Industry ... 51

An Overview of the Current Latin American
    Automotive Industry   60
Conclusion   66
Notes   66

4   A MODEL OF THE DEVELOPMENT OF THE
    SECTOR OF PRODUCTION IN A PERIPHERAL
    ECONOMY   69

A General Overview: The Growth of the Sector
    of Production   69
Competition Within an Industry: The Steindl
    Model   72
Intraindustry Competition in a Peripheral
    Economy   75
Behavioral Assumptions of the Model   79
The Complete Model   81
Conclusion   83
Notes   84

5   AUTOMOTIVE INDUSTRY TECHNOLOGY,
    SUPPLY CONDITIONS, AND COST DIFFERENTIALS   88

Technology   89
Changes in Supply Conditions in Argentina,
    Chile, and Mexico   92
Cost Differentials   103
Conclusion   113
Notes   114

6   THE DEMAND FOR CARS AND DEPENDENT
    INDUSTRIALIZATION   117

Theoretical Considerations   117
Income Distribution and the Demand for Cars   126
The Demand for Cars in Some Latin American
    Countries   129
Conclusion   140
Notes   141

7   CONCENTRATION AND DENATIONALIZATION
    IN THE AUTOMOTIVE INDUSTRY   144

Changes in the Industrial Structure   144

Chapter   Page

           The Mechanisms of Concentration and
              Denationalization   152
           Conclusion   169
           Notes   170

    8   THE PATTERN OF DEPENDENT INDUSTRIAL-
         IZATION IN THE AUTOMOTIVE INDUSTRY   173

           A Model of the Dependent Sector of Production   173
           Capital Flows   178
           Market Structure and the Forms of Competition   181
           Market Fragmentation and Local Costs   197
           The Utilization of Capacity   208
           The Possibilities of Developing Exports   212
           Capital Accumulation and Employment Creation   217
           Conclusion   219
           Notes   220

    9   ALTERNATIVE PATTERNS OF AUTOMOTIVE
         INDUSTRY DEVELOPMENT   226

           Policies in Argentina, Chile, and Mexico   227
           New Developments in the Latin American
              Automotive Industry   229
           The Japanese Model   239
           The Soviet Union and Eastern Europe   244
           Conclusion   247
           Notes   248

    10   CONCLUSIONS: DEPENDENT INDUSTRIALIZATION
         AND LATIN AMERICAN DEVELOPMENT   251

           The Pattern of Dependent Industrialization   252
           Notes   259

APPENDIX

    A   ECONOMIES OF SCALE IN THE AUTOMOTIVE
         INDUSTRY   263

           Notes   270

    B   STATISTICAL TABLES   273

	Page
INDEX	295
ABOUT THE AUTHOR	299

LIST OF TABLES AND FIGURES

Table		Page
1.1	Number of New Manufacturing Subsidiaries of U.S. Multinational Corporations in Latin America	6
1.2	Industries in Which the Participation of Foreign Subsidiaries Is Greater than 50 Percent	7
1.3	Ranking of Automotive Manufacturers Among Largest Firms, 1970	11
2.1	Car Exports by Leading Countries, 1950-70	24
2.2	Imported Passenger Cars as Percent of Total New Car Registrations	25
2.3	Number of Assembly Contracts by Country of Origin, 1969	26
2.4	Distribution of Sales of the Major European Automotive Manufacturers, 1973	27
2.5	Leading Vehicle Producers (Including Subsidiaries), 1973	29
2.6	Average Annual Growth of New Registrations (Sales) of Vehicles, 1950-71	35
2.7	Market Prices of Cars in Foreign Markets as Percent of Domestic Market Price, 1966	36
2.8	Number of Assembly Contracts by Major Firms, 1968	39
3.1	Local Content Requirements in the Brazilian Automotive Industry	53
3.2	Permitted Imports in the Argentinian Automotive Industry	54
3.3	Local Content Requirements for Chilean Cars, 1963-70	56

Table		Page
3.4	Local Content Requirements for Chilean Commercial Vehicles, 1966-70	57
3.5	Degree of Local Integration in the Latin American Automotive Industry, 1973	61
3.6	Production and Employment in the Latin American Automotive Industry, 1973	62
3.7	Total Vehicle Production by Firm in Latin America, 1973	63
3.8	Percentage Equity in Affiliate	65
5.1	Savings in Foreign Exchange from Local Assembly	90
5.2	Investment in Fixed Assets by Terminal Plants, Argentina, 1959-70	94
5.3	Annual Increase in Fixed Assets, Mexico, 1961-69	95
5.4	Annual Increase in Fixed Assets, Chile, 1964-70	96
5.5	Capital Intensity in the Argentinian Automotive Industry, 1959-64	98
5.6	Capital Intensity in the Mexican Automotive Industry, 1960-69	99
5.7	Capital Intensity for 13 Chilean Automotive Manufacturers, 1964-72	100
5.8	Cost Structure of the Argentinian Automotive Industry	101
5.9	Cost Structure of the Mexican Automotive Industry	102
5.10	Cost Structure of a Chilean Car	103
5.11	Profitability of Selected Argentinian Firms, 1964-66	104

Table		Page
5.12	Profitability of Selected Chilean Firms, 1970	105
5.13	Cost of Imported CKD Pack in Chile	107
5.14	Profitability of Selected Mexican Firms, 1966–73	110
6.1	Expenditure on Cars by Income Group in Argentina, 1963	127
6.2	Ownership of Cars by Income Group in Mexico, 1963	128
6.3	Expenditure on Transport Equipment by Income Group in Chile, 1969	128
6.4	Imports of Cars into Argentina, 1920-54	130
6.5	Relative Prices of New and Used Cars in Argentina, 1963–66	132
6.6	Growth of Car Output and Gross Domestic Product in Argentina, 1960-73	134
6.7	Growth of Car Output and Gross Domestic Product in Mexico, 1960-73	141
7.1	Indices of Concentration in the Argentinian Automotive Industry, 1960-73	146
7.2	Indices of Concentration in the Chilean Automotive Industry, 1962-73	148
7.3	Indices of Concentration in the Mexican Automotive Industry, 1963-71	149
7.4	Income-Cost Relation in the Automotive Industry	155
7.5	Chilean Trade with LAFTA Countries Under Compensation Arrangements, 1965-73	162
7.6	Breakdown of Local Content, 1972	163
8.1	Prices of Argentinian Cars by Market Segment, 1971	183

Table		Page
8.2	Average Price and Dispersion by Market Segment	184
8.3	Advertising in the Argentinian Automotive Industry, 1964-73	186
8.4	Total Output of Most Popular Argentinian Cars, 1959-73	188
8.5	Examples of Credit Terms Offered to the Consumer, 1971	188
8.6	Prices of Chilean Cars by Market Segment, July 1970	190
8.7	Average Price and Dispersion by Market Segment	191
8.8	Fiat Advertising Expenditure, 1965-73	191
8.9	Credit Terms to Dealers in Chile	193
8.10	Prices of Mexican Cars by Market Segment, 1971	193
8.11	Average Price and Dispersion by Market Segment	194
8.12	Distribution of Sales by Dealers According to Length of Credit Granted, 1968	196
8.13	Structure of Costs in the Chilean Automotive Industry, 1969	201
8.14	Index of Costs in the Assembly of Vehicles	203
8.15	Direct Cost Structure in the Mexican Automotive Industry, Late 1960s	205
8.16	Economies of Scale in the Mexican Automotive Industry	206
8.17	Exports by the Argentinian Automotive Industry, 1965-74	213
8.18	Exports of Parts from Chile, 1965-73	215

Table

Page

8.19 Exports by the Mexican Automotive Industry,
1967-73
216

9.1 Circulation of Cars and All Vehicles, 1970
245

A.1 Estimates of Economies of Scale in the Automotive
Industry
268

B.1 Licensees and Subsidiaries of Major Automotive
Manufacturers, 1970
275

B.2 Production of Vehicles in Latin America, 1955-73
279

B.3 Vehicles in Circulation in Latin America, 1955-72
280

B.4 Imports of Vehicles to Latin America, 1955-69
281

B.5 Gross Domestic Product per Capita and Cars per
1,000 Inhabitants in 26 Countries, 1958 and 1969
282

B.6 Demand for Cars and Commercial Vehicles in
Argentina, 1960-74
283

B.7 Vehicles in Circulation, Argentina, 1951-74
284

B.8 Index of Vehicle Prices, Argentina, 1960-74
285

B.9 Production and Imports of Motor Vehicles,
1960-74
286

B.10 Vehicles in Circulation, 1955-72
287

B.11 Demand for Cars in Mexico, 1950-73
288

B.12 Growth of Vehicle Production and Gross Fixed
Investment, Argentina, 1959-74
290

B.13 Market Shares by Firm in the Argentinian
Automotive Industry, 1960-73
291

B.14 Market Shares by Firm in the Chilean Automotive
Industry, 1962-73
293

Table   Page

B.15   Market Shares by Firm in the Mexican Automotive
        Industry, 1963-73   294

Figure

2.1   The Formation of British Leyland, 1960-68   21

2.2   Interpenetration of the Major Automotive Manu-
        facturers, 1975   31

4.1   The Steindl Model of Intraindustry Competition   74

4.2   Intraindustry Competition in a Peripheral Economy   81

5.1   Cost Increase as a Function of Local Content   93

6.1   "Repressed" and "Backlog" Demand   122

7.1   Alternative Production and Marketing Strategies   158

8.1   Intraindustry Competition in a Foreign-Dominated
        Sector   175

A.1   Economies of Scale with Different Cost Curves   265

LIST OF ABBREVIATIONS

ACARA	Asociación de Concesionarios de Automotores de la República Argentina
ACCIA	Asociación Chilena de Importadores de Automoviles
ADEFA	Asociación de Fabricas de Automotores (Argentina)
AMIA	Asociación Mexicana de la Industria Automotriz
ANDA	Asociación Mexicana de Distribuidores de Automóviles
ANFAVEA	Asociacão Nacional dos Fabricantes de Vehiculos Automotores
BCRA	Banco Central de la Republica Argentina
CAFA	Camara Argentina de Fabricantes de Automotores
CESO	Centro de Estudios Socio-Economicas de la Universidad de Chile
CFIA	Comisión para el Fomento de la Industria Automotriz (Chile)
CIF	Cost, insurance, and freight
CIFARA	Camara Industrial de Fabricantes de Autopiezas de la Republica Argentina
CKD	Completely knocked down (vehicles)
CONADE	Consejo Nacional de Desarrollo (Argentina)
CORFO	Corporación de Fomento (Chile)
DIRINCO	Dirección de Industria y Comercio (Chile)
ECLA	Economic Commission for Latin America
EEC	European Economic Community
FLACSO	Facultad Latinoamericana de Ciencias Sociales
FOB	Free on board
GEIA	Grupo Ejecutivo de la Industria Automovilistica (Brazil)
GDP	Gross domestic product
GNP	Gross national product
IASF	Industria Automotriz Santa Fe (Argentina)
ICHA	Instituto Chileno del Acero
IKA	Industrias Kaiser Argentina
ILDIS	Instituto Latinoamericano de Investigaciones Sociales
IME	Industrias Mecanicas del Estad
LAFTA	Latin American Free Trade Area
MITI	Ministry for International Trade and Industry (Japan)
NEDO	National Economic Development Office (United Kingdom)
ODEPLAN	Oficina de Planificación Nacional (Chile)
OECD	Organization for Economic Cooperation and Development
SKD	Semiknocked down (vehicles)
SMMT	Society of Motor Manufacturers and Traders
SOMEX	Sociedad Mexicana de Crédito Industrial
UDC	Underdeveloped country
UNCTAD	United Nations Conference on Trade and Development
UNIDO	United Nations Industrial Development Organization

Dependent Industrialization
in Latin America

The underdevelopment of Latin America can only be understood if the continent is seen in relation to the international economy of which it is an integral part and has been since the Conquest. This is not to assert that the external relationships are the determining factor in the development of the region, but rather that they form a conditioning situation that "determines the limits and possibilities of action and behaviour of men."[1] Because the internal dynamics of the Latin American economy has taken different forms in response to changes in the structure of the world economy, development and underdevelopment cannot be seen as two stages in a single growth path common to all societies. They are two sides of the same coin, part of a single system whose dynamics can only be explained in terms of their interaction. This broad perspective, which has been used by Latin American economists, sociologists, and political scientists to analyze the continent's underdevelopment, provides the framework within which this study is written. It is an attempt to see the way in which external relationships have manifested themselves in a specific instance over a short period of time, and the effect that this has had on the internal dynamics of the economy.

THE CONTEXT OF THE STUDY

The earliest form in which the link to the world economy established itself in Latin America was through the plunder of the conquistadores, which supplied a basis for primary accumulation in Europe during the early phase of capitalist development. The first two or so centuries of colonization saw the development of a series of mining cores and the export of gold and silver to Spain that acted as an intermediary between Latin America and the rest of Europe.[2] The postindependence period of the nineteenth century saw the consolidation of what has become known in Economic Commission for Latin America (ECLA) terminology as "desarrollo hacia afuera," loosely translated as "foreign-oriented development." This traditional form of external dependence was characterized by monoexport for the world market from a primary producing enclave showing little integration with the local economy. Although regional differences existed within Latin America that affected the pattern of development in a number of ways, for example, in the impetus given to local manufacturing activities and the extent of local infrastructure development, the basic elements of the system remained the same. Internal expansion was dependent on the world market for the particular country's exports. In the event of a crisis, such as that of the early 1930s, or a gradual deterioration of the terms of trade, as occurred from about 1950, the dynamism of the economy was seriously impaired.

The first real break with this pattern of development came in the 1930s when a number of factors came together to initiate the so-called "desarrollo hacia adentro" (inward-oriented development). The world economic depression that led to a sharp fall in Latin American exports and to an adverse movement in the terms of trade, reducing the continent's capacity to import by more than 30 percent between 1930 and 1934,[3] was the major factor behind this change. In the most advanced Latin American countries* this provided a stimulus to a process of industrialization that had begun during the period of "desarrollo hacia afuera" and to a breakdown of the old oligarchic system of domination, already under pressure. Thus, although appearing as a sharp break with the past, the crisis of the 1930s only accentuated trends already evident both at the level of the international economy (the reversal of the upward trend in the import coefficient of the industrialized countries and the deterioration of primary product prices) and internally in Latin America (industrialization and the changing balance between different classes).[5]

After World War II the strategy of import-substituting industrialization was given a theoretical underpinning by ECLA, which saw it as a means of lessening the dependence of the Latin American

---

*Argentina, Brazil, Chile, Colombia, Mexico, and Uruguay, which began their industrialization at the end of the nineteenth century or in the early twentieth century. The need to distinguish these countries from those that did not begin their industrialization until after World War II has been emphasized by V. Bambirra.[4]

countries on the world economy through a reduction in the import coefficient. Only in the 1960s did it become evident that this very policy had led to the creation of "the new dependence."[6] This involved the penetration of the Latin American industrial structure by foreign capital and technology, either through direct investment or licensing agreements, and corresponded to a new phase in the integration of the world economy based on the operations of the multinational corporation.

The new forms of external dependence have a number of characteristic features. First, import substitution tends to take place in finished consumer goods, so that there has been a shift in the composition of Latin American imports away from such products toward capital goods, raw materials, and intermediate inputs. In 1968, imports of consumer goods for Latin America as a whole were only 16.2 percent of total imports (compared with 20.7 percent in 1955) and were less than 10 percent in Argentina, Brazil, and Colombia, while intermediates and raw materials came to 45.8 percent and capital goods were 37.5 percent of all imports.[7] This means an increased rigidity in imports that becomes very difficult to reduce when exports decline because they are now essential for the maintenance of capacity utilization and employment and for the expansion of productive capacity and the creation of new employment. Thus, although quantitatively (in terms of the import coefficient) dependence on foreign trade has been reduced, qualitatively (in terms of the structure of imports and hence the effect on internal growth) it has increased. As a result, it has been necessary to preserve a traditional export sector as a source of foreign exchange, especially in view of the limited development of manufactured exports.*

A second feature is the growing importance of foreign indebtedness in Latin America. Payments related to the presence of foreign capital (both private and public) are absorbing an increasing share of the continent's export earnings. This has risen from just over 20 percent in the early 1950s to more than 40 percent of total current income in the late 1960s.[9] Thus, as well as finding import requirements becoming increasingly rigid with the industrialization of the postwar period, the capacity to import has been compressed by having a growing burden of financial payments imposed upon it.

The latest phase in Latin America's relationship to the world economy has also been characterized by the increased importance of direct foreign investment in manufacturing industry, as opposed

---

*Exports of manufacturers, although increasing, accounted for only 7.5 percent of the region's total exports in 1968.[8]

to the traditional areas where it was located, mainly in the extractive industries and public utilities. The proportion of total U.S. investment in Latin America in the manufacturing sector increased from 6.3 percent in 1929 to 16.5 percent in 1950 to 20.3 percent in 1961, reaching a record level of 36.3 percent in 1971.[10] In the most industrialized countries of the region, Argentina, Brazil, and Mexico, a much higher proportion of U.S. investment was in the manufacturing sector, and in 1971 it was more than 60 percent of total U.S. investment in each of these countries.[11] U.S. investment accounted for only 49.1 percent of the total direct foreign investment in Latin America in 1950 and 59 percent of the total in 1969,[12] so that this trend is not necessarily representative. Nevertheless, what evidence exists suggests that the share of European investment in manufacturing is also increasing. In the case of British investments in Latin America, manufacturing increased its share from 56.3 percent in 1962 to 68 percent in 1968.[13]

This trend is reflected in the growing participation of foreign capital and technology in the manufacturing sector, which has aroused considerable concern in Latin America. The increasing involvement of foreign technology is indicated by the rapid growth of technical assistance and royalty payments in recent years. It has been estimated that payments for technology grew at an annual average rate of 27 percent in Argentina (1965-70), 21 percent in Brazil (1965-69), and 15 percent in Mexico (1953-68).[14] The use of foreign technology is even more extensive than the penetration of foreign capital. For example, in Chile, one study of 281 large firms found that while 43 percent of the firms had some foreign shareholding, a further 17 percent with no foreign capital paid royalties.[15]

The growth of foreign investment has tended to attract more attention than foreign technology because of the displacement of national firms that it has involved.

> The inflow of private foreign capital in the form of direct investment or in association with national enterprises, while constituting a contribution of capital and often of technical know-how, represents excessively stiff competition for national investors, who have gradually been displaced from those industrial activities that offer the best financial prospects. Thus the initial capital contribution usually severely limits the ultimate possibility of capital formation by national entrepreneurs.[16]

There is considerable evidence of the extent of penetration of Latin American manufacturing by foreign capital in the 1960s. In 1964, foreign firms in Argentina accounted for 28 percent of industrial output,[17] while in Brazil, four years earlier, foreign capital controlled an estimated 31 percent of industry.[18] Not surprisingly, considering its proximity to the dominant world capitalist power, the most heavily penetrated of the major Latin American economies is Mexico, where, by 1970, according to one estimate, multinational corporations accounted for 34.9 percent of industrial production.[19] In Chile, foreign companies accounted for 20.3 percent of the total share capital of all manufacturing Sociedades Anonimas in the year before the Unidad Popular government came to power.[20] Thus, it appears that between one fifth and one third of industry in a number of Latin American countries is in the hands of foreign capital. R. Vernon estimates that, for the continent as a whole, about one sixth of manufacturing sales is accounted for by U.S. subsidiaries,[21] to which must be added European and Japanese investment, suggesting that the share of all foreign firms would be around 25 to 30 percent.

The tendency for foreign firms to increase their participation in Latin American manufacturing is the local manifestation of the internationalization of capital that has occurred during the past two decades. In Chile, during the late 1960s, foreign firms increased their participation in the total share capital from 16.6 percent in 1966 to 20.3 percent in 1969, while in Mexico one study found that foreign firms increased their share of production from 19.6 percent in 1962 to 27.6 percent in 1970.[22] Although no data are available on changes in foreign participation for industry as a whole, the share of foreign firms in the sales of Argentina's largest 100 firms increased from less than half in 1956 to two thirds in 1971, at the same time as increasing concentration raised the share of the largest hundred in total production.

The process of denationalization can take three forms. One form is the direct takeover of locally owned firms by foreign groups. As Table 1.1 indicates, the proportion of new subsidiaries formed by acquisitions of existing firms has increased sharply, particularly since the late 1950s. This trend is particularly marked in the most advanced countries of the region where there is a considerable nucleus of preexisting locally owned industry. Some writers have gone so far as to compile lists of firms taken over by foreign enterprises in Argentina and Brazil during the 1960s.[23] These amount to more than 50 acquisitions in each case and do not pretend to be exhaustive. They are particularly concentrated in advanced technology sectors, such as the automotive industry, chemicals, pharmaceuticals, and machinery and metallurgical products.

The second form taken by denationalization is that of a competitive struggle that drives local firms out of a particular industry. Over time there tends to be increasing concentration in most of the newly established import-substituting industries that takes the form

TABLE 1.1

Number of New Manufacturing Subsidiaries of
U.S. Multinational Corporations in Latin America

	Pre-1946	1946-57	1958-67
Latin America			
Total	206	340	750
Acquisitions	47	97	331
Argentina			
Total	45	34	79
Acquisitions	11	13	42
Mexico			
Total	46	90	216
Acquisitions	9	31	116

Source: J. W. Vaupel and J. P. Curhan, The Making of Multi-national Enterprise: A Sourcebook of Tables Based on a Study of 187 Major U.S. Manufacturing Companies (Cambridge: Harvard University Graduate School of Business Administration, 1969), p. 256.

of the displacement of nationally owned firms by the multinational corporations with their superior financial, technological, or manager-ial resources. This phenomenon of denationalization within a sector has not been studied in any great detail, but appears to have occurred in the pharmaceuticals industry, and, as will be discussed later, in the automotive industry to some extent.[24]

Finally, the location of foreign investment in the fastest growing sectors of industry means that the natural process of differential growth rates alone leads to an increasing penetration by foreign capital. There is ample empirical evidence of such a concentration of foreign investment, which also, incidentally, suggests that global figures for the share of foreign subsidiaries in the manufacturing sector tend to underestimate their strategic significance. As Table 1.2 shows, foreign firms account for more than half of the invested capital or output in a number of industries in each of the major Latin American economies. Despite the different universe taken in the studies represented, the table shows the same sectors turning up time and time again: rubber, transport equipment, tobacco, and pharmaceuticals.

The tendency for foreign subsidiaries to be large firms also adds to their strategic significance. Thus, typically, the share of foreign capital in the output of the larger firms in a particular

TABLE 1.2

Industries in Which the Participation of Foreign Subsidiaries Is Greater than 50 Percent

Argentina	Brazil	Chile	Mexico	Venezuela
Rubber	Rubber	Tobacco	Rubber	Rubber
Pharmaceuticals	Chemicals	Rubber	Tobacco	Electrical equipment
Vehicles and parts	Machinery	Transport equipment	Pharmaceuticals	Transport equipment
Tractors	Electrical products		Nonelectrical machinery	
"Frigorificos"	Pharmaceuticals		Electrical machinery	
	Vehicles and parts		Transport equipment	
	Other (including tobacco)			

Sources: Argentina: Share of value of production for all industry, 1964, from Consejo Nacional de Desarrollo (CONADE), La Concentración en la Industria Argentina en 1964 (Buenos Aires, 1969), pp. 71–78. Brazil: Share of assets of 500 largest manufacturing firms, late 1960s, from F. Fajnzylber, Sistema Industrial y Exportación de Manufacturas, ECLA (E/CN.12/), 1970, Table 2.7. Chile: Share of assets of all manufacturing limited companies, 1968–69, from G. Gassic, "Concentración, Entrelazamiento y Desnacionalización en la Industria Manufacturera," unpublished (Documento de Trabajo, CESO), 1971, Table 38. Mexico: Share of production for all industry, 1970, from F. Fajnzylber and T. Martínez Tarrago, Las Empresas Transnacionales, Expansión a Nivel Mundial y Proyección en la Industria Mexicana (Versión Preliminar) (Mexico, 1975), p. 256. Venezuela: Share of paid-up capital of all firms employing more than 100 persons, 1966, from CORDIPLAN, II Encuesta Industrial (Caracas, 1968).

country is higher than its share of the output of all firms. In
Argentina, for example, whereas in 1963 it was estimated that
foreign firms accounted for 22.8 percent of industrial production, [25]
a few years later it was found that within the group of the largest 50
firms in the country their share was 51 percent. [26] Similarly, in
Mexico, the share of production accounted for by foreign firms rose
from 26.7 percent for a group of 938 firms to 47 percent for the
largest 100. [27]

These, then, are the characteristic features of what has come
to be known as the "new dependence." In the last few years, a
number of global studies of the extent of foreign capital penetration
in various Latin American economies have given empirical substance
to what were previously little more than vague generalizations,
concerning, for example, the domination of dynamic sectors of the
economy by foreign capital. [28] There has also been a vast literature
of a theoretical nature on the economic, sociological, and political
aspects of dependence that has refined further the general concepts
and analytical framework used. The main criticism of the theory
is that it has remained at a high level of generality and abstraction.
Those empirical studies that have been undertaken within its framework, at least as far as economic studies are concerned, have
confined themselves to analyzing what has been described above
as the characteristic feature of dependence, that is, its phenomenal
form. What are missing are concrete studies of the mechanisms
involved in the new relationship between Latin America and the
world economy, and a working through of the implications of these
mechanisms for the development of the region. [29]

THE INDUSTRY AS A FOCUS FOR STUDY

This study is an attempt to make more specific those mechanisms that integrate Latin America with the world economy and the
way in which the region has been conditioned by the development
and expansion of the advanced industrialized countries. The choice
of an industry as the field for study requires some explanation,
however. One may contrast it with two alternatives, either the
study of the economy as a whole or the study of the individual firm.
A number of global studies of Latin American economies have
already been undertaken, but, as was suggested in the previous
section, these have failed to go beyond a fairly descriptive analysis
of the main features of dependence. This is a consequence of im-
posing an artificial framework, that of the nation-state, on the
analysis of what is essentially an international phenomenon. This
is to say that dependence is not a bilateral relationship between, say

Mexico and the developed world, but a much more complicated multi-
lateral relationship within a single world system. The second problem
of such an approach is that it loses the variety of mechanisms involved
in the relationship by looking at global aggregates. These mechanisms
are, at least in part, specific to individual industries and can only be
examined in detail through a number of industry studies.30
        The other alternative is to look at the operations of the individual
firm. As has been pointed out by C. Palloix, this, too, is an inappro-
priate level at which to analyze the process of internationalization
(and hence dependence, which is an aspect of this process), the
reason being that it confines key factors, such as the market, to the
theoretical level as explanations that are not themselves explained.31
This is particularly obvious in the work of Vernon, who explains the
development of multinational enterprises in terms of exogenous
factors, such as the protection of markets and the search for raw
materials.32 The individual firm is no more an appropriate focus
for the analysis of internationalization than it is for the study of
concentration within a particular economy. In the chapters that
follow, it will be argued that the process of competition within an
industry is an essential factor in explaining the features of the "new
dependence."
        The advantage of an industry study is that it gives a well-defined
field for analysis at the international level that can be articulated
with the periphery, avoiding both the extremes of generality of a
global study and of specificity of a firm study. It brings out the
way in which multinational corporations are established and consolidated and makes it possible to study the operations of the international
oligopoly. Factors normally exogenous, such as competition between
firms, concentration, and denationalization, can be considered as
endogenous. Such an approach is able to go beyond the examination
of forms (patterns of investment in the case of country studies or
organizational setups in the case of firm studies) to look at dynamic
processes.
        At the same time, one must recognize the limitations and
dangers inherent in choosing the industry as the focus of study.
J. Schumpeter, in discussing capitalist development, summarizes
the problem:

> Since we are dealing with an organic process, analysis
> of what happens in any particular part of it—say, in an
> individual concern or industry—may indeed clarify
> details of mechanisms but is inconclusive beyond that.
> Every piece of business strategy acquires its true signi-
> ficance only against the background of that process and
> within the situation created by it.33

In discussing the automotive industry in the following chapters, it must always be borne in mind that it is part of the global process of dependent industrial development that has been sketched out in the preceding pages. As Schumpeter adds later, "the problem that is usually being visualized is how capitalism administers existing structures whereas the relevant problem is how it creates and destroys them. As long as this is not recognized, the investigator does a meaningless job."[34]

THE CHOICE OF A SPECIFIC INDUSTRY

A number of factors led to the choice of automobiles as the industry to be studied. In the first place, it is a quantitatively important sector in terms of the proportion of industrial value added that it generates, both in the advanced industrial countries and in those Latin American countries where it has been developed to the fullest extent, namely, Argentina, Brazil, and Mexico.* The importance of the industry as far as foreign investment is concerned is even more pronounced. The transport equipment sector, of which the automotive industry is the major component, accounted for 20.6 percent of the total sales of U.S. manufacturing affiliates in Latin America in 1966.[36] In Argentina almost 20 percent of the foreign investment approved by the government between 1958 and 1969 was in the transport equipment industry.[37] In Chile the same sector accounted for almost 10 percent of the total funds received from abroad by subsidiaries and affiliates of multinational corporations between 1961 and 1969,[38] and in Mexico it represented 16 percent of gross fixed investment by foreign firms in the industrial sector.[39]

Another indicator of the importance of the automotive industry from the point of view of the multinational corporation is the share of the industry in the total payments made by the various countries for foreign technology. In Argentina the automotive industry accounted for 37 percent of all royalty payments in 1970.[40] The proportion was even higher in Brazil where the terminal industry alone paid 46.3 percent and, together with the parts industry, 55.3 percent of the total in the late 1960s.[41] In Mexico and Chile the fact that a significant proportion of the parts used in the automotive industry is still imported makes royalty payments less important

*In Argentina and Brazil the industry accounts for about 12 percent of industrial production, and in Mexico for over 6 percent. See Chapter 3. In Britain the industry accounted for about 7.5 percent of the gross output of manufacturing in 1963.[35]

TABLE 1.3

Ranking of Automotive Manufacturers Among
Largest Firms, 1970

United States	General Motors (1)	Ford (3)	Chrysler (8)
United Kingdom	British Leyland (8)	Ford (12)	Vauxhall (59)
France	Renault (1)	Peugeot (14)	Citroen (17)
West Germany	Volkswagen (1)	Daimler-Benz (4)	Opel (19)
Japan	Toyota (3)	Nissan (8)	Honda (17)
Argentina	Fiat (2)	Ford (6)	General Motors (10)
Brazil	Volkswagen (2)	General Motors (6)	Ford (8)
Mexico	Automex (12)	Ford (13)	DINA (17)

Source: United States, United Kingdom, France, West Germany, and Japan
from the London Times Index of Leading Companies; Argentina from Mercado;
Brazil from Quem e Quem na Economica Brasileira, August 1070, and Mexico
from Coocña, Anexo 1.

as a means of transferring funds. In Mexico the automotive industry
accounted for almost 12 percent of total royalty payments in 1968,[42]
while in Chile they are extremely low.

The automotive industry has exhibited a substantial internationalization of capital during the postwar period that has been
reflected in a rapid growth of both manufacturing and assembly
operations in Latin America since the mid-1950s. It seems particularly suitable, therefore, as an industry in which to study the relationship of the region to the world economy and its consequences.

Another reason for choosing this particular industry is that it
is dominated at the international level by a relatively small number
of large firms. In each country where they operate, the automotive
manufacturers are among the largest firms, both in the developed
world and in the more advanced Latin American countries. (See
Table 1.3.) This not only serves to underline the importance of the
industry in each of these countries but also makes it easier to cope
with the analysis. Since ten companies account for 82 percent of
the world's vehicle output, it makes it possible to build up a picture
of the industry as a whole from individual company data in a way
that would not be possible with an industry having a large number
of firms.

A final reason for choosing the automotive industry is that it
represents a well-defined sector with a particular product or a
limited number of products. Therefore, it does not pose the same
practical problems as would an industry with a much more diversified
output, such as chemicals. Moreover, the fact that for all the major
companies in the industry vehicle production is their main or only
activity means that certain problems are avoided (at least to some

extent) in the use of company data. The small number of firms and products is also the main reason for limiting the study to the terminal industry, and only considering the parts and components industry in passing in relation to it, since the parts industry is highly diversified both in terms of the firms that comprise it and the products that it produces.

NOTES

1. T. Dos Santos, "The Crisis of Development Theory and the Problem of Dependence in Latin America," in Underdevelopment and Development: The Third World Today, ed. H. Bernstein (New York: Penguin, 1973), p. 77.

2. S. J. and B. H. Stein, The Colonial Heritage of Latin America: Essays in Economic Dependence in Perspective (New York: Oxford University Press, 1970), pp. 3-27.

3. Economic Commission for Latin America (ECLA), Economic Survey of Latin America, 1949 (E/CN. 12/164/Rev. 1), 1951, Table 28.

4. V. Bambirra, "Integración Monopólica Mundial e Industrialización: Sus Contra—dicciones," Sociedad y Desarrollo 1 (1972): 53-55.

5. See C. Furtado, Economic Development of Latin America: A Survey from Colonial Times to the Cuban Revolution, trans. S. Macedo (C.U.P., 1970), pp. 39-42, for the changes in the international economy; F. Cardoso and E. Faletto, Dependencia y Desarrollo en América Latina: Ensayo de Interpretación Sociológica (Mexico City: Siglo XXI, 3rd ed., 1971), pp. 54-101; and A. Bianchi, "Introducción: Notas sobre la Teoría del Desarrollo Económico Latinoamericano," in Ensayos de Interpretación Económica, ed. A. Bianchi (Santiago: Editorial Universitaria, 1969), pp. 17-31, on industrialization before 1930.

6. T. Dos Santos, El Nuevo Carácter de la Dependencia (Santiago: Centro de Estudios Socio-económicos, 1968).

7. ECLA, Economic Survey of Latin America, 1970 (E/CN. 12/868/Rev. 1), 1971, Table 71.

8. ECLA, Economic Survey, 1970, op. cit., Table 69.

9. O. Caputo and R. Pizarro, Imperialismo, Dependencia y Relaciones Económicas Internacionales (Santiago: Centro de Estudios socio-económicas, 1970), Table II-6. See also A. G. Frank, "Invisible Foreign Services or National Economic Development," in Latin America: Underdevelopment or Revolution, Essays on the Development of Underdevelopment and the Immediate Enemy (New York: Monthly Review Press, 1969), pp. 181-91.

10. ECLA, External Financing in Latin America (E/CN. 12/649/Rev. 1), 1965, Table 15; and U.S., Department of Commerce, Survey of Current Business (various issues).

11. U.S., Department of Commerce, Survey of Current Business 53 (1972).

12. ECLA, Economic Survey of Latin America, 1971 (E/CN. 12/935/Rev. 1), 1972, Table 8.

13. Board of Trade Journal (various issues).

14. United Nations, Conference on Trade and Development (UNCTAD), Major Issues Arising from the Transfer of Technology to Developing Countries (TD/B/AC. 11/10), 1972, Table III-3.

15. E. Acevedo and H. Vérgara, "Concentración y Capital Extranjera en la Industria Chilena," Economía y Administración, no. 15 (1970), Table 12.

16. "Industrial Development in Latin America," EBLA 14 (1969).

17. Cuadernos de Cicso, El Poder Económico en la Argentina (Buenos Aires: Cicso, n.d.), Table 9.

18. Ruben Medina, Desnacionalização: Crime Contra o Brasil? (Sao Paulo: Editôra Saga, 1970).

19. F. Fajnzylber and T. Martinez Tarrago, Las Empresas Transnacionales, Expansión a Nivel Mundial y Proyección en la Industria Mexicana, mimeographed (Versión Preliminar)(México, Centro de Investigacion y Docencia Economica, 1975), p. 258.

20. L. Pacheco, "La Inversión Extranjera y las Corporaciones Internacionales en el Desarrollo Industrial Chileno," in Proceso a la Industrialización Chilena, CEPLAN (Santiago: Ediciones Nueva Universidad, 1972), Table 2.

21. R. Vernon, Sovereignty at Bay, the Multinational Spread of U.S. Engerprises (New York: Penguin, 1973), p. 34.

22. B. Sepulveda and A. Chumacero, La Inversión Extranjera en México (Mexico City: Fondo de Cultura Económica, 1973), Table 14. It is not clear why the estimate for 1970 is lower than that previously quoted.

23. E. Galeano, "The Denationalization of Brazilian Industry," Monthly Review 22 (1969): 11-30; and Rogelio Garcia Lupo, Contra la Ocupación Extranjera, 3rd ed. (Buenos Aires: Editorial Centro, 1971), pp. 177-78.

24. See Furtado, op. cit., on the pharmaceuticals industry, p. 176.

25. Consejo Nacional de Desarollo (CONADE), La Concentración en la Industria Argentina en 1964 (Buenos Aires, 1969), pp. 71-78.

26. G. Martorell, Las Inversiones Extranjeras en la Argentina (Buenos Aires: Editorial Galerna, 1969), Chap. 6.

27. Ricardo Cinta G., "Burgesía Nacional y Desarrollo," in El Perfil de México en 1980, vol. 3, Instituto de Investigaciones Sociales, Universidad Nacional Autónoma de México (Mexico City: Siglo XXI, 1972), Table 10.

28. In addition to the studies already quoted, see F. Gasparian, "The Internationalization of the Brazilian Economy," mimeographed, on Brazil; L. Pacheco, "La Inversión Extranjera en la Industria Chilena" (Diss., University of Chile, 1970), on Chile; J. A. Mayobre, Las Inversiones Extranjeras en Venezuela (Caracas: Monte Avila Editores, 1970), on Venezuela; and J. L. Ceceña, México en la Órbita Imperial (Mexico City: Ediciones "El Caballito," 1970), on Mexico.

29. For a similar criticism, see P. O'Brien, "A Critique of Latin American Theories of Dependency," in Beyond the Sociology of Development, ed. I. Oxaal, T. Barnett, D. Booth (London: Routledge Kegan Paul, 1975), pp. 7-27.

30. See, for example, Vaitsos' findings on the use of different mechanisms for transferring profits abroad in different industries. C. V. Vaitsos, Transfer of Resources and Preservation of Monopoly Rents, Economic Development Report No. 168 (Cambridge: Harvard University, Development Advisory Service, 1970).

31. C. Palloix, Note de Recherche sur le Proces d'Internationalisation, mimeographed (Grenoble, 1972), p. 11.

32. See the comments of Palloix in R. Vernon, "Future of the Multinational Enterprise," in C. P. Kindleberger, The International Corporation: A Symposium (Cambridge, Mass: MIT Press, 1970); Palloix, op. cit., pp. 8-9.

33. J. Schumpeter, Capitalism, Socialism and Democracy, 4th ed. (London: Allen & Unwin, 1954), pp. 83-84.

34. Ibid.

35. See National Economic Development Office, Motor Manufacturing E.D.C., The Effect of Government Policy on the Motor Industry (M.M.S.O., 1968), p. 6.

36. H. K. May, The Effects of U.S. and Other Foreign Investment in Latin America (New York: Council for Latin America, 1970), Table 5.

37. S. M. MacDonnell and M. R. Lascano, La Industria Automotriz, Aspectos Económicas y Fiscales (Buenos Aires: Departmento de Estudios, Division Planes, 1974), p. 1.

38. UNCTAD, Major Issues Arising from the Transfer of Technology: A Case Study of Chile (TD/B/AC.11/20), 1974, Table 15.

39. Sepulveda and Chumacero, op. cit., Tables 12 and 13.

40. B. C. Raddavero, "Análisis de la Transferencia de la Tecnología Externa a la Industria Argentina," Economica 18 (1972): 367-88.

41. ECLA, The Transfer of Technology in the Industrial Development of Brazil: General Aspects of the Problem (E/CN. 12/937), 1974, Table 6.

42. UNCTAD, Major Issues in Transfer of Technology to Developing Countries: Addendum (TD/B/AC 11/10/Add. 1), 1972, p. 30.

THE INTERNATIONAL
AUTOMOTIVE INDUSTRY

In this chapter the development of the automotive industry is traced back to the early twentieth century. The opening section analyzes the growth of a mass production industry in a few centers, namely, the United States and Western Europe, up to World War II. In the following sections the changes observed in the industry in the postwar period, at both the national and international levels, are described and explained. This later period, which is of central interest from the point of view of this thesis, it will be argued, has been characterized by the emergence of a world industry dominated by a few international firms. It is no longer possible to analyze the development of the automotive industry in a particular country without taking this fact into account. An understanding of the growth and structure of the Latin American automotive industry hinges on the nature of oligopolistic competition at the international level.

THE AUTOMOTIVE INDUSTRY BEFORE
WORLD WAR II

In the early stages of the industry's development, its technology was fairly simple, scales of production low, and capital requirements small. In the United States, car producers were, in the main, assemblers that bought most of their parts and components from outside suppliers. Even in Britain, where the supplier industry was less well developed, "it was not difficult to enter the industry. A knowledge of general engineering techniques and a modest amount of capital were all that were required."[1] In the United States it has been estimated that there were 181 companies in the industry during the early 1900s,[2] while in Britain, 198 different makes of

cars had been put on the market up to 1913, of which over 100
quickly disappeared.[3] This period corresponds to the initial phase
in the introduction of a new product as described in the product cycle
theory, characterized in the literature by high unit costs, labor-
intensive production processes, and short runs.[4]

The major technological innovation that changed this was the
introduction of mass production by Henry Ford, coinciding as it
did with the changeover from wood to metal bodies around 1910 in
the United States.[5] Europe, with its smaller, less standardized
markets, was slower than the United States in adopting these techniques. Mass production methods did not begin to be introduced
until the 1920s and then not on such an impressive scale as on the
other side of the Atlantic. In the mid-1930s, large pressed items
were first used, increasing scale requirements considerably.

The consequences of the assembly line were felt throughout
the world automotive industry. Between 1909 and 1921, Ford
increased his output from 12,000 to almost 2 million cars a year
and his share of the U.S. market from 10 to 55 percent.[6] In the
five-year period following the introduction of the conveyor belt, he
was able to make a 50 percent saving in the production costs of the
Model T. In order to achieve this expansion, the price of the
Model T was cut to less than one third of its initial level over a
period of several years. At the same time, for the American
automotive industry as a whole, the capital-labor ratio index rose
sharply from 58.5 in 1909 to 93.6 in 1919 (1929 = 100).[7] In Britain,
too, similar trends became evident from the mid-1920s onward,
although not on such a spectacular scale. The Society of Motor
Manufacturers and Traders (SMMT) index of prices, however, fell
from 100 in 1924 to 52 ten years later.[8]

As a result, the interwar period saw a considerable increase
in concentration in both the United States and Western Europe. The
number of firms in the industry fell from the early 1920s in both
Britain and the United States. In the latter it declined from 108 in
1923, to 44 in 1927, to 35 in 1931, and to only 12 in 1941,[9] and
General Motors, Ford, and Chrysler accounted for 75 percent of
the market by 1929, increasing in 1930 to 90 percent. In Britain
the number fell from 88 in 1922 to 31 in 1929 and 22 by 1938.[10]
Three firms (Morris, Austin, and Singer) accounted for 75 percent
of output in 1929 and in 1938 six firms produced 90 percent of the
total. Similar trends appeared in the other two major producing
countries, France and Germany. Here the industry was even more
fragmented than in Britain during the early 1920s, with 150 firms
in France (1921) and more than 200 in Germany (1925). Significant
levels of concentration were attained by the late 1920s in France,
where three firms made 68 percent of sales in 1928, and the late

1930s in Germany where by 1937 three firms produced 74 percent of all cars.[11]

Undoubtedly, the main factor behind the increased concentration of the interwar period was the new technology of mass production. The comments of G. Maxcy and A. Silberston in their classic study of the British automotive industry sum up this process neatly and apply with equal force to the other major producing countries:

> The factor that sealed the fate of the smaller concerns was the growth of mass production techniques on the part of companies such as Morris and Austin which had succeeded in producing models that were successful with the public. . . . [and further] The concentration of some 75 percent of car production in the hands of these manufacturers and the elimination of many small producers during the 1920s had been brought about by the competitive pressure exerted by a few rapidly expanding companies benefiting from the economies of scale that accompanied the introduction of elementary mass-production techniques.[12]

A secondary factor leading to intensified competition in the European automotive industry was the entry of subsidiaries of Ford and General Motors into the British and German industries during the 1920s.[13] In the United States a change in the nature of the car market to become primarily a replacement market from the mid-1920s onward led to a slowdown in the rate of growth of the industry and intensified competition for market shares. (Peak output was attained in 1929 and was not surpassed until after World War II.)

Thus, the rise in concentration during the interwar years can be explained in terms of the classic mechanism of competition with increasing returns. Economies of scale and technical progress combine to give the largest and fastest growing firms a cost advantage, which enables them to expand further and faster than their competitors. The introduction of mass production considerably increased the scale at which costs were minimized and this, reinforced by the other factors tending to increase competition, created the concentration movement observed.

The development of the industry in the major producing countries was reflected internationally in several ways. The earlier introduction of mass production techniques in the United States meant that the U.S. firms enjoyed a considerable competitive advantage over the European producers in the years immediately after World War I. This led the European countries to adopt tariffs and other measures to protect their infant automotive industries against U.S. competition. This created an international structure, with the United States, Britain, France, Germany, and Italy dominating as exporters while at the same time enjoying virtually isolated domestic markets. International trade in vehicles, therefore, was almost exclusively directed toward the less industrialized countries.[14]

The same factors that led to increased concentration within national boundaries also caused firms to look for new markets. The preferred form of expansion was through exports, although some assembly plants were set up during this period. In 1929, the U.S. companies exported 536,000 vehicles, to which can be added a further 200,000 or more assembled abroad. In the same year the foreign sales of the four main European producing countries came to only 122,000, all through exports.[15] This brings out both the dominance of exports vis-a-vis foreign assembly operations and of the United States vis-a-vis Europe. The introduction of mass production in Europe improved the continent's competitive position and increased its share of world exports from 15 percent in 1929 to 40 percent by 1938. This did not represent a significant intensification of competition at the international level, however. Britain, for example, only exported 15 percent of its car output in 1938, and 75 percent of this was to areas where the United Kingdom enjoyed tariff preferences.[16]

CONCENTRATION IN THE POSTWAR PERIOD

Since World War II there have been further increases in concentration in each of the major car-producing countries. In the United States the independents, those companies other than the Big Three (General Motors, Ford, and Chrysler), managed to obtain about 22 percent of the total market in the early postwar years. This was made possible by the shortage of both new and used cars in this period, following several years with virtually no production. With the return to normal market conditions in 1953, however, their share fell sharply to only 7.6 percent.* This led to a spate of mergers, first between Kaiser-Frazer and Willys-Overland in 1953, followed a year later by the Nash-Hudson and the Studebaker-Packard mergers.[18] In 1963, Studebaker-Packard stopped production in the United States, and, in 1970, Kaiser-Willys, which had stopped

---

*In the immediate postwar years, secondhand cars were selling at above the list price for new cars, and as late as 1952 car dealers were selling new cars at list prices and making a profit on their used car resales, all of which indicate abnormal market conditions.[17]

producing cars during the 1950s, sold its remaining jeep operations to American Motors (the outcome of the Nash-Hudson merger), the only surviving independent.

The same process has been evident throughout Europe and has intensified considerably since 1960. A number of small European producers either have gone out of business or have been taken over by their larger competitors. Concentration seems to be tending toward a situation in which each major producing country has one nationally owned firm dominating the market, competing against a number of smaller foreign subsidiaries.

This process has reached its logical conclusion in the United Kingdom, where British Leyland is now the only major locally owned automotive manufacturer and competes against the subsidiaries of the U.S. Big Three, Ford, Vauxhall, and Chrysler. The formation of a major British company dates back to the early 1950s when the merger of Austin and Morris created the British Motor Corporation, but it is only since 1960 that virtually all the independent British companies, that is, those that are not American subsidiaries, have been brought under one roof. In 1960, the four leading producers accounted for 82.7 percent of British car production, and now four firms dominate the entire industry, with only a few thousand units produced by specialists, such as Rolls Royce and Aston Martin.

The early 1960s saw a number of mergers and takeovers (see Figure 2.1). Jaguar took over Daimler and Guy in 1960 and 1961, respectively. In 1960, too, Leyland made its first venture into the passenger car field by taking over Standard-Triumph International, and in the following year it merged with ACV, its major rival in heavy trucks. In 1966, the industry was further consolidated through the BMC-Jaguar merger and the takeover of Rover, which had previously absorbed Alvis, by Leyland. Finally, in 1968, British Motor Holdings (the product of the BMC-Jaguar merger) and Leyland merged, with considerable government encouragement, to form the British Leyland Motor Corporation. These mergers were not sufficient, however, to create a viable British automotive company, and, in 1975, the government was forced to intervene directly by taking a shareholding in the firm.

At the same time, the U.S. companies were tightening their hold on the British automotive industry. General Motors had held all Vauxhall's shares since the 1920s. In 1960, Ford bought out the 45 percent of British Ford's shares held by minority shareholders in order to "obtain greater operational flexibility and enable us better to co-ordinate our European and American manufacturing facilities and integrate further our product lines and operations on a world-wide basis."[19] In retrospect it can be seen that this was an important step in the internationalization of the automotive industry.

FIGURE 2.1

The Formation of British Leyland, 1960-68

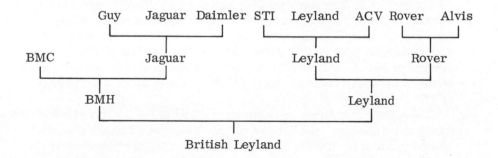

Source: Compiled by the author.

Four years later Chrysler gained a foothold in the British
market through buying up 30 percent of Rootes' shares. Since then,
it has increased its participation, first to give it overall control
(despite initial resistance from the British government) and eventually
almost complete ownership.

France had already achieved a high degree of concentration by
1960, with 96.1 percent of passenger car output being accounted for
by four firms, so that concentration during the 1960s and early 1970s
was not as marked as in Britain. It did, however, see the elimination of Facel-Vega in 1964 and the disappearance of Panhard as an
independent make, so that, in 1973, Renault, Citroen, Peugeot, and
Simca accounted for all French car production save some 4,000 units.
More significant, however, were the changes in ownership of Simca
and Citroen during this period. Chrysler had already obtained a
minority holding in Simca in 1958; in 1963, it achieved majority
control and since then has increased its share further. Citroen has
experienced a series of difficulties as an independent company, and,
in 1968, Fiat obtained a 15 percent share in the company, but General
de Gaulle vetoed the Italian company's attempt to gain control. Although Fiat was able to increase its holding to 49 percent during the
early 1970s, it subsequently divested itself of its holding. In 1974,
heavy losses by Citroen led to a government-sponsored takeover of
its car operations by Peugeot and a merger of its commercial
vehicle subsidiary, Berliet, with Renault's Saviem. These moves,
together with the close cooperation between Peugeot and Renault,
which have a number of jointly owned factories producing parts and

components, suggest that the French car industry is moving toward a situation in which there is one major national firm as in Britain.

The 1950s and 1960s also saw a dramatic reduction in the number of French commercial vehicle producers, with firms such as Chenard et Walker disappearing completely. There were also a number of takeovers and mergers, such as those involving Salmson and Saviem, Delahaye and Hotchkiss, and the takeover of the largest French commercial vehicle firm, Berliet, by Citroen in 1967. The merger of Berliet with Saviem reduced the number of firms producing medium and heavy trucks to two, the other being Unic, a subsidiary of Fiat.

In 1960, four firms in Germany accounted for 86.9 percent of total car production, and here again there has been further concentration, so that by 1973 these same companies were producing 94.0 percent of German output. The main stimulus to concentration has been Volkswagen's failure to expand its range from the Beetle on which it has relied for so long. This has led the company to collect other German firms in an attempt to diversify its product line. In 1964, it bought a half share in Auto Union, which had previously been completely owned by Daimler-Benz, and, in 1966, took full ownership of the company. In 1969, NSU, which had been responsible for the development of the Wankel engine, was taken over. Volkswagen also has a joint company with Porsche. With Borgward's failure in 1961 and BMW's takeover of Hans Glas in 1967, there remain three German companies, Volkswagen, Daimler-Benz, and BMW, competing against the subsidiaries of General Motors and Ford.

A similar increase in concentration has occurred in the commercial vehicle industry in Germany. In 1969, Daimler-Benz strengthened its position as the market leader by buying Hanomag and Henschel from Rheinstal. MAN's merger with Bussing, the decision of Krupp to abandon commercial vehicle production, and the failure of International Harvester in its attempt to enter the German market in the mid-1960s has left only three major truck-producing groups in Germany: Daimler-Benz, MAN, and Magirus Deutz, which merged with Fiat in early 1975.

Fiat dominated the Italian market in 1960, having taken over Autobianchi three years earlier, with 86.5 percent of total production. The four leading firms—Fiat, Alfa Romeo, Lancia, and Innocenti—accounted for 99.8 percent of Italian output. Although Fiat attempted to consolidate its position by taking over Lancia and Ferrari in 1969, increased competition from the state-owned Alfa Romeo reduced its market share slightly to 84.2 percent in 1973. Its only competitors in the domestic market (apart from imports) are Alfa Romeo and Innocenti, which was taken over by British Leyland in 1972. In commercial vehicles the position of Fiat is even more dominant. Together with its subsidiaries OM and Autobianchi, the company controls more than 99 percent of all Italian production.

To a greater or lesser extent, increased concentration has characterized the automotive industries of all the major car-producing countries of Western Europe during the 1960s. Although Sweden is not a major producing country, the same has been true there. At the beginning of the decade there were three firms producing vehicles in the country: Volvo, Saab, and Scania Vabis. In 1968, the truck firm Scania Vabis and the car firm Saab merged, so that Sweden now has two diversified groups producing both passenger cars and commercial vehicles.

The Japanese automotive industry expanded spectacularly during the 1960s. In the late 1960s and early 1970s there were signs that the growth of the domestic market was slowing down and the industry was becoming increasingly dependent on exports for its dynamism. In 1961, the then leading firms of Nissan, Toyota, Toyo-Kogyo, and Fugi Heavy Industries accounted for 82 percent of Japanese car production. By 1971, the four largest firms, which now included Mitsubishi in place of Fuji, produced 93.8 percent of Japan's cars. This concentration has taken place since the mid-1960s, smaller firms being absorbed by Toyota and Nissan, which, by 1970, were accounting for 70 percent of the home market and 90 percent of Japanese exports.

The government, through the Ministry for International Trade and Industry (MITI), has played a leading role in promoting concentration in the Japanese automotive industry. The first step was the takeover of Prince Motors by Nissan in 1966, although two years previously the Mitsubishi companies (Mitsubishi Japan and Shin Mitsubishi) had come together to form one group. Attempts to form a Mitsubishi-Isuzu-Fuji group failed, and, in 1968, Fuji joined Nissan. The Toyota group includes both Hino and Daihatsu Motors, and it seems likely that Suzuki will also join it in the near future. A major change occurred in the industry in the early 1970s with the liberalization of the Japanese foreign investment code, and, in 1971, Chrysler was permitted to take a 35 percent shareholding in Mitsubishi, the fourth largest Japanese automotive company. It was followed by General Motors with a similar arrangement with Isuzu, but the projected Ford-Toyo-Kogyo deal fell through. This means that apart from the Big Two, there are now only two Japanese producers, Honda and Toyo-Kogyo, without foreign participation. (For further details on the Japanese automotive industry, see Chapter 9.)

THE INTERNATIONALIZATION OF THE
AUTOMOTIVE INDUSTRY

The term "internationalization" in this context is used to
describe the increasingly worldwide nature of the automotive industry
in the postwar period, in contrast to its largely national structure
during the interwar years. This is reflected not only in the considerable expansion of trade in motor vehicles but also in the interpenetration of the markets of the leading producing countries, a feature
notably absent before. It is also reflected in the growth of foreign
assembly operations by the major multinational companies and by
the increasing number of links between these firms.[20]

Table 2.1 indicates the considerable growth that has taken
place in international trade in cars over the last two decades.[21]
In the 1950s, prior to the formation of the European Economic
Community (EEC), the European car producers continued to enjoy
substantial tariff protection, as they had since World War I. The
British and French tariffs stood at 30 percent; the Italian at 35 to 45
percent, depending on the type of car; and the German at 17 to 21
percent. During this period, exports expanded rapidly between
1953 and 1959, when they trebled, mainly as a result of the boom
in U.S. car imports, which increased from a negligible 25,000 in
1954 to a peak of 614,000 in 1959.[22] In the next two years, world
exports stagnated as a result of the contraction in U.S. imports
following the introduction of the compacts, but the 1961-64 period
saw a renewed growth of trade, probably due to the trade-creating

TABLE 2.1

Car Exports by Leading Countries, 1950-70
(thousands of units)

1950	720	1958	1,765	1966	3,269
1951	839	1959	2,178	1967	3,226
1952	703	1960	2,264	1968	4,304
1953	746	1961	2,008	1969	4,811
1954	943	1962	2,487	1970	5,361
1955	1,162	1963	2,893	1971	6,608
1956	1,175	1964	3,124	1972	6,633
1957	1,434	1965	3,150		

Sources: Society of Motor Manufacturers and Traders (SMMT)
1950-58; National Economic Development Office Data Book, Motor
Industry Statistics, 1959-70 (London: Her Majesty's Stationery
Office, 1971), and author's compilation.

TABLE 2.2

Imported Passenger Cars as Percent of Total
New Car Registrations

	1958	1973
West Germany	10.4	25.8
France	1.4	20.9
Italy	4.2	28.0
Britain	2.5	27.4
United States	9.3	17.9

Sources: 1958: E. Mahler, L'Industrie Automobile et ses
Perspectives d'avenir dans le Nouvel Equilibre Europeen et Mondial
(Lausanne: L'ere Nouvelle, 1966); 1973: Economist Intelligence
Unit, Motor Business (various issues, 1974).

effects of the formation of the Common Market. By 1965, the EEC's
common external tariff was 22 percent and internal tariffs had been
reduced to about 30 percent of their initial level, while intra-EEC
trade in cars had increased 378 percent since 1958.[23] The final
period of rapid growth from 1967 onward was associated with a
reduction of the British tariff to 22 percent in 1968 and the Kennedy
Round, which subsequently halved tariffs to 11 percent in both Britain
and the EEC.

Exports grew at a faster rate than production, so that the
vehicle exports of the eight leading countries increased as a share
of world output from 10.1 percent in 1950 to 17.9 percent in 1960,
reaching 26.2 percent by 1970.

A particular feature of the growth of trade in cars has been
the increasing interpenetration of markets among the leading producing
countries, breaking with the prewar pattern of exports to less industrialized countries from a heavily protected home base, which
persisted into the 1950s. This, of course, has been particularly
marked among the Common Market countries. Between 1958 and
1970, the market share of French cars in West Germany increased
from 1.9 to 13.8 percent, while correspondingly in France, German
cars were up from 0.9 to 10.9 percent and Italian cars from 0.2 to
6.3 percent. In Italy the market penetration of German cars rose
from 1.3 to 16.1 percent and that of the French from 0.7 to 10.9
percent.

The same pattern emerges if one looks at the share of all
imports in new registrations for the major producing countries,
as shown in Table 2.2. As can be seen from the table, imports

have increased their share markedly, so that in 1973 between 18
and 28 percent of the cars sold in the major producing countries
(apart from Japan) were foreign made. Even without membership
in the EEC, British imports of cars reached almost 20 percent of
total sales in 1971, with imports from the Common Market trebling
between 1965 and 1970. The less spectacular increase in U.S.
imports may be explained by the fact that the United States always
has been a relatively low tariff market for cars and because of the
sharp increase in imports in the years immediately preceding 1958
from only 1.6 percent of the market in 1956. The figure for West
Germany also gives a misleading impression of the growth in market
penetration by imports, since the 1958 figure was almost double the
1957 level of 5.3 percent.

Another aspect of the internationalization of the motor industry
is the growth of the overseas assembly and manufacturing operations
of the major companies.[24] The number of assembly contracts in
operation increased from 170 in 1960 to 430 at the end of 1968, and
the number of countries with assembly operations increased from
42 to 70 over the same period.[25] Table 2.3 indicates the considerable extent of overseas operations by the major car-producing
countries.

The spread of the multinational automotive companies is
reflected not only in their manufacturing and assembly operations
but also in the extension of their sales networks.[26] Indeed, for the
major European and Japanese companies, exports are as, if not
more, important than overseas production (see Table 2.4), although,
for the U.S. companies, the reverse is true.

TABLE 2.3

Number of Assembly Contracts by
Country of Origin, 1969

	Number	Countries
United States (including subsidiaries)	133	43
France	77	39
West Germany	56	26
United Kingdom	48	34
Italy	30	27
Japan	59	28

Source: United Nations Industrial Development Organization
(UNIDO), The Motor Vehicle Industry (ID/78), 1972, p. 8.

TABLE 2.4

Distribution of Sales of the Major
European Automotive Manufacturers, 1973
(percent)

	Domestic Sales	Exports	Overseas Production
Citroen	49	26	25
BLMC	52	27	21
Volkswagen	27	48	25
Fiat	44	27	29
Renault	43	26	31
Peugeot	55	20	25
Daimler-Benz	51	37	12

Note: Data refer to volume, except for BLMC and Daimler-Benz, for which only value data were available.

Sources: Company annual reports.

All the major European firms do almost half or more of their business abroad either through exports or overseas production, with exports accounting for at least 20 percent of total output and overseas production between 21 and 31 percent (apart from Daimler-Benz). The U.S. producers do not export a significant proportion of their U.S. output, but both Ford and Chrysler have about one third of their total production outside the United States and Canada, while General Motors has about one fifth of its production overseas. Compared to the prewar position, this reflects a considerable increase in their foreign involvement for the European producers and a decided shift away from exports and toward overseas assembly in terms of the composition of foreign sales.

A different aspect of the internationalization of the automotive industry is the steps that have been taken recently by the U.S. companies in the integration of their worldwide operations, which have been developed most fully by Ford.[27] Ford has been working toward the increased integration of its European operations since the early 1960s when it bought out the minority shareholders in Ford U.K. with the avowed intention of obtaining greater flexibility of operations.[28]

The setting up of Ford of Europe around 1967 represented a further decisive step. The immediate advantage that the company

gained from this move was the addition of the Escort to the Ford
Werke model range, which improved Ford's weakening position in
the German market. At first, the Escort was assembled at Genk,
Belgium, from British components; later, it was manufactured in
Cologne. The introduction of the Capri showed the advantages of
greater integration of the company's European operations. The
development of the same car for both the British and German markets
meant that it was possible to cut engineering and design time by half.
Further economies could be obtained through the pooling of research
between the two subsidiaries. Ford also gained additional flexibility
in marketing through having two different sources of supply for the
same model, especially in the face of strikes (at least until the
automotive industry unions are able to organize themselves multi-
nationally to meet this threat).

The other U.S. companies have not gone as far as Ford in the
integration of their European operations. Not until late 1970 did
General Motors follow Ford in setting up European headquarters.
It recently opened an automatic transmission plant in Strasbourg,
and it is to be expected that in future there will be greater use of
common design and components between Opel in Germany and
Vauxhall in Britain. Chrysler, after gaining control of Simca and
Rootes in the mid-1960s, was able to increase its exports significantly by integrating its marketing outlets. Integration in production
has not been developed fully, however, partly because of the financial
difficulties faced by the parent company in the United States, which
have resulted in the curtailment of expansion plans. These financial
difficulties also led Chrysler to decide to import the Hillman Avenger
(together with the Mitsubishi Colt) and sell it on the U.S. market as
the Plymouth Cricket rather than to develop a subcompact in the
United States, the tooling costs of which were estimated at around
$200 million.

The decision of Ford and General Motors to produce subcompacts in the United States represents a backward step in the
international integration of their operations. This is especially
true for Ford, which originally had planned to manufacture the
1,600 cc engine in Britain and the 2,000 cc engine in Germany, as
well as importing various other components from Europe. Partly
as a result of the uncertainty of supply because of strikes and partly
because sales reached the minimum output level of 400,000 to
500,000 units required to justify such an investment, Ford decided
to build an engine plant in the United States. It is also certain that
there are political pressures against selling "international" cars
on the U.S. market, which may have encouraged Ford to transfer
operations from Europe.

THE PRESENT STRUCTURE OF THE
WORLD AUTOMOTIVE INDUSTRY

The level of concentration in the major vehicle-producing countries has already been discussed. As was mentioned, all these countries have at least one independent producer, that is, a firm that is not a foreign subsidiary. It is not surprising to find, therefore, that when one looks at the world as one market, concentration is less than in any one country taken in isolation. Nevertheless, it is still true that the industry is dominated by a small nucleus of companies (see Table 2.5). Between them, General Motors and Ford accounted for 38.4 percent of world vehicle production in 1973, while the largest 13 companies in the world made up 87 percent of total output. It is evident that concentration on a national scale has been reflected in concentration in the international market.

The movement toward cross-country mergers has not progressed very far as yet, but this underestimates the extent of links among the world's leading vehicle producers, since the main form that these have taken has been through joint companies or agreements involving no ownership. One of the most significant joint companies linking

TABLE 2.5

Leading Vehicle Producers
(Including Subsidiaries), 1973
(thousands of units)

		Percent
General Motors	8,684	22.9
Ford	5,871	15.5
Chrysler	3,450	9.1
Toyota	2,692	7.1
Volkswagen	2,335	6.1
Fiat	2,278	6.0
Nissan	2,271	6.0
Renault	1,452	3.8
British Leyland	1,161	3.1
Peugeot	795	2.1
Citroen	773	2.0
Toyo-Kogyo	739	1.9
Daimler-Benz	548	1.4
Total	38 million	

Source: Company reports.

major car manufacturers is the Societe Franco-Suedoise de Moteurs in which Renault, Peugeot, and Volvo each has one-third share. The company is intended to produce 1 million engines a year. At first, these will be to the individual specifications of the partners, but eventually it is planned to produce an integrated range. Another important cross-country link through a joint company is that between Citroen and NSU. These two companies have owned Comobil jointly since 1965, which was intended to develop Wankel engine cars, and they set up another company, Comotor, in 1967. In Japan, Toyo-Kogyo and Nissan have collaborated with Ford to build a joint automatic transmission plant. See Figure 2.2 for a diagram illustrating these links among the companies.

Jointly owned companies have also been used to link major car manufacturers within national boundaries. The close cooperation between Renault and Peugeot has been realized in a number of joint companies, the most important of which are Societe des Transmissions Automatiques and Francaise de Mecanique. Similarly, in Germany, Volkswagen and Daimler-Benz for a number of years have had a joint research company going under the grandiose title of the Deutsche Automobil GMBH.

Other agreements, not involving common ownership, can take a number of forms, such as the exchange of parts, production of common parts, or assembly and/or marketing of one firm's vehicles by another. Such agreements tend to be particularly common in the commercial vehicles sector of the industry, possibly because a greater number of small firms have survived than in the case of car production, and it is the first step toward further rationalization of the industry. Thus MAN in West Germany has a production and marketing agreement with Saviem, the commercial vehicles subsidiary of Renault. This involves the exchange of parts between the two firms with MAN producing engines and Saviem supplying truck bodies in return, while MAN also sells Saviem trucks in West Germany through its own dealers. Saviem also has an agreement with the Dutch firm DAF, the Swedish Volvo, and the West German Magirus Deutz in order to develop, produce, and buy their truck components in common.

THE CAUSES OF CONCENTRATION
AND INTERNATIONALIZATION

It was argued in the first section of this chapter that the major factor underlying the increase in concentration in the main producing countries during the interwar years was the effect of economies of scale, leading individual firms to expand output and drive out competi-

FIGURE 2.2

Interpenetration of the Major Automotive Manufacturers, 1975

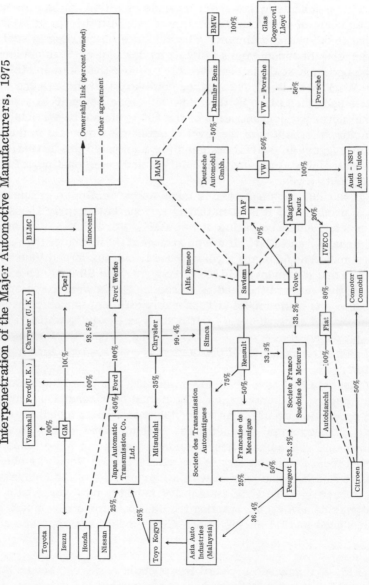

Source: Compiled by the author.

tors in order to achieve lower costs. Can this drive for production
economies at plant level explain the developments that have occurred
during the postwar period? Such a drive could lead to mergers at
the national level followed by a reduction in the number of models
produced and an increase in average production volumes. It could
also lead to international cooperation in such areas as engine production and to increased exports.

    This mechanism, however, depends on either an increasing
optimum scale of production over time or an initial level of production that is below the optimum. The evidence on changes in scale
requirements in recent years is by no means clear. It is obvious
that the optimum scale is considerably greater than immediately
before World War II.[29] It appears, however, that most of the
increase had taken place by the mid-1950s (see Appendix A), so
that the increased concentration of the 1960s cannot be attributed to
this factor. Estimates of the level of economies of scale in the
industry suggest an overall optimum for integrated production,
that is, assembly, pressing, machining, and some casting, of around
400,000 units a year.*

    If 400,000 cars per year is taken as the minimum efficient
scale of production, it is seen that in Europe in the early 1960s
six firms had achieved such a scale: BMC, Ford U.K., Volkswagen,
Opel, Renault, and Fiat. If a less stringent definition of the minimum
scale of only 200,000 cars a year is used, one might add Vauxhall,
Rootes, Ford (Germany), Citroen, Peugeot, and Simca. This
suggests that most of the leading European firms were large enough
to produce one basic model at reasonably efficient scales of production during the early 1960s. A firm such as Renault, which, in
1961, produced almost 400,000 units of one model, the Dauphine,
would gain little in terms of production economies by a larger volume
of output.

    The data that have been reviewed here are purely technical
in their nature, and only indicate the actual cost conditions under
which production occurs. As such, the data takes account of tooling
costs and fixed capital expenditures, such as those for design and
development. These have now assumed a degree of importance far
removed from the early days of the industry when Ford was able to
put its first car on the market within four months of the company
being formed.[30] The U.S. automotive industry now works on a
three-year design cycle, starting the sketches for a new model to
be introduced in 1971 during 1968. Clay models are approved about

---

    *This is discussed in detail in Appendix A where various studies
of economies of scale in the industry are compared.

two years before the planned introduction date, after which the cost
of any change in design increases considerably.[31] In Britain, the
development lag seems to be even longer, estimated at between
three and a half and five years.[32] It took Ford four years to develop
the Capri, for example.

Estimates of the design and development costs of a new model
seem to be difficult to ascertain with any degree of accuracy. This
difficulty is illustrated by the different estimates made by two
analysts of Ford's expenditure on the development of the Mustang.
John Kenneth Galbraith[33] puts the engineering and styling costs of
the car at $9 million, with a further $50 million on tooling costs,
while L. J. White[34] suggests a total figure of around $40 million,
roughly equally divided between design and development, and tooling.
In Britain, estimates have put the design, development, and tooling
costs of the Austin Allegro at £17 million and of the Morris Marina
at £15 million.[35] White's estimate puts the cost of design and
development per car at about $100. If these broad orders of magni-
tude are accepted, then taking account of these expenditures would
tend to add to the importance of scale economies, above what would
be expected from technological data, by increasing fixed costs. But
since they only amount to about 5 percent of the total cost for a
successful car, they will not make a great deal of difference.

The key word here is "successful." The costs of failure are
extremely high. In 1970, only four car firms enjoyed profits of
more than $100 million, so that the need to write off development
expenditures of say $30 to $50 million on an unsuccessful car, even
over a period of several years, would be a severe financial strain.
The importance of the increased gestation period between the first
designs and actual production of a model is not so much its impact
on cost curves as its effect on risk. Again, however, the phenomenon of a long gestation period seems to have been characteristic of
the entire postwar period and cannot, per se, be responsible for
the observed developments. In fact, the most recent developments,
such as the use of numerically controlled machine tools and electrical discharge and electrochemical machining in making tools and
dies, and the use of computerized systems to automate the entire
engineering-design function, have led to increased flexibility in the
preproduction period and a reduced lead time.[36] Computer control
of die cutting, for example, has been estimated to cut the average
lag time between approval of the clay model and startup of production
from 21 or 22 months to 17 months.[37]

Since the developments that have taken place in the automotive
industry since 1960 cannot be explained by technological changes in
the area of supply, one must look for an alternative explanation.
The lack of car production during World War II meant that the industry

was faced with very favorable demand conditions in the immediate postwar years both in the United States and Europe. In the United States, this period, which saw used cars selling at prices above the list price for new cars, came to an end in 1953 and would probably have ended sooner had it not been for the effect of the Korean War. In Britain, the return to normal market conditions has been put slightly later, around 1956,[38] having been delayed by the government's policy of putting priority on car exports rather than meeting home demand. A similar situation existed in the other major producing countries in Europe.

As Table 2.6 shows, the rate of growth of new registrations in the major European countries was particularly high between 1950 and 1955, while demand conditions were extremely favorable, and fell in the next five-year period except in the relatively immature Italian market. The first half of the 1960s saw a further fall in growth in all countries except France and the period 1965-71 saw growth decline further in all countries. This slowdown in the rate of growth of the major markets has meant an increase in competition within each national industry.

The increased concentration that has taken place in the U.S. automotive industry since World War II has been analyzed by a number of authors.[39] Here we shall only summarize some of their findings that are relevant. J. A. Menge has suggested that the annual model change has been an important factor in driving the independents out of the U.S. market. These changes impose an additional cost on the smaller firms, which have to replace the dies used for stamping the car body before they are worn out, whereas the larger firms have to change these dies, which have an useful life of up to a million bodies anyway, so that the cost of a style change is correspondingly lower. Since model changes have a considerable effect on sales, the independents found themselves in a vicious circle of being repeatedly forced back along their cost curves away from volumes of production that would justify frequent model changes, by the model changes of the Big Three.

The second important factor is the need to supply a full range of models in order to attract dealers and to prevent customers from changing to another firm when they change price class. This led Studebaker-Packard to attempt to maintain a full line of products after the merger, but the difficulties of doing so at the levels of production that the firm was obtaining led it to abandon the effort after two years.

In Europe, two factors have led to increased competition in the automotive industry. First was the return of a buyer's market in the major producing countries in the late 1950s, leading to the emergence of excess capacity as the unusual postwar conditions were

TABLE 2.6

Average Annual Growth of New Registrations
(Sales) of Vehicles, 1950-71
(percent)

	1950-55	1955-60	1960-65	1965-71
West Germany	17.9	12.4	9.0	5.8
France	17.8	7.1	9.6	5.9
Italy	14.1	17.2	17.0	8.3
United Kingdom	22.4	9.3	5.8	1.8
United States	1.7	-1.6	7.6	1.3

Source: Motor Vehicle Manufacturers Association of the U.S.
Inc., 1971 World Motor Vehicle Data, p. 8.

finally eliminated. Second, as was indicated in the previous section,
tariff reductions led to a growth of international trade in vehicles,
and for the first time the major producers had to face competition
from imports in their domestic markets. That this competition was
in fact extremely vigorous is illustrated by the discriminatory pricing
policies of the companies, which, in their anxiety to penetrate new
markets, frequently sold their cars at lower prices abroad than in
their domestic markets (see Table 2.7).

From the end of World War II to the late 1950s, an European
car firm with a well-protected home market and an excess demand
for cars had little need to worry about consumer acceptance of its
product. As one observer put it, "Up until the early Sixties, car
manufacturers had only one problem: keeping up with demand."[40]
The leading firms, such as Renault and Volkswagen, survived and
grew, producing only one basic model, and were large enough to
reap all the significant economies of scale. Moreover, the favorable
market conditions of the 1950s reduced the risk involved in introducing
new models. The situation began to change as early as 1954. Until
that date, the major car-exporting countries concentrated on different geographic areas, with West Germany, Italy, and France having
their main markets in Europe and in its colonies, in the case of
France, while the United States supplied the Americas and Britain,
the Commonwealth.[41] In 1955, West German companies, particularly Volkswagen, began a vigorous worldwide export drive, and the
old pattern of market division started to break down.

The increased competition extended to Europe itself and to
the domestic markets of the major producers with the return of a
buyer's market and the lowering of tariffs during the late 1950s.
Wierzynski has summarized the consequences:

TABLE 2.7

Market Prices of Cars in Foreign Markets
as Percent of Domestic Market Price, 1966

	United Kingdom	France	Germany	Italy	Switzer-land
Mini	n.a.	124	95	95	93
Anglia	n.a.	96	–	100	96
Cortina	n.a.	97	–	126	99
Viva	n.a.	99	86	106	98
Imp	n.a.	108	94	110	97
Citroen DS	153	n.a.	95	120	117
Renault 10	122	n.a.	94	100	108
Volkswagen 1300	141	110	n.a.	116	122
Taunus 12M	162	117	n.a.	112	125
Fiat 500	138	126	101	n.a.	109
Fiat 1500	118	99	82	n.a.	102
Volvo 122S	91	98	77	82	81
Saab Sedan	83	91	69	85	81

Source: J. Paranson, Automotive Industries in Developing Countries, World Bank Staff Occasional Paper No. 8, 1969, Annex Table 10.

The new configurations in Europe have led manufacturers to put a new emphasis on marketing. The accent on engineering remains, but the shift towards styling, with annual changes has begun. . . . The life of a given model is coming down sharply; "facelifts"–small changes in styling and engineering–don't prolong life expectancy much any more.[42]

The increase in the range of models offered by the leading European firms is striking evidence of this. In 1961, Renault produced only one model, the Dauphine, on a large scale. In 1962, the Renault 4 and Renault 8 were introduced. Three years later, the company added two more models, the Renault 10 and the Renault 16, and, in 1968, the Renault 8S and 16TS. 1969 saw the introduction of the Renault 6-850 and 1970 two more models, the Renault 12 and the Renault 6-1100. Finally, in 1971, the Renault 12 Estate came on the market, and since then more new models have been added. Thus, in the space of a decade, the company moved from complete reliance on a single model to a whole new range of ten cars.

Renault is only the most spectacular illustration of the general tendency in the European automotive industry. Even a relatively small producer, such as Peugeot, increased its range from two to four basic models between 1960 and 1971. As mentioned above, Volkswagen's efforts to expand its range of models led to the take-over of Auto Union and NSU during the 1960s. Even without including models produced by the Audi-NSU-Auto Union subsidiary, the company had increased its model range from two in 1960 to eight by 1971. The heads of the leading companies are quite explicit regarding their policies of increasing the range of cars that they offer.[43]

On the marketing side there are two reasons why firms require a full line of models. First, there is the observed fact that when customers trade up to a more expensive car, they tend to buy the same make as they owned previously.[44] Thus, if a firm has a gap in its model range it will tend to lose customers who are then difficult to regain. Second, manufacturers prefer exclusive dealerships since this gives them greater control over, and bargaining power vis-a-vis, the dealers. This becomes difficult to impose without a full range since dealers wish to be able to meet the requirements of all customers. As the companies' operations become increasingly international, the need for a wide range of models in order to attract new dealers grows.

As well as the marketing advantages involved in a full line of models, such a policy also reduces risks. As indicated above, the costs of design and development for a new model are considerable and failure extremely expensive. The more competitive environment in which the European car manufacturer has operated for the last decade or more has tended to increase the risk of a new model being unsuccessful. For a one-model company such a failure would probably be fatal, whereas a more diversified firm is able to spread the risk. The future of Chrysler U.K. in the late 1960s hinged very much on the success or failure of the Avenger, and the situation would obviously have been much graver had it been an independent company.

For all the major European companies there is an evident conflict between the need to provide a full range of models and the need for large volumes to take advantage of scale economies. This is partially resolved by giving an appearance of diversity while using common parts in different models in order to attain longer runs. To take the example of Renault again, its range of 11 vehicles (including a van derivative) could be broken down into five different body styles and four different engines. Fiat, which has one of the widest model ranges in Europe, exchanges parts between different models and also has a policy of gradual alterations to keep its models up to date, which cuts both development costs and the gestation lag. Another method used to resolve this conflict is for two companies to get together to produce certain parts, as, for example, the Societe Franco-Suedoise de Moteurs, formed by Renault, Peugeot, and Volvo, which is intended eventually to produce an integrated range of engines.

A full model range and a shorter life for individual models have meant an increased rate of introduction of new models, which again makes life more difficult for the small firm. It is noticeable that mergers often occurred in the 1960s at a time when a new model needed to be introduced. The Chrysler takeover of Rootes came when the British company had recently introduced the Hillman Imp, the tooling for which had cost £9 million, and needed to replace the Minx range, which would have been a severe strain on the firm's financial resources. In fact, the problem can be traced back to an excessive initial dependence on a narrow range of 1,500 cc cars. The merger between BMC and Jaguar also came at a time when the latter needed to introduce a new engine and give a face-lift to most of its models. Similarly, in France, Fiat bought into Citroen when the latter needed to obtain capital in order to finance the introduction of the GS and fill the gap in its range, around 1,500 cc, which happened to be the most popular size class.

Thus it is possible to say that the explanation of concentration in the postwar period does not lie primarily in economies of scale at the plant level as it did before the war. Larger scales of produc- tion are not sought in order to reduce production costs but rather to enable a wider range of models to be offered and changes in models to be made more frequently. This drive has been brought about since the late 1950s by the increased competitiveness of the world automotive industry—a result of the slowdown in the rate of growth of demand in the major producing countries and the lowering of protective tariffs.

THE EXPANSION OF THE AUTOMOTIVE
INDUSTRY IN THE UNDERDEVELOPED AREAS

Despite the small share of the underdeveloped countries of Africa, Asia, and Latin America in world vehicle production, which was only 4.9 percent in 1969, and in the number of vehicles regis- tered, which was only 8.8 percent of the world total in the same year, the industry has been growing faster in these areas than in the developed countries. Between 1955 and 1969, the production of the developing countries increased at a rate of 18.9 percent per year, as compared to only 5.7 percent for the developed countries.[45]

TABLE 2.8

Number of Assembly Contracts by
Major Firms, 1968

	Total	Caribbean and Latin America	Asia	Africa
General Motors	24	9	6	2
Ford	32	8	8	4
Chrysler	31	10	9	2
Volkswagen	16	5	3	–
Fiat	28	5	5	5

Source: United Nations Industrial Development Organization
(UNIDO), The Motor Vehicle Industry (ID/78), 1972, p. 8.

The period since 1950 has seen a tremendous expansion of both
assembly and manufacturing operations in the underdeveloped
countries, with nearly 50 countries starting some form of automotive
industry.[46] As Table 2.8 indicates, this has involved a substantial
international extension of the operations of the major international
companies, which have set up assembly plants in countries previously
supplied by exports of assembled vehicles.

The more detailed breakdown of assembly operations by company and country given in the Appendix Table A.1, shows even more
clearly the way in which the operations of the leading companies have
been extended to the underdeveloped countries. Typically, the small
markets of the less developed countries are supplied by a number of
firms, with as many as 10 or more of the 15 firms listed operating
assembly plants either through licensed producers or subsidiaries.

What is the explanation of this rapid expansion of the automotive
industry in developing countries and especially the proliferation of
companies in a number of small markets? Unlike exports, expansion
into these areas through licensing agreements and subsidiaries
cannot be attributed to plant economies. There may, of course, be
economies in the initial stages through supplying parts to a local
assembly plant, although this may be a fairly small and short-lived
gain. There may also be economies for plant design work and some
overheads where plants duplicate production facilities and there is
no gain in terms of plant economies. Model design and development
costs, too, can be spread if the subsidiaries produce the same

models as the parent company.* Where markets are small, however, the effect on total costs for the firm will be insignificant, especially if account is taken of the higher costs of local production in the under-developed country.

The explanation is to be found in the nature of oligopolistic competition in the international automotive industry. As has been shown in the preceding sections, the industry has come to be domi-nated by a handful of firms at the world level. Competition has not ceased as a result, but has taken particular forms, such as model diversification and model changes. The firms in the industry are all conscious of the interdependence of their actions, but are not in a position to engage in collusion.

This situation can be clarified in terms of the theory of games.[47] For simplicity, it is assumed that there are only two players, A and B (representing two companies). Each player has a choice of two strategies, either to export finished vehicles to a particular under-developed country or to assemble them locally. Because of the small size of the local market, assembly costs are higher than the costs of direct exports. If any firm sets up an assembly plant, however, it will receive tariff protection from competing exports. The payoffs, which can be assumed to represent rates of return, can be set out as follows:

| | Player A | |
Player B	Export	Assembly
Export	20, 20	25, 10
Assembly	10, 25	15, 15

As can be seen, the collusive situation is for both firms to continue exporting. However, each firm has an incentive to set up an assem-bly plant, because if the other firm does not do so, its profit rate will be increased. If both firms follow mini-max strategies, however, they will both assemble locally and both be worse off than in the cooperative solution. This is the classic case of the "prisoner's dilemma."

The example is oversimplified in two respects. In the first place, the situation will not be one of duopoly, but of oligopoly. This will tend to reduce the likelihood of a cooperative solution being attained, since it only needs one firm to choose the assembly strategy

---

*General Motors and Ford planned to introduce small cars in the United States in 1946, but these were canceled and appeared in 1948 as the Australian Holden and the French Ford Vedette.

for all others to be better off if they follow suit. This is just another way of saying that the more firms there are in an industry, the less likely they are to be able to arrive at a joint-profit maximizing solution. The second qualification is that these decisions are not made once and for all, as in the case of the prisoner's dilemma. Although a decision to assemble locally might be regarded as irreversible, at least over a period of several years, the decision to continue exporting can be changed within a year or two. There will still be an incentive to set up a local assembly plant if the short-run profits that can be made before other firms enter are sufficiently large.

The analysis can be brought nearer to the real world by considering a small underdeveloped country, say Uruguay, which it is assumed imports fully assembled cars from the United States, Britain, France, West Germany, and Italy. A company that exports to Uruguay knows that if one of its competitors should invest in an assembly plant there, it will obtain tariff protection that would make finished imports prohibitively expensive. The first company to invest, moreover, will be able to make large profits until other firms enter the market, so that there is an incentive to attempt to preempt the market by entering first. This will be accentuated if a Japanese company that does not at present export to Uruguay is interested in setting up a plant in order to break into the market. Thus, although the optimum situation from the point of view of the firms at present exporting is to continue to do so because of the small size of the market, this situation is not stable. If the oligopoly was sufficiently stable for collusion, either explicit or implicit, then the result would be different. There would be no local investment until the market was large enough for all (or most) of the firms to enter.[48]

There is considerable evidence available by now to support such a model of foreign investment. It has been tested empirically by F. T. Knickerbocker with data from the Harvard Multinational Enterprise Project.[49] Using a measure of the extent to which firms in the same industry followed each other into particular markets, he concluded that such "oligopolistic reaction" increased with industry concentration, except at very high levels of concentration when it fell somewhat as a result of collusion becoming possible. A second important determinant of the extent of oligopolistic reaction was the stability of the industry in terms of the number of firms becoming overseas manufacturers for the first time in the postwar period.

Knickerbocker's analysis, of necessity, is limited since he was only able to use data relating to the foreign operations of U.S.

multinational corporations and related these data to data on concentration in the U.S. economy. Looking at the international automotive industry (which, it has been argued, is the relevant unit) rather than the U.S. automotive industry, it appears that the level of concentration and relative lack of stability as a result of the entry of West European and Japanese companies as international producers have given rise to a high level of oligopolistic reaction. This model of defensive investment by international oligopolists in order to protect export markets threatened by local assembly by their competitors is further supported by studies of the decision to invest abroad, based on interviews or questionnaires, which have shown it to be an important motive in many cases.[50] As a result, considerations of market size are not important in the decision of follower firms to expand abroad.[51] In Nigeria, for example, P. Kilby found that there was no necessary relationship between the size of the local market relative to the minimum efficient scale of plant and the decision of foreign firms to set up in certain industries, but that there was a tendency for several firms to follow the first entrant.[52]

It seems, therefore, that oligopolistic interdependence can explain a considerable amount of foreign investment in manufacturing industry. It also seems a plausible explanation of the rapid growth of overseas assembly and manufacturing operations by the major automotive companies in the postwar period. The evidence suggests that many underdeveloped countries could be supplied at a lower cost from the point of view of the companies by exports, but the choice is not usually one between exports and investment, but one between investment and losing the market to competitors. As General Motors Vice-President T. A. Murphy said in evidence to the Senate Subcommittee on International Trade, "There is no question that if General Motors or other U.S. automotive firms were to turn their backs on market participation through overseas facilities, multinational firms based in other countries would be alert and quick to act to fill the need."[53] In practice, the situation is also complicated by the role played by host governments that may actively try to precipitate the decision to invest, either by restricting imports or by playing on the fears of the major companies that a rival will steal a march on them.[54] Host governments also have frequently been persuaded by the large number of companies that have invested in an excessively small market to pass on the costs to the local consumer by providing sufficient tariff protection to enable them to charge correspondingly high prices. Thus, the losses to the companies of failing to achieve a cooperative solution are minimized.

THE OIL CRISIS AND FUTURE DEVELOPMENTS IN THE INTERNATIONAL AUTOMOTIVE INDUSTRY

Since 1973, the sharp increase in the price of gasoline has had a major impact on the development of the automotive industry. The most obvious manifestation of this has been the substantial reduction in sales and production of cars in 1974 when the effects of price increases made themselves felt. In that year, production was down on 1973 levels by 22 percent in West Germany, 5 percent in France, 11 percent in Italy, 12 percent in Great Britain, 24 percent in the United States, and 12 percent in Japan. Not surprisingly, demand shifted toward cars with a lower fuel consumption so that, whereas sales of most models fell, those with an engine capacity of less than 1 liter tended to increase. The commercial vehicle market remained much firmer and production increased in France, Italy, and Japan and fell less sharply than car production in the other countries.

It has already been noted that the reduction in the growth of car sales in the main producing countries during the 1960s and early 1970s led to increased competition and concentration in the industry. The recession of 1974 is likely to accentuate this trend, putting pressure on the smaller firms that will find it difficult to maintain their profitability and facing shrinking markets and the attempts of the larger firms to maintain their production levels. Moreover, the smaller firms are less able to carry losses if these are sustained for any length of time. Already the financial difficulties of Citroen in France have led to the government-sponsored takeover by Peugeot and the merger of Berliet with Saviem, together with an injection of F130 million in cash to stave off bankruptcy. In the Netherlands, the national automotive company DAF only survived through being taken over by Volvo, while in the United Kingdom the already serious problems of British Leyland have been accentuated by the crisis.

A number of alternatives face the automotive manufacturers in this situation. Further mergers, both within countries where possible and across national boundaries as in the case of Volvo and DAF, seem likely. Alternatively, the weaker producers may seek closer links with the state, as in the case of British Leyland. A third alternative of diversification into nonautomotive products is difficult because of low profits, which means that firms have only limited funds for new investment. Thus, the most likely outcome of the present crisis for the industry is a reduction in the number of firms and closer links with the state.

One significant aspect of the developments observed in the international automotive industry during 1974 is the continued expansion of car production in a number of peripheral economies despite the recession in the major producing countries. In Brazil, for instance, car production was up by 11 percent and production of all vehicles by 18 percent, while in Mexico the number of cars produced increased by 24 percent over 1973. Other countries in which vehicle output increased were the USSR, Spain, Australia, Czechoslovakia, and Poland. This suggests that another effect of the crisis will be a further internationalization of the automotive industry as production expands outside the traditional centers of the United States, Western Europe, and Japan. Further growth for the major companies is likely to depend increasingly on participation in the automotive industries of Eastern Europe and the underdeveloped countries. Fiat, for instance, saw the sales of its domestic plants drop by 12 percent in 1974, while its production overseas increased by 12 percent.

The need to internationalize further is also likely to accentuate the trend toward concentration among the major companies. Firms such as British Leyland, which has been forced to withdraw from expanding markets in Spain and Australia, are likely to find themselves under increasing pressure at home as their worldwide production falls behind that of more favorably placed companies. Thus, an intensification of competition, both at home and abroad, appears likely in the immediate future until a more tightly knit oligopoly emerges in the industry.

CONCLUSION

This chapter has indicated the way in which an international automotive industry had been formed by the 1960s, in contrast to the primarily national industries of the interwar years. A consequence of this development has been the expansion of the operations of the major companies to a large number of underdeveloped countries, which provide the best prospects for rapid future growth. In order to survive, companies have had to become international, and the need to operate on an international scale has led to further concentration of production. Despite its oligopolistic structure, however, the industry has remained competitive and the struggle between the major producers is occurring in every corner of the world.

NOTES

1. G. Maxcy and A. Silberston, The Motor Industry (London: Allen & Unwin, 1959), p. 11.

2. R. F. Lanzillotti, "The Automobile Industry," in The Structure of American Industry, 3rd ed., ed. W. Adams (New York: Macmillan, 1961), p. 312.

3. G. Maxcy, "The Motor Industry," in Effects of Mergers, ed. L. Cook (London: Allen & Unwin, 1958), p. 360.

4. S. Hirsch, Location of Industry and International Competitiveness (Oxford: Clarendon Press, 1967), Chap. 2.

5. J. B. Rae, American Automobile Manufacturers (New York: Chilton, 1959), Chap. 1.

6. Lanzillotti, op. cit., Table 2.

7. D. Creamer, "Capital and Output Trends in Manufacturing Industries, 1880-1948," National Bureau of Economic Research, Occasional Paper 41 (New York, 1954). Quoted in Maxcy and Silberston, op. cit., pp. 207-09.

8. D. G. Rhys, The Motor Industry: An Economic Survey (London: Butterworths, 1972), pp. 15-17.

9. Rae, op. cit., Chap. 3.

10. Maxcy, op. cit., Table II.

11. I. Svennilson, Growth and Stagnation in the European Economy (Geneva: Economic Commission for Europe, 1954), p. 15.

12. Maxcy and Silberston, op. cit., pp. 14, 99.

13. Svennilson, op. cit., p. 151.

14. Ibid., pp. 150-51.

15. Ibid., pp. 151-52.

16. Rhys, op. cit., p. 376.

17. L. J. White, The Automobile Industry Since 1945 (Cambridge, Mass.: Harvard University Press, 1971), p. 13.

18. For more details on the elimination of the independents, see C. E. Edwards, Dynamics of the United States Automobile Industry (Colombia, S.C.: University of South Carolina Press, 1965).

19. Letters from Ford U.S. to Ford U.K., quoted in The Economist 197 (November 19, 1960), p. 803.

20. For a detailed theoretical analysis of internationalization, see C. Palloix, "The Internationalization of Capital," mimeographed. Palloix distinguishes the internationalization of the circuit of commodity capital, the circuit of productive capital, and the circuit of money capital.

21. This corresponds to the internationalization of the circuit of commodity capital in Palloix's terminology. Palloix, ibid., pp. 11-12.

22. White, op. cit., Tables A.2 and A.3.

23. W. J. Karssen, "Concentration in the Automobile Industry of the EEC," in U.S., Congress, Subcommittee on Antitrust and Monopoly, Economic Concentration, vol. 7a, 1968, pp. 3915-25.

24. This corresponds to the internationalization of the circuit of money capital in Palloix's terminology. See Palloix, op. cit., pp. 5-9.

25. UNIDO, The Motor Vehicle Industry (ID/78), 1972, p. 8.

26. As early as 1963, the Economist Intelligence Unit commented on this phenomenon. See "Changes in the Ownership of the European Motor Industry," Motor Business 36 (1963).

27. This corresponds to Palloix's concept of the internationalization of the circuit of productive capital. See Palloix, op. cit., pp. 9-11.

28. See letters from Ford U.S. to Ford U.K., op. cit., p. 25.

29. Hoffman estimated an optimum of 100,000 units per year in 1939. See White, op. cit., p. 51. Rhys contrasts the optimum output of presses today of 2 million with a figure of 250,000 before 1939. See Rhys, op. cit., p. 289.

30. See J. K. Galbraith, The New Industrial State (London: Hamilton, 1967), p. 11.

31. For further details, see White, op. cit., Chap. 3.

32. See Rhys, op. cit., p. 300.

33. See Galbraith, op. cit., p. 11.

34. White, op. cit., p. 37.

35. D. G. Rhys, personal communication, 1973.

36. U.S., Department of Labor, Bureau of Labor Statistics, Technological Trends in Major American Industries, Bulletin No. 1474 (Washington, D.C.: Government Printing Office, 1966), pp. 97-102.

37. White, op. cit., p. 33.

38. Rhys, op. cit., pp. 309-10.

39. C. E. Edwards and H. G. Vatter, "The Closure of Entry in the American Automobile Industry," Oxford Economic Papers (1952): 213-34; J. A. Menge, "Style Change Costs as a Market Weapon," Quarterly Economic Journal 76 (1962): 632-47.

40. G. H. Wierzynski, "The Battle for the European Auto Market," Fortune 77 (1968): 119.

41. Rhys, op. cit., p. 383.

42. Wierzynski, op. cit., p. 121.

43. See the statements by Lotz of Volkswagen and Dreyfus of Renault in Wierzynski, ibid., 142.

44. In the United States, between 40 and 70 percent of car purchases are repeats, that is, from the same firm as the previously owned car. See White, op. cit., p. 103.

45. J. Baranson, "International Transfer of Automotive Technology to Developing Countries," United Nations Institute for Training and Research (UNITAR), Research Reports, no. 8 (New York, 1971): 81-83.

46. UNIDO, op. cit., p. 39.

47. For the application of game theory to oligopolistic
situations, see M. Shubik, Strategy and Market Structure: Competition, Oligopoly and the Theory of Games (New York: Wiley, 1959).

48. This is similar to White's analysis of the introduction
of the compact by the U.S. companies. See White, op. cit.,
pp. 171-78.

49. F. T. Knickerbocker, Oligopolistic Reaction and Multinational Enterprise (Cambridge, Mass.: Harvard Graduate School
of Business Administration, 1973).

50. See F. J. Robinson, The Motivation and Flow of Private
Foreign Investment (Stanford, Calif.: Stanford Research Institute,
1961); and Y. Aharoni, The Foreign Investment Decision Process
(Cambridge, Mass.: Harvard Graduate School of Business Administration, 1966).

51. Knickerbocker, op. cit., pp. 125-38.

52. P. Kilby, Industrialization in an Open Economy: Nigeria,
1945-1966 (Cambridge: Cambridge University Press, 1969),
pp. 53-80.

53. U.S., Senate, Subcommittee on International Trade of
the Committee on Finance, 1973.

54. Most of the automotive industry development programs
in Latin America involved restrictions on imports of assembled
vehicles. A recent example of a host government playing on
company fears that a rival will preempt the market is the Lebanonese
where the government and local bankers have encouraged British
Leyland to set up an assembly plant by suggesting that if it does
not do so, the Japanese will. See Counter Information Service,
British Leyland: The Beginning of the End? CIS Anti-Report, No. 5,
1973, p. 40.

CHAPTER

3

THE SPREAD OF
THE AUTOMOTIVE
INDUSTRY TO
LATIN AMERICA

Chapter 2 discusses the major developments that have taken place in the international automotive industry over the last half century, and more especially since about 1960. Chapter 3 now gives a brief explanation of the way in which these developments have affected the area that is the main focus of interest of this study—Latin America. In this chapter, therefore, the main features of the spread of the automotive industry to Latin America are set out and the chief characteristics of the industries as of the early 1970s are summarized.

THE ASSEMBLY PHASE

The historical origins of the automotive industry in Latin America can be traced back to the first Ford plant set up in Buenos Aires in 1916 (although there had been some previous attempts at local assembly*). Ford was the leading firm in the early development of the industry, opening assembly plants in Chile (1924), Brazil (1925, 1926, and 1927), and Mexico (1926); by 1927, there were 11 Ford companies and branches in Latin America.[1] During the late 1920s and early 1930s, Ford was followed by the other major U.S. companies, General Motors and Chrysler. In some cases, such as the original Ford plant in Argentina, local assembly occurred because of the savings in transport costs that could be made without any tariff protection.[2] By the early 1930s, however,

---

*Between 1906 and 1911, a local entrepreneur, by the name of Anasagasti, had assembled vehicles using Bleriot parts imported from France.

48

Argentina, Brazil, and Mexico all provided some degree of protection for local assembly. For example, in Argentina in 1931 the
tariff on imports of unassembled cars was 30 percent less than that
on assembled vehicles and 15 percent less than that on semiassembled
vehicles.[3]

As was suggested in Chapter 2, the growth of vehicle exports
during the interwar period can be explained by the drive to achieve
lower costs in the face of economies of scale on the part of the major
companies. Since the most important scale economies were in
processes other than final assembly, given a certain volume of
demand, local assembly could prove profitable. Estimates for
Argentina during the early 1930s suggest that a firm needed sales
of about 3,000 to 4,000 cars a year for assembly operations to be
worthwhile.[4] Only Ford, General Motors, and Chrysler enjoyed
sufficiently large demand; moreover, the European companies that
still had room for expansion in their domestic markets were less
concerned to find overseas outlets. As a result, the Latin American
automotive industry came to be completely dominated by the U.S.
companies during the interwar period.

As noted, the traditional division of world markets began to
break down around 1954. The implication of this for U.S. hegemony
in the Latin American automotive industry is vividly demonstrated
by the case of Argentina. In the 1920s and 1930s, the United States
accounted for over 90 percent of Argentina's imports of vehicles.
The postwar period saw a reduction in U.S. dominance, and, during
1951-54, its share of vehicle imports fell to 61.6 percent. After
1954, the fall became even more pronounced, so that, in 1955-58,
the United States accounted for only 22.3 percent of the total. The
dollar shortage, gasoline rationing, and, after 1956, lower import
duties on small vehicles all tended to favor the European producers.
Because the Big Three imported cars from their European (especially
German) subsidiaries, these figures exaggerate the reduction in
their market share. Nevertheless, they do indicate the way in which
Latin America became a battleground in the competitive struggle
within the automotive industry.

Another development that had its origins during World War II,
when Latin American imports of cars and parts were cut off, was
the growth of a substantial industry manufacturing spare parts, in
order to keep the existing fleet of vehicles operating. These began
as small workshops, operating virtually as cottage industry, but
they provided a basis on which a supplier industry could later be
developed. In the postwar period, some of these parts began to be
used by the assembly plants as original equipment.

The increased competition within the world automotive industry
and its extension to Latin America during the 1950s, together with

the development of an embryonic parts industry, meant that the circumstances were particularly propitious for governments that wished to develop a local industry during this period. The drive for overseas expansion was such that even relatively small markets (in 1955, the Latin American market absorbed less than 200,000 vehicles, equally divided between cars and commercial vehicles) could not be ignored. Thus, when governments began to use tariffs and local content requirements to cut off imports and started to offer incentives to firms to manufacture vehicles locally, a stream of defensive investments was forthcoming.

In the prewar period, protective measures were not able to do more than shift final assembly to Latin America, the incorporation of local parts being minimal, since the underlying dynamic of overseas expansion was the need of the parent company to achieve economies of scale in production. The new dynamic behind expansion in the postwar period, in which plant economies played a less crucial role, made it possible for the larger countries to enforce extremely high local content requirements and still attract the major multinational companies. (It is interesting to note in this context that both Ford and General Motors had sales approaching 20,000 units a year in Argentina in the late 1920s and continued to assemble vehicles, whereas, in the postwar period, many companies have begun manufacturing operations in Latin America at much lower levels of output.)

Another aspect of the relationship between the competitive struggle in the advanced countries and the development of the automotive industry in Latin America was the export of plants by companies that had been driven out of the industry in the developed countries in order to set up subsidiaries or independent companies. This is illustrated by the case of Industrias Kaiser Argentina, the first company to start manufacturing, as opposed to assembling, motor vehicles on the continent.

Kaiser-Frazer had attempted to enter the U.S. market immediately after World War II, but was one of the first of the independents to be hit as a result of the return of normal market conditions in 1953. Kaiser originally submitted a proposal to set up a factory to the Argentinian government in September 1954 but, with the fall of Perón a year later, some amendments had to be made and the contract was finally signed in January 1956. Kaiser provided the plant that was shipped from the United States in its entirety, and full production was planned at 40,000 vehicles a year with a local content of 60 percent of total vehicle weight. The company setup had a majority local shareholding, part private and part government, while Kaiser had a minority holding. (A similar strategy was followed in setting up Willys-Overland de Brasil.)

In Mexico, a local group of businessmen bought the Borgward plant after that company's failure in Germany in an attempt to set up an independent Mexican automotive company.

GOVERNMENT POLICY AND THE GROWTH OF THE LATIN AMERICAN AUTOMOTIVE INDUSTRY

A number of factors prompted the governments of the large Latin American countries to develop local manufacture of vehicles and the other countries to require assemblers to incorporate gradually local parts. In most cases the dominating consideration was the need to save foreign exchange, since either vehicle imports were a substantial share of total imports or they were being kept down by quotas or prohibitive tariffs with the result that the supply was extremely restricted. During the 1950s, imports of vehicles and parts accounted for 11 percent of Mexico's total imports,[5] and in Brazil there was a similar proportion during the immediate postwar period (1945-52).[6] In Argentina, on the other hand, vehicle imports were strictly controlled, and, as a result, there was a severe shortage of new vehicles and a deterioration in the age structure of the existing stock. (See Chapter 6.) Over time, these problems were accentuated as the demand for vehicles grew with rising incomes.

Despite the existence of some potential parts suppliers, the incorporation of locally produced parts was extremely limited during the early postwar years. The existing assembly plants were organized in order to assemble imported knocked-down units and failed to act as a catalyst for the development of local suppliers.[7] In Mexico, for example, the few parts that were bought locally, such as tires or batteries, were usually the result of government incentives or requirements. Consequently, there was little saving in foreign exchange as a result of local assembly operations.

A rough estimate of the total amount saved by the Mexican automotive industry in 1961 illustrates this point. The total output of cars assembled in the country in that year, valued at prices in the country of origin, came to $69 million, while direct imports of parts for local assembly were $42.5 million, to which one might add an estimated $5.7 million in indirect imports. The valuation of output was made at prices to the public in the country of origin, however, rather than at wholesale prices, which are the relevant ones for calculating the foreign exchange saving.

A deduction of 20 percent was made to allow for the dealer's margin and local taxes (this would seem to be a very conservative estimate). In order to take account of transport costs to Mexico, this deduction was reduced to 15 percent. (An estimate of 5 percent for the additional costs of delivery to Mexico does not seem excessively low since most vehicles were of U.S. origin.) This reduces the value of local production to $58.6 million and the exchange saving to $10.4 million.

So far, no account has been taken of capital flows resulting from local production. If royalty and license payments are 5 percent of the price to the public of a vehicle, there is a further $3.5 million outflow, leaving a net saving of only $6.9 million to offset against that part of the $10.2 million profit remitted abroad. Assuming that 50 percent of profits were remitted, the total saving for foreign exchange would be only $1.8 million.[8]

A second important motive behind government measures to promote vehicle manufacturing in Latin America was a desire to create new employment opportunities. Assembly plants alone had little employment-generating effect since they depended almost entirely on imports of parts. For example, in Argentina, in 1956, the terminal industry employed 4,449 people,[9] and in Mexico it employed about 4,000 in 1949,[10] increasing to 7,000 by 1960.[11] It was felt, moreover, that automotive manufacture was a particularly appropriate industry to develop from this point of view because of its backward and forward linkage effects that would stimulate the parts industry, the steel industry, petroleum refining, and so on.

A further consideration that recommended the automotive industry for import substitution was its technological progressiveness, which appealed to governments anxious to modernize their industrial structure. The intercountry demonstration effect cannot be left out of the analysis altogether. Given the political rivalry between Argentina and Brazil for influence in Latin America, it was inevitable that if one developed an automotive industry, the other would soon follow suit. Similarly, the development of the automotive industry in these countries both indicated the possibilities open to Mexico and put pressure on the Mexican government to develop its own industry in order to withstand Argentinian and Brazilian efforts within the Latin American Free Trade Area (LAFTA) to open the Mexican market to their car exports.

As a result of these internal pressures and the favorable external environment, the Latin American countries began to require higher levels of local content in their vehicles from the mid-1950s onward. The first country to undertake a systematic development of the automotive industry was Brazil with a decree passed in 1956 that set up the Grupo Ejecutivo de la Industria Automovilística (GEIA) and formulated the norms that were to be applied to the industry.

TABLE 3.1

Local Content Requirements in the Brazilian
Automotive Industry
(percent weight)

1956	35 - 50
1957	40 - 60
1958	65 - 75
1959	75 - 85
1960	90 - 95
1961	95 - 99

Sources: Comisión de Estudios Económicos de la Industria
Automotriz, La Industria Automotriz Argentina; Asociación de
Fálsricas de Automotores, Informe Económico 1969 (Buenos Aires:
ADEFA, 1969), p. 93.

The level of local content aimed at initially was 35 percent
for trucks and 50 percent for cars, rising to 90 and 95 percent by
1960 and 98 and 99 percent, respectively, by 1961, which was, to
all intents and purposes, achieved by 1962 (see Table 3.1). The
basis on which this content was to be calculated was the weight
of the vehicle. Companies setting up in Brazil were offered a
number of incentives, including exemptions from duties for the
permitted imports of parts and from duties and taxes for imported
machinery and equipment, as well as classification as basic industries to qualify for assistance from the National Development Bank.
Argentina soon followed suit with Decree 3693 in 1959, which
set a framework for the organization of the industry over a five-year
period. It gave certain advantages to firms that submitted production
plans for the local manufacture of cars and trucks and met a required
level of incorporation of local parts. Table 3.2 indicates the maximum percentage of the CIF (cost, insurance, and freight) value of
vehicles that could be imported at a preferential rate under the
decree.
In category A, the duty charged on the percentage indicated
in each year was to be 20 percent on the CIF value, while a further
5 percent could be imported at a 100 percent duty and the remainder
up to 60 percent at 300 percent. For the other categories, the
preferential rate was 40 percent and again the remainder up to
60 percent could be imported at 300 percent. A further 10 percent
of the annual amount imported was allowed to cover losses and
replacement of parts with an import duty of 100 percent. In 1960,

TABLE 3.2

Permitted Imports in the Argentinian
Automotive Industry
(percent CIF value)

		1960	1961	1962	1963	1964
A	Commercial vehicles	45	40	35	30	20
B	Cars 190-750 cc	45	40	35	25	10
C	Cars 750-1,500 cc	40	35	30	20	10
D	Cars 1,500-2,500 cc	35	30	25	15	10
E	Cars more than 2,500 cc	30	25	20	15	10
F	Others	20	15	10	5	5

Source: Industrias Kaiser Argentina, La Industria Automotriz Argentina (Buenos Aires: 1963), pp. 34-35.

imports of assembled vehicles were prohibited, although a nominal rate of protection was fixed at between 400 and 500 percent for cars and 35 to 40 percent for trucks.[12]

Foreign firms setting up in the automotive industry also benefited from Law 14,780 of 1958, which had been passed by the Frondizi government to attract more foreign investment to Argentina. This law permitted foreign companies to make their investment in the form of goods and equipment or patents and immaterial goods necessary for the firm's production, as well as in foreign exchange, and guaranteed equal judicial treatment to foreign and local capital. This law led to a substantial inflow of foreign investment to Argentina. Between 1959 and 1961, almost U.S. $400 million was approved by the government, of which 25 percent was in the automotive industry.[13]

The Mexican government, worried by the large variety of makes being assembled in the country (44 in 1960), began to reorganize the automotive industry by prohibiting imports of cars selling at over 55,000 pesos, so that by 1962, the number had been reduced to 22. This was followed by the decree of August 25, 1962 that required 60 percent of the direct costs of vehicles* to be accounted for in Mexico, included in which had to be the engine, by 1964. A further decree in 1963 completely exempted the automotive industry from paying import duties on machinery and equipment for five years

---

*Direct costs is defined as raw materials and parts, lubricants and power used in production, wages of workers employed directly in production, and depreciation.

and on raw materials, parts, and components for four years, followed by two three-year periods during which exemptions of 50 and 25 percent were granted on imported inputs. Finally, the federal assembly tax was reduced by 80 percent. The industry remained subject to government quotas unless a level of local integration in excess of 70 percent was achieved. Thus, by the mid-1960s, there were three Latin American countries that could be said to be manufacturing and not assembling vehicles.

This same period, the late 1950s and early 1960s, saw the development of assembly industries with varying degrees of incorporation of locally produced parts in a number of other countries in the region. The initial development of an automotive industry in Chile during the 1950s occurred in Arica in the extreme north of the country. The area had been declared a free port in the early 1950s, essentially for political reasons.* However, this did not prove a very satisfactory mechanism for integrating Arica into the Chilean economy, the main consequence being the development of a considerable illicit traffic in imported luxury consumer goods.

The government response was to attempt to promote industrial development in the region, and a number of promotional decrees were passed that led to several assembly plants being set up in Arica during the late 1950s and early 1960s. In 1962, Decree 835 attempted to introduce a semblance of order into this system. The Comisión para el Fomento de la Industria Automotriz was set up as the government body in charge of the development of the automotive industry. National content requirements were set on the basis of FOB (free on board) prices in the country of origin and a certain percentage for assembly and finishing (see Table 3.3). Equally significant, vehicles were removed from the list of permitted imports in January of the same year.

This decree applied only to cars, vans, station wagons, and pickups, and it was not until Decree 507 of 1966 that similar conditions were laid down for the assembly of chassis for trucks and buses. This set the local content requirements given in Table 3.4.

Venezuela had a vehicle assembly industry from 1948, but until 1963, the main source of supply continued to be imports of completely assembled vehicles. In December 1962, imports were prohibited almost completely and a local content requirement

---

*It had been taken from Peru in the War of the Pacific in 1884 and many of the inhabitants still looked northward to Lima rather than toward Santiago. Moreover, it was also a part of the country where the left attracted considerable support and was thus doubly sensitive politically.

TABLE 3.3

Local Content Requirements for
Chilean Cars, 1963-70
(percent FOB value)

1963	30.0	1967	55.0
1964	36.6	1968	57.9
1965	41.1	1969	57.9
1966	50.0	1970	57.9

Source: Gamma Ingenieros, Estudio de la Industria Automotriz Chilena, UNIDO (ID/WG 76/6), 1970, p. 10.

imposed. Initially, this was extremely low, but, by 1969, it had reached 38.5 percent of the weight of the vehicle for cars. Local assembly did not begin in Peru until 1965 under a decree issued two years earlier that required a 30 percent national content to be achieved within five years of starting production. Colombia relied mainly on imports for its supply of vehicles for most of the period. Two firms were set up in the early 1960s under special contracts with the government, but production only began to achieve significant levels toward the end of the decade. There are no precise local content requirements, but in practice it appears to vary between 23 and 30 percent. Of the other Latin American countries, Uruguay and Costa Rica have some local assembly but at extremely low levels of output.

The most immediate consequence of these developments was the mushrooming of firms in virtually every country following the passing of the various promotional laws. Argentina attracted more firms than any other country, with 21 automotive manufacturers in 1960. It was closely followed by Chile with 20 (1962); then came Venezuela (16), Peru (13), and Brazil (11). Only in Mexico, where two of the firms authorized to produce withdrew, was the number kept below double figures with eight firms starting production. (As noted, Colombia did not have any specific automotive industry legislation.)

It was suggested in Chapter 2 that the nature of competition in the international automotive industry is such that the decision of one firm to invest in a particular country will precipitate a similar decision on the part of a number of other firms, giving rise to exactly this kind of market fragmentation. It is relevant here to ask whether government policy could have prevented market fragmentation. Some writers have suggested that the large number of firms attracted to the automotive industry in these countries was the result of excessively generous incentives offered by host governments,[14] and that a better solution would have been achieved if only a more appropriate level of incentives had been offered.

Such a conclusion implicitly assumes a continuous function relating the number of firms attracted (or, even more dubiously, the amount of investment generated, which assumes perfect divisibility of capital) to the level of incentives and, by extension, to the expected rate of profit. This may be true under conditions of perfect competition, but under oligopoly the interdependence of firm reactions makes nonsense of such conclusions, as was seen above. In fact, the relation between the number of firms entering the industry and the level of government incentives is highly discontinuous. At a low level of incentives, no firms are likely to enter, but once a certain level is reached and one firm finds it profitable to enter, its competitors will tend to follow suit to avoid seeing the market preempted. This appears to be the characteristic form of oligopolistic behavior exhibited in the automotive industry.

Of course, it is impossible to know in any given case what would have happened at a given moment in time had the level of incentives offered been different from what they were. The uniformity of the response in the different Latin American countries suggests that there must be some systematic mechanism at work rather than merely each country in turn offering excessively generous incentives. One of the main features of the legislation in each of the countries concerned was that it was accompanied by measures to ban or severely limit imports of vehicles, and that this meant that international firms were faced with the choice of either investing locally or abandoning the market.

TABLE 3.4

Local Content Requirements for Chilean
Commercial Vehicles, 1966-70
(percent FOB value)

4/29/66 to 12/31/66	25.0
1/1/67 to 6/30/67	30.0
7/1/67 to 6/30/68	37.5
7/1/68 to 6/30/69	47.5
7/1/69 to 6/30/70	50.0

Source: Gamma Ingenieros, Estudio de la Industria Automotriz Chilena, UNIDO (I D/WG 76/6), 1970, p. 10.

The importance of this fact is well illustrated by the statements of F. G. Donner, chairman of General Motors, concerning the decision of his company to invest in Argentina. After World War II, the General Motors Overseas Policy Group concluded that assembly would be economically more sound than manufacturing, given the lack of auxiliary industry and essential raw materials in the country. The reason why this decision was revised was the prohibition of imports. "For General Motors, and a number of other vehicle producers, the question was whether to manufacture in Argentina or abandon the market."[15] Of course, there had been previous periods of severe import restrictions in Argentina. The difference this time was that the creation of a domestic industry threatened to exclude from the market permanently firms that did not invest, since high entry barriers, both natural and artificial, were likely to develop, preventing entry at a later date. This seems to indicate a pattern of interdependent behavior of the kind that was suggested above.

If, then, the oligopolistic international industry leads to a large number of firms wishing to enter the market when an under-developed country begins to develop a local automotive industry, the question then arises of why the host governments did not take direct measures to limit the number of firms entering the industry, for example, through investment licensing. Even such staunch opponents of government intervention as I. Little, T. Scitovsky, and M. Scott admit the need for investment control in such a case and specifically mention the automotive industry as an example.[16] The extent of which governments attempted to screen investment proposals varied from country to country. Argentina and Brazil, for example, were particularly lax, permitting all firms that met the legal requirements to start production. In Mexico, on the other hand, only 10 of the 18 projects put forward to the government were approved, and 2 subsequently withdrew. (Among the firms that submitted proposals but did not start production in Mexico were Peugeot, Volvo, Hillman, Citroen, Toyota, and Mercedes-Benz.)

Despite attempting to screen the proposals submitted, it is noticeable that even the Mexican government failed to reduce the number of companies to the level that the market would have been able to support at a reasonably efficient scale of production. The government ignored detailed work by its own technicians on exactly this point, which showed that the maximum number of models that should be produced in the country was five.[17]

The reason usually given for not limiting the number of entrants is that competition would eliminate the least efficient firms and, at the same time, bring about price reductions.[18] But, as the same semiofficial Mexican study pointed out, the objection to this is that foreign subsidiaries can produce at a loss in the hope of achieving a larger market in the future while offsetting these losses against the tax liabilities of the parent.[19] The real reason for failing to adopt stricter measures of control is the inability of host governments to withstand external pressure and the effect that such measures would have on the "climate for foreign investment."[20]

The effect of the various promotional programs has been a substantial growth of vehicle production in Latin America. The output of cars and trucks rose from 60,912 in 1955 to 1,478,150 in 1973, an increase of 24 times in less than two decades.* What is more, the vehicles produced in 1955 were mainly only assembled locally, most of the parts being imported, whereas, by 1973, almost 90 percent of local production was manufacturing production, in the sense of having over 60 percent national content. The increase in value added in Latin America is, therefore, even more spectacular. At the same time, there has been a shift in emphasis from commercial vehicles to passenger cars. Whereas in 1955 slightly more than half of total production was of commercial vehicles, by 1973, passenger cars accounted for approximately two thirds of output (see Appendix Table B.2).

There was also a sharp rise in the number of vehicles in circulation in Latin America from 2,727,542 in 1955 to 12,453,934 in 1972, a more than fourfold increase (see Appendix Table B.3).† Until the late 1950s, the stock of vehicles had grown relatively slowly at only about 7 percent per year, whereas since then the rate of growth has been stepped up to about 10 percent. As a result, the Latin American share of the world's automotive vehicles increased from 2.7 to 4.4 percent over the period. As might have been expected from the data on production, passenger cars have shown a more rapid growth than commercial vehicles.

Local production still has not completely replaced imports of vehicles to the continent, and, in the late 1960s, these were running at about 100,000 a year, a relatively small decrease under the circumstances from the 135,000 imported in 1955 (see Appendix Table B.4). Despite the virtual closure of the two major markets, Argentina and Brazil, to imports since local production began, other countries, mainly Mexico and the Central American republics,

---

*These figures refer to seven countries in Latin America—Argentina, Brazil, Colombia, Chile, Mexico, Peru, and Venezuela—which account for virtually all the area's vehicle production.

†The figures refer to Bolivia, Ecuador, Panama, Paraguay, Uruguay, and the member countries of the Central American Common Market, as well as the seven countries mentioned in the previous footnote.

have continued to absorb a significant number of foreign cars and
commercial vehicles.

AN OVERVIEW OF THE CURRENT
LATIN AMERICAN AUTOMOTIVE INDUSTRY

It is convenient to separate the countries of Latin America into
three groups according to the technological level and degree of local
integration of their automotive industries, since, as will be seen
in later chapters, such technological differences have important
economic repercussions in terms of economies of scale, capital
intensity, and so on. The local content requirements imposed in
the major Latin American countries have already been discussed
and are summarized for convenience in Table 3.5.

The first group that can be identified are those countries that
have almost complete local integration, producing the engine, other
parts and subassemblies, and body stamping. Both Argentina, with
a local content requirement of 96 percent for cars and 90 percent
for commercial vehicles (calculated on a standard value-weight
relation for each group of parts), and Brazil, where, until 1972,
the requirement was 98 percent for trucks and 99 percent for cars
(measured as a percentage of total vehicle weight), fall into this
category. In Brazil, the local content was reduced in 1972 in order
to permit greater flexibility in the interchange of parts between
foreign subsidiaries. Both the engine and the stamped body parts
are generally produced by the terminal manufacturers, that is, the
assembly companies.

Mexico, although it by now has a market almost as large as
that of Argentina, comes into the intermediate group. As in Argentina
and Brazil, the engine, other parts, and subassemblies are produced
locally, but body stampings are mainly imported. The local content
requirement is 60 percent of the direct cost of the vehicle, which
has enabled the subsidiaries of U.S. companies in Mexico to follow
the annual model changes of the parent rather than having to keep
the same model in production for several years, as in Argentina and
Brazil.

The third, somewhat heterogeneous, group includes Colombia,
Chile, Peru, and Venezuela. These have in common the import of
both body stampings and engines, but some local production of
various other parts. Local content varies from 23 to 30 percent
in the case of Colombia and to 70 percent in Chile. It should be
noted, though, that the Chilean figure includes a 5 percent allowance
for final assembly, and special legislation regards parts imported
from other LAFTA countries as local content. In effect, therefore,

TABLE 3.5

Degree of Local Integration in the
Latin American Automotive Industry, 1973

Group	Country	Local Content	Measurement Basis
1	Argentina	Cars 96 percent; commercial vehicles 90 to 93 percent	Value
	Brazil	Cars 85 percent; commercial vehicles 78 to 82 percent[a]	Value
2	Mexico	Average 65 percent	Direct cost
3	Colombia	23 to 30 percent	Value
	Chile	70 percent[b]	Value
	Peru	25 to 35 percent	Value
	Venezuela	45 percent	Value

[a]Imports only permitted if compensated for by exports.

[b]Parts imported from other LAFTA countries considered as local content when compensated for by exports. Actual local content varies from 27 to 72 percent.

Source: Ministerio de Fomento, Dirección de Industrias, Algunos Aspectos Sobre la Integración Latinoamericana de la Industria Automotriz (Bogota, 1973).

the terminal firms in these countries are assemblers, importing the body stampings and engines from the parent company or its affiliate in another country and buying other parts from local suppliers (although the Unidad Popular government planned to take the step to manufacturing production in Chile).

This grouping by level of national integration also reflects the ranking of countries by size of automotive industry, whether measured in terms of the number of vehicles produced, the value of production, or the numbers employed in the terminal industry (see Table 3.6). Argentina and Brazil together accounted for almost 70 percent of the vehicles produced in Latin America in 1973. These two countries are also the most important in terms of value of output and employment generation. Mexico accounted for about 19 percent of the vehicles produced in the region and is only slightly behind Argentina in terms of value of output (although this does not take account of the higher import content of Mexican vehicles). The remaining four countries accounted for less than 12 percent of total output and have correspondingly low levels of employment.

TABLE 3.6

Production and Employment in the
Latin American Automotive Industry, 1973

Country	Units Produced	Value of Production	Number Employed (millions of $ U.S.)
Brazil	729,136	1,946.6[a]	88,625
Argentina	293,742	1,369.6	50,626
Mexico	283,250	1,137.6	35,551
Venezuela	96,951	170.5[a]	7,463
Peru	31,741	155.1	3,154
Colombia	26,315	49.0[b]	1,599[b]
Chile	17,015	n.a.	4,550

n.a.: not available.
[a]1972.
[b]1969.

Sources: Industry trade association publications.

A similar ranking emerges if one considers the relative
importance of the industry within each country. In Argentina and
Brazil, the automotive industry represents an important part of
the total economy and especially the industrial sector, accounting
for about 4 percent of GNP and 12 percent of industrial production
in both countries during the early 1970s.[21] In this respect, too,
Mexico occupies an intermediate position with the industry, accounting for almost 7 percent of the total value of production in the manufacturing sector in 1973.[22] Of the other countries, it has been
estimated that the value of production of the automotive industry
in Chile in 1969 was 2.8 percent of manufacturing output[23] and
in Venezuela in 1968 it came to 4.4 percent of total manufacturing
output.[24]
    A further feature of the Latin American automotive industry
that deserves comment at this point is the extent to which it has
been penetrated by the major international companies. Table 3.7
ranks 13 companies according to their size in the world market
and gives the output of their vehicles in each of the major Latin
American countries. Reading along the rows, it is possible to see
the spread of each company's Latin American operations. Thus,
for example, Chrysler has affiliates in all seven countries listed

TABLE 3.7

Total Vehicle Production by Firm in Latin America, 1973

Firm	Argentina	Brazil	Chile	Colombia	Mexico	Peru	Venezuela	Total	Percent of Worldwide Production
General Motors	29,681	140,567	–	–	37,170	–	17,911	225,329	2.6
Ford	62,374	147,986	–	–	44,512	–	29,337	284,209	4.8
Chrysler	27,671	36,826	24	11,406	47,864	9,897	21,817	155,505	4.5
Toyota	–	645	–	–	–	6,096	3,840	10,581	0.4
Volkswagen	–	365,472	–	–	87,361	8,867	5,244	466,944	20.0
Fiat	66,648	–	5,232	1,690	–	–	2,099	75,669	3.3
Nissan	–	–	440	–	24,635	6,025	1,814	32,914	1.4
Renault	41,892a	–	1,650	11,453	15,912	–	6,695b	77,602	5.3
BLMC	–	–	2,039	–	–	–	780	2,819	0.2
Peugeot	29,102	–	1,562	–	–	–	–	30,664	3.9
Citroen	17,489	–	6,068	–	–	–	–	23,557	3.0
Daimler-Benz	7,689	32,564	–	–	–	–	2,702	42,955	7.8
American Motors	4,236	–	–	–	16,993	–	3,227	24,456	
Total	293,742	729,136	17,015	26,315	283,250	31,741	96,951	1,478,150	100.0
Percent	19.9	49.3	1.2	1.8	19.2	2.1	6.6		

aIncludes 8,016 Torinos; Industrias Kaiser Argentina and Renault also produce Rambler and Jeep under license.
bIncludes unspecified number of AM vehicles.

Source: Industry trade association publications.

63

and Renault produces in five countries. Until recently, Ford and
General Motors operated in six countries, but the closure of their
plants in Chile and Peru as a result of government rationalization
policies has left them with plants in only four countries, the same
number as Fiat and Volkswagen.

If the rankings of the companies in Latin America are compared
with their rankings worldwide, one sees that Volkswagen is relatively
more favorably placed in Latin America, while Ford also comes
ahead of General Motors. Other points to be noticed are the relatively
poor performance of the Japanese companies, since only local production is included and they have relied more on exports from Japan,
and of British Leyland, which has chosen to concentrate its efforts
in the Commonwealth. The spread of operations seems to suggest
that there is no agreed division of the Latin American market between
the major companies as has been observed in some other industries.

It is also worth noting that, apart from Volkswagen and possibly
Daimler-Benz, their Latin American operations are strictly marginal
from the point of view of the major automotive manufacturers. Latin
American production usually amounts to less than 5 percent of the
worldwide output of these companies. The importance of the continent
has been increasing, however, and, as was suggested in Chapter 2,
the oil crisis may accentuate this tendency. Volkswagen, which has
20 percent of its production in Latin America, mainly from its large
Brazilian subsidiary and Mexico, may foreshadow the development
of the other companies. At present, however, no other firm has a
Latin American subsidiary of a substantial size relative to the parent
company.

Table 3.8 indicates the insistence of both General Motors and
Ford on having 100 percent ownership of their subsidiaries. (The
apparent exception of Ford in Brazil is due to having bought Willys-
Overland do Brasil.) Chrysler has shown a greater willingness to
opt for less than complete ownership and even minority participation,
while some of the other companies, notably Renault, have used
licensing. What is not seen in the table are the changes that have
been taking place over time with a tendency for foreign ownership
to rise as capital participation replaces licensing and majority
ownership replaces minority holdings.

The preceding tables give some idea of the extent to which
the fragmentation of the Latin American markets between a large
number of companies has continued, despite host government hopes
to the contrary. The full extent of this fragmentation is not captured
because of the exclusion of a number of firms. If each company in
each country is considered separately, there were a total of 73
terminal firms in the Latin American automotive industry in 1972.
Of these, 22 had an annual output in that year of less than 1,000

TABLE 3.8

Percentage Equity in Affiliate

Firm	Argentina	Brazil	Chile	Colombia	Mexico	Peru	Venezuela
General Motors	100	100	–	–	100	–	100
Ford	100	51	–	–	100	–	100
Chrysler	100	92	License	80	91	100	100
Volkswagen	–	80	–	–	100	License	License
Fiat	89	–	99	26	–	–	40
Toyota	–	100	–	–	–	100	License
Renault	40*	–	50*	49	License	–	License
BLMC	–	–	53	–	–	–	–
Nissan	–	–	60	–	100	75	License
Peugeot	93	–	50*	–	–	–	–
Daimler–Benz	100	100	–	–	–	–	License
Citroen	91	–	100	–	–	–	–
American Motors	8*	–	–	–	46	License	100

*Same company.

Sources: Banque Francaise et Italienne pour l'Amérique du Sud, "L'industrie Automobile en Amérique Latine," Etudes Economiques, no. 3 (1972); J. Behrman, The Role of International Companies in Latin American Integration; Autos and Petrochemicals (Lexington, Mass.: D. C. Heath, 1972), Appendix A; company reports.

vehicles, while a further 21 had an output of between 1,000 and 10,000.[25] At the other end of the scale, only three firms had production figures of more than 100,000 vehicles, with another three between 50,000 and 100,000.

CONCLUSION

This chapter has described the origins and development of the automotive industry in Latin America, indicating the relationship between the growth of the industry on the continent and the tendencies in the international industry of which it forms a part. It has shown the way in which the oligopolistic structure of that industry, together with the policies adopted by host governments to promote the development of a local industry, gave rise to a large number of relatively small-scale producers being set up and the persistence of this structure to the present. It has also indicated the existence of three different levels of automotive industry development in the area: total integration, integration excluding major body stampings, and local assembly with the incorporation of some parts. The remainder of this study concentrates on three case studies, Argentina, Mexico, and Chile, one from each of the three groups identified. This will permit a more detailed consideration of the key features of the development of the Latin American automotive industry during the 1960s.

NOTES

1. M. Wilkins and F. Hill, American Business Abroad (Detroit: Wayne State University Press, 1964), pp. 145-49.

2. Ibid., p. 91. This may also have been the case with the Ford plant in Mexico. Wilkins and Hill state that Ford's head in Mexico was able to negotiate important concessions of railway freight rates, customs duties, and taxes for the company, but the original investment decision may have preceded this (p. 147).

3. G. Wythe, Industry in Latin America, 2nd ed. (New York: Columbia University Press, 1949), p. 119. If one estimates that the value added in the assembly of completely knocked down vehicles represents 10 percent of total costs, and that the value added in assembling semiknocked down vehicles is 5 percent, then this tariff would represent an effective rate of protection in the region of 300 percent.

4. D. M. Phelps, The Migration of Industry to South America (New York: McGraw-Hill, 1936).

5. Jorge Orvananos Lascurain, "Aspectos de la Demanda y Oferta Automotriz" (professional thesis, Instituto Tecnológico Autónomo de México, 1967), Chap. 2b (ii).

6. Economist Intelligence Unit, "The Brazilian Motor Industry," Motor Business, no. 18 (1959): 28-36.

7. This is the conclusion of a study of the procurement practices of U.S. firms operating in the Mexican automotive industry. See G. S. Edelberg, "The Procurement Practices of the Mexican Affiliates of Selected United States Automobile Firms" (D.B.A. thesis, Harvard University, 1963).

8. The value of output at prices in the country of origin was calculated using AMIA (Asociación Mexicana de la Industria Auto-motriz) data for the average prices of five different size groups of cars in their country of origin and weighting them by an estimate of their market share in 1961. A similar estimate of the foreign exchange saved in 1960 put the sum even lower at U.S. $1.3 million. See C. Sánchez-Marco, Introduction to the Mexican Automobile Industry (Paris: OECD Development Centre, 1968), pp. 7-8.

9. Consejo Nacional de Desarrollo (CONADE), La Industria Automotriz (Analisis Preliminar) (Buenos Aires, 1965), Table 23.

10. Carlos Octavio Gómez y Linares, "Papel de la Política Fiscal en el Desenvolvimiento de la Industria Automotriz" (profes-sional thesis, Universidad Nacional Autónoma de México, 1970), Chap. 2b.

11. Asociación Mexicana de la Industria Automotriz (AMIA), "La Industria Automotriz de México en Cifras" (Mexico City: 1972), p. 69.

12. S. J. Parellada, La Industria Automotriz en la Argentina, UNIDO (ID/WG 76/9), 1970, p. 174.

13. "The Motor-Vehicle Industry in Latin America," Bank of London and South America Quarterly Review 2 (1962): 124.

14. See, for example, O. Altimir, H. Santamaria, and J. Sourrouillo, "Los Instrumentos de Promoción Industrial en La Postguerra," Desarrollo Económico 6 (1966): 99-105.

15. F. G. Donner, The World-wide Industrial Enterprise: Its Challenge and Promise (New York: McGraw-Hill, 1967), pp. 64-67.

16. I. M. D. Little, T. Scitovsky, and M. Scott, Industry and Trade in Some Developing Countries: A Comparative Study (Oxford University Press for OECD, 1970), p. 342.

17. Nacional Financiera, Elementos para una Política de Desarrollo de la Fabricación de Vehículos Automotrices en México (Mexico City, 1960).

18. See G. M. Bueno, "La Industria Siderúrgica y la Industria Automotriz," El Perfil de México en 1980, vol. 2 (Mexico City: Siglo XXI, 1971), p. 95.

19. Nacional Financiera, op. cit., p. 56.

20. King suggests that to have refused to allow General Motors and Ford to continue operating in Mexico would have seriously harmed the country's image with foreign investors. See T. King, Mexico, Industrialization and Trade Policies Since 1940 (Oxford: Oxford University Press for OECD, 1970), pp. 61-62. It is, of course, difficult to get any hard facts on the pressures brought to bear on host governments, but some general suggestions are indicative. In 1961, the Argentinian government revised the automotive industry promotional legislation through Decree 6567. The most significant changes involved were an increase in the permitted imported content of cars over 2,500 cc and a measure to make it easier to introduce new models. It appears that part of the motivation behind these changes was to give an added incentive to U.S. companies to start producing passenger cars in Argentina. In Mexico, it is believed that the Japanese government applied pressure in favor of Nissan's investment proposal being accepted. There is a striking similarity between the behavior described here and that that has been observed in South Africa. Here, too, no attempt was made to limit the number of firms, and the explanation given was that the "exclusion of firms from some countries while those from other countries were granted exclusive manufacturing rights might have had political implications," and that the exclusion of any of the existing foreign subsidiaries would have been interpreted as enmity toward foreign investors. See S. J. Kleu, "Import Substitution in the South African Automobile Industry" (D.B.A. thesis, Harvard University, 1967), pp. 223-53.

21. Figures given by Asociacão Nacional dos Fabricantes de Vehiculos Automotores (ANFAVEA) for Brazil; for Argentina, see Banque Francaise et Italienne pour l'Amérique du Sud, "L'industrie Automobile en Amérique Latine," Etudes Economiques, no. 3 (1972): 9.

22. AMIA, op. cit.

23. Gamma Ingenieros, Estudio de la Industria Automotriz Chilena, UNIDO (ID/WG 76/6), 1970, p. 2.

24. Hector Hurtado, La Industria Automotriz en Venezuela, UNIDO (ID/WG 76/7), 1970, p. 6.

25. R. Jenkins, "International Oligopoly and Dependent Industrialization in the Latin American Motor Industry," unpublished (Cambridge, 1974).

4

A MODEL OF THE DEVELOPMENT OF THE SECTOR OF PRODUCTION IN A PERIPHERAL ECONOMY

In Chapter 3 the fragmentation of the Latin American automotive industry among a large number of firms and the predominant position enjoyed by the major international companies were described. The main body of this work is an analysis of the way in which this structure has been generated in three countries, Argentina, Chile, and Mexico, and some of the further consequences to which it has given rise. This chapter presents a model of structural change within an industry for an underdeveloped economy. In the chapters that follow, empirical evidence is presented to support the theoretical generalizations made and to illustrate the specific operation of the model in each of the three cases.

A GENERAL OVERVIEW: THE GROWTH OF THE SECTOR OF PRODUCTION

The analysis of the development of an individual industry over time, or, as A. Cotta calls it, "the growth of the sector of production,"[1] has been a relatively neglected area of economic theory. This, no doubt, reflects, to some extent, the neglect of dynamic analysis on the part of microeconomic theory, which has remained tied by the limitations imposed by the static, or at best comparatively static, approach.[2] Industrial organization theory has been noticeably reluctant to go beyond description and classification of different market structures, to make generalizations about changes over time within an industry.[3] Conventional economic theory, therefore, does not have much to offer in the way of models to analyze the problem under consideration.

One exception, however, is the product cycle theory. This theory has been used by certain authors in the context of international trade and capital flows, but it also has a wider applicability.4 According to this theory, products, like men, have a life cycle passing from infancy through maturity to old age. When a product is first introduced, it is characterized by high unit costs and a relatively limited market. Production processes tend to be labor intensive, techniques change rapidly, and production runs are relatively short since constant modifications are being made to the product. For these reasons scientific and engineering expertise are essential if the product is to be successful, and the factor limiting entry into the industry is know-how rather than capital.

The industry at a certain point passes into a growth phase with sales beginning to expand rapidly and mass production techniques being introduced with a consequent increase in the capital-labor ratio. The number of firms in the industry rises as new firms are attracted by the growing market and entry is made easier by the expiry of patents and the acquisition of manufacturing skills. Casualties and mergers also tend to increase since many of the entrants are ill-equipped to supply the market. Management, defined to cover administrative skills and marketing, now becomes the crucial labor input.

Ultimately, the exhaustion of new markets and the appearance of substitutes lead to a slowing down of the rate of growth of sales and possibly a reduction in demand. Production techniques in this period become even more capital intensive because of the large quantity of specialized machinery and the optimal size of plant increases making economies of scale an important factor in determining the competitive strength of individual manufacturers. The number of firms tends to decline, and since there are few new innovations, unskilled and semiskilled labor are the most important human inputs.

This model cannot be applied directly to the development of an industry in a dependent underdeveloped economy, but it is possible to suggest an alternative scheme concentrating on the same basic variables. Typically, the initial source of supply of a particular product comes from imports rather than from a large number of small manufacturers. In this case, local operations will only involve sales and servicing so that the capital investment required is low. This initial phase will also tend to be associated with a diversity of sources of supply. In contrast to the initial phase of the product cycle in a developed country, the key human input will be knowledge of the local market rather than engineering skill. Moreover, the dependence on imports means that supply may well fluctuate in response to changes in the particular country's balance of payments position.

For many products it is possible to move from importing the finished good to local assembly of imported parts. Such a development may occur fairly early in a country's evolution when transport costs and tariff barriers make it profitable. This can be done with a minimum increase in capital investment at fairly low levels of output. It tends to create additional employment compared to the case where the assembled product is imported, and hence holds some appeal for host country governments, although it can easily give rise to cases of negative value added at international prices.*

Not all products are such that they can be assembled from imported parts; for these, only two stages may be identified, imports or local production. With assembled products, however, local assembly of imported parts represents an intermediate stage between importing the finished product and manufacturing it locally using locally produced parts. This last stage requires a much greater investment in fixed assets than either of the previous two stages since the transformation of materials generally requires more machinery and equipment. It also involves a much larger scale of production than is necessary for assembly, which tends to lead to greater concentration. It creates major new sources of employment while at the same time freeing the supply of the product from its previous dependence on the balance of payments position; and a sudden upsurge in sales can be a result of this.

In the manufacturing phase of an industry's development, access to foreign technology becomes a crucial factor. As long as products are imported or only assembled locally, the operations that take place in the underdeveloped country do not involve very complex processes since the technology is already embodied in the imports. What is more, since local value added is low, the competitive disadvantage of using inferior techniques is small. The transition to manufacturing production not only increases local value added and hence the importance of efficiency in production but also requires the use of complex techniques that are not usually possible to develop locally.

The need for foreign technology gives a new role to international corporations in the development process. The companies that previously supplied the market with imports are able to take advantage of the fact that their trademarks are already well known

---

*Negative value added occurs when the output of an industry valued at international prices is less than the value of the inputs used at international prices. This situation is most likely to arise in assembly processes where local value added at domestic prices is relatively small when these activities are heavily protected.5

and of their ability to mobilize local and foreign sources of credit,
as well as almost always receiving various forms of government
incentives. As Furtado points out, there is an initial stage of high
profits when the product becomes freely available, and then, "Once
supply returns to normal, the market tends to be controlled by one
or more financially powerful groups, nearly always linked to the
international consortia that had traditionally controlled imports."[6]
It is this phenomenon that recent writers on Latin American development have labeled the "new dependence."[7]

COMPETITION WITHIN AN INDUSTRY:
THE STEINDL MODEL

The previous discussion illustrates broad lines along which
an industry might be expected to develop in a peripheral economy.
Further analysis of the problems posed in Chapter 3 requires the
development of a model of intraindustry competition that will explain
the unequal growth rates of different firms. These questions have
been tackled by Josef Steindl in his two major books.[8] The remainder
of this section will be devoted to an exposition of Steindl's model of
competition within an industry.

Steindl bases his arguments on the existence of significant
cost differentials between firms within the same industry, claiming
that the existence of considerable cost differentials is of crucial
importance to the theoretical analysis of price formation.[9] These
cost differences are related to the size of firms, and their primary
cause is to be found in the existence of economies of scale.[10] This
assumption gives rise to the concept of the marginal producer,
which is the highest cost producer in an industry, analogous to the
least fertile land under cultivation in Ricardo's theory of land rent.
In Steindl's formulation, the scarcity of big units of capital plays
the role of the scarcity of better land. In an industry where competitive pressure is acute, the marginal firm earns only normal profits,
whereas in an industry where entry is difficult such firms may earn
a surplus. Thus, it is necessary to distinguish between "competitive"
industries, where there is freedom of entry and exit and excess
capacity is eliminated in the long run by price-cutting, and "monopolistic" industries, where this mechanism is not operative.

In addition to the assumptions concerning cost differentials
and the marginal producer, the other assumptions made are that
firms invest only in their own industry (an assumption that is later
relaxed), that firms invest because they have saved in the past, and,
finally, that the rate of growth of the market is exogenously given
for the industry as a whole.

Let us consider first the case of an industry where the marginal producer earns only normal profits. Larger firms, tending to have higher profit margins as well as a higher rate of profit (unless the increase in the capital-output ratio with scale more than offsets the higher profit margin), will accumulate funds at a faster rate than small firms. Three alternative situations can be distinguished. First, the internal accumulation and hence the expansion of the large firms may be no faster than the rate of growth of the market, so that large firms are not increasing their market share and new entries are maintaining the share of small firms (since it is assumed that marginal firms do not accumulate). Second, large firms expand faster than the industry as a whole and then they increase their market share, but small firms may still be able to grow in absolute terms. Finally, the rate of growth of the favorably placed firms may be so fast relative to the growth of demand, or their initial market share may be so large, that they are only able to expand by driving out marginal producers.

The three alternative situations can be expressed algebraically as follows:

$$x'_f < x'; \qquad x'_d > x' \tag{a}$$

$$x' > x'_d > 0; \quad x'/S_f > x'_f > x' \tag{b}$$

$$x'_d < 0; \qquad x'/S_f > x'_f \tag{c}$$

where x' is the rate of growth of the market, x'_f the rate of growth of favorably placed firms, x'_d the rate of growth of marginal producers, and S_f the market share of favorably placed firms.

In order to expand their market share, the favorably placed firms must undertake a "sales effort," which can take the form of heavier advertising expenditures or price or quality competition. Such a sales effort will result in a reduction in the net profit margin of these producers and hence the funds available for internal accumulation. If one then assumes that new capacity involves lower costs than existing capacity as a result of technical progress, one can identify two factors in the dynamics of the industry's development. These are cost reductions by progressive firms, which tend to increase the profit margin by expanding the cost differential between them and the marginal producer, and the excessive internal accumulation by the former, which leads to the elimination of high cost firms and tends to reduce the profit margin.

Figure 4.1 helps to illustrate the interaction of these two factors. The output of the various firms is arranged in the declining order of their costs, from left to right along the horizontal axis.

FIGURE 4.1

The Steindl Model of Intraindustry Competition

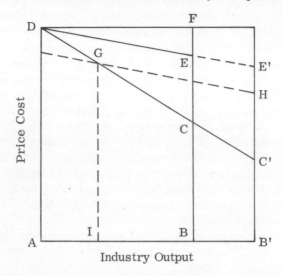

Source: Compiled by the author.

The cost curve of the industry is given by CD. If EF represents
the sales effort, then the price curve is given by DE. If progressive
firms expand output from B to B', costs fall to C' and the profit
margin increases to C'E'. This is the first of the two effects considered above. If this leads to a higher level of internal accumulation
than can be supported by the expansion of the industry as a whole,
there is a competitive struggle and the price line is driven down to
GH, thus eliminating the high cost producers AI and driving down
the profit margin of the most progressive firms to C'H.

In a monopolistic industry, marginal firms earn abnormal
profits since they tend to require capital equipment on a scale that
makes it impossible to refer to them as small firms. Moreover,
since they are not small, marginal firms are likely to have larger
financial resources and hence are able to offer more resistance to
any attempt to drive them out of the industry. This increases the
costs to the progressive firm in attempting to increase its market
share and thus reduces the incentive to do so. In many cases,
therefore, the sales effort required for expansion would be so large
as to offset the advantage obtained by innovation and accumulation.
As Steindl puts it, "Oligopoly is grit thrown in the mechanism of
competition previously described."[11]

INTRAINDUSTRY COMPETITION IN A
PERIPHERAL ECONOMY

As was indicated above, the key factor underlying cost differentials for Steindl was economies of scale in conjunction with size
differences between firms. Although he does not emphasize the fact,
his data indicating a positive correlation between size and gross
profit margins refer to plants, and it is an assumption on his part
that interplant cost differences are reflected in differences between
firms.[12] In the case of a dependent industry in a peripheral economy,
however, the essential factor distinguishing favorably placed firms
is not their size of plant but their foreign ownership. This may be
thought of as the size of the total operation into which the individual
company is integrated, since foreign subsidiaries are part of a
worldwide unit, while locally owned firms are, at the most, part
of a national conglomerate. This is clearly not the same concept
as the technical economies of scale that Steindl sees as the primary
cause of cost differentials.

There are a number of reasons why one might expect foreign
subsidiaries that are part of a worldwide organization to enjoy lower
costs than national firms in the same industry. These derive in the
main from the scale of the total operation and the increased flexibility
that access to an international parent company and its affiliates gives.
(Chapter 7 discusses two examples of this flexibility at work in the
cases of Chile and Mexico.) Two of the most general advantages
enjoyed by subsidiaries are access to the parent company's technology
(understood in a wide sense to include trademarks, marketing skills,
administrative skills, and so on) and to its financial support.[13]

Generally, only the multinational corporations are in a position
to undertake large-scale industrial research, and local firms in the
periphery are obliged to rely on licenses in order to obtain the technology that would be expensive to develop locally.* In order to bring
out the significance of this fact, it is necessary to consider briefly
the nature of the international market for technology.

It has now come to be recognized that the market for technology
does not approximate the perfect competition model. This is partly

---

*This obviously does not apply to all industries but only to
those high technology industries normally considered dynamic.
It should also be borne in mind that one is considering the cost to
the individual firm of developing its own technology. Divergences
between private and social cost might mean that it would still be in
the national interest to develop the technology locally.

a consequence of the inherent ambiguity in any market for information, since the perfect competition model assumes perfect knowledge.[14] It is also a consequence of the empirical fact that international transfers of technology usually occur in sectors dominated by international oligopolists.[15] C. Vaitsos has argued that the marginal cost of transferring technology from the point of view of the firm making the transfer is zero, since it already possesses the technology that has been developed for other markets, or close to zero where there are some local adaptation costs. On the other hand, the marginal cost to the recipient of developing an alternative is either very large or even infinite.[16] Between these two limits the price is set by relative bargaining strength.

Jorge Katz[17] has developed a model of bilateral monopoly to determine the price at which technology will be sold by a monopolistic supplier to a recipient that enjoys a monopoly position in the supply of a final good in the domestic market. The point is that part of the monopoly profit that the final good producer is able to make by its position in the domestic market is appropriated by the technology supplier. The supplier cannot, however, appropriate the whole of the benefit of his customer's monopoly position since an increase in the royalty charged as a percentage of sales will lead to a reduction in output and an increase in the price of the final good. The only way in which the technology supplier can secure the entire monopoly profit available is through direct investment.

J. Katz assumes a single monopolist in both the technology and the final goods market. In practice, oligopoly is a more likely situation, and this will affect the price according to whether competition is stronger in the technology market or in the product market (on the supply side). Even so, it remains true that the foreign investor appropriates the whole of the monopoly profit available from facing a downward sloping demand curve, while the licensed producer yields part of this profit to the licensor. Since royalty and licensing charges of 5 percent on sales are common, this factor can lead to significant cost differentials between foreign subsidiaries, which do not have to pay for technology supplied by the parent company, and nationally owned firms, which do.[18]

Technology is usually thought of as know-how related specifically to production. In this context, however, one is interested in a much broader spectrum of advantages that a foreign firm enjoys over local competitors. Thus, trademarks, technical assistance in administration, the use of advanced marketing techniques, and so on must be included. The local firm has to obtain these in exactly the same way as it must obtain technical assistance in production and design, rights to use blueprints, and so on.[19] Without them, the local firm suffers a productivity disadvantage. With them, it has to cede part of its profit to the foreign supplier.

The second important source of advantage to foreign subsidiaries is differential access to capital. This can take two forms: either access to debt and equity capital on preferential terms reflected in lower interest charges and higher share prices or greater access to credit reflected in a higher gearing ratio. As far as the first form is concerned, the scale of the multinational corporation gives it a double advantage. It is able to raise capital in countries where interest rates tend to be lower, whereas national firms are usually forced to raise capital locally since they are virtually unknown outside the home country.[20] Moreover, even when foreign firms raise capital in the country where their subsidiary operates, as they often do,[21] they are able to do so on more favorable terms than their national competitors because of the security the parent company represents.[22]

Suppose that a nationally owned company must pay an interest rate of 16 percent on capital it raises locally, while a foreign subsidiary can obtain capital at an 8 percent rate of interest either locally or abroad. Assume further that both companies have a debt-equity ratio of 1 and a capital-output ratio also of 1. Then the additional cost of capital to the local firm represents a cost disadvantage of 4 percent on sales. With a capital-output ratio of 2, then the cost disadvantage would be increased to 8.

In this example it was assumed that the gearing ratios for foreign subsidiaries and local firms were the same. In practice, the backing of the parent company means that a subsidiary is not subject to the same restrictions on its gearing ratio as a locally owned enterprise. Thus, where local finance is available at low real rates of interest, the foreign subsidiary may use a high gearing ratio in order to increase its rate of return on the parent's own capital.[23] This can be illustrated by maintaining the assumption that local companies must pay a rate of interest of 16 percent and that foreign subsidiaries pay only 8 percent and introducing an assumed rate of return on total assets of 20 percent for all firms and a debt-equity ratio of 2:1 for foreign subsidiaries and 1:1 for local firms. It can then be shown that local firms will have a rate of return of 24 percent on their own invested capital as compared with 44 percent for foreign firms. Thus, the combined effect of differences in the cost of finance and its availability can be considerable.

The differential costs of capital and technology would appear to be the most significant sources of cost differentials between firms in dependent economies. What then of the other major inputs into the productive process, labor and materials? It is possible that the overall size of multinational corporations gives their subsidiaries greater bargaining power vis-a-vis both their suppliers and their labor force. In theory, this could lead to lower prices for their materials and lower labor costs as a result of lower wage rates.

Lower prices could arise where suppliers are also multinational in the scope of their operations so that the customer is able to use its purchases in the home market as a lever in order to obtain better terms from the supplier in other markets where they both operate. Lower labor costs could arise from the creation of a docile labor force through threats to move production elsewhere* and a greater ability to withstand union pressure for wage increases since the company's operations in any one country is only a small part of its total activities, whereas unions are still fragmented by national boundaries.

There does not appear to be any empirical evidence to support the hypothesis that subsidiaries have used their potential bargaining power in this way. As far as labor is concerned, the evidence suggests that foreign firms tend to pay their workers higher wages, thus creating a privileged elite within the local working class.[24]

Although it has been argued that differences exist in the cost of technology and finance to locally owned firms and foreign subsidiaries, it must be emphasized that these are not necessarily reflected in differences in the payments actually made by the two kinds of firms. While the payments made by national firms reflect the cost to them of the inputs that they use, the same cannot be held to be true for wholly owned subsidiaries, since charges appearing as royalties in company accounts are a way of transferring resources from the affiliate to the parent, which has no connection with the cost of the technology provided. Similarly, where the parent provides loan capital to a subsidiary, the financial charges that the latter has to pay may bear no relation to the opportunity cost of capital to the multinational corporation as a whole. This, needless to say, makes it difficult to test the underlying relationships empirically.

The above analysis concentrates on one particular type of indū .stry, namely, that in which foreign and local firms both produce basically similar products using similar foreign techniques. This seems to be a fair characterization of the so-called "dynamic" industries ("so-called," as "dynamic" refers not to their actual performance, which may be quite undynamic, but to the expectation, based on the experience of the developed countries, that they would be dynamic). Another broad type of industry is that in which foreign subsidiaries compete with local artisan-type production, where both the technology and the product are different for the two groups of

---

*Compare Henry Ford II's threat to the workers at Dagenham to concentrate Ford's expansion on the continent.

firms. In a dynamic industry, it is possible to concentrate on differences in the costs of inputs, whereas in the second case comparison of the two groups of firms would be much more complicated, requiring consideration of both technology and the demand side.

In summary, it is possible to say that economies of scale (as they can be referred to in the broad sense of scale in its global context) accruing to favorably placed firms in a peripheral economy tend to be pecuniary economies, whereas in a developed economy they are real economies. The modification of the Steindl model in order to apply it to a dependent economy requires changes in the behavioral as well as the structural hypotheses.

BEHAVIORAL ASSUMPTIONS OF THE MODEL

The key behavioral assumptions made by Steindl are that firms invest what they have saved in the past and that they tend to do so in their own industry because it is easier to expand in a branch of production with which one is already familiar than to go into new industries. In view of recent developments in the advanced capitalist economies (especially the formation of conglomerates), the latter assumption has come to be extremely doubtful in the context in which it was formulated, as Steindl himself has admitted.[25]

The only model of foreign investment that shares Steindl's behavioral hypothesis is the gambler's earning theory associated with Barlow and Wender, Penrose, and others, according to which profits made abroad are reinvested locally. This may be a reasonable assumption during the early stage of a national company's transition into a multinational corporation,[26] but ceases to be a rational model for corporate behavior once international operations have become widespread.[27] Moreover, the empirical evidence does not support the assumption of subsidiary independence but is consistent with a model of global maximization.[28] Thus, instead of the firm's investment decisions being made on the basis of past profits, they are made on the basis of future profit expectations compared to those in the other countries in which it operates and the total available resources of the parent company.*

If the gambler's earning hypothesis is rejected as a model of behavior for the foreign subsidiary, then it is necessary to introduce an alternative behavioral postulate that will relate the rate of expansion of these firms to internal conditions in the country that is being

---

*This model applies to the expansion of existing capacity rather than the initial investment decision.

studied, making ceteris paribus assumptions concerning conditions elsewhere for the time being.

It is then possible to identify a number of important variables. First, there is the current and past rate of profit of the firm, which is an indicator of expected future profits. Second, the rate of growth of the market determines the ease with which firms are able to expand. Third, there is the cost to the firm of driving out its competitors in order to increase its market share, which is determined by the profit rate of marginal firms and the cost advantage of favorably placed firms, as well as the financial strength of marginal firms. Finally, one must introduce a risk factor that leads foreign corporations to limit the amount of their own capital transferred to the subsidiary, particularly during the early stages of the investment. 29

The main points can be shown diagramatically as in Figure 4.2. In the initial situation, the total output of the industry is AC, AB of which is produced by local firms and BC by foreign firms. As in Figure 4.1, firms are ranked according to costs, with the difference that there is now a sharp discontinuity in the cost curve corresponding to the cost differential between local and foreign firms. If the market is expanding by, say CM, then foreign firms are able to expand their output by an equal amount without reducing the sales of locally owned firms.

Given a stagnating market, however, if foreign firms wish to expand output to BM, then the output of local firms must be reduced by AP. In order to do this, prices must be lowered from HK to RV. (This may also be thought of as a sales effort of KV per unit rather than a price-cut.) In deciding whether or not to undertake such an expansion, the profit-maximizing firm must compare the area JTUN, which represents the profit lost as a result of the price-cut (or sales effort), with UELV, the gain from the expansion. This can be seen to depend on the profit margin of the marginal firm that gives the amount by which prices have to be cut or sales effort increased to effect a given increase in output, the initial profit of foreign firms, and the lowering of costs as a result of the expansion.*

Despite their complexity, the above relationships represent an oversimplification as far as the behavior of a foreign subsidiary is concerned, ignoring as it does the effects of the parent company's liquidity and its alternative opportunities for investment elsewhere. It is, however, an improvement over the gambler's earning theory. In the case of locally owned companies, Steindl's assumption that

---

*Figure 4.2 suffers from being a tool of comparative statics. It is also impossible to show the financial strength of different firms in two dimensions.

FIGURE 4.2

Intraindustry Competition in a
Peripheral Economy

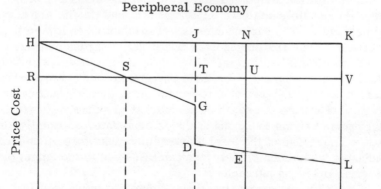

Source: Compiled by the author.

firms expand by reinvesting the profits that they have earned in the
past would seem satisfactory. The possibilities of outside finance
are limited by the low degree of development of the capital market
in most underdeveloped economies so that firms expand by plowing
back profits.[30]

THE COMPLETE MODEL

It is now possible to set in motion a dynamic two-sector model
of structural change within an industry in a peripheral economy.
The nature of interfirm cost differentials has been identified and
behavioral assumptions have been made about the investment decisions
of the two groups of firms. All that remains is to link these to the
changes over time in demand and supply conditions, which were
discussed at the beginning of this chapter, and which are exogeneous
from the point of view of the model of competition. It was pointed
out that the startup of local production in underdeveloped economies
was likely to be followed immediately by a rapid growth of sales
where there had previously been import restrictions. It was also
indicated that local manufacturing tended to be associated with
increasing capital intensity and scale requirements. Firms require
more working capital to finance local suppliers and more fixed
capital for their own operations. Similarly, the rate of royalty pay-

ment on sales increases with local content since royalties are frequently not charged on imported components.

In the initial period of rapid growth of the industry, prices tend
to be high, possibly up to the tariff barrier, and profits are correspondingly high. The capital intensity of production is low so that
local firms do not find themselves at a great cost disadvantage compared to foreign subsidiaries. Moreover, their greater knowledge
of the local environment gives them certain advantages over subsidiaries so that they are able to earn a more than adequate rate of
return.[31] The rate of growth of the market is sufficiently great for
both groups of firms to expand at the desired rate, especially since
a lack of knowledge of the local market may make foreign companies
reluctant to risk much of their own capital, even to the extent of
preferring licensing agreements.

Over time, however, two factors enter to influence the dynamic
of the situation. On the demand side, if the rate of growth of the
market slows down, increased competition for market shares tends
to drive down the rate of profit. Let us put it another way. The rate
of growth of the two sectors taken together must, in the long run,
equal the exogenously given rate of growth of demand. Since the
rate of growth of supply is a function of the rate of profit in the two
sectors and the changing level of capital intensity, then these variables
must be adjusted to bring about the equality of supply and demand.
But the rate of change in capital intensity, it is assumed, is also an
exogenous variable, so that the entire burden of adjustment falls on
the profit rates. Thus a slowdown in the rate of growth of demand
tends to lead to a fall in the rate of profit.*

On the supply side, two factors appear to be important. First,
there is a tendency for the cost disadvantage of local firms to increase
over time. This is in part owing to the increasing level of capital
intensity, either through an increase in fixed investment or in working
capital, which affects nationally owned firms to a greater extent than
local firms because of the higher cost of capital to them (discussed
above) and, in part, because of increased royalty payments. This
increase in cost disparity is, as was suggested above, an incentive
for foreign firms to expand at the expense of locally owned firms.
The second factor is the change in the perception of risk on the part
of the foreign companies as they become more familiar with the local

---

*"Tends," since in certain periods exogenous changes in the
capital-output ratio may be sufficient to offset demand changes.
Also, if the changes in capital intensity are not to be exogenous,
changes in the rate of growth of demand may be offset by changes
in capital intensity.

environment, which makes them prepared to make a greater capital contribution, manifesting itself in a more rapid growth of subsidiaries and a replacement of licensees by joint ventures and joint ventures by wholly owned subsidiaries.

Let us suppose for the moment that the rate of growth of demand is unchanged, perhaps because it is controlled by the government through a quota system, prices also being controlled. Then the changes described in the previous paragraph will lead unambiguously to an increase in the rate of growth of foreign firms, since demand growth and profit rates remain unchanged. This will lead to increased competition and tend to drive down profits. Thus, a new equilibrium will be established with a lower rate of growth for domestic firms and a higher rate of growth for foreign subsidiaries. If now it is assumed that the rate of growth of demand slows down, then this serves only to accentuate the process described above.

So far the analysis has assumed implicitly constant returns to scale and full (or at least constant) utilization of capacity for all firms. Although economies of scale have not been assigned the role of primum mobile in our model as they were in that of Steindl, they do undoubtedly exist and reinforce the tendencies described above. Thus, economies of scale, by reducing the costs of expansion, increase the incentive to expand market shares. There is a cumulative process whereby an initial cost advantage leads to a faster rate of growth and thus larger scale, which further increases the original cost advantage.

Underutilization of capacity plays a similar role to economies of scale (indeed, it may be thought of as its short-run equivalent). This is likely to be particularly important in industries where there are significant plant indivisibilities so that capacity tends to be expanded ahead of demand. Fajnzylber makes the point that in dynamic industries, foreign subsidiaries tend to build excess capacity in order to obtain an optimum scale of plant and then use various mechanisms in order to increase utilization.[32] In view of their limited financial resources, local firms may well be unable to both invest in an optimum scale plant and undertake the necessary expenditures in terms of advertising or consumer credit to achieve reasonable levels of utilization. Thus, they are forced to adopt suboptimal positions.[33]

CONCLUSION

This chapter has presented a model of competition and growth within a sector of production that can be used to explain the development of the Latin American automotive industry during the 1960s.

Three main features have been identified in the operation of the model. The first is the change involved in the move from importing or assembly operations to local manufacturing, particularly the increased capital requirements and importance of foreign technology that this implies. Also on the supply side, there is the existence of significant cost differentials between foreign subsidiaries and national firms as a result of the advantage that the former enjoy in terms of access to finance and technology. Finally, on the demand side, there is the rate of growth of the total market that determines the expansion possibilities for firms and the degree of pressure toward the elimination of some existing firms. In Chapters 5 and 6, some evidence is presented to illustrate these points in the context of the automotive industry in Argentina, Chile, and Mexico.

NOTES

1. A. Cotta, "The Growth of the Sector of Production," in Problems of Economic Dynamics and Planning: Essays in Honour of Michel Kalecki (Oxford: Pergamon, 1966), pp. 79-105.

2. The "new theories of the firm" represent a partial exception to this generalization, but, although they attempt to provide a dynamic analysis of the individual firm, they do not go beyond the single firm, that is, they do not deal with industry dynamics. For a discussion of these theories, see R. Marris, "An Introduction to Theories of Corporate Growth," in The Corporate Economy: Growth, Competition and Innovative Potential, ed. R. Marris and A. Wood (New York: Macmillan, 1971), pp. 1-36.

3. Bain, for instance, in his basic text, Industrial Organization, states that no single pattern of concentration typifies all industries. Rather, he believes that a fairly common situation is one where initially there are a fairly large number of small firms, concentration then increasing in maturity, reaching a peak that is subsequently maintained or falls off slightly, but in either case tends to stabilize at a relatively high level. This, significantly, is the only aspect of industrial structure about which Bain even attempts such a generalization. See J. Bain, Industrial Organization, 2nd ed. (New York: Wiley, 1968), pp. 159-62.

4. The following summary of the product cycle theory is based on S. Hirsch, Location of Industry and International Competitiveness (Oxford: Clarendon Press, 1967), pp. 16-42. See also R. Vernon, "International Investment and International Trade in the Product Cycle," Quarterly Journal of Economics 80 (1966): 190-207.

5. See I. M. D. Little, T. Scitovsky, and M. Scott, Industry and Trade in Some Developing Countries: A Comparative Study (Oxford: Oxford University Press for OECD, 1970), pp. 423-27.

6. C. Furtado, Economic Development of Latin America: A Survey from Colonial Times to the Cuban Revolution (Cambridge: The University Press, 1970).

7. F. Cardoso and E. Faletto, Dependencia y Desarrollo en America Latina: Ensayo de Interpretación Sicológica (Mexico: Siglo XXI, 1971); V. Bambirra, "Integracion Monopolica Mundial e Industrialización: sus contradicciones," Sociedad y Desarrollo 1 (1972); O. Caputo and R. Pizarro, Imperialismo, Dependencia y Relaciones Económicas Internacionales (Santiago: Centro de Estudios Socio-Economicos, 1970); T. dos Santos, El Nuevo Carácter de la Dependencia (Santiago: Centro de Estudios Socio-Economicos, 1968).

8. See his two major works, Small and Big Business: Economic Problems of the Size of Firms (Oxford: Blackwell, 1945) and Maturity and Stagnation in American Capitalism (Oxford: Blackwell, 1952). A model which is similar to that of Steindl in many respects has been developed by P. Sylos-Labini. Unlike Steindl, who emphasizes accumulation, Sylos-Labini's main concern is with the determination of the equilibrium price under oligopoly. Consequently, although the issue of intraindustry competition and the elimination of small firms is discussed by Sylos-Labini, it is not as fully developed as in Steindl's writings. For clarity of exposition, the discussion has been couched entirely in terms of Steindl's model. It is also worth mentioning here that Sylos-Labini's analysis is carried out in terms of a homogeneous oligopoly, but he indicates that it can be extended to differentiated oligopoly. See P. Sylos-Labini, Oligopoly and Technical Progress (Cambridge, Mass.: Harvard University Press, 1962), pp. 53-56.

9. Steindl, Maturity, op. cit., p. 18.

10. Steindl, Small and Big, op. cit., pp. 13-21; Maturity, op. cit., pp. 18-40.

11. Steindl, Maturity, op. cit., p. 55.

12. Ibid., p. 37. In fairness to Steindl, it should be pointed out that, in Small and Big, op. cit., pp. 14-15, he mentions the importance of economies of scale in industrial research and other factors that are related to firm rather than plant scale.

13. An empirical study comparing the factors perceived as obstacles to their expansion by local and foreign (United States and Canadian) firms in El Salvador indicated the availability of capital and the availability of technical and administrative skills as the two areas where the advantage of foreign firms was most marked. See W. J. Bilkley, Industrial Stimulation (Lexington, Mass.: Heath Lexington Books, 1970), pp. 171-74.

14. K. Arrow, "Economic Welfare and the Allocation of Resources for Invention," in The Rate and Direction of Inventive Activity: Economic and Social Factors, National Bureau for Economic Research (Princeton, N.J.: Princeton University Press, 1962), pp. 609-25.

15. This is well established for technology transfers through direct foreign investment. See J. N. Behrman, Some Patterns in the Rise of Multinational Enterprise, Research Paper 18 (University of North Carolina, 1969). The same appears to be true for all contractual transfers of technology. See United Nations, Conference on Trade and Development (UNCTAD), Major Issues Arising from the Transfer of Technology to Developing Countries (TD/B/AC. 11/10), 1972, pp. 7-10.

16. C. V. Vaitsos, Transfer of Resources and Preservation of Monopoly Rent, Center for International Affairs, EDR No. 168 (Harvard University, 1970), pp. 17-23.

17. J. Katz,"Importación de Tecnología, Aprendizaje Local e Industrialización Dependiente," Centro de Investigaciones Económicas, Documentos de Trabajo No. 59 (Instituto Torcuato di Tella, 1972), pp. II 7-18.

18. For Argentina, see Katz, ibid., pp. VIII 11-15. For Mexico, see M. S. Wionczek, G. M. Bueno, and J. E. Navarrete, "La Transferencia Internacional de Tecnología al Nivel de Empresa: El caso de México," mimeographed (Mexico: Fondo de Cultura Económica, 1974), pp. 91-94. It should be noted that a royalty of 5 percent on sales implies a higher rate on the value added by the firm, and may be greater than the profit margin that remains after the royalty has been paid.

19. F. Fajnzylber, Estrategia Industrial y Empresas Internacionales: Posición Relativa de América Latina y Brasil, ECLA, UN E/CN 121 12/ (1970), pp. 125-26.

20. S. Rose, "The Rewarding Strategies of Multinationalism," Fortune 78 (1968): 100-05, 180-82.

21. See M. Z. Brooke and H. L. Remmers, The Strategy of Multinational Enterprise: Organization and Finance (London: Longman, 1970), Chap. 2, p. 6. U.S. manufacturing subsidiaries in Latin America raised 40 percent of their capital from local external sources (more than in any other area) in the period 1957-65. See Fajnzylber, op. cit., Chap. 2.

22. See D. Chudnovsky, Empresas Multinacionales y Ganancias Monopólicas (Buenos Aires: Siglo XXI, 1975).

23. Ibid.

24. It is well known that workers of foreign companies in the export sector in underdeveloped economies are often paid higher wages than prevail in the economy as a whole; for example, the case

of the Chilean copper miners. It also appears that even within one
industry, foreign companies pay higher wages. See R. C. Maddox,
Wage Differences Between U.S. and Guatemalan Industrial Firms
in Guatemala, Studies in Latin American Business no. 10 (University
of Texas, 1971).

25. See Josef Steindl, "On Maturity in Capitalist Economies,"
in Problems of Economic Dynamics and Planning: Essays in Honour
of Michel Kalecki (Oxford: Pergamon, 1966), pp. 423-32.

26. See Rose, op. cit.

27. For a criticism of the gambler's earning theory, see
S. Hymer, "The International Operations of National Firms" (Ph.D.
thesis, Massachusetts Institute of Technology, 1960), pp. 169-79.

28. Stevens has carried out an econometric test of this hypothe-
sis. See Guy V. G. Stevens, "Fixed Investment Expenditures of
Foreign Manufacturing Affiliates of U.S. Firms," Yale Economic
Essays 9 (1969): 136-98.

29. See Y. Aharoni, The Foreign Investment Decision Process
(Cambridge, Mass.: Harvard Graduate School of Business Administration, 1966), especially Chap. 6.

30. G. di Tella, "The Behaviour of the Firm with a Financial
Restriction," Journal of Industrial Economics 27 (1969): 119-31.

31. Bilkley concluded that the areas where local firms
apparently enjoyed an advantage over foreign firms were those
related to the superior contacts and better knowledge of local conditions of the former. See Bilkley, op. cit., p. 171.

32. F. Fajnzylber, Sistema Industrial y Exportación de
Manufacturas, ECLA (E/CN. 12.), 1970, pp. 280-98.

33. See di Tella, op. cit.

5

AUTOMOTIVE INDUSTRY TECHNOLOGY, SUPPLY CONDITIONS, AND COST DIFFERENTIALS

It was argued in Chapter 4 that the development of the Latin American automotive industry could be explained by a model of intraindustry competition. This chapter concentrates on two of the main features of the model that relate to the supply side of the industry's development, that is, the changeover from assembly to manufacturing and the existence of cost differentials between foreign subsidiaries and local firms.

As was discussed previously, there is a tendency for the capital intensity and technological complexity of production to increase as an industry moves from assembly operations to full manufacturing. This generalization is made more specific by reference to the technology of the automotive industry. It will be shown that the introduction of automotive manufacture requires a considerable increase in investment on the part of firms that wish to continue production. This is a reflection of the rising capital requirements that result from the greater capital intensity and higher minimum scale requirements of the other processes involved in production as compared to assembly.

In the latter part of this chapter, the existence of significant cost differentials between foreign subsidiaries and locally owned firms is discussed. Since these differences are related to the preferential access to capital and technology enjoyed by subsidiaries of multinational corporations, it is to be expected that the differential will widen with the introduction of manufacturing production, as well as the rising capital requirements and technological level that this involves.

TECHNOLOGY

It is possible to identify a number of stages of automotive industry development.[1] In the first stage, local activities related to the automotive industry are confined to distribution, servicing, and possibly the production of some replacement parts, such as batteries and tires, while the vehicles themselves are imported "on wheels," that is, fully assembled. During this phase, the supply of vehicles comes from a variety of different sources and there may be significant competition.

Transport costs or tariffs may soon lead to assembly plants being set up. It is only a small step to move on to the final assembly of semiknocked down (SKD) vehicles, which can be carried out in rudimentary buildings with a minimum amount of machinery and equipment. Capital requirements tend to increase when the vehicles are painted locally and, at a more advanced stage, with completely knocked down (CKD) assembly, which includes local welding and body-building shops. The necessary capital investment is, nevertheless, still within reach of local entrepreneurs, and often the assemblers are the previous importers. The protection received from imports and the limited number of firms setting up plants imply a reduction in competition, and this, taken together with the fact that the greater part of the final product is imported from a parent company or licensor, gives considerable scope for overpricing.[2]

As was seen in Chapter 3, the impact of purely assembly operations on the local economy tends to be limited. There is little if any saving in foreign exchange, and the effect in terms of backward and forward linkages and employment creation is small. It has been estimated that the labor and materials required to pack a Renault 10 cost as much as it would to assemble the car.[3] Even with a minimal incorporation of local parts of, say, 5 or 10 percent, there may not be any significant foreign exchange saving, especially when it is remembered that the system of deletion allowances practiced by the exporting firms reduces the gains from omitting items from a CKD pack.* Table 5.1 indicates the situation with a 5 percent local content.

---

*This is the system by which the omission of a part from a CKD kit leads to a reduction in the price of the pack of less than the value of the omitted part. This leads to the logical possibility that a firm imports an empty CKD pack and pays, say, 50 percent of what it would pay for a complete pack.

TABLE 5.1

Savings in Foreign Exchange from
Local Assembly
(dollars)

	Imports	SKD	CKD
Ex-factory price	1,000	980	950
Minor deletions		-50	-50
	1,000	930	900
Packing and FOB charges	} 40	110	} 100
Freight and insurance		80	
Total	1,040	1,120	1,000

Source: A. S. El Darwish, "The Establishment of an Automotive Industry in Developing Countries," in UNIDO, Establishment and Development of Automotive Industries in Developing Countries (ID/36 vol. 2, 1970), pp. 59-72, Table 2.

The first locally manufactured parts to be incorporated are those, such as batteries or tires, that already have been developed in order to meet the demand for replacements. The sum total of these parts, however, would only account for between 5 and 10 percent of a vehicle's price. There is a limitation on the use of local parts at this stage since basic parts, such as bearings, cannot be bought locally unless main parts, for example, engines, are imported in unassembled form, which would increase their volume and consequently transport costs. There are some other parts that can be supplied locally with little additional investment. Examples of such parts are shock absorbers, small stampings, and electrical parts that in many cases can be produced by existing manufacturers.

The incorporation of these items, taken together with an allowance for assembly costs, permits the achievement of a local content of about 35 percent in this stage of automotive industry development. This is illustrated by the following cost breakdown (in percent) of a low-cost, medium-sized car found in a Chilean study:[4]

Wheels and tires	4.4
Windows	1.6
Brake operating system	1.2
Upholstery	7.0
Raw material for paint	2.9

Radiator	1.9
Small mechanical parts	3.4
Body accessories	4.6
Total	27.0

Add to this an estimated 5 to 10 percent for assembly costs, and the total is in the region of 35 percent.

During this period, the industry finds itself with increased requirements of working capital in order to finance the newly developed local suppliers. Dependence on local parts may prove a new source of supply bottlenecks and lead to excess capacity in the terminal sector. On the other hand, new sources of employment are created.

Further local integration involves the engine and transmission, which raises content to some 60 percent. Finally, local stamping of the major body parts brings the industry properly into the final stage of development with an almost entirely domestically produced vehicle.* It is only in the later stages of local integration that the terminal manufacturer becomes involved in machining, pressing, and possibly foundry activities. In the previous stage, the terminal producer is still basically an assembly plant, although in some cases it may integrate backward into part production. The essential difference between this and the import and CKD assembly stages is that the terminal plant now buys some parts locally instead of importing them.

Since an increase in national content involves the introduction of new production processes at the local level, it has repercussions on economies of scale, investment requirements, and costs in the automotive industry. The different processes undertaken in an integrated car factory, that is, assembly, machining, stamping, forging, and casting, are subject to different cost schedules and, hence, scale requirements. It is generally agreed that economies of scale are most significant, and the additional costs of low volume

---

*It should be noted that these figures are only estimates of the shares of the various groups of parts in the cost of the final product and will not correspond exactly to the percentages in particular countries or individual firms. They do not necessarily conform with the local content requirements set down in government legislation since these are measured in a variety of ways. There are also differences between individual models; for example, the use of an overhead camshaft engine in the Fiat 128 increased the share of the engine in total cost relative to the body, which is made from four major pressings.

operations, therefore, greatest, in the stamping process, which requires expensive dies and presses. Machining is also subject to large-scale economies, but to a somewhat lesser extent than stamping. The other processes also have decreasing costs, especially foundry work (see Appendix A).

As a result, the disadvantages of small-scale production tend to increase with local content. Up to a level of local content of about 20 to 25 percent, different scales of production make relatively little difference to costs over a range of 8,000 to 50,000 units a year (see Figure 5.1). Above this level, the disadvantages of small scale becomes more important. Finally, when local content exceeds 65 percent, they are overwhelming, reflecting again the importance of scale economies in body stamping. This is the pattern that one would have predicted from the nature of the basic production processes.

Not only do the different processes involved in vehicle production enjoy differing economies of scale, they also require different initial investments. At an output of 10,000 cars a year, it has been estimated that the investment for an assembly plant would be around $6.4 million. Partial integration, involving some machining and foundry operations, would increase investment requirements to $19.1 million. A fully integrated factory, however, would involve a total investment in the region of $49 million, of which $15 million would be in the machining department and $21.1 million in stamping.[5] During the initial stages of local integration, when the changeover is made from CKD assembly to use some local parts, the terminal firm does not need to make much additional capital outlay (at least as far as investment in fixed assets is concerned). Further integration to include the engine and bodywork, on the other hand, means the creation of machining and stamping departments and hence a considerable increase in investment.

CHANGES IN SUPPLY CONDITIONS IN ARGENTINA, CHILE, AND MEXICO

From the general features of automotive industry technology discussed above, it is to be expected that the developments of the 1960s in Argentina, Chile, and Mexico would have increased the capital requirements of the automotive industry considerably. This is likely to be most marked in Argentina, which has the highest level of local integration, and least striking in Chile. An indication of the extent to which this has occurred can be obtained from several different sets of data. First, it is possible to observe the growth of investment in the industry during the period in which local content

FIGURE 5.1

Cost Increase as a Function of Local Content

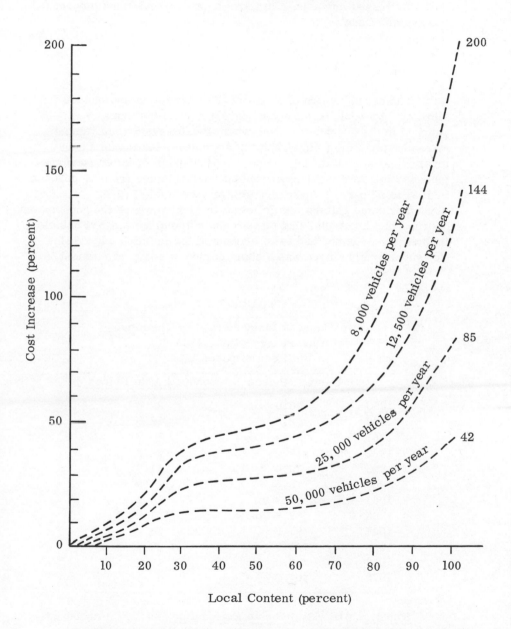

Source: Asociación de Fabricas de Automotores, Informe Económico 1969 (Buenos Aires: ADEFA, 1969), p. 24.

was being increased. Second, the increase in the amount of capital employed per unit produced can be calculated. Finally, the relationship between variable and fixed costs can be estimated as an indication of the increased importance of those cost elements most subject to economies of scale.

The Time Profile of Investment

The broad pattern of investment in Argentina and Mexico is similar. As would be expected, investment in the industry is bunched in the few years during which local content requirements were sharply increased. Thus, in Argentina, there was a heavy level of investment during the period 1960-63 in order to meet the increase in government local content requirements from 40 percent in 1961 to 90 percent three years later (see Table 5.2).

The same pattern was followed in Mexico where the government decreed in August 1962 that 60 percent of the direct cost of vehicles, including the engine, had to be accounted for in Mexico by 1964. Not surprisingly, there was a short period of heavy investment in

TABLE 5.2

Investment in Fixed Assets by Terminal
Plants, Argentina, 1959-70
(millions of pesos ley)

	Current Prices	Constant 1960 Prices
1959	20.0	22.3
1960	42.0	42.0
1961	56.0	50.7
1962	110.0	76.3
1963	90.0	51.3
1964	48.7	23.9
1965	55.8	19.6
1966	87.8	24.9
1967	94.9	20.9
1968	118.2	23.9
1969	245.9	47.8
1970	407.2	n.a.

Sources: ADEFA, Informe Estadístico, no. 588 (August 28, 1974), Table 12, and own elaboration using BCRA implicit price deflator for total investment in fixed assets.

TABLE 5.3

Annual Increase in Fixed Assets,
Mexico, 1961-69
(millions of pesos)

	Current Prices	1960 Prices
1961	21	21
1962	15	14
1963	105	93
1964	594	511
1965	286	229
1966	154	117
1967	147	109
1968	133	98
1969	81	58

Sources: Asociación Mexicana de la Industria Automotriz,
"La Industria Automotriz de México en Cifras" (Mexico City: 1972),
p. 69, and own elaboration using Bank of Mexico implicit price
deflator for investment in fixed assets.

1964 and 1965 while firms endeavored to build the necessary capacity
to meet these requirements. As Table 5.3 indicates, almost 60
percent of the total investment in fixed assets by the Mexican automotive manufacturers during the 1960s occurred in the two years
1964 and 1965.[6]
   The Chilean automotive industry remained essentially an
assembly industry throughout most of the 1960s. Consequently,
the value added in the terminal industry was low and virtually all
the parts and components that make up the vehicle were bought,
either from the parent company and its affiliates or from local
suppliers. It has been estimated that the terminal sector accounted
for only 16.8 percent of the total costs of Chilean cars in 1969, the
remainder being distributed in the following manner: 29 percent
local materials, 11.8 percent imported from other LAFTA countries,
and 42.4 percent imported from outside LAFTA. Despite government local content requirements, therefore, the Chilean terminal
producers have not found it necessary to make major investments
in fixed capital.
   As Table 5.4 indicates, it was only from 1970 that investment
appeared to increase sharply, reflecting important new investments
in productive capacity, particularly the expansion of the Citroen
plant in Arica and the new factory at Los Andes built by Automotores
Franco-Chilena, a joint venture between Renault and Peugeot.

TABLE 5.4

Annual Increase in Fixed Assets,
Chile, 1964-70
(millions of escudos)

	Current Prices	1965 Prices
1964	6,732	8,684
1965	11,188	11,188
1966	3,264	2,481
1967	16,890	10,303
1968	17,289	8,126
1969	37,190	12,645
1970	76,499	19,125
1971	101,886	20,377
1972	228,145	n.a.

Note: The firms were Citroen, Chilemotores (Ford), EMSSA
(BMC), Federic (NSU), Fiat, Imcoda (Skoda), Importsur (Volvo),
Nissan, Indauto (Renault), Indumotora (General Motors), Nun y
German (Chrysler), San Cristobal (Peugeot), and Teona (CM).
Between them, they accounted for 95.1 percent of total production
in 1963 and 100 percent in 1972. The original data came from the
balance sheets of the companies and were adjusted to achieve a
common closing date.

Source: Oficina de Planificacion Nacional (ODEPLAN),
Cuentas Nacionales de Chile, 1960-71 (Santiago: ODEPLAN, n.d.),
Tables 6 and 15, and author's compilation.

The Capital Intensity of Production

The increased investment brought with it an increase in the
capital intensity of production and therefore in the total amount of
capital required to produce a given output. This was partly a result
of a higher proportion of in-plant manufacture and partly a result of
the more capital-intensive nature of the processes introduced. Any
attempt to measure capital-output ratios at an industry level is faced
with a number of problems. While the measurement of output can
be reasonably unambiguous, the measurement of capital is fraught
with difficulties. A number of alternatives have been used by
different authors. These can be divided broadly into three categories:
those using the value of the stock of capital, those using depreciation,
and those using a physical index, such as installed horsepower or
electricity consumed.[7]

Each approach is subject to particular problems and none represents an entirely satisfactory measure. The valuation of capital will be subject to competitive distortions, which make it possible for the same physical capital to be valued differently at different times or different places. This is a particularly salient point in discussing an industry where foreign investment and foreign technology are important elements, so that the value placed on a particular item of physical capital is either a monopoly price charged by a technology supplier or a transfer price charged by a parent company to its subsidiary. Depreciation calculations can be based either on an assumed standard rate of depreciation, given a value of the capital stock, in which case the same objections apply as did in the case of the first measure, or on the actual depreciation of individual firms, in which case it becomes an arbitrary measure depending on the particular accounting practices of the firms studied. Finally, installed horsepower or electricity consumption, although much easier to measure unambiguously, may not be a good proxy for capital. Because it does not indicate the mechanical efficiency of machinery, similar horsepower or electricity consumption figures may be associated with completely different physical capital. Moreover, with electricity consumption figures, there is the additional complication that they do not take into account capacity utilization; thus, physical capital and this proxy may diverge even further.[8]

Strictly speaking, what is relevant from the point of view of the argument being developed here is that the capital outlays that firms were required to make increased as a result of the rising content requirements imposed by governments. Thus, the relevant measure of capital intensity is one based on the value of the stock of capital, whether or not this represents an increase in capital intensity in physical terms. The problem of dealing with the investment of foreign companies in their local subsidiaries (mentioned above) makes this a less than completely satisfactory measure. As a check, therefore, a second measure of capital intensity based on electrical energy consumed has also been used.

Table 5.5 shows four indicators of the capital intensity of the Argentinian automotive industry, the first three based on the output and the fourth on value added. These indices all agree in showing a considerable increase in capital intensity over the period, the increase being more marked in the case of the capital stock measurements than in the case of electricity consumption. The increase observed in the ratio of capital to value added indicates the increased capital intensity of the production processes, so that the increase observed in the other measures cannot be attributed solely to a higher level of vertical integration.

TABLE 5.5

Capital Intensity in the Argentinian
Automotive Industry, 1959-64

	Capital per Unit	Capital/ Output	Kilowatt-hour Output	Capital/ Value Added
1959	794	0.20	458.6	0.49
1960	537	0.12	636.6	0.74
1961	812	0.18	578.6	0.77
1962	1,312	0.28	633.9	1.47
1963	2,478	0.53 (0.32)	980.0	1.91
1964	1,863	0.45	820.7	1.66

Source: Consejo Nacional de Desarrollo (CONADE), "La
Industria Automotriz: Análisis Preliminar" (Buenos Aires: CONADE,
1966), and own elaboration.

One further point deserves comment, namely, the sharp rise
in all indices in 1963 and the subsequent fall in 1964. This reflected
a substantial decline in vehicle production in 1963 of about 20 percent
compared with 1962 that led to considerable excess capacity in that
year. An alternative calculation, based on full capacity utilization,
gave a capital-output ratio of 0.32 as opposed to the actual ratio of
0.53, indicating a steady increase in capital intensity through to
1964. Thus, it seems reasonable to conclude from these figures
and the previous discussion of automotive industry technology that
the period of increasing local content in the Argentinian automotive
industry during the early 1960s was accompanied by an increase in
the amount of capital required to produce a given number of vehicles.

In Mexico, as in Argentina, there is evidence to support the
contention that capital intensity rises sharply as the automotive
industry makes the transition from assembly to manufacturing.
In the Mexican case, as has already been seen, this occurred during
the years immediately following the 1962 decree. Table 5.6 shows
that the capital-output ratio, whether measured in terms of the
value of output or the number of units produced, and the ratio of
capital to value added more than doubled between 1963 and 1965.
Unfortunately, it has not been possible to obtain a continuous series
for electricity consumption, but the available figures are consistent
with the estimates in the other three columns. During the second
half of the decade, when local content remained unchanged, capital
intensity declined somewhat as output expanded without any major
new investments.

Unlike the two preceding cases, there was no evidence of a tendency for capital intensity to rise in Chile; indeed, there appears rather to have been a fall during the mid-1960s and a subsequent recovery toward the end of the decade (see Table 5.7). Data on electricity consumption for the industry as a whole are not available, but the figures for one of the leading firms, Citroen, confirm the general pattern, with electricity consumed per car produced falling until 1968 and then starting to increase.

As was indicated previously, the Chilean industry remained an assembly industry during the 1960s despite an increasing incorporation of locally produced parts. As a result, the greater part of the assets of the terminal firms was in the form of working capital, either stocks or short-term credits.[9] Working capital grew much faster than fixed assets. In the four years to 1969, fixed assets increased by only 30.8 percent in real terms as compared to 234 percent for working capital.[10]

It is tempting to attempt a comparison of capital intensity in the three countries considered. In doing so, however, the problems of measurement discussed earlier are further compounded owing to different accounting practices, different prices of both capital goods and vehicles, and the difficulties of finding suitable exchange rates for local currencies. Any comparative analysis of the three cases,

TABLE 5.6

Capital Intensity in the Mexican
Automotive Industry, 1960-69

	Capital per Unit	Capital/ Output	Kilowatt-hour Output	Capital/ Value Added
1960	440	0.17	n.a.	0.38
1961	416	0.17	n.a.	0.39
1962	421	0.16	n.a.	0.40
1963	435	0.16	241	0.35
1964	888	0.28	268	0.63
1965	1,101	0.33	n.a.	0.86
1966	1,043	0.30	421	0.95
1967	1,032	0.30	n.a.	1.08
1968	964	0.27	417	0.82
1969	899	0.25	n.a.	0.77

Source: Asociación Mexicana de la Industria Automotriz, "La Industria Automotriz de México en Cifras," (Mexico City: 1972), pp. 69-71. Secretaría de Industria y Comercio, and own elaboration.

TABLE 5.7

Capital Intensity for 13 Chilean Automotive
Manufacturers, 1964-72

	Capital per Unit ($)	Capital/ Output
1964	766	0.12
1965	897	0.14
1966	964	0.15
1967	820	0.11
1968	491	0.09
1969	496	0.10
1970	607	0.12
1971	n.a.	0.16
1972	n.a.	0.07

Source: Corporación de Fomento, company accounts, and own elaboration.

therefore, must be extremely tentative. Bearing this in mind, it might be suggested that the changeover from assembly operations increases the value of fixed assets required per car produced to over $1,000 and raises the capital-output ratio above 0.25. This took place in Argentina in 1962, in Mexico in 1964, and has yet to occur in Chile.

In comparing Argentina and Mexico, one could expect the higher level of local content in the former to give rise to a higher level of capital intensity, a view confirmed by all the indicators used. In Chile, capital intensity is significantly lower than in the other two countries, although in the mid-1960s it was higher than expected. But this could be explained by different accounting practices or higher relative prices for fixed assets, which would inflate the figures for capital intensity. As noted earlier, calculations such as these are extremely tricky, and their interest lies in the fact that they are consistent with the conclusions drawn in the earlier part of this section.

The Structure of Costs

The previous section suggested that the amount of capital required to produce a given output increased as a result of the transition to manufacturing production. In the earlier discussion,

it was seen that such a step would also increase the importance of
economies of scale since new processes of production are introduced.
Thus, not only does the capital intensity of production increase but
so, too, does the disadvantage of low volumes of output, creating
a double tendency toward an increase in the total capital needed by
a firm.

One of the main factors leading to economies of scale in production are large initial costs (see Appendix A). It is to be expected
that an increase in local content requirements in the automotive
industry will result in a rise in the share of fixed costs in total
costs.[11]

The available data for Argentina (see Table 5.8) are not
sufficiently detailed to make an exact estimate of the share of fixed
costs. This would require a more detailed breakdown of labor,
administration, finance, and sales costs. It would also require
the subtraction of profits from the last row of the table. Nevertheless, the figures do give some indication of the changes that took
place between 1960 and 1967.

From the table, there appear to have been three major changes.
First, nationally produced materials were substituted for those
previously imported, leading to an increase in the share of the
former, while the total share of material inputs in costs remained
more or less constant. This was obviously a direct result of the
government's local content measures. Second, the share of administrative, finance, and sales costs fell by more than half. This can
be attributed to the doubling of output over the period, thus spreading

TABLE 5.8

Cost Structure of the Argentinian
Automotive Industry
(percent)

	1960	1967
Local materials	35.1	52.3
Imported materials	28.0	11.2
Labor	11.3	12.5
Other inputs (energy, and so on)	1.1	1.8
Administration, finance, sales	16.4	7.8
Profits, depreciation, interest	8.1	14.4

Source: Asociación de Fabricas de Automotores (ADEFA),
Informe Económico 1969 (Buenos Aires: ADEFA, 1969), pp. 7-10.

the cost of administrative overheads, which had to be incurred from the outset, over a greater volume. Finally, payments to capital, that is, profits, depreciation, and interest, almost doubled their share of costs. Thus, although the data are not as detailed as they could be, they do suggest that fixed costs have increased.

A clearer picture can be obtained from the Mexican data. These, again, show an increase in the share of national materials at the expense of imported materials between 1960 and 1969. It has also been possible to estimate the share of fixed costs, which increased more than fourfold over the period. Table 5.9 gives a much better idea of the differences between an assembly and a manufacturing industry, since the Mexican automotive industry in 1960 was still quite clearly in the assembly phase, whereas in Argentina by that year the industry was already in transition.

The case of Citroen in Chile provides confirmation of the hypothesis that fixed costs tend to increase with local content. Between 1968 and 1974, the local integration of the models considered rose from 38.6 to 64.8 percent, on the Chilean government's definition. This manifested itself in terms of actual costs to the firm in a substantial fall in the share of foreign parts and an increase in the share of locally purchased parts. At the same time, there was a substantial increase in fixed costs, which almost trebled their share of the total* (see Table 5.10).

TABLE 5.9

Cost Structure of the Mexican
Automotive Industry
(percent)

	1960	1969
Local materials	12.7	42.0
Imported materials	66.1	30.4
Labor	9.9	14.9
Other variables	8.8	1.6
Fixed	2.5	11.1

Sources: Banco de México, La Estructura Industrial de México en 1960 (Mexico City: 1967), pp. 215-18; Asociación Mexicana de la Industria Automotriz, unpublished data; and own elaboration.

---

*Although figures have been adjusted to make them comparable in the case of the two years for each country, they are not comparable between countries.

TABLE 5.10

Cost Structure of a Chilean Car
(percent)

	1968	1974
Foreign parts	50.4	33.6
Local parts	26.0	31.1
Other variables	14.0	8.4
Fixed	9.7	26.9

Source: Based on data provided by Oficina de Planificación Nacional. The vehicles in question are the Citroen A2L in 1968 and the Citroen AX in 1974.

COST DIFFERENTIALS

In this section some initial evidence is presented to support the hypothesis that significant cost differentials of the kind discussed in Chapter 4 do in fact exist as between local and foreign firms in the Latin American automotive industry. Ideally, one should like a complete breakdown of costs for each company in order to analyze interfirm differences in costs.[12] Such a study, especially had it been attempted for all three countries under consideration, would have involved a complete study in itself, and since the intended scope of this work is much wider, would not have been justified. Moreover, it is extremely doubtful whether a single researcher could have obtained all the information necessary for such a project, considering the suspicion with which some companies view such investigation of their activities. This presents particular problems in both Argentina and Mexico where foreign subsidiaries, whose shares are not quoted on the local stock exchange, are not obliged to publish their balance sheets. Therefore, in the section that follows, the investigation has been restricted to a comparison of those cost elements that the a priori analysis above has suggested as significant sources of cost differentials.

A further difficulty arises from the nature of the problem being analyzed. As noted in Chapter 4, it is by no means easy to isolate the gains to a multinational corporation of the operations of a subsidiary in a particular country. Since transactions between parent and subsidiary are not usually of an arm's-length nature, the declared profitability of a subsidiary is not necessarily an accurate indicator of the contribution it makes to the international company's global profits. Payments such as royalties, which appear

as costs from the point of view of the subsidiary, are profits from
the point of view of the multinational corporation. Moreover, practices such as transfer pricing make it difficult to estimate costs of
production for the subsidiary, particularly where the products being
sold are specific to the firm and do not have a market price. Similarly, interaffiliate loans may be made at rates of interest above the
opportunity cost of capital to the parent company. Problems such
as these mean that a comparative analysis of costs can at best only
be suggestive of the underlying situation, which may be distorted
by transfer accounting.

Bearing all this in mind, it is not to be expected that an
examination of the declared rates of return of locally owned and
foreign firms will necessarily indicate that the latter are more
profitable. Six foreign subsidiaries and three firms with majority
local ownership for which data were available were compared for
1964 and 1965. The firms were Citroen, Ford, General Motors,
Chrysler, Fiat, and Mercedes-Benz (foreign owned) and Industrias
Kaiser Argentina (IKA), Industria Automotriz Santa Fe (IASF), and
Siam di Tella (locally owned); and the average rate of return on
capital plus reserves was calculated for both groups.* As can be
seen from Table 5.11, the foreign firms made higher profits in
1964 and showed substantial profits in 1965 when the local firms had
a loss.

Since the declared profitability of foreign subsidiaries is such
a poor indication of their contribution to the parent company, this

TABLE 5.11

Profitability* of Selected Argentinian Firms,
1964-66
(percent)

	1964	1965
Local firms (declared)	12.9	-3.8
Foreign firms (declared)	16.0	25.8
Foreign firms (effective)	22.4	32.3

*Rate of return on capital plus reserves.
Sources: Company balance sheets and own elaboration.

———————

*Mercedes-Benz, IKA, and IASF had a financial year ending
on June 30, so the averages of two financial years were taken to
get figures for calendar years.

TABLE 5.12

Profitability of Selected Chilean Firms, 1970
(percent)

	Declared Profits	Effective Profitability Assuming Overpricing of	
		25	10
Local firms	4.9		
Joint ventures	-11.2	9.8	-0.7
Foreign firms	-2.9	48.4	23.1

Sources: Company balance sheets and own elaboration.

gives no idea of the cost advantage enjoyed by subsidiaries, except that effective profitability is almost certain to be greater than declared profitability. Overpricing of imported intermediate inputs is not likely to have been a very significant factor in the Argentinian automotive industry because of the relatively high local content requirements, which had reached 90 percent by 1964, limiting the scope for such practices. Moreover, since under the Argentinian legislation, content was measured in value terms rather than by weight, as in Brazil, increasing the price of imported parts would reduce the quantity that could be imported. This, together with the high costs of producing locally those parts that could no longer be imported, acted as a disincentive to overpricing. The lack of any data on overpricing is not likely, therefore, to be an important omission.

Royalty payments, while representing costs to locally owned firms, are part of the effective profits of foreign subsidiaries. In the third row of Table 5.11, therefore, the rate of return for the six foreign subsidiaries has been recalculated to include royalties as well as declared profits.* As a result of including royalty payments, the rate of return of foreign companies increased considerably, making it significantly higher than that of the locally owned companies in both of the years considered. Even these figures may underestimate the effective profitability of foreign subsidiaries, since it has not been possible to allow for other channels of profit repatriation.

_____

*Royalty payments were estimated on the basis of the payments actually made by some companies and on extrapolation for other companies from the percentage royalty on sales paid in later years.

As in Argentina, a number of Chilean automobile manufacturers were selected and grouped according to ownership. The larger number of firms made it possible to distinguish three groups: 100 percent locally owned firms, joint ventures, and 100 percent foreign firms. The firms selected were Nun y German and Imcoda (local), British Leyland, Indauto, and Automotres San Cristobal (joint ventures), and Citroen, Fiat, General Motors, and Nissan (foreign).* The declared rate of return on capital plus reserves was found to be positive only for the locally owned firms, while the joint ventures and foreign subsidiaries had losses. There certainly appears to be no reason on this evidence for supposing that foreign firms are more profitable than their local competitors, a conclusion that was supported by a general study of the largest manufacturing firms in Chile that found that the profitability of foreign subsidiaries was similar to that of local firms.[13]

As was indicated above, calculations of the profitability of foreign investment from the point of view of the parent company should also include royalty payments made by the subsidiary. It appears that such payments have not been widely used by car assemblers, however, possibly because the Comisión Revisora de Contratos de Regalias, set up in 1967, has put a maximum royalty of 5 percent on the "despiece" value of national integration for the assembly of vehicles.

Unlike Argentina, where the high level of local integration meant that there was relatively little scope for overpricing of intermediate inputs, Chilean car assemblers are heavily dependent on parts imports from parent companies or associated producers so that this possibility cannot be ignored. This requires consideration of the pricing policies of multinational automobile companies regarding the CKD packs they export. As was mentioned above, the normal practice is for a price to be set for the entire CKD pack and then a deletion allowance is granted for those parts omitted from the pack, which tends to be less than the share of that part in the pack's total value. One possibility is that the deletion allowance for a part is based on its marginal cost, whereas the entire pack is priced at average cost. Another possibility is that the deletion allowance equals the cost of production of the part but does not include the profit margin.[14] All this points to the difficulty of determining what exactly is the world market price for the CKD pack of a particular firm and so to determine the extent of overpricing.

---

*British Leyland's financial year closed on June 30 so the averages for 1969-70 and 1970-71 were used.

In the particular case of Chile, one does have some basis on which to work. The Chilean legislation, under which the automotive industry operates, specifies local content requirements in terms of the "despiece" value of the vehicle. This is a breakdown of the FOB price of the vehicle in the country of origin allocating a certain percentage of the total cost to each part and component. If a foreign company wished to overvalue some part it intended to import, there would have to be a corresponding undervaluation of some other part. If the other part were also to be imported, then the company would have gained nothing by overpricing the first part. If, on the other hand, it were to have been produced locally, the total number of locally produced parts would have to be increased in order to attain the required content level. Consequently, the scope for overpricing seems rather limited.*

However the foreign subsidiary does not import CKD packs at FOB prices, but at CIF prices. Therefore, the prices actually paid do not necessarily correspond with those indicated in the "despiece" value of the car. In practice CIF prices in Chile appear to be about 50 percent above FOB prices.15 Most reasonable estimates of these charges for vehicle exports do not put them above 20 to 25 percent.16 Peugeot, for example, in the tender it submitted to the Chilean government for the franchise to build a medium-sized car, indicated the breakdown in Table 5.13 for CKD pack imports from France. Taking the FOB price as 100 and the CIF price as 150, it would appear, therefore, that between 17 percent (25/150) and 20 percent (30/150) of the CIF value of parts imported represents overpricing; or, to put it another way, parts are overpriced by between 20 percent (25/125) and 25 percent (30/120).

TABLE 5.13

Cost of Imported CKD Pack in Chile

	U.S. $	Percent
CKD	466.90	100
Packing	32.60	7.0
Freight	48.54	10.4
Insurance	3.74	0.8

Source: Corporación de Fomento, unpublished data.

---

*The whole question is complicated, however, by the need to allocate overheads.

In the second and third columns of Table 5.12, the effective return to the foreign company has been calculated, first assuming what appears to be a reasonable estimate of overpricing of 25 percent, and then with a much lower rate of only 10 percent, as a sensitivity text in view of the lack of any direct evidence on the level of overpricing. In the first case, the rate of return for foreign subsidiaries is increased to almost 50 percent, while overpricing of only 10 percent would give a return of over 20 percent. For joint ventures, the rate of return on the foreign company's own capital (which was slightly more than half of the total share capital) was calculated. This turned a large loss in terms of declared profits into an effective profitability of almost 10 percent with an assumed overpricing of 25 percent and a small loss with overpricing of only 10 percent. This second finding suggests that there are considerable gains to the foreign company from complete ownership, while the general conclusion must again be that wholly owned subsidiaries have a significant cost advantage over their local competitors.

The Mexican data, which cover the eight firms in operation throughout the period under consideration, provide confirmation of the higher profitability enjoyed by foreign subsidiaries. A comparison of declared profits indicates a higher rate of return for this group of firms from 1969 on. If royalties are also included in the calculation, as was argued above, foreign firms had higher returns from 1968.

As in the case of Chile, the fact that Mexican vehicles have a substantial import content makes it necessary to consider the possibility of declared profits underestimating effective profitability because of transfer pricing. Data on two Mexican firms (Automex and Ford) indicated that, in 1964, the output of the two companies, valued at international prices, was less than the tradable value of the imported and local parts that they incorporated.[17] Since the prices of local parts already had been adjusted to take account of the higher cost of such parts compared to world prices, the only reasonable explanation appears to be that the prices of the imported parts are also higher than the international market price. (An alternative explanation is that some parts got lost in transit, but this does not seem very plausible.) This is consistent with what is known about the system of deletion allowances used by the automotive manufacturers.

The assumption that transfer pricing may be an important source of income is given further support by the finding that some technology contracts in the automotive industry specify a 10 percent markup on the price of components sold to the Mexican firm over the price of original equipment. The rate of return of foreign subsidiaries, therefore, was recalculated using an assumed level of overpricing of 10 percent of the value of imported parts. As indicated in Table 5.14, this resulted in a substantial increase in the rate of profit, which contributed to a further divergence between the profitability of the two groups of firms.

It is equally difficult to unravel the elements that account for the differences in the profitability of foreign subsidiaries and local firms as it is to illustrate the existence of those differences. In Chapter 4 it was suggested that better access to capital, both in terms of being able to borrow more and of being able to obtain finance on better terms, was one of the key advantages enjoyed by foreign subsidiaries. For several reasons, it is not easy to show this empirically. First, better access to capital is a factor affecting only the supply of funds to the two groups of companies, whereas actual gearing ratios are affected not only by the supply of funds but also by the demand for external finance of each firm. Thus, foreign firms, which generate more funds internally because of their higher profitability, have, as a result, a lower demand for external funds. It cannot be predicted a priori, therefore, how gearing ratios would differ. In the early years of a firm's existence, before it has been able to accumulate much capital internally, or during periods of major expansion relative to the existing size of the firm, the difference should be easier to see.

Second, it is not easy to say much regarding access to funds from a comparison of interest payments. A large part of a foreign subsidiary's debt may be held with the parent company, so that interest charges are a form of interaffiliate transfer pricing, determined by the need to move funds within the international firm. Thus, high interest rates paid by such firms may represent a method of repatriating capital rather than the high cost of capital, per se. The lack of any systematic relationship between interest payments (deflated by liabilities) and ownership, which was found in the three cases studied, does not necessarily contradict the hypothesis that the opportunity cost of outside finance differs for the two groups of firms, and, as will be seen in Chapter 7, shortage of capital played an important part in the failure of a number of companies.

Bearing in mind these difficulties, an attempt was made to compare the gearing ratios of foreign and local firms. For Argentina, the date chosen for such a comparison was June 30, 1962, this being the earliest date for which information was available for sufficient companies. It was found that the average gearing ratio for three local firms (Industria Automotriz Santa Fe, Industrias Kaiser Argentina, and Siam di Tella Automotores)* was 1.52. For the

---

*For Siam, the average for 1961 and 1962 was used since the financial year ended on 31 December.

TABLE 5.14

Profitability of Selected Mexican Firms, 1966–73
(percent)

	1966	1967	1968	1969	1970	1971	1972	1973
Local firms	11.5	6.6	6.7	8.0	-3.8	-17.9	-11.1	-3.6
Foreign firms	4.9	-5.0	5.2	9.6	10.3	6.7	6.1	8.5
Foreign firms (profits & royalties)*	7.1	-2.9	7.6	11.4	12.2	9.0	8.7	11.7
Foreign firms (profits & royalties + 10% average overpricing)	17.8	7.1	18.5	19.0	19.9	17.8	18.2	n.a.

*Royalty payments in 1966–67 and 1969–70 were calculated on the basis of the ratio of royalties to sales found in 1968.

Sources: Asociación Mexicana de la Industria Automotriz, unpublished data and own elaboration.

industry as a whole, the gearing ratio was 2.32,[18] implying that
foreign subsidiaries have gearing ratios considerably higher than
those found for the local firms. The evidence, therefore, does
indicate a considerable difference in gearing ratios between foreign
and local firms.

For Chile, the latest year for which data were available, 1970,
was chosen for comparison, because this, as indicated earlier,
permits three groups of firms to be compared and because, despite
some of the firms having existed for a number of years, considerable
investments were being made. The results here are even more
striking than those for Argentina, and confirm the findings of a study
of foreign investment in Chilean industry, that foreign firms tend
to commit less of their own capital and rely more heavily on outside
finance than their Chilean counterparts.[19] The same nine firms
were selected as before in considering profitability. It was found
that the unweighted average of the gearing ratio was a remarkable
7.49 for the four foreign subsidiaries considered. If one looks at
the other two groups of firms, the joint ventures have a gearing
ratio of 4.54, while the local wholly owned companies have the
lowest gearing ratio of all at only 1.20. Another feature of the
financial structure of vehicle producers in Chile that bears on the
access to capital of different firms is the virtual absence of long-
term liabilities, particularly in the case of locally owned firms.
In fact, the only firm to use long-term debt on a significant scale
has been Citroen, although the other foreign-owned firms also used
some.

In Mexico there is an interesting new element in the situation.
In 1965, the gearing ratio of the foreign subsidiaries operating in
the Mexican automotive industry was 1.24, somewhat less than the
average for the industry as a whole, which stood at 1.44 in that
year.[20] This appears to contradict the initial hypothesis, especially
since the year in question represented an early stage in the development of the industry when, according to the earlier argument, it
might have been supposed that significant differences would exist
between local and foreign firms.

A more detailed examination reveals that, in fact, it is
possible to distinguish two types of firms among those that have
majority Mexican ownership, namely, those with state participation
and those that have private Mexican capital. The former have a
gearing ratio that is much higher than for the industry as a whole,
2.41, while the latter have a lower than average gearing, only 0.82.

The high gearing of the former group of companies can be
explained by the advantages that state ownership give to the two
companies, Dina and VAM, in terms of access to credit, either
because government credit was channeled to these firms or because

private sources of credit considered government backing as good a guarantee of their loans as the backing of a foreign parent. The private Mexican firms are in the same position as their Argentinian and Chilean counterparts with lower gearing.*

Another indication of access to capital is the share of inter-affiliate loans in a company's total liabilities. The wholly owned subsidiaries in Mexico tend to have a much higher percentage of their liabilities in the form of loans from the parent company, for example, Ford, 95.3 percent; General Motors, 51.3 percent; Volkswagen, 42.6 percent; whereas Automex, which only had a minority foreign shareholding, only got 15.3 percent of its total loans from its foreign affiliate.[21] As was mentioned earlier, this does not show up necessarily in the form of lower interest charges as it may be used as a form of interaffiliate transfer pricing. Unfortunately, the data are not available to determine the extent to which the liabilities of subsidiaries take the form of interaffiliate loans in Argentina and Chile.

Nevertheless, as has been seen, there is suggestive evidence to support the hypothesis that foreign subsidiaries do enjoy better access to outside sources of finance than do their local competitors in all three countries considered. This is most evident from the higher gearing ratios characteristic of foreign subsidiaries, as well as from other indicators, such as the proportion of long-term liabilities and the percentage of liabilities that are loans from the parent company. Unfortunately, this is not reflected in differences in interest payments between different types of firms.

Apart from access to capital, the other major factor contributing to differential costs, it was suggested in a previous chapter, was access to the parent company's technology. The latter appeared either directly as royalty payments or indirectly incorporated in the costs of imported parts. Again, it is difficult to measure with any precision the advantage this represents from the point of view of the subsidiary. For the purpose of comparison, the royalty payments made by local firms can be regarded as an additional cost and any such payments by foreign subsidiaries can be ignored since they form part of the effective profitability of the parent.

---

*It is, of course, possible that the higher gearing ratios of foreign subsidiaries compared to local firms is a result of factors other than preferential access to capital. It may be the case that local firms are prepared to raise capital by issuing shares on the local stock market, whereas a foreign company, which wishes to maintain complete ownership of its subsidiary, prefers to borrow locally.

One point that needs to be made in this context is that royalty payments are often made on a scale that increases with local content. What appears, therefore, as a low rate of royalty payments in relation to the sales of the local company often represents a much higher proportion of the value added and a substantial part of the total profit before paying royalties. As local content, and hence value added, increase, the royalty charge increases as a percentage of the firm's total sales.

It is often difficult to obtain data on the amount of royalties paid, especially payments from subsidiaries to parent companies. In this case, as indicated above, the problem can be partly avoided since it is only payments by locally owned companies that are relevant, and these are often more willing to disclose the sums involved. In the Argentinian case it was possible to obtain an estimate of royalty payments as a percentage of sales for the three local companies for which estimates of profitability and gearing were given earlier. The largest of these, Industrias Kaiser Argentina, made royalty payments, which amounted to about 2 percent of the total value of sales in 1968, to American Motors, Kaiser-Willys, and Renault. Of the other two companies, Industria Automotriz Santa Fe paid a rather high rate of 5 percent of sales to DKW, while Siam di Tella paid an estimated 3 percent for its BMC license.

In Chile it is necessary to take an additional factor into account, namely, the high cost of imported parts as a result of transfer pricing. Overpricing of intermediate inputs can be thought of as a form of payment for technology, like royalties, since it arises from the dependence of a local firm on a foreign technology supplier. As was seen earlier, this represented a considerable amount and should be considered as a cost from the point of view of the local firm. To this sum must be added the further costs in terms of any royalty charges that have to be paid by the local firm. Nun y German, for example, paid royalties of about 1.5 percent on sales in 1970, but this accounted for more than 30 percent of the company's profits before paying royalties.

In Mexico the rate of royalty charges was roughly similar to those found in Argentina. One estimate puts them at between 3.5 and 5 percent on sales, although higher rates may be charged in the case of more sophisticated components.[22] Any overpricing of imported components would have to be added to the royalty payments in order to arrive at the total cost disadvantage of locally owned firms.

CONCLUSION

This chapter has sought to establish two main points. First, it was seen that policies that raised the local content of vehicles produced in underdeveloped countries led to an increase in the capital intensity of production and in the economies of scale to which the automotive industry is subject. Together, these two factors have led to considerable increases in the total amount of capital required by an automotive manufacturer. Even in Chile, which remained at a lower level of local content, there was a growing need for working capital to finance suppliers. Second, some evidence was presented to support the hypothesis that foreign subsidiaries enjoyed a cost advantage over local firms as a result of the better access they have to capital and technology.

NOTES

1. A similar classification of stages in the development of the automotive industry in underdeveloped countries can be found in I. Griffiths, The Motor Industry in Developing Countries: Patterns of Growth and Location, Makerere Institute of Social Research, EDRP no. 143 (1968), pp. 5-16.

2. Overpricing refers here to the practice of charging subsidiaries or licensees prices that are above the competitive world price for inputs supplied by the parent company or licensor. The work that brought this to the attention of development economists is C. V. Vaitsos, Transfer of Resources and Preservation of Monopoly Rent, Center for International Affairs, EDH No. 168 (Harvard University, 1970).

3. F. L. Picard, The Rationale of the Gradual Development of the Automotive Industry in Developing Countries. From Assembly of Imported Parts to Complete Local Production, UNIDO (ID/WG. 13/3), 1968, p. 23.

4. Quoted in UNIDO, The Motor Vehicle Industry (ID/78), 1972, p. 48.

5. Economic Commission for Latin America (ECLA), Prespectivas y Modalidades de Integración Regional de la Automotriz en América Latina, ECLA/DI/DRAFT/92, División de Desarrollo Industrial (1973), Table 2.5.

6. Although not strictly relevant to the point under consideration, that is, the increased capital requirements of the terminal industry, it is of interest to note that investment in the automotive parts industry also followed the same pattern. In Argentina, almost 40 percent of the total investment in the parts industry between 1960 and 1967 (both years inclusive) was in the two years 1961 and 1962, while in Mexico, the total assets of the parts industry more than doubled between 1962 and 1964, from 2,000 million pesos to 4,500 million pesos. See Comisión de Estudios Económicos de la Industria

Automotriz, La Industria Automotriz Argentina: Informe Económico 1969 (Buenos Aires: ADEFA, 1969), Table 11; and Manuel Franco Rosas, "Problemas y Perspectivas de la Industria Automotriz en México" (Thesis, Universidad Nacional Autónoma de México, 1971), Chap. 1.

7. See, for example, Mario M. Cortes, "Technological Absorption and Unemployment: A Comparative Analysis" (Ph.D. thesis, Washington University, 1973), quoted in D. Felix, "Technological Dualism and Late-Late Industrializers: On Theory, History and Policy" (Paper delivered at the Economic History Association Annual Meeting, Atlanta, September 1973), p. 4, who uses mainly installed horsepower; J. Katz, Importación de Tecnología, Aprendizaje Local e Industrialización Dependiente, Centro de Investigaciones Económicas, Documentos de Trabajo No. 59 (Instituto Torcuato di Tella, 1972), pp. VI 3-6, who uses the value of the capital stock; and C. Cooper, Employment, Incomes and Equality: A Strategy for Increasing Productive Employment in Kenya (Geneva: 1972), pp. 446-52, who uses depreciation.

8. For a further discussion of these points, see R. Sutcliffe, Industry and Underdevelopment (Reading, Mass.: Addison-Wesley, 1971), pp. 140-46.

9. Instituto de Costos, Estudio Sobre la Industria Automotriz (Santiago, 1969), Anexo 28.

10. Ibid., Chap. 2b.

11. It has been observed in the motor industry in advanced countries that the more vertically integrated a firm, the higher the ratio of fixed to total costs. See G. Maxcy and A. Silberston, The Motor Industry (London: Allen C. Unwin, 1959), pp. 62-63.

12. An example of the kind of analysis that we have in mind is the study of the Argentinian tractor industry by José María Dagnino Pastore and others, the third volume of which is devoted entirely to a comparison of the cost structure of the different firms. José María Dagnino Pastore et al., La Industria del Tractor en la Argentina, Centro de Investigaciones Económicas, Trabajos Internos, No. 21 (Instituto Torcuato di Tella, 1966).

13. See L. Pacheco, "La Inversión Extranjera en la Industria Chilena" (professional diss., University of Chile, 1970), Chap. 7.

14. See S. J. Kleu, "Import Substitution in the South African Automobile Industry" (Thesis, Harvard University, 1967), pp. 67-73, for this and other examples.

15. See Felix Gil Mitjans, "Un Modelo de Programación de la Industria Automotriz Chilena" (Thesis, Universidad de Chile, 1969), Table C; and Instituto Chileno del Acero, Problemas y Perspectivas de la Industria Automotriz Chilena (Santiago, 1969), Anexo II.

16. See J. Behrman, The Role of International Companies in Latin American Integration; Autos and Petrochemicals (Lexington, Mass.: D. C. Heath, 1972), on the relatively low costs of transporting parts.

17. C. Sanchez-Marco, Industry Study, Cost-Benefit Analysis of Car Manufacturing in Mexico (1) (Paris: OECD, Development Center, 1968), Tables VI and IX.

18. C. M. Jiménez, "Contribución al Estudio Crítica sobre la Política de Radicación de Capitales en la República Argentina: La Industria Automotriz" (Ph.D. thesis, University of Buenos Aires, 1964), Chap. 2b (i). Average figures for 1961 and 1962 were again used.

19. Pacheco, op. cit., Chap. 4.

20. Emilio Kawage Vera, "La Industria Automotriz y la Política Gubernamental" (professional thesis, Universidad Autónoma de México, 1968).

21. Rafael Vizcaino Velasco, La Industria Automotriz Mexicana: Análisis Evaluación y Perspectivas (professional thesis, Escuela Superior de Economía, 1969), Chap. 4.

22. M. S. Wionczek, G. Bueno, and J. E. Navarrette, "La Transferencia International de Tecnología al Nivel de Empresa: El Caso de México," mimeographed (Mexico: Fondo de Cultura Económica, 1974), pp. 92-93.

6

THE DEMAND FOR
CARS AND DEPENDENT
INDUSTRIALIZATION

It was noted in Chapter 4 that the rate of growth of market demand was an important element in explaining the extent to which competition led to an increase in concentration within an industry. If expansion is rapid, then it will enable all firms to grow and perhaps even encourage new firms to enter the industry. When a market is stagnating or only growing slowly, however, foreign firms can only grow by driving out other companies, and there will be a tendency for increased concentration and denationalization.

In this chapter, the characteristic features of the demand for cars in underdeveloped countries are discussed, and the typical pattern of growth of demand over time traced. The analysis concentrates on the market for passenger cars to the exclusion of that for commercial vehicles. This seems justified since the dynamic role in automotive industry development almost always has been played by the former (with the exception of the socialist bloc and the earliest phase of development in some countries). Moreover, the passenger car sector is, analytically, the more interesting of the two since it is here that the distinction between developed and underdeveloped countries is most marked.

THEORETICAL CONSIDERATIONS

The most significant characteristic of the car from the point of view of demand is that it is a consumer durable. In economic terms, this means that the product is not entirely consumed during the period in which it is bought. In other words, at any given moment in time there is a stock of cars in existence on the roads that is different from the new purchases of cars over, say, the

117

preceding 12-month period. Consequently, most of the models that have been used to analyze and predict car demand in the developed countries are based on the stock-adjustment principle.[1] New car purchases are a function of the difference between the existing number of cars in circulation at the end of the previous period and a desired, optimum stock of cars and the rate of depreciation.

Although it is possible to apply the same kind of model to underdeveloped countries, it is necessary first to consider a number of important characteristics that differentiate the demand for cars in such countries. The models that explain the demand for cars in terms of a few variables, such as income, price, and the existing stock, represent a simplification of a much more complex phenomenon. A satisfactory formulation would need to take account of a number of other variables, such as the cost of car ownership (and not just the price of new cars), the cost and availability of alternative forms of transport, the development of the road network, the extent of consumer credit, advertising, expectations, the time pattern of the development of ownership of consumer durables, and the distribution of income.[2] It appears from the goodness of fit of the equations used in developed countries that the omission of these variables is not serious, either because they have remained constant or because they are well approximated by the included variables. In other cases some of these variables, such as credit terms, have been explicitly included.[3] It cannot be assumed a priori, however, that the same will apply in underdeveloped countries.

The usual model applied in the developed countries makes the desired car stock (S^*) a function of income and price, and demand for new cars a proportion of the difference between desired and actual stocks.

$$X_t = a(S^*_t - S_{t-1}) - dS_{t-1} \tag{1}$$

$$S^*_t = m + bY_t + cP_t \tag{2}$$

where X is the demand for new cars, Y is income, and P is price.

The desired car stock is also a function of the development of the road network and the availability and cost of other forms of transport. Whereas in developed countries these may be relatively unchanging, in underdeveloped countries it is not possible to make the same assumption. Therefore, it may be necessary to introduce a time trend to catch these variables. The advantage of using a time trend in this context, rather than a more direct proxy, is that one can thus also catch the typical pattern of growth of demand for a new commodity, which is partly a function of the availability of complementary commodities (such as roads on which to drive cars)

but also a function of the diffusion of knowledge and changes in consumer tastes.[4] Thus, we may rewrite Equation 2 in the form

$$S^*_t = m + bY_t + cP_t + gt \tag{3}$$

Another feature that usually has been ignored in car demand
studies in developed countries but that may be important in underdeveloped countries is the distribution of income. If one thinks of
the desired stock of cars, S^*, as the maximum level of car ownership
(the term used by Roos and von Szleiski), then it can be seen more
clearly that this will be determined by the number of households
with an income above a certain minimum required for car ownership;
that is, it will be a function of both income level and distribution and
not just per capita income as was previously assumed. This does
not present much of a problem when income is fairly equally distributed and does not change significantly over time. If, however,
there are sharp discontinuities in income distribution, or if it
changes during the period under study, then per capita income will
not be such a good explanatory variable. As income increases,
the number of households pushed over the threshold of car ownership
will vary. Thus, a highly unequal income distribution may give rise
to rapid initial growth of demand, but a subsequent slowing down
because increases in per capital income do not bring many additional
households over the threshold. Similarly, regressive changes in
favor of upper and middle income groups will increase the number
of potential consumers, while income increases for the lowest
income groups will not. Where cars are mass consumption goods,
explicit inclusion of income distribution is likely to be a less
important consideration than where car ownership is just beginning
to penetrate the upper and middle income groups.

One of the few studies of car demand in an underdeveloped
country to consider income distribution explicitly is one of Brazil
by the Confederacão Nacional da Industria.[5] The following equation
was used to forecast the growth of car sales:

$$1 + q = (1 + r)^\alpha / (1 + p)^{\alpha - 1}$$

where q is the potential rate of growth of the car stock, p is population growth, r is the rate of growth of GNP, and α is Pareto's
income distribution coefficient (the parameter of the income distribution curve calculated as the elasticity of the number of income
receiving units to the lower income limit). A higher value of α
implies a more equal distribution of income, so that, given the
above equation, greater income equality tends to lead to a faster
potential rate of growth of the car stock.[6] In view of the criticisms

that have been leveled at Pareto's law, however, this does not appear
to be a very satisfactory method for dealing with the effects of income
distribution on the demand for cars.

The demand for a consumer durable can be divided into two
components, that part that goes to increase the stock of the product
and that that goes to replace existing units. In the specific case of
cars, part of sales goes to increase the number of vehicles on the
road, while the remainder goes to replace scrapped vehicles. The
relative importance of these two components of demand differs
greatly between developed and underdeveloped countries. For
example, in the United States, in the mid-1960s, scrappage represented 70 percent of new registrations; that is, of total sales, 70
percent went to replace scrapped units, while only 30 percent
contributed to an increase in the number of vehicles in circulation.
In Britain, in 1965, scrappage was 42 percent of new registrations.
The equivalent ratio for Argentina in 1965 was about 10 percent and
that for Mexico 7.2 percent in the same year.

Another respect in which the demand for cars in underdeveloped
countries may differ from that in developed countries is in the proportion accounted for by business demand for passenger cars. This
is particularly important in the earliest stages of the development
of car ownership. Data for South Korea[7] in 1965 indicated that 66.5
percent of all cars registered in the country were either business
or government vehicles as compared to only 19 percent in Britain.[8]
Unfortunately, there are no corresponding figures available on the
share of business registrations in the total stock in the Latin American countries that interest us, but, bearing in mind the considerably
higher level of car density in those countries, it would probably be
much lower than in South Korea.

By far the most important factor to be taken into account when
considering car demand in an underdeveloped country as opposed to
a developed country is the question of constrained supply. This can
be ignored in developed countries where the greater flexibility of
the economy means that, when they do arise, supply constraints
are of short duration. In an underdeveloped country, on the other
hand, they can persist over long periods because of a low capacity
to import or bottlenecks in certain key sectors, for example,
electricity, or, in the case of the automotive industry, the parts
industry.

Supply constraints assume a special significance in the case
of consumer durables, since, unlike the case of nondurable consumer
goods, they give rise to a backlog demand for the goods concerned.
In terms of the model discussed above, there is a growing divergence
between the desired and the actual stock of vehicles in circulation.
In cases of particularly severe shortages prolonged over a consider-

able period of time, the stock of vehicles may fall as scrapped units are not replaced, while per capita income and the desired stock of vehicles increase. The classic example of this process is Argentina where the number of cars per 1,000 inhabitants fell from 24 in 1928 to 19 in 1958, despite the growth of income during the period.

Backlog demand is not necessarily identical with repressed demand, although the two concepts have been confused. Backlog can arise with or without repressed demand, as the latter is conventionally understood. The best way of bringing out the distinction between the two concepts is through some simple examples.

The first possible situation is one where the supply of cars is controlled either by import quotas or by production quotas and prices are also controlled by government policy. In this case, if the demand at the fixed price exceeds the given supply, or to put it another way, if the market clearing price is in excess of the controlled price, then there will be repressed demand that will manifest itself in waiting lists for cars, advance payments, and other forms of nonprice rationing. This will also clearly lead to backlog demand, since there will develop a divergence between the actual stock and the desired stock of cars.

A second situation is again one with a supply constraint in the sense that the government attempts to keep down the level of car sales. But, in this case, it uses the price mechanism to do so, either directly by using import duties rather than quotas or indirectly with import or production quotas, by allowing prices to rise to the level that equates demand with the available supply. This is not a situation of repressed demand in the conventional sense, but it is one of backlog demand in the sense of a gap between actual and desired car stocks.

The last situation that can be identified is one where neither supply is restricted nor prices controlled. This is the usual situation of developed countries and here there is neither repressed nor backlog demand.

Figure 6.1, a diagramatic representation, can help to clarify the different situations even further. Let us suppose that in period 0, given the existing stock of cars and the level of income in the country concerned, the demand for new cars is given by the line DD_0. Supply is limited by the government to the level S_0. The first example, discussed above, is that where the price of cars is also controlled at the level $\bar{P}$, below the market clearing price P_0, and the indicated repressed demand is given by MN. In the second case, prices are allowed to rise to the level P_0 so that repressed demand is eliminated. In the third case, supply is increased to S_1 so that repressed demand is also eliminated.

FIGURE 6.1

"Repressed" and "Backlog" Demand

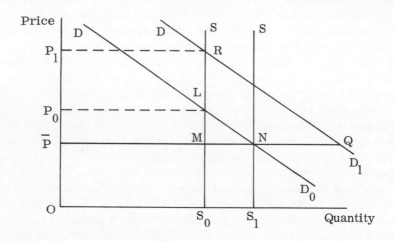

Source: Compiled by the author.

So far, however, the analysis has been confined to one period, so that it has not been possible to discuss whether or not there is also backlog demand in these cases. As was mentioned above, DD_0 was drawn for a given level of income and stock of cars. Over time, however, these factors will change, increases in income pushing the curve outward and increases in the stock of cars pushing the curve inward. If there is a backlog of demand, the stock will not grow sufficiently fast to match the growth of income and the curve will be pushed outward to DD_1. If supply remains constrained at S_0, repressed demand at the official price $\bar{P}$ increases from MN to MQ and the market clearing price rises from P_0 to P_1. This shift in DD as a result of backlog demand will occur independently of whether or not it is accompanied by repressed demand and will continue as long as a backlog exists.

The same point can be made with a numerical example. Suppose for simplicity that the demand equation takes a log-log form:

$$\log X_t = a \log Y_t - b \log P_t - c \log S_{t-1}$$

a, b, and c are thus the elasticities of demand with respect to the variables to which they are attached. Let us assume for the sake

of the example that a = 3, b = 1, and c = 2. Assume further that
Y_t is growing at a rate of 5 percent per year. In the long run both
new purchases and stock must grow at the same rate. If this is
assumed initially to be 5 percent, then P_t can remain constant.

Rates of Growth of Variables

Year	Y_t	X_t	S_t	P_t
0	5%	5%	5%	0
1	5%	4%	4.8%	1.0%
2	5%	4%	—	1.4%
.	.	.	.	.
.	.	.	.	.
.	.	.	.	.
.	.	.	.	.
n	5%	4%	4%	3%

If the rate of growth of supply is reduced to 4 percent, then
the market clearing price rises initially by 1 percent and the rate
of growth of the stock of cars falls below 5 percent. Eventually,
the rate of growth of the stock of cars falls to the new equilibrium
rate of 4 percent. The rate of growth of market clearing prices will
then level off at 3 percent per year. It makes no difference if actual
prices are allowed to rise by this amount or not; there will be a
backlog of demand in either case.

Whether or not repressed demand exists together with the
backlog demand, the effect is the same when the supply constraint
is removed. Either way demand is very buoyant for a period while
this backlog is being met. In the case where there is no repressed
demand, because prices have been allowed to rise to the market
clearing level, this can be thought of simply as a price effect, since
the startup of local production, for example, is likely to be accompanied by a fall in price compared to the previous import price plus
duty.[9] In practice, some combination of the two cases is likely to
be found. In the first case there is no visible price effect but
queuing and so on are eliminated and the gap between the desired
and actual stock closed.

Having defined backlog demand in this way, it is not simple
to identify when it may have existed and even more difficult to
attempt to quantify it. The problem arises from the fact that the
phenomenon is not necessarily accompanied by queuing and that it
is not easy to know how high prices have to be to choke off demand
so that there is no repressed demand observable.

One approach to the problem is that of international comparisons. It is assumed initially that the most important single factor

determining the level of car ownership within a country is its per capita income. The regression line relating car density to income was calculated using the data available for 26 capitalist economies. The use of cross-section analysis in such a situation presents a number of problems. A regression calculated in this way may simply be the result of linking points on each country's individual growth path relating car density to income.

For a curve derived from cross-section data to be meaningful, it is necessary to postulate a universal relationship between the two variables. This is a strong assumption but may not be implausible in economic terms. What it does imply is that as incomes rise, consumption follows the same pattern in all countries. This is the equivalent of saying that, as a result of the international demonstration effect, the desired level of car density is the same in countries at the same level of income. In fact, it would appear that the international demonstration effect is very strong in the case of passenger cars.

If it were the case that no universal relation existed between income and the number of vehicles in circulation, but that the relationship observed using international cross-section data was simply the result of linking points on individual country curves, then this observed relationship would show no constancy over time. If, on the other hand, there was such a universal relationship, then the curve would not change significantly over a number of years.

The hypothesis that a universal relation exists was tested by calculating the regression equations relating the log of the number of cars per 1,000 inhabitants to the log of per capita gross domestic product for 26 countries on which data were available both for 1958 and 1969. The equations thus derived were as follows:

$$1958 \quad \log S = 1.63 \log Y - 3.10 \qquad r^2 = 0.83$$
$$(0.16) \qquad (0.44)$$

$$1969 \quad \log S = 1.74 \log Y - 3.38 \qquad r^2 = 0.90$$
$$(0.11) \qquad (0.33)$$

These were tested to see if the coefficient of log Y, that is, the income elasticity of the number of vehicles in circulation, had changed significantly over the period, and it was concluded that it had not.

It has already been mentioned, in discussing the demand for new cars, that per capita income is by no means the only factor determining this demand, and the same is true of the stock of cars. The most important variable, apart from income, is likely to be the cost of car ownership, composed of the purchase price of the car and its running cost over its entire lifetime. It has not been possible to find any data on international comparisons of the cost of running a car, so that the purchase price of a new car has been taken to represent the cost of car ownership. Using data for 16 countries in the mid-1960s, it was found that introducing the price variable, the data for which were admittedly not very good, did not add anything to the explanatory power of the regression using only per capita income.

It seems possible, therefore, to use the equations presented earlier to give a rough indication of the expected level of car ownership in a country, given its per capita income. If the actual car density falls well below the predicted level, this would be a priori evidence of backlog demand.

Taken together, these factors tend to make the pattern of demand found in the car market of the underdeveloped countries rather different from that found in developed countries. As has just been seen, there is likely to be a significant upward time trend in the demand for cars in underdeveloped countries, as the road network develops and the use of cars becomes more widespread. This would not be the case in the developed countries since they have already passed through the comparable phase in the development of the car market. Thus, the number of cars in circulation and even the number of new registrations may continue to grow in recession years when per capita income falls. This tendency for growth independently of income and price movements is likely to be accentuated during the early years of the development of the industry in many countries because of the existence of considerable backlog demand along the lines just described.

It is not clear what the consequences of the various individual characteristics of the market for vehicles in underdeveloped countries will be for the income and price elasticities of demand. A. Nowicki has suggested that income and price elasticities will tend to be higher in underdeveloped countries than in developed countries.[10] He bases his argument on the differential weights of expansion and replacement demand in the two groups of countries. If one assumes that the income elasticity of demand for increases in the stock of vehicles is the same in developed and underdeveloped countries, and that the rate of scrappage is less sensitive to income changes than new demand, then the higher weight of the latter in underdeveloped countries will make total demand more sensitive to income changes.

It is not clear that either of these assumptions holds, however. In the first place, the tendency for demand to grow regardless of changes in income, the greater importance of demand for cars for business as opposed to private use, and the more unequal income distribution may mean that the income elasticity of demand for new car purchases is not the same in developed and underdeveloped countries. Moreover, despite the relative importance of replacement purchases in the advanced countries, demand still fluctuates considerably from year to year, reflecting perhaps the role of expectations and the ability to postpone the acquisition of a new car, which may make a replacement market more volatile.

In developed countries, the high proportion of demand that goes to replace scrapped units tends to dampen the price elasticity of demand, since used cars tend to be traded in when making new purchases. It is not necessarily true, however, that the lower ratio of replacement to expansion demand in underdeveloped economies will lead to a higher price elasticity. The fallacy here lies in equating sales to new owners with sales that increase the number of cars in circulation. In practice, new cars tend to be bought by previous owners and those who are buying for the first time tend to buy used cars. Even if it were true that a higher proportion of new car buyers were entering the market for the first time in underdeveloped countries, one could still not conclude that this would lead to a higher price elasticity without taking into account a number of other factors. The importance of business demand or the importance of supply constraints might make demand relatively inelastic with respect to small changes in price.

INCOME DISTRIBUTION AND THE
DEMAND FOR CARS

In the previous section it was indicated that the distribution of income was an important variable in explaining the growth of car ownership in underdeveloped countries. Since it is unfortunately rather difficult to include it in an econometric model of car demand, the general pattern of ownership or expenditure by income group will be discussed before going on to consider the growth of demand and changes in demand conditions in each country individually. Unlike the developed countries where car ownership is by now widespread, in the underdeveloped countries a mass market has not developed and ownership reaches down only as far as medium-sized business owners and professional workers. As Nowicki puts it, "a country which shows signs of having mass consumption in motor cars is becoming a developed country."[11]

In Argentina, the most developed of the countries under consideration, more than half the households covered by a family expenditure survey in 1963 spent virtually nothing on car purchases, accounting for only 5 percent of total expenditure on cars, while

TABLE 6.1

Expenditure on Cars by Income Group in
Argentina, 1963
(thousands of pesos)

Family Income	Percent Families	Percent of Car Expenditure	Cars as Percent of Total Expenditure
Less than 200	53	5.3	0.5
200 to 350	29	23.1	2.5
350 to 750	15	38.4	5.1
More than 750	3	33.2	10.9
Total	100	100.0	3.3

Sources: Camara Industrial de Fabricantes de Autopiezas de
la Republica Argentina, Estudio Técnico-Económico de la Industria
Nacional de Transporte (Buenos Aires, 1970), pp. 232-35. Comisión
de Estudios Económicos de la Industria Automotriz, La Industria
Automotriz Argentina, Informe Economico, 1969 (Buenos Aires,
1969), pp. 197-98.

more than 70 percent of such expenditure is made by the top 18 percent of households. Thus, even in this country, with its large middle
class, the car is still by no means a mass consumer good. Families
with an income below 70,000 pesos do not spend on cars, while those
between 70,000 and 200,000 pesos spend only 0.5 percent of their
total expenditure on cars. It is only in the highest income group,
which accounts for 3 percent of all families, that the proportion
rises above 10 percent (see Table 6.1).

The Mexican case (Table 6.2) shows a high concentration of
automobile ownership among the highest income groups. The lowest
76 percent of families by income account for only 14 percent of all
the cars owned in the country, while the highest 9 percent, with
40 percent of total income, own 59 percent of all cars. It can be
seen from these figures that cars, as would be expected of a luxury
consumer durable, are more highly concentrated than total income.
Even these figures underestimate the extent to which car ownership
is concentrated, since they refer only to the number of units owned,
whereas the lower income families will tend to have secondhand
cars and cheaper models and the high income groups will have newer
and larger cars. Data on car ownership that took account of the
value of the vehicles owned or data on new purchases would show
even higher concentration.

TABLE 6.2

Ownership of Cars by Income Group
in Mexico, 1963

Family Income (pesos monthly)	Percent Families	Percent Total Income	Percent Cars Owned
Less than 1,500	76.01	35.4	14.2
1,501 to 3,000	15.00	24.7	26.8
3,001 to 4,500	4.55	13.0	15.6
4,501 to 10,000	3.56	17.6	32.5
More than 10,000	0.88	9.3	10.9

Source: Banco de México, S. A., Encuesta sobre lugresos y Gastos Familiares en México, 1963 (Mexico City, 1966).

Unfortunately it was not possible to obtain statistics of car sales or ownership by income group for Chile. As an approximation, data on the consumption of transport equipment in general had to be used, which tend to underestimate the true extent to which car owner-ship is concentrated, since they include other items, such as bicycles, which tend to be consumed by lower income groups. Even so, the figures in Table 6.3 show that car purchases only assume a signifi-cant proportion of total expenditure for the top 5 percent of house-holds and that these account for more than 75 percent of total

TABLE 6.3

Expenditure on Transport Equipment by
Income Group in Chile, 1969

Family Income (sueldos vitales)	Percent Families	Percent of Car Expenditure	Transport Equipment and Percent of Total Expenditure
0 to 2	31.2	0.5	0.1
2 to 4	35.0	1.1	0.1
4 to 6	14.6	8.1	1.2
6 to 8	14.3	14.8	1.6
More than 8	4.9	75.5	13.2

Source: S. Pitar and E. Moyano, Redistribución del Consumo y Transición al Socialismo, Cuadernos de la Realidad Nacional no. 11 (1972), pp. 25-44.

purchases of transport equipment. The lowest two thirds of all households consume only 1.6 percent of the total, which in all likelihood includes no cars whatsoever.

These three studies, despite the differences in the concepts they employ (car ownership, sales), all show that car ownership in Latin America is concentrated in the hands of a small minority of the population, while the vast majority is virtually excluded from participating in this market. The second point that emerges is the discontinuity in car consumption, which increases sharply as a percentage of total consumption in the upper income groups. In the two studies that refer to car purchases (that is, those on Argentina and Chile), more than 10 percent of total expenditure by the highest income group is on cars, while the proportion is significantly less among lower income groups. (This would seem to indicate a lack of trickle down from the high income groups as far as car consumption is concerned.)

THE DEMAND FOR CARS IN SOME
LATIN AMERICAN COUNTRIES

This section attempts to utilize some of the theoretical concepts discussed in previous sections in order to analyze the pattern of growth of car output in a number of Latin American economies and the factors contributing to it. Where possible, econometric analysis is used, but emphasis is given to statistical material of a more descriptive nature.

As has already been seen, a number of factors may underlie the growth of output. As with all commodities, there is both an income elasticity and a price elasticity effect. There is also an added factor derived from what has been called backlog demand, that is, the adjustment of the car stock to its normal level, below which it has been kept by a supply constraint. In the early stages of the industry's development, this is likely to be the most important factor at work in a number of countries. Finally, there is the import-substituting effect of replacing cars previously imported, the importance of which depends on how far imports were permitted before the initiation of local production.

Of the three countries to be considered, Argentina and Chile are obviously cases where imports of cars have been subject to severe restraint so that there is an a priori reason for supposing that the supply constraint and backlog demand have been important factors. This is not so readily apparent in Mexico, which has enjoyed a more favorable balance of payments position since World War II and has been able to maintain imports and local assembly at

relatively high levels. Nevertheless, even Mexico had a considerably
lower number of cars in circulation in 1960 than might have been
expected on the basis of international comparisons.

Argentina

As was indicated above, Argentina appears as a classic case
of a country where control of imports of cars over a long period of
time led to a considerable divergence between the actual and desired
number of vehicles in circulation. As Table 6.4 indicates, the
crisis of 1929 brought a sharp fall in the country's car imports.
Up to 1956, the main method used to restrict imports of cars was
a quota system, which was subsequently replaced by high tariff
duties. Car prices rose considerably in real terms from 1929
onward, especially after World War II. Thus, small cars in the
early 1960s cost between 1.6 and 2.5 times more than in 1929 and
medium and large cars varied from 2.8 to 4.3 times the 1929 price.[12]
Presumably the differential was even higher during the 1950s before
the start of local production. These comparisons, it should be
remembered, take no account of quality and design improvements
over the period.
    If the stock of cars in Argentina in 1960 is compared with the
level predicted on the basis of international comparison, it appears
that it fell short by more than 40 percent. Another consequence and
indication of the shortage of new vehicles from the 1930s onward
was the lengthening of the life of the existing vehicles. Whereas in
1933 more than half the cars in Argentina were less than 5 years

TABLE 6.4

Imports of Cars into Argentina, 1920-54

1920-24	105,854
1925-29	267,766
1930-34	70,443
1935-39	125,334
1940-44	36,150
1945-49	48,985
1950-54	25,759

Source: Asociación de Fabricas de Automotores (ADEFA),
Industria Automotriz Argentina (Buenos Aires, 1970).

old and all cars were less than 10 years old, by 1954 the situation
had so deteriorated that 65.7 percent of all cars were more than
15 years old and only 7.3 percent were less than 5 years old.[13]
This lengthening of the life of cars meant that the real stock of
vehicles in circulation, taking account of depreciation, was less
than the apparent stock calculated simply in numerical terms.

Until 1960, imports had been the major source of cars in
Argentina. Nevertheless, the absolute level was low and fluctuating.
The only years during the 1950s in which they surpassed 15,000 were
in 1951 and 1958. Import substitution, in the literal sense of the
phrase, therefore, did not provide much scope for the growth of
local production. The initial backlog demand and the age structure
of the existing stock, on the other hand, did. The number of cars
per 1,000 inhabitants rose from 23 in 1960 to around 75 by 1971.
By 1967, the proportion of cars less than ten years old had risen
to 70 percent compared to less than 25 percent in 1954 and less
than 40 percent in 1960.[14]

It is impossible to say exactly when the initial backlog demand
was eliminated. Some industry sources put the elimination of excess
demand as early as the end of 1962,[15] but it is difficult to disentangle
the effect of the recession in general economic conditions from the
secular evolution of the automotive industry. By 1969, however,
the car density in Argentina was higher than its expected level by
almost 20 percent.

These developments had a number of market manifestations.
New car prices fell by almost 25 percent in real terms between 1960
and the mid-1960s. At the same time, used cars, whose value
depreciated by only 5 percent per year up to 1960, began to depre-
ciate at a faster rate.[16] As Table 6.5 indicates, there was a
considerable increase in depreciation rates up to 1963 that continued
during the mid-1960s.

The same forces of increased supply and competition that
tended to drive down the prices of new cars and the trade-in values
of secondhand cars also led to increased utilization of sales finance.
Initially, the manufacturers found little need to extend credit to
their customers in order to sell their cars. But between 1959 and
the first half of 1963, the percentage of total units sold for which
credit was granted rose from 32 to 84 percent, while the average
period for which credit was extended lengthened from 10 to 24 months
and the monthly interest rate fell from 2.0 to 1.6 percent.[17] In the
mid-1960s, the normal deposit was estimated at between 40 and
50 percent of the car's price.[18] This was a period during which
the manufacturers or their dealers began to set up finance companies
in order to provide credit to their customers. One of the earliest

TABLE 6.5

Relative Prices of New and Used Cars
in Argentina, 1963–66

		Age (years)			
Year	New	1	2	3	4
1963	100	84	80	76	72
1964	100	82	78	74	70
1965	100	78	73	70	66
1966	100	73	68	63	59

Source: Asociación de Concesionarios de Automotores de la
República Argentina, El Concesionario de Automotores en la Argentina 2 (Mar de Plata, 1967).

established companies, Permanente, which operated on behalf of
IKA, grew rapidly during the first half of the decade, especially
between 1963 and 1964.

In order to try and gain further understanding of the factors
contributing to the growth of car production in Argentina during
this period, a statistical demand function was estimated for the
years 1960 to 1971. A stock adjustment model of the form discussed
above incorporating a time trend was used.

$$X_t = aY_t + bP_t + cS_{t-1} + dt \tag{1}$$

In order to avoid the problems posed by multicolinearity
between income, price, and stock, first differences of the variables
were taken and the equation became

$$DX_t = aDY_t + bDP_t + cDS_{t-1} + d \tag{2}$$

The equation was estimated using both absolute and per capita values
of sales, income, and stock, the best fit being obtained with the
latter, which gave the equation

$$D(X/N)_t = 31.35D(Y/N)_t - 0.02DP_t - 0.36D(S/N)_{t-1} + 1.56$$
$$(7.06) \qquad (0.04) \qquad (0.14) \qquad (0.63)$$

$$R^2 = 0.79$$

A number of interesting observations can be drawn from this
equation. In the first place, per capita income, car density, and

the constant term are all significant. If one assumes a rate of
depreciation of the stock of cars of 2 or 3 percent per year, then
the adjustment coefficient can be estimated at slightly less than
0.4, remembering that the coefficient c is composed of the rate of
depreciation minus the adjustment coefficient. The estimated income
elasticity at the mean values of the variables comes to approximately
3.1. The calculated price elasticity of demand is extremely low,
only 0.3 and not significantly different from zero, although it does
have the correct sign. The constant term in the equation is significant, indicating an upward trend in demand not explained by income
and price changes. In fact, this appears to be the most important
factor explaining the growth of output during the period, followed by
the growth of per capita income.

It is of interest to compare these findings with the results
obtained in a number of studies of car demand in the United States.
Ten studies quoted by L. White[19] found income elasticities ranging
from 1.0 to 4.0, with 3.0 as a center point, and price elasticities
between -0.5 and -1.5. The lower income elasticities were obtained
using variables such as Roos and von Szelski's "supernumary income,"
rather than total income, as the independent variable. Where
personal disposable income was used, the elasticity estimates were
all greater than 3. The Suits study, which is the one most akin
in its methodology to the equation used here, suggested an income
elasticity of 4.59.[20] As Suits points out, the use of first difference
analysis tends to bias the income elasticity upward and the price
elasticity downward. Thus, it appears clear that the income elasticity of demand is lower in Argentina than in the United States, and
that the price elasticity is also probably lower.

As the initial backlog of demand was eliminated in Argentina,
it was to be expected that further growth in output would come to
depend more closely on growth of income. In fact, the correlation
coefficient between per capita income and car sales per head
increased from 0.62 in the period 1960-65 to 0.85 for the entire
period 1960-71. This suggests that from the mid-1960s onward the
expansion of the market came to depend on the growth of the economy
as a whole. This, in turn, led to a slowing down of the rate of
growth of both car production and the number of cars in circulation.
Whereas car production grew at an average of 27.2 percent per year
between 1960 and 1965, it fell to 6.4 percent for 1965-73.

Another indication of the reduced dynamism of the industry
is obtained if one compares annual changes in car output to changes
in gross domestic product (GDP).* As can be seen from Table 6.6,

---

*A similar pattern is found in the case of commercial vehicles.
The rate of growth of commercial vehicle output slowed down from

TABLE 6.6

Growth of Car Output and Gross Domestic
Product in Argentina, 1960-73

	Cars (percent)	GDP (percent)	Cars/GDP
1961	95.0	7.1	13.4
1962	15.8	-1.7	+
1963	-16.9	-2.4	7.0
1964	52.1	10.4	5.0
1965	16.7	9.1	1.8
1966	0.1	0.7	0.1
1967	-2.6	2.5	−
1968	-1.8	4.6	−
1969	19.6	8.4	2.3
1970	9.1	4.4	2.1
1971	15.6	3.7	4.2
1972	4.0	3.8	1.1
1973	9.2	4.8	1.9

Key: + Increase in numerator accompanying decrease in
denominator. - Decrease in numerator accompanying increase in
denominator.

Sources: Banco Central de la República Argentina (BCRA)
data as quoted in Fundación de Investigaciones Economicas Latino-
americanas, Indicadores de Coyuntura (Buenos Aires), various
issues; ADEFA, 1974 Industria Automotriz Argentina (Buenos Aires:
ADEFA, 1975); and own elaboration.

not only does the coefficient relating the growth of car output and
GDP fall significantly in the second half of the decade but one gets
a new phenomenon of car output falling in years when GDP increased
(1967, 1968), whereas in the first half of the decade, car output
increased while GDP fell (1962). The same tendency for the rate
of growth to fall during the second half of the decade was also evident
in the case of the number of cars in circulation. The reduction from
14.1 percent per year in 1960-65 to 10.4 percent per year in 1965-73

4.5 percent per year in 1960-65 to 2.5 percent per year in 1965-73.
There was also a tendency for the ratio of changes in commercial
vehicle output to changes in gross fixed investment to decline during
the 1960s. See Appendix Table A.12.

was not, however, on such a dramatic scale as that observed for
output.*

Chile

The Chilean situation cannot be described in the same terms
as the Argentinian one, of a severely restricted supply of cars being
eased as a result of the setting up of local production facilities leading
to the elimination of the backlog of demand that had built up during
the period when imports were the major or only source of supply.
Until 1960, the supply of new cars in Chile depended entirely on
imports that fluctuated around 2,500 units a year between 1955 and
1960. As a result, the number of cars in circulation grew by an
average rate of only 3.6 percent per year and the number of cars
per 1,000 inhabitants remained more or less constant at around
7.5. Those cars that were imported were subject to a tax of 200
percent on their FOB value from 1956 onward. Thus, in 1960, the
stock of cars in Chile was extremely low relative to the country's
per capita income, less than 40 percent of the level that would have
been expected on the basis of international comparison.

The startup of local production in 1960 by no means removed
the supply constraint, as it did in Argentina, although it did increase
the apparent consumption of cars threefold. Supply remained constrained for a number of reasons. First, since the local content
requirement was only 30 percent in 1963, the industry was still
highly dependent on imports during the early years of its development.
Second, as the foreign exchange constraint was removed through
increasing national integration to 57.94 percent in the late 1960s,
a new restriction came into play with the limited capacity of suppliers
to provide parts.[21] Firms replying to the Rol Industrial annual
questionnaire in the period 1967-70 gave deficiencies in the quantity
or quality of inputs as an important factor causing underutilization
of capacity.[22] A third problem derived from the special agreement
with Argentina by which Argentinian-produced parts qualified as
local content if compensated for by exports of Chilean parts. This
has introduced another bottleneck, and some firms mentioned the
difficulties of increasing these exchanges as a further cause of excess
capacity.[23]

Despite an average annual increase of slightly less than 10
percent in the number of cars in circulation in Chile during the 1960s,

---

*For commercial vehicles the period of most rapid growth of
number in circulation was 1959-64. The rate of growth fell from
7.9 percent per year in 1960-65 to 6.1 percent per year in 1965-73.

the evidence seems to suggest that, for the greater part of the period, supply fell short of demand. Official and semiofficial bodies have suggested that the demand for cars had not been met up to 1968 or 1969.[24] This is borne out by the fact that for the greater part of the period, consumers had to wait a long time and make advance payments for cars, especially those models in greatest demand, such as the Mini or Renault 4. Moreover, some of the manufacturers were able to finance part of their operations by requiring advance payments from dealers. Not surprisingly, no firm mentioned a deficiency of demand as a cause of excess capacity.[25] The existence of official price control from 1966 onward meant that supply had to be rationed through queuing rather than through the price mechanism.

Nevertheless, there were some signs that from about 1967 onward, market conditions were easing as supply and demand came increasingly into balance. One indication is that the average period for which credit was granted increased from 6 months in 1966, 9 months in 1967, 12.7 months in 1968, and to 14 months in 1969. Another is the growth of credit outstanding at the beginning of each year from 44 million escudos in 1967 to 246 million escudos in 1969, at 1969 prices.[26] This is confirmed by evidence on the initial deposit and length of the period for which credit is extended both to dealers and to the public for various models.[27]

These trends were reversed with the election of the Unidad Popular in 1970. The large increase in effective demand and the inflationary climate led to an upsurge in the demand for cars. By 1971, all sales were being made for cash, and there was such a long waiting list for cars that the government was forced to intervene, setting up Estanco Automotriz to deal with the distribution of cars. This situation persisted until the military coup of September 1973, but the deflationary policies pursued by the junta led to a sharp reduction in demand, the reemergence of sales credit, and considerable sales difficulties for the motor companies.

The main factors underlying the growth of car production in Chile were the substitution of imports by locally produced vehicles in the early 1960s and the subsequent elimination of the accumulated backlog of demand. The volume of sales was determined by supply factors rather than demand. On the demand side, relative prices have increased rather than fallen since 1964[28] and changes in car sales were negatively correlated with income changes.* As the remaining imports are replaced and the backlog of demand eliminated,

---

*The partial correlation coefficient relating changes in car sales per inhabitant to changes in income per capita between 1962 and 1970 was -0.61.

further growth of output comes to depend increasingly on income and price changes, leading to a slower rate of expansion.

Although not as spectacular as in Argentina, the initiation of local production has had a considerable effect in Chile. The increased rate of growth of the car stock has already been mentioned. Moreover, there has also been some improvement in the age structure of the stock so that, by 1971, 42 percent of all cars were less than five years old as opposed to only 22 percent in 1959, and the number of cars over ten years of age fell from 58 to 35 percent over the same period.[29] In addition, local production replaced imports as the main source of supply in 1962, and, by the early 1970s, most cars were produced locally, although about half the supply of commercial vehicles was imported.

By 1969, the number of cars in circulation in Chile was over 80 percent of its expected level, more than double what it had been at the beginning of the decade. It seems possible that the remaining 20 percent differential could be accounted for by the extremely high price of cars in Chile, where in the period 1964–68 costs averaged 4.2 times those in the country of origin.[30] The main point to be remembered for later analysis, however, is that for the greater part of the period under consideration, demand conditions were extremely favorable and that, a priori, one would not expect competition in the market to be the most important factor explaining the development of the industry.

Mexico

Throughout the 1950s, the demand for cars in Mexico was met in almost equal proportions by imports of completely builtup vehicles and by local assembly of imported parts and components. Until 1958, a rigid quota system imposed by the government had led to the creation of considerable unsatisfied demand. The system was then liberalized somewhat and the apparent consumption of cars (that is, imports plus local assembly) rose by 31.8 percent in 1959 and by a further 26.8 percent in 1960, imports increasing somewhat more sharply than assembly. Despite the increased supply of cars in these two years, the stock of cars in Mexico in 1960 was still more than 30 percent below what would have been expected given the country's level of income.

From 1951 to 1958, prices had been subject to official control, but in practice requests from manufacturers to increase them were usually granted. As a result, prices were able to increase by about 10 percent annually, especially since luxury cars were not subject to the price control. Subsequently, a stricter system of control was introduced by which prices were to be determined on the basis of costs. In 1960, therefore, the government controlled both the price at which cars were sold and their number by means of a quota, a system that has been maintained in operation since then. Government control has permitted a steady growth in the number of cars on the road in Mexico. Between 1955 and 1960, the increase was 9.4 percent per year, in the next five-year period it was slightly higher at 9.8 percent per year, and between 1965 and 1970 there was a further rise of 9.9 percent per year.* This growth of the stock of cars has only closed the gap slightly between the actual and predicted level, since per capita income and population both have grown rapidly over the same period.

As a result of the quota system and the control of prices, Mexico has not seen a situation comparable to that of Argentina in the early 1960s. There is, however, evidence to suggest that cars are not as easy to sell as they once were in Mexico. The car dealers association, Asociación Mexicana de Distribuidores de Automóviles (ANDA), has been making alarmist noises. At the 23rd Annual Convention, there were complaints that more cars were available than the market could absorb, and, since the mid-1960s, ANDA has been complaining in its publications that dealers are being squeezed between a market that is becoming saturated and the demands of the manufacturers. Such statements have to be discounted as a common grievance among intermediaries such as car dealers, but nevertheless they do contain a kernel of truth. There does appear to have been a tendency for their profits to be squeezed. Dealers' net profits on invested capital fell from 7.3 percent in 1965 to 6.1 percent in 1968 and 5.1 percent in 1971, although profits did recover somewhat to 5.7 percent in 1972.[31] Moreover, the pressure from the manufacturers is understandable when it is remembered that they have also been squeezed by rising costs and government price control measures.

The market is still a seller's market, however, in the sense that total output is determined by the government's production quotas rather than by demand. Since quotas refer to the model year beginning at the end of November and sales figures to the calendar year, it is not possible to make an exact comparison of the two. It seems to be the case, however, that in 1969 all firms, apart from VAM and FANASA, filled or almost filled their quota and that total output

---

*Statistics of the number of cars in circulation are published by the Departamento General de Estadisticas of the Secretaría de Industria y Commercio and by the Asociación Mexicana de la Industria Automotriz. The figures are not identical, so the official government figures are used here.

was thus constrained. (FANASA was on the verge of ceasing production altogether in any case.) It should be mentioned here that only the basic quota is set by the government and that the firms can increase their quota by exporting, increasing local content, or maintaining low prices. Thus, for firms that have export possibilities, for example, the full utilization of quotas may not necessarily mean that they cannot produce more but simply that it is not profitable for them to do so given the state of the market and the cost of exports.

On the other hand, it is not a seller's market in the sense that all firms can sell their vehicles regardless of quality, credit terms, advertising, and so on. As far as credit goes, about 31 percent of cars are sold with a repayment period of more than a year, between 21 and 27 percent (depending on the size of the car) with credit for three to twelve months, and 42 to 48 percent for cash (1968 figures).[32] As mentioned before, not all firms have filled their quota. VAM, for instance, deliberately has kept production below the quota limit in order to avoid sales problems, and Automex began to suffer sales difficulties in the late 1960s. Contrary to the assertions of ANDA, advertising has not played a major role in maintaining the level of demand. Between 1960 and 1968, advertising expenditure as a percentage of the total value of production and per car produced has remained more or less constant, which would seem to contradict the picture of the Mexican car market as one which is approaching saturation point.

An attempt was made to estimate a statistical demand function for cars similar to that obtained for Argentina. The available data go back to 1950, so that the equation of the form

$$DX_t = g + aDP_t + bDY_t + cDS_{t-1}$$

was estimated for t = 1951 to t = 1970. Unlike the Argentinian case, better results were obtained using absolute rather than per capita data, but even so the equation gave an R^2 of only 0.56 as opposed to 0.79 for Argentina. The inclusion of a dummy variable RP, set at 1 up to 1960 and 0 subsequently, increased R^2 to 0.63 and gave the following equation.

$$DX_t = -14,060 - 864DP_t + 1.47DY_t - 0.001DS_{t-1} + 962ORP \quad R^2 = 0.63$$
$$\quad (7,990) \quad (380) \quad (0.58) \quad (0.017) \quad (5,550)$$

As well as giving a lower R^2 than was obtained in the Argentinian case, it was also found that the existing number of vehicles in circulation was not a significant explanatory variable. Both income and price were significant explanatory variables with the income elasticity of demand in the region of 3.5 and price elasticity around -1.2 at the mean values of the variables. Nevertheless, this still left a large part of the growth of demand unexplained.

A second attempt to obtain more satisfactory results was made for the period 1960-70 without any dummy variable.

$$DX_t = -10,530 - 103DP_t + 1.67DY_t + 0.006DS_{t-1} \quad R^2 = 0.71$$
$$(6,390) \quad (720) \quad (0.53) \quad (0.014)$$

As can be seen, this gave a slightly better result in terms of R^2, which was 0.71 for absolute values and 0.64 for per capita values. Here, however, only the income coefficient proved to be significantly different from zero, with an elasticity of 3.8. The term for vehicles in circulation in the previous period has the wrong sign (that is, is positive) in the case of absolute values.

The failure to derive a meaningful statistical demand function for cars is not surprising in view of the control exercised by the government over both prices and output. The use of the quota system in Mexico meant that there was no period of rapid growth of car production followed by a period of relative stagnation, as was the case in Argentina. As Table 6.7 shows, output grew steadily through the 1960s, but in the early 1970s the growth rate fell, and in 1972 and 1973 was only slightly greater than the growth of GDP. This may indeed be an indication that the Mexican car market is now approaching the saturation point.

CONCLUSION

This chapter has shown that the automotive industry in an underdeveloped country enjoys particularly favorable demand conditions during the early years of its development as a result of the accumulated backlog of demand created during a previous period of constrained supply. This manifested itself in a rapid growth of output during the early 1960s in Argentina and in a seller's market in both Chile and Mexico throughout the greater part of the 1960s. Once the backlog has been eliminated, demand conditions begin to change as occurred in Argentina in the mid-1960s, with an increase in consumer credit, greater depreciation on used cars, and so forth. Further growth then depends on the normal parameters of a demand function, income, and price. As was seen in the Argentinian case, however, the income elasticity of demand for cars is less than in the United States, and the price elasticity is not significantly different from zero. Moreover, the unequal income distribution means that the potential market is limited to only a fraction of the population. Thus, after a short period of growth, the industry is likely to lose its dynamic impetus.

TABLE 6.7

Growth of Car Output and Gross Domestic
Product in Mexico, 1960-73

	Cars (percent)	GDP (percent)	Cars/GDP
1961	26.9	4.9	5.5
1962	4.6	4.7	1.0
1963	19.8	8.0	2.5
1964	24.3	11.7	2.1
1965	9.2	6.5	1.4
1966	21.3	6.9	3.1
1967	7.5	6.3	1.2
1968	17.0	8.1	2.1
1969	12.4	6.3	2.0
1970	15.8	6.9	2.3
1971	11.8	3.7	3.2
1972	10.2	7.3	1.4
1973	8.9	7.6	1.2

Sources: AMIA, La Industria Automotriz de México en Cifras
1971 (Mexico City: 1972), p. 53; AMIA, La Industria Automotriz
de México en Cifras 1973 (Mexico City: 1974), p. 62; Banco de México,
S.A., Informe Anual, 1974 (Mexico City: 1975), Statistical Appendix,
Table 1; own elaboration.

In the following chapter the way in which the different demand
conditions observed in each of the three countries interacted with
changing supply conditions to bring about changes in the structure
of the industry is discussed. These demand conditions have also
influenced the form that interfirm competition has taken at different
times and in different countries, as will be seen in Chapter 8.

NOTES

1. See, for example, C. F. Roos and V. von Szeliski,
"Factors Governing Changes in Domestic Automobile Demand," in
The Dynamics of Automobile Demand (New York: General Motors
Corporation, 1939); G. C. Chow, Demand for Automobiles in the
United States (Amsterdam: North-Holland Publishing, 1957);
D. P. Suits, "The Demand for New Automobiles in the United States,
1929-56," REStat. 11 (1958): 273-80.
2. See D. Llarena and R. Trovarelli, Demanda de Automóviles
en el Peru (Lima: Universidad Nacional "Federico Villarreal,"

Centro de Investigaciones Económicas y Sociales, 1971), pp. 7-14, for a discussion of the macro- and microeconomic variables influencing the demand for cars.

3. Suits, for example, has a term to measure credit facilities (op. cit.).

4. For a long time, consumer demand theory has remained within a static framework, but some attempts have been made to develop a dynamic theory of secular demand growth. See R. Marris, The Economic Theory of "Managerial" Capitalism (New York: Macmillan, 1967), pp. 133-203, and J. Duesenberry, Income, Saving and the Theory of Consumer Demand (Cambridge, Mass.: Harvard University Press, 1949).

5. Quoted by A. G. Nowicki, Automobile Demand in Developing Countries, UNIDO (ID/WG, 13/23), 1968, pp. 18-19.

6. A discussion of Pareto's law can be found in J. Pen, Income Distribution, trans. T. S. Preston (London: Allen Lane, 1971).

7. See Nowicki, op. cit., pp. 11-12.

8. D. G. Rhys, The Motor Industry: An Economic Survey (London: Butterworths, 1972), p. 238.

9. On this point see C. Diaz-Alejandro, Essays on the Economic History of the Argentine Republic (New Haven, Conn.: Yale University Press, 1970), p. 317.

10. Nowicki, op. cit., pp. 7-13.

11. Ibid., p. 28.

12. Industrias Kaiser Argentina S. A., División Planificación Comercial, La Industria Automotriz Argentina, vol. 1, unpublished (1963), pp. 97-98.

13. Consejo Nacional de Desarrollo (CONADE), La Industria Automotriz (Análisis Preliminar) (Buenos Aires, 1966), Table 2.

14. Ibid., Table 2; and Banque Francaise et Italienne pour l'Amérique du Sud, "L'Industrie Automobile en Amérique Latine," Etudes Economique, no. 3 (1972), p. 12.

15. Camara Argentina de Fabricantes de Automotores, Significación Económica de la Industria Automotriz, 1963 (Buenos Aires, 1963).

16. Industrias Kaiser Argentina, op. cit., p. 114.

17. Ibid., p. 134.

18. Asociación de Concesionarios de Automotores de la República Argentina (ACARA), El Concesionario de Automotores en la Argentina. Examen de Su Situación Jurídica, Impositiva y Económico-Financiera (Mar del Plata, 1965), p. 144.

19. L. J. White, The Automobile Industry Since 1945 (Cambridge, Mass.: Harvard University Press, 1971), Table 7.2.

20. Suits, op. cit.

21. Corporación de Fomento (CORFO), División de Planificación Industrial, Desarrollo del Consumo Interno de Automotores, Publicación No. 13a/69, 1969, p. 5.

22. Ministerio de Economía, Rol Industrial.

23. Ibid.

24. CORFO, op. cit., pp. 3-4; Instituto de Costos, op. cit., Chap. I.

25. Rol Industrial.

26. Centro de Investigaciones Económicas de la Universidad Católica de Chile, "Efectos Económicos de la Industria Automotriz," Asociación de Industriales Metalúrgicos, Primer Seminario Nacional de la Industria Automotriz (Santiago: 1969), pp. 101-03.

27. Instituto de Costos, op. cit., Tables 73 and 74; own investigations.

28. Instituto de Costos, op. cit., Table 81.

29. ASIMET, Anexo 5; own calculation on the basis of data provided by the Comisión Automotriz.

30. Instituto de Costos, op. cit., Chap. II. 2b.

31. Héctor Vazquez Tercero, "Análisis Financiero del Sector Distribuidor, 1971 y 1972," in Estudio de Comercialización (Mexico City: Asociación Mexicana de Distribuidores de Automóviles, 1973).

32. J. Foncerrada Moreno and H. Vázquez Tercero, Informe Económico (Mexico City: Asociación Nacional de Distribuidores de Automóviles, 1969), p. 84.

CONCENTRATION AND DENATIONALIZATION IN THE AUTOMOTIVE INDUSTRY

In the last two chapters it has been seen that a number of the conditions that were assumed in the model presented in Chapter 4 were in fact fulfilled in the Argentinian, Chilean, and Mexican automotive industries during the 1960s. The model predicted that there would be a tendency for concentration within the industry, and that this would take the specific form of denationalization, that is to say, the elimination of locally owned firms. In this chapter, the overall developments in the industrial structure of the three countries are first examined in order to verify the extent to which the predictions of the model were realized. In the second part, more detailed attention is given to the experience of individual firms in order to adduce additional evidence on the advantages enjoyed by foreign subsidiaries over their domestic competitors.

CHANGES IN THE INDUSTRIAL STRUCTURE

The traditional analysis of concentration applied in the developed countries sees increases in concentration mainly as a function of the optimum size of plant or firm rising at a faster rate than the growth of the market, and the desire of firms to restrict competition, or what has been called "monopolization considerations."[1] In the case of the Latin American automotive industry increases in local content have played the same role as that attributed to technical progress in the advanced countries by causing the minimum optimum scale of plant and the initial capital requirement to rise, or by increasing the amount of working capital needed to finance suppliers. The Latin American experience differs from that of the developed countries in that changes in local content requirements make themselves felt much more rapidly than technological changes, although the latter may also lead to sharply discontinuous changes in the minimum scale of production.

In measuring industrial concentration, two fundamental choices have to be made: the variable to be considered and the measurement of concentration to be used. The first is largely governed by considerations of data availability, and for this reason the number of vehicles produced or sold has been used for Argentina and Mexico, whereas the value of production has been used for Chile. It could be argued that the use of units rather than values underestimates the importance of companies producing trucks or the larger, more expensive cars and overestimates the market share of medium and small car producers. As far as the measurement of concentration is concerned, there is no reason to believe that the two will differ greatly, and in any case there is no a priori reason for supposing that the share of the market in value terms is a better indicator of monopoly than the share in volume terms.

In measuring concentration, one wishes to throw up two dimensions of the problem, the inequality of size distribution and the total number of firms. It is easy to see that neither of these measures on its own gives a satisfactory measure of concentration. The first fails to distinguish between the situation where the market is shared between two firms of equal size and the case where it is divided equally by 1,000 firms. The second fails to distinguish between an industry in which 1,000 firms share the market equally and one where one firm has 50 percent of the market, leaving the remaining 50 percent to be distributed between 999 firms.

An interesting attempt to incorporate both these factors in a single measure is the Herfindhal index.[2] An alternative measure frequently used is the percentage of the market accounted for by the largest three, four, or eight firms, or the number of firms to account for, say, 80 percent of the market. In the following analysis of the automotive industry in Argentina, Chile, and Mexico, three indicators of concentration have been used, the absolute number of firms, the Herfindhal index, and the market share of the four leading firms.

The most striking evidence of increased concentration in the Argentinian automotive industry is the reduction in the total number of firms in operation from 21 in 1960 to 10 at present (see Table 7.1). Most of the exits from the industry occurred during the first half of the decade and, already by 1964, the number of firms had fallen to 13. The other two indices calculated both indicate a sharp rise in concentration during the recovery from the 1964 recession. Since the mid-1960s, concentration has remained more or less constant, as indicated by the four-firm concentration ratio, although

TABLE 7.1

Indices of Concentration in the Argentinian
Automotive Industry, 1960-73

	Number of Firms	Herfindhal Index	Four Firm Concentration (percent)
1960	21	0.1839	67.6
1961	20	0.1428	61.1
1962	18	0.1429	60.1
1963	15	0.1398	61.5
1964	13	0.1631	71.9
1965	13	0.1623	72.5
1966	12	0.1491	71.5
1967	11	0.1566	73.4
1968	10	0.1535	71.2
1969	11	0.1447	68.7
1970	10	0.1441	66.8
1971	10	0.1513	69.6
1972	10	0.1500	68.1
1973	10	0.1547	69.7

Source: Appendix Table B.13.

there was a slight fall in 1969 and 1970 as a result of a continuing
decline in the market share of IKA-Renault not being offset by an
increasing share of the other three leading firms. The Herfindhal
index also declined somewhat during the late 1960s, indicating the
faster growth of the medium-sized firms, which offset the elimination of some of the smaller firms.

It is, of course, somewhat misleading to treat vehicles as a
homogeneous product since cars and trucks are not close substitutes
and even small and large cars may not be directly competitive.
Since the same firms are involved in producing different kinds of
vehicles, it is difficult to determine what the "industry" is for the
purpose of analyzing concentration. A more detailed breakdown by
category of vehicle indicates that concentration increased during
the early 1960s in all categories except large cars, where the late
entry of the U.S. Big Three reduced concentration.[3]

Perhaps more significant than the quantitative increase in
concentration has been the change in the ownership of the Argentinian
automotive industry that this process has involved. Of the 21 firms
in operation in 1960, only 4—Fiat, Ford, General Motors, and
Mercedes-Benz—were under majority foreign ownership, the remain-

der being either entirely or majority Argentinian owned and producing under license from a foreign firm. In 1963, locally owned firms accounted for more than 50 percent of total production, and as late as 1965, 6 of the 13 firms in operation were locally owned. The threat to their existence was recognized in 1964, and plans were presented to the government for a merger between the five local companies (excluding IKA) in order to form a company able to hold its own against foreign competition. These plans came to nothing, however, and at present there only remains the state-owned IME under local control. Some of these Argentinian firms, such as Siam di Tella, Isard, and Metalmecanica, which had no foreign capital participation, were driven out of the industry by competitive pressures. Others, like IKA and IAFA, were taken over by multinational corporations under whose license they had previously operated. In no case, however, was a foreign-controlled firm driven out of the industry.

During the early 1960s, the Chilean automotive industry was even more fragmented than that of Argentina. In 1962, there were a total of 20 firms, the leading 4 of which accounted for only just over half of the value of output. Some of these firms led a very unstable existence, producing 20 or 30 cars a year, and suspending production entirely in some years. Thus, the total number of firms fell from 20 in 1962 to 14 in 1963, recovering again to 18 in 1964 (see Table 7.2). By 1970, there had been a substantial increase in concentration with the number of firms being cut by half, the share of output accounted for by the four largest firms increasing by almost 20 percent and the Herfindhal index going from 0.1017 to 0.1491. The Unidad Popular government reduced the number of firms even further as part of its policy to rationalize the automotive industry. By 1973, four firms accounted for nearly the whole of Chile's production.

A detailed examination of Table 7.2 indicates a sharp upsurge in concentration in 1966 when a number of firms, including Indauto (Renault), EMSSA (BMC), and Nissan Motor Chile, were forced to suspend production because they were unable to meet the increase in local content from 41.1 to 50.0 percent required in that year. This was followed by a reduction in concentration during the next two years when these firms began production again, but further concentration in the last two years of the decade reestablished the peak of 1966. It should be noted in this context that it was the conscious policy of the Frei government to bring about increased levels of concentration in the industry through the control of prices and increasing local integration requirements.[4] Subsequently, the Allende government used more direct measures to increase concentration to a much higher level.

TABLE 7.2

Indices of Concentration in the Chilean
Automotive Industry, 1962–73

	Number of Firms	Herfindhal Index	Four Firm Concentration (percent)
1962	20	0.1017	53.2
1963	14	0.1173	60.6
1964	18	0.0842	49.1
1965	18	0.0817	44.5
1966	10	0.1551	70.2
1967	12	0.1397	67.1
1968	12	0.1203	59.0
1969	11	0.1415	68.4
1970	10	0.1491	71.9
1971	9	0.2159	82.8
1972	7	0.3966	93.4
1973	6	0.3132	96.4

Source: Appendix Table B.14.

As in Argentina, concentration has been accompanied by
increasing foreign ownership in the industry. In the early years,
only Fiat and Nissan of the world's major car companies invested
their own capital in the Chilean automotive industry. In 1963,
Citroen took an 80 percent shareholding in Importadora e Industrial
José Lhorente y Cia. Ltda., which had run into financial difficulties.
Other firms followed suit, with Ford taking a 50 percent holding in
Chilemotores in 1965, Renault a majority holding in Indauto in 1967,
and British Leyland and Peugeot majority holdings in EMSSA and
San Cristobal, respectively, in 1969. At the same time, both
General Motors and Ford replaced their local licensees, Indumotora
del Pacifico and Chilemotores, by wholly owned subsidiaries. Con-
currently, a number of locally owned firms, such as Federic and
Importsur, were being driven out of the industry. Thus, of the nine
firms remaining at the end of 1970, when the Allende government
assumed power, five were entirely foreign owned—Citroen, Fiat,
Ford, General Motors, and Nissan—two were majority foreign owned—
Automotores Franco-Chilena (Renault and Peugeot) and British
Leyland Automotores de Chile—and two were entirely locally owned,
producing under license—Nun y German (Chrysler) and Imcode
(Skoda).

In 1971, Ford and General Motors withdrew from Chile as a direct result of the political change and U.S. hostility to the Unidad Popular government, and, in 1972, Imcoda, which had produced on a very small scale, closed down.

A somewhat different picture emerges in Mexico from that in the other two countries studied. If one looks at the pattern since 1963 (see Table 7.3), the year in which the Mexican automotive program began to take effect, it can be seen that there has been little change in the level of concentration. The four-firm concentration ratio, in fact, fell slightly from 76.8 to 76.6 percent, while the Herfindhal index increased slightly. There was also a reduction in the total number of firms in the industry, but this could hardly be regarded as significant.*

Not only has concentration been less pronounced but so, too, has the elimination of locally owned firms. During the assembly

TABLE 7.3

Indices of Concentration in the Mexican
Automotive Industry, 1963-71

	Number of Firms	Herfindhal Index	Four Firm Concentration (percent)
1963	10	0.1731	76.8
1964	10	0.1867	80.1
1965	10	0.1888	81.5
1966	9	0.1850	82.2
1967	9	0.1725	78.3
1968	10	0.1619	75.9
1969	10	0.1616	74.5
1970	10	0.1615	74.2
1971	9	0.1646	74.9
1972	9	0.1667	74.8
1973	9	0.1750	76.6

Source: Appendix Table B.15.

---

*Of course, if one were to look back to the earlier period of car assembly, a significant increase in concentration would indeed emerge, since the number of firms producing cars alone, without taking into account commercial vehicles, was 17 in 1960. This fell to seven by 1973, while the share of the four largest car firms increased from around two thirds to three quarters of the total market.

period, most of the firms were either wholly or majority Mexican owned. Thus, for example, of the 12 assembly plants in operation in mid-1961, only 3 (Ford, General Motors, and International Harvester) were entirely foreign owned, the remainder having complete or majority Mexican ownership. Of the companies that began manufacturing cars under the government's local content decree, four—Ford, General Motors, Volkswagen, and Nissan—were entirely foreign owned, two—Automex (Chrysler) and VAM (American Motors)— were joint ventures with Mexican capital having the major share, and two—DINA and FANASA—were entirely Mexican owned. FANASA, which was an attempt to set up a completely Mexican car company independent of foreign licenses, by buying the Borgward plant after the failure of that company in Germany, eventually closed down in 1970 without ever really having got off the ground. Furthermore, in 1971, Automex, the most important of the Mexican-owned firms, was taken over by Chrysler, which increased its shareholding from 45 to 90.5 percent.

The market share of Mexican-owned firms fell from 38.3 percent in 1963 to 14 percent in 1973, and the only remaining locally owned firms are the state-owned companies Vehiculos Automotores Mexicanos and Diesel Nacional, and Trailers de Monterrey with a small output of commercial vehicles. Nevertheless, this is still a more significant local participation than exists in either of the other two countries considered.

The explanation for the lack of concentration in the Mexican automotive industry is to be found in the quota system imposed by the government on all firms that benefit from the legislation to promote the development of the industry. Each firm is granted a basic quota on the basis of the requests of the companies, their market penetration, an estimate of market potential, and the degree of local integration and volume of sales in the previous year. The basic quota has remained frozen since 1967.

Firms are able to increase their quota above the basic quota set in three ways. The most widely used method is through exports. Firms are permitted to import additional parts to a value equal to their exports from Mexico and to increase their quota correspondingly. This system has been used extensively by both Ford and Volkswagen in order to increase their output. In 1969, for the industry as a whole, about 10 percent of the total quota was accounted for by the export quota. The second most important method of increasing the quota is to raise local integration above the 60 percent minimum required by the 1962 decree. An additional 500 units is granted for each percentage point increase in local content, but, generally speaking, this has not proved such an attractive incentive as that for exporting owing to the increasing costs of local production.

Finally, additional quotas are granted for maintaining or reducing prices below the official prices set for vehicles. This has been of little importance, since the companies have complained frequently that official prices are set too low to permit them to obtain a reasonable profit.

Such a quota system has provided a degree of protection for the smaller producers from the larger firms, which are not able to expand their market shares at the former's expense. This is clearly seen by all the parties concerned. The foreign companies put pressure on the Mexican government to remove the quotas, while the Mexican firms argued that they were necessary to protect them against the greater financial strength of the multinational corporations. The minister of industry and commerce supported this latter view of the usefulness of the quota system.[5] The attitude of the government toward the smaller producers is in marked contrast to the complete lack of concern shown by the Argentinian and Chilean governments, no doubt partly as a result of the fact that two of these firms are controlled by government agencies.

Had the quota system been completely rigid, market shares would have been determined directly, and since prices were controlled by the government, cost differentials would lead to differences in profits without the possibility of being reflected in higher rates of investment and more rapid growth. As has just been seen, however, a degree of flexibility is introduced into the quota system as a result of the additional quotas authorized in return for exports, increased local content, or price reductions. Once this is the case, firms are able to increase their market share by undertaking to comply with one of these three alternatives.

In the previous model, the investment decision of foreign subsidiaries was based on their own profit rate and the ease with which market shares could be expanded. This latter was a function of the cost advantage enjoyed by foreign firms and the rate of profit of local firms. Now it is clear that the Mexican quota system imposes an additional cost (assuming that firms would not do any of the three things otherwise) on those firms desirous of expanding their market shares. Thus, for any given rate of profit of foreign and domestic firms, and differential cost advantage, foreign firms will increase their market share and eliminate local firms at a slower rate in the presence of this kind of quota system.

In the absence of a quota system, the increase in capital requirements in the Mexican automotive industry, which was observed in the period 1963-65 (see Chapter 5), would have resulted in a process of concentration and denationalization similar to that observed in Argentina during the first half of the 1960s. In fact, however, as the analysis of the previous paragraph would suggest, the process has been much less spectacular in Mexico.

In 1969, the Mexican government introduced new legislation that would eventually render the quota system obsolete. (In 1972, these measures were consolidated in a new decree, which replaced that of 1962.) In view of the continued outflow of foreign exchange to which the automotive industry gave rise, the government decided that the industry should no longer be a net foreign exchange loser. The intention was that all imports of parts and components for the automotive industry should be matched by exports of automotive products within ten years. This was to be achieved by gradually increasing the percentage of the imports of parts required for each firm's basic quota, which had to be covered by exports from 5 percent in 1970, 15 percent in 1971, 25 percent in 1972, and so on. As the free foreign exchange available to the industry is reduced through time, the significance of the basic quota diminishes, as does the protection the quota system affords to the smaller firms. At the same time, these firms are likely to experience relatively more difficulty in expanding exports than are the foreign subsidiaries. Consequently, the outlook for the Mexican automotive industry is likely to be further denationalization.

THE MECHANISMS OF CONCENTRATION
AND DENATIONALIZATION

In this section, the experience of a number of individual firms in the countries studied will be examined in order to illustrate the way in which the general tendencies of concentration and denationalization worked themselves out in specific cases. It will be seen that the model presented in Chapter 4 operated in its purest form in Argentina, whereas in both Chile and Mexico, government intervention assumed much greater significance.

Argentina

In Chapter 6, it was seen that during the first few years of the 1960s, say, up to 1963, the automotive industry in Argentina enjoyed very favorable demand conditions, it being essentially a seller's market. The same period up to 1963 also saw a very significant rise in the capital intensity of production as a result of the increase in local content requirements from 40 percent in 1960 to 90 percent by 1964 (see Chapter 5). Furthermore, as has just been indicated in the preceding section, these developments were accompanied by a significant reduction in the number of firms operating in the industry. This section will interpret the Argentinian experience and the cases of particular firms in the light of the model developed previously.

It was indicated in Chapter 4 that considerations of risk and lack of information in operating in an unfamiliar environment enter into the multinational corporation's investment decision, so that in the early stages it tends to keep its capital commitment as low as possible. This leads to the use of joint ventures and licensing arrangements and raising of loan capital locally.

There is considerable evidence of this phenomenon in the Argentinian case. Of the total amount invested in the Argentinian automotive industry between 1960 and 1962, only 17.3 percent was financed from foreign sources, the remaining 82.7 percent being raised locally.[6] Even those firms that set up wholly owned subsidiaries kept their actual cash investment to a minimum. General Motors is a case in point. By Decree 11625/59, it was authorized to make an investment of $20 million in order to manufacture trucks and diesel engines. This was to be divided into $6 million of local expenditure financed from reinvestment of profits earned by General Motors in Argentina and $14 million in machinery, equipment, and special tools provided by General Motors from Detroit. The fact that the parent company did not have to make any cash contribution was a crucial factor in deciding to go ahead with the investment.

> It was our expectation that the investment in expanded
> plant facilities could be accomplished without any con-
> siderable dollar outflow from the U.S. relying, in part,
> upon earnings generated within Argentina, and in part,
> upon the shipment of machinery and equipment from our
> U.S. operations in return for capital stock of the Argen-
> tine subsidiary.[7]

Similarly, Ford, by decrees in 1959 and 1961 (to manufacture trucks and cars, respectively), was authorized to invest $74.3 million, of which less than half was provided by Ford (U.S.).

Other firms chose to enter the market initially in joint ventures with locally owned companies. Chrysler, for example, formed a joint venture with the local firm of Fevre y Basset, a national dealer organization. Citroen, too, was initially a joint venture. A number of other firms chose to make no direct investment, preferring to operate through a local license. These included BMC, Peugeot, and BMW, which concluded licensing agreements with Siam di Tella, IAFA, and Metalmecanica, respectively.

A further indication of the desire not to commit too much capital initially was the decision of the three American companies not to produce cars, concentrating their efforts on truck production.

If anything, truck production was less risky than car production. There was a well-established market, whereas the exact size of the future car market was rather difficult to predict following the long period of import restrictions. (The U.S. companies also followed a policy of investing first in trucks and then in cars in Brazil.)

Over time, the foreign firms increased their participation in the joint ventures until they obtained almost complete ownership, while local licensees either ceased production or were taken over. These developments can be attributed to two basic factors. First, the takeover of local licensees by their foreign technology suppliers or joint-venture partners can be explained in part by the strategies pursued by the latter in order to minimize their risk during the initial stages of the industry's development. Second, the changes in supply and demand conditions described previously have acted to the detriment of locally owned firms in the ways suggested in Chapter 4.

The changes that have been described in both supply and demand conditions during the early 1960s led to a cost-price squeeze especially in the period 1961-62 (see Table 7.4). This tendency was reflected in a fall in profit rates for almost all companies in 1962 or 1963.*

The mechanisms at work can be best illustrated by looking at the experience of some of the nationally owned companies in order to see how the model described above operated in practice. Siam di Tella was one of Argentina's leading firms, producing domestic appliances, electrical machinery, and a variety of industrial equipment from bread- and spaghetti-making machines to equipment for the oil industry.[8] The company decided to enter into car production in response to the government's promotional decree of 1959, and obtained a license from BMC. Initially, the only serious competition faced by the new company, Siam di Tella Automotores, came from Industrias Kaiser Argentina and Fiat, but 1961 saw the entry into the market of General Motors, Ford, and Chrysler with larger more powerful cars.

In 1962, Siam di Tella approached BMC to try and get it interested in investing in the company, offering up to a 50 percent share in the equity, and discussions between the two firms dragged on for several years. The difficulties faced by the company had a

---

*Of course, this was partly attributable to the general recession in 1963. This illustrates the difficulty of distinguishing between secular and cyclical changes, especially since the total time period being considered is so short.

TABLE 7.4

Income–Cost Relation in the Automotive Industry
(1961 = 100)

	1960	1961	1962	1st half 1963	2nd half 1963
Price of vehicles	92.9	100.0	115.8	133.5	134.9
Unit costs	92.9	100.0	131.9	152.5	157.9
Local supplies	90.8	100.0	132.6	156.2	162.8
Foreign supplies	100.0	100.0	137.4	162.5	165.9
Labor	86.5	100.0	110.3	113.5	118.3
Transfers to government	91.9	100.0	134.5	153.8	159.3
Income/cost	100.4	100.0	87.8	87.5	85.4

Source: Cámara Argentina de Fabricantes de Automotores (CAFA), Significación Económica de la Industria Automotriz (Buenos Aires, 1963), Table 2.

number of causes, but all derived basically from a shortage of financial resources. Initially, Siam had financed itself in part by buying components on credit and paying suppliers at 90 or 180 days. Ford and General Motors came in and started paying suppliers cash down, which created problems for Siam.

At the same time as this source of credit was being cut off, there was an increasing need for installment finance in order to place cars in the market. In fact, even as early as 1961, sales were being limited by lack of more ample finance to the public.[9] The difficulties of sales financing are illustrated by the fact that the ratio of net sales to credit for the company was 4.97 in 1964, compared to 2.03, 1.91, and 3.23 for three foreign firms in the same year.[10] Not only was Siam able to offer less credit than its competitors but it also did so on less favorable terms.[11] As a result, the company found its market share declining after 1961 and was unable to achieve anything like full utilization of capacity.

On the supply side, Siam had obtained suppliers' credit from Britain, the United States, and West Germany to finance the company's imports of machinery and equipment, including a credit of $4.2 million from the Ex-Im Bank. These credits imposed a significant burden on the company in terms of financial charges, which was accentuated by devaluation since they were denominated in foreign currency. By 1963, interest charges were absorbing almost 5 percent of the total value of sales; and by the time the company was taken over by IKA, the monthly interest charges were running at over m$n 70 million,* while the gross profit of producing 50 cars a day (almost as much as the highest rate ever attained) before paying interest was only m$n 30 million.[12] The company, therefore, was caught in a vicious circle, whereby it was unable to cover its interest charges without expanding output and unable to expand output without consumer credit, which further worsened the firm's debt position. Thus, a program of expanded production in 1965 did not achieve the anticipated results because of a lack of credit lines.

Royalty payments do not appear to have played a crucial part in the difficulties of Siam. Although these were calculated as a percentage of the value of the vehicle produced locally, and hence tended to rise as local content increased from 49 percent in 1960 to 78 percent in 1963,[13] payments were suspended from 1962 onward. Thus, the financial difficulties appear to have been more important in this context. In 1965, Siam had heavy losses, and in the following year it was taken over by Industrias Kaiser Argentina.

---

*The expression "m$n" refers to "pesos monedanacional," the Argentinian currency at the time, which was later replaced by "pesos ley" at the rate of m$n 100 = 1 peso ley.

Another firm that was almost entirely locally owned and went out of business was Industria Automotriz Santa Fe, which produced under license from DKW, the latter also having a minority shareholding as a result of a $1 million investment. In addition, IASF obtained credit from the Banco Industrial de la República Argentina, the Banco de la Provincia de Santa Fe, the Deutsch Sudamerikanische Bank, and the Bank fur Gemeinwirtschaft en Alemania at rates of interest varying between 9.5 and 12 percent.[14] The firm enjoyed very favorable demand conditions for its car, the Auto Union 1000, and operated virtually without a stock of cars, the customer having to pay in advance of delivery. IASF was able to do this because of its low sales, which were only around 6,000 in the company's peak year. A policy of low production meant a saving on sales financing, but also involved a considerable underutilization of the plant's capacity of 14,000 units a year working two shifts.

It is interesting to compare the strategy adopted by IASF with that of Siam. The former, by accepting high unit costs of production, was able to economize on finance for consumer credit and hence achieve a low level equilibrium with considerable excess capacity. The latter attempted to push its demand curve outward through offering hire purchase facilities in order to reach a high level equilibrium point with low production costs, since capacity would be fully utilized, but with high financial charges. Figure 7.1 shows this strategy in a diagram.

The Siam strategy proved unviable, since the company did not have sufficient financial resources to arrive at the high level equilibrium point. In reality, so, too, did the IASF strategy, the problem being that, over time, competition from other firms was pushing the demand curve inward so that it became necessary to run in order to stand still. Moreover, despite the policy of low output, rising material costs following the 1962 devaluation led to a shortage of working capital, which, owing to the collapse of the stock market at the same time, it was impossible to obtain. By 1964, interest charges were running at 4 percent of the total value of sales. The problems of the company were further accentuated by a relatively high royalty charge of 5 percent on sales.

IASF's difficulties arose not merely from its problems within the Argentinian automotive industry but also from developments in the international industry.* In 1964, Daimler-Benz sold its majority shareholding in Auto Union, from whom IASF held the DKW license, to Volkswagen. The latter stopped making the Auto Union 1000,

---

*This illustrates the importance of an international perspective when analyzing the industry in Latin America.

FIGURE 7.1

Alternative Production and Marketing Strategies

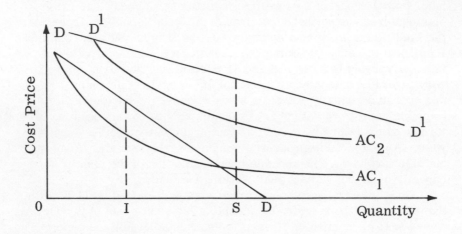

Source: Compiled by the author.

which meant an end to any technical evolution in the model. It has been suggested that since Volkswagen's major interest in Latin America was in Brazil, it wanted to use IASF to make parts for Brazil, which would explain why it refused to grant IASF rights to produce a new Auto Union model.

The final collapse of the company came about at the end of 1968 when it had debts reaching 3 billion pesos, the major creditors being the Argentinian government and Volkswagen, which were owed m$n 1 billion and m$n 700 million, respectively. It was widely expected that Volkswagen would take over the company and use it as a way of getting into the Argentinian market, but it was preempted by Fiat, which bought the company, mainly it seems, to exclude Volkswagen and converted the factory to tractor production.

Industrias Kaiser Argentina, despite large foreign share-holdings (mainly by Kaiser, but also by American Motors and Renault), could in many respects be regarded as a local firm in the early 1960s, since it did not comprise an integrated part of a multinational car company. It also had its shares quoted on the Buenos Aires stock exchange. Until 1967, when it was overtaken by Fiat, IKA was the largest firm in the industry in terms of units produced, although its relative position had been declining since 1964. The company's most successful year was 1965 when output reached 56,625 cars and light commercial vehicles.

During the early 1960s, IKA had been able to operate with negligible sales credit, but as the market tightened, this became more and more imperative. In the 1960-61 financial year, the ratio of sales to sales credit was more than 25:1, but it declined considerably to less than 5:1 during 1962-63.* Nevertheless, as in the case of Siam di Tella, IKA was unable to achieve such a low ratio of sales to credit as the foreign subsidiaries. This was reflected in the less favorable credit terms that the company was able to offer its customers.[15]

The difficulties of the company were accentuated during the 1965-66 financial year, however, as tighter government monetary policy led to a curtailment of consumer credit for IKA vehicles. Problems continued in the following year with a general recession in the demand for vehicles and increasing sales difficulties, despite the introduction of the Torino, especially designed for IKA by Pinanfarina, at the end of 1966. As a result, output fell to 40,085 in 1966 and 37,226 in 1967, and the company's market share declined from 29.1 percent in 1965 to 22.3 percent in 1966 and 21.2 percent in 1967, a decline that continued until 1970.

One consequence of these developments was the growing burden of interest charges. These had risen gradually during the first half of the 1960s and then rose sharply to 4.3 percent of the value of sales in the financial year 1966-67, increasing further to more than 7 percent by the early 1970s. If one examines the deterioration in IKA's performance in 1966-67, it can be seen that the rise in interest payments was only part of the problem. More important than this, however, was the drop in the gross profit margin, which resulted from a fall in the value of sales of m$n 3 billion, while there was no substantial change in the costs of products sold. A squeezing of the gross profit margin was, of course, to be expected as a result of the fall in output that reduced capacity utilization from 84 percent in 1965 to 60 percent in 1966 and 55 percent in 1967.

The company's position was further worsened by the takeover of Siam di Tella, which led to a loss of over m$n 1.4 billion in 1966-67. At the end of that year it was announced that Renault would take over control of the company.

The losses incurred in the bankruptcy of Siam were more than covered by the sale of Transax to Ford. The new management

---

*For the growth of consumer credit in response to changing market conditions, see above Chapter 6.

attempted to deal with the more fundamental problems facing the
company through a program of investment to modernize and rationalize the firm's production capacity, and by issuing new stock in
December 1967, which was taken up by the firm's majority shareholders in order to reinforce the company's financial structure.
This latter move was intended to reduce the firm's burden of financial
charges, but these continued to rise into the early 1970s. In 1972,
the company capitalized debts of U.S. $40 million with Renault in
order to reduce interest payments. Renault also succeeded in
reducing the ratio of sales to sales credit below 4:1 after taking
over the company, but despite these moves and Renault's intention
of using the company as the center of its Latin American operations,
IKA's position is still somewhat precarious.

Chile

It has been pointed out in previous chapters that the automotive
industry in Chile remained largely an assembly industry, buying the
greater part of its components and parts either locally or from
foreign associates or parent companies throughout the period under
consideration. The explanation given for concentration and denationalization in Argentina, therefore, does not fit the Chilean case,
insofar as it rests on the increased quantity of fixed capital required
for manufacturing production as opposed to assembly and the greater
dependence on foreign technology that this also implies.

As was seen in Chapter 5, however, there was a substantial
increase in working capital employed in the Chilean automotive
industry that would have similar effects to the increase in fixed
capital. In order to explain this increase, it is necessary to consider
the relationship that exists between the terminal industry in Chile
and its parts suppliers.

It has been estimated that about 29 percent of the value of
Chilean cars is made up of locally produced parts, that is, parts
not produced by the automotive manufacturers themselves.[16] The
parts industry, however, is still relatively underdeveloped. By
the late 1960s, the Register of Manufacturers of National Parts of
the Ministry of Economics contained around 250 firms, although
this probably overestimates the number of firms actually producing
parts for the industry. The parts produced tend to be technologically
unsophisticated and are produced not by specialist firms, but by
companies that manufacture a whole range of parts. Out of 230
locally produced parts and pieces classified by the Instituto de
Costos, only 19 were considered to embody a high technological
content, while 148 were classified as low technology parts.[17] In

the late 1960s and early 1970s, however, more specialized producers began to set up, such as Wobron producing clutches, Rockwell Standard producing springs, and Conjuntos Mecanicos Los Andes producing gear boxes. As well as lacking technological sophistication, the firms that comprise the local parts industry tend to be extremely small. According to the Fourth Census of Manufacturing (1967), the average number employed per enterprise was only 8.3.

The small size and relative financial weakness of the firms that produce parts have made it necessary for the terminal firms to supply them with credit facilities if they are to be able to meet the latter's demands. It is usual for suppliers to require 50 percent or more in cash in advance. One firm estimated that about 70 percent of its suppliers had to be paid 50 percent or more in cash, as much as four or five months in advance in some cases, [18] while another company cited payments of as much as 80 percent in advance of delivery. [19] This is reflected in a predominance of short-term credits in the balance sheets of the terminal firms. A. Aguilera found that the largest single use of funds made by these firms in the period 1965-68 was in short-term loans to nonfinancial enterprises, which accounted for 42 percent of the total uses of funds over the period. [20]

As well as requiring finance from the terminal producers, the low level of development of the parts industry in Chile led some firms in the late 1960s and early 1970s to begin production of parts themselves. Between 1968 and 1970, Citroen invested $6 million in Chile in order to produce parts locally. Similarly, Renault and Peugeot formed a joint venture with the Corporación de Fomento (CORFO), Conjuntos Mecánicos Los Andes, involving an investment of $12 million. Fiat, through its subsidiary, Agrotécnica, produced about a quarter of its requirements of Chilean parts internally.* Moreover, in 1970, Fiat took an 80 percent holding in the Chilean firm Fundición Cassali. Thus, while during the greater part of the 1960s, the capital requirements of the terminal producers were mainly for working capital in order to be able to finance suppliers, by the end of the decade investment in fixed assets was becoming increasingly important (see Chapter 5).

The growing requirements of working capital were not, however, the main reason underlying concentration and denationalization in the Chilean automotive industry. A more important factor was the increasing of the local content requirement, from 30 percent

---

*In 1969, Agrotécnica supplied 13.9 of the 52.9 percent of Chilean parts for the Fiat 600 and 9.3 of the 40.4 percent for the Fiat 1500 according to the Comisión Automotriz breakdown.

in 1963 to 57.9 percent five years later, coupled with a particular feature of Chile's policy toward the industry, namely, the special treatment accorded to parts imported from other LAFTA countries. Law 14,824 of 1962 permitted such parts to be considered national if they were compensated for by an equal value of parts exports from Chile; and by a subsequent decree in 1967, import duties on such parts were eliminated. Exchanges of parts and pieces under this legislation were started with Argentina in 1965 and followed by Mexico in 1968. As a result, a considerable volume of trade in vehicle parts has been generated, mainly between Chile and Argentina. (See Table 7.5.)

As a result of these exchanges, a large part of the legally required local content is not produced in Chile at all. Thus, in 1969, out of a required local content of 58 percent, and an achieved content slightly above this (59.1 percent), parts imported from LAFTA under compensation agreements accounted for 13.7 percent.[21] This average hides considerable variations between firms and models, as Table 7.6 shows.

Under these conditions, the response of most companies to a higher required local content was to increase imports of parts from Argentina rather than to produce new parts in Chile. This made it difficult for those firms that produced models and makes not manufactured elsewhere in Latin America to meet the content requirements and remain competitive. A number of firms did in fact go out of business because they were unable to meet the entire

TABLE 7.5

Chilean Trade with LAFTA Countries Under
Compensation Arrangements, 1965-73
(thousands of dollars FOB)

	Imports	Exports
1965	752.1	32.1
1966	3,548.0	689.0
1967	7,107.9	1,370.7
1968	7,446.7	5,572.0
1969	7,765.2	9,243.5
1970	5,733.7	8,443.7
1971	7,808.7	4,477.7
1972	4,692.0	4,121.1
1973	2,135.3	3,131.6

Source: Comisión Automotriz (unpublished data).

TABLE 7.6

Breakdown of Local Content, 1972
(percent)

	Chilean	LAFTA	Total
Citroen AX-H	53	15	68
Fiat 600/E	65	*	65
Renault R4S	44	21	65
Peugeot 404	48	18	66
Fiat 125/S	59	7	66
Nissan Datsun	43	22	65

*Parts for the Fiat 600 are imported from Argentina but these are not compensated for by exports.

Source: Comisión Automotriz (unpublished data).

local content requirement from Chilean parts. Importsur, which assembled Volvo cars, found it impossible to continue after 1966 since the make was not produced elsewhere in Latin America.22 Similar problems were faced by Federic, which assembled the NSU Prinz and went out of business in 1968. By 1970, the only firms that met the entire local content requirements with Chilean parts were British Leyland and Imcoda. The former was able to do so by producing a fiberglass body locally, while the latter was experiencing considerable difficulties.

For those firms whose models were produced in other LAFTA countries, a new problem arose from the nature of the compensation operation itself. The basic difficulty is caused by the fact that the prices of Chilean-produced parts are significantly higher than those of Argentina, with which most of the relevant exchanges take place. Given a price differential of this sort, it is possible for such interchanges to be valued in one of three different ways.

1. At the price of the part in the country of origin of the model, independently of the prices in Argentina or Chile

2. At the prices in the country with which the interchange takes place, that is, at Argentinian prices

3. At the prices of the producing country, that is, Chilean exports at Chilean prices and imports at Argentinian prices*

---

*A further logical possibility is that exchanges occur at Chilean prices, but this method has not apparently been used.

The different alternatives can be analyzed in a number of
stages. The first is the direct way in which it appears in the accounts
of the terminal company in each country. Thus, where exchange
occurs at prices below the ruling prices in the country under consideration, the company will register a loss on the transaction
because it must buy the parts that are to be exported at a higher
price from local suppliers. That is to say, if the export was not
matched by an import, it could be said unequivocally that the company
had made a loss. As a second step, however it is necessary to look
at the compensating import to see if this, too, does not take place
at prices that are below the market prices of the exporting country.
Finally, the price paid for the imported product must be compared
with the price that would have had to have been paid in order to buy
it locally (that is, in the importing country).

In order to clarify what this means, it is worth taking a simple
numerical example. Suppose that the parts that are exported from
Argentina to Chile have a price inefficiency with respect to the
country of origin of 1.5, while the same parts in Chile have an
inefficiency of 3.0. Similarly, suppose that the parts that are
exported from Chile to Argentina have an inefficiency of 2.5, while
the same parts in Argentina have an inefficiency of 2.0. Let us now
consider the situations listed.

Case 1. Argentina exports to Chile $100 worth of parts valued
at prices in the country of origin. The terminal firm in Argentina
buys these parts from a local parts producer paying $150 (or the
peso equivalent) and hence loses $50 on making the export to Chile.
In Chile, $100 worth of parts for export to Argentina costs the firm
$250 to buy locally, so that it makes a loss on the transaction of
$150. However, it is receiving parts from Argentina at $50 below
the cost to the Argentinian firm so that the net loss is only $100.
On these terms, therefore, there would appear to be a transfer of
$100 to Argentina. If, however, one compares what the Chilean
firm pays for Argentinian parts with what it would have had to pay
to buy them locally, that is, $300, then it makes a gain of $200 on
the operation ($300 less $100) and a net gain, after subtracting the
loss on its own exports of $50. Thus, the gains are equally divided,
with Argentina also saving $50 compared to the situation had it
produced the parts locally.

Case 2. Argentina exports to Chile $150 worth of parts,
valued this time at Argentinian prices (and representing, therefore,
the same volume of parts as in the previous example) and receives
a similar value of exports from Chile, also valued at Argentinian
prices (representing only $75 worth at prices ruling in the country
of origin). The Argentinian company obviously makes no losses or

gains from the operation. The Chilean company sells $150 of parts to Argentina but it costs $187.50 to buy them in Chile and it therefore makes a loss of $37.50 on the transaction. Since Argentina sells to Chile at cost, it receives no subsidy from Argentina so that the net loss is $37.50. Compared to purchasing the parts locally however, which would have cost $300, there is a net gain of $112.50 ($150 less $37.50) for Chile.

Case 3. If Argentina again exports to Chile $150 worth of parts valued at Argentinian prices, it now receives $150 of Chilean parts valued at Chilean prices (that is, $60 of parts valued at international prices). Neither company makes a loss on its export transaction since both take place at existing prices. Argentina could have bought the same parts locally, however, for $120 and so makes a loss of $30, while it would have cost Chile $300 to make the same parts and so it gains $150 with no offsetting loss since it sells at cost.*

It can be seen from these analyses that there has been some confusion among writers on the complementation arrangements between Chile and Argentina concerning its exact effects. It is frequently argued in Chile[23] that the higher cost of parts in that country means that it makes a loss as a result of the exchange in each of the three situations, although case 3 is the least unfavorable. One can see how this misconception arises if one fails to compare the amount paid by the Chilean company for imports from Argentina with the amount that would have had to have been paid if the parts had been bought locally. In case 1 there appears to be a loss of $100 and in case 2 a loss of $37.50. In fact, however, as the example shows, in case 1 both Argentina and Chile gain from the arrangement, in case 2 Chile gains, while Argentina is unaffected, and in case 3 Chile gains at the expense of Argentina.

The significant point, however, is that different policies with regard to the prices at which transactions are made will involve different distributions of the gains between Argentina and Chile. If the two firms involved are both wholly owned subsidiaries of the same multinational corporation, it will not matter how the gains

---

*This discussion is logically equivalent to the theory of comparative advantage in international trade, with the difference that in the latter case the international price ratio must, it is assumed, come between the two extremes represented by the national price ratios. The discussion has been purely static and has assumed constant returns to scale in order to concentrate on the effects of different pricing arrangements.

are distributed.* If, however, one firm is a subsidiary and the other
a local firm producing under license, then the parent company will
wish to see that profits are realized in the country in which the
subsidiary operates and this may become a source of conflict.
General Motors, Ford, Peugeot, and Chrysler all had licensed
producers in Chile and subsidiaries in Argentina, and were therefore in a situation that could generate this kind of conflict.

It is also interesting to note that only with two wholly owned
subsidiaries would it be possible to operate the third type of system,
which imposes an absolute loss on one or other of the parties. Were
the producers independent of each other, it would pay one to break
the arrangement in exactly the same way as the theory of comparative advantage indicates that mutually advantageous trade will occur
at prices that lie between the relative price ratios in the two countries concerned, and that if prices lie outside this limit, trade will
not occur. It is not surprising, therefore, to find that only those
multinational companies that have wholly owned subsidiaries in
Chile have used this third system.[24]

It is possible to identify two reasons why, given this situation,
a move toward wholly owned subsidiaries would be expected. First,
none of the three arrangements discussed enables all the benefits of
complementation to be realized in Argentina. Thus, by having a
licensee in Chile rather than a wholly owned subsidiary, the parent
company loses some of the benefits of its multinationalism. Second,
the takeover of the licensee might be seen as a way of resolving
conflict in the same way as taking over local shareholders in a joint
venture is often necessary.

It is not surprising, therefore, that during the late 1960s,
Ford, General Motors, and Peugeot all took over their local licensees. In each of these cases, it was forseen that the replacement
of a licensee by a subsidiary would ease the operation of LAFTA
complementation arrangements. Both in the cases of Industria
Automotores del Pacífico the General Motors licensee, and of
Automotores San Cristobal, the Peugeot licensee, the advantages
from the point of view of these exchanges were mentioned specifically
as the major factor leading to the takeover by the licensor.[25] In
the case of the Ford licensee, Industrias Chilenas de Automotores,
LAFTA exchanges were made at international prices up to the end

---

*This should not be taken to imply that the parent company will
necessarily be indifferent to which of the two countries its profits
will be realized in. Tax and other considerations may well mean
that it prefers to realize its profits in one country or the other. The
distribution of profit will not be a source of tension, however.

of 1966, this being the most advantageous arrangement from the point of view of Ford, which had a wholly owned subsidiary in Argentina. This led to a considerable accounting loss on Chilean exports in the 1966-67 financial year, and from 1967 on, exchanges were made at commercial prices.[26] Subsequently, in 1969, Ford acquired all the company's shares, having held 50 percent since 1965, and put it into liquidation. The only company with a subsidiary in Argentina that still had a licensee in Chile by the early 1970s was Chrysler. Here, too, there had been conflict between the local company, Nun y German, and Chrysler over the prices at which complementation exchanges were made, and generally they occurred at Argentinian prices.[27]

Mexico

As was seen in the first section of this chapter, the quota system enforced by the Mexican government played an important part during the 1960s in limiting the extent of concentration and denationalization in the automotive industry. Despite this, there have been some developments that parallel those in Argentina and Chile, as can be seen from a more detailed examination of the experience of individual companies.

The most striking evidence to support the hypothesis that the same underlying forces were at work in Mexico as in the other two countries is the case of Fábricas Automex, which was set up in 1939 to assemble vehicles under license for Chrysler. At the time of the government decree that initiated manufacturing of vehicles in Mexico, Chrysler held 33 percent of the company's shares. The company's declared profitability has been low since then, and has tended to deteriorate over time. In the two years 1970 and 1971, the company had losses amounting to 180 million pesos, while its share capital came to only 300 million pesos. At the same time, Automex became increasingly indebted to the Chrysler group. In 1968, it had short-term debts to Chrysler of over 260 million pesos and in 1969 of 350 million pesos. In 1969, too, it contracted a long-term debt of 73 million pesos, which rose to a further 191 million in 1970. In 1970, Chrysler increased its participation in the company from 33 to 45 percent, and in December 1971 invested a further U.S. $14.5 million to hold 90.5 percent of the company's share capital, at which point it became a consolidated subsidiary.[28] This pattern of increasing indebtedness to the foreign corporations whose license is held, leading to a takeover, is a fairly typical mechanism for the denationalization of locally owned firms.[29]

The main problem lying behind these difficulties appears to have been the company's falling market share, which declined from 29 percent of the vehicle market in 1965 to 17 percent in 1971. In 1968, the company opened a new industrial complex in Toluca, with an assembly plant capacity of 126,000 units, that has been utilized at levels far below this potential maximum. Although Automex has fully utilized its quota, it appears to have had difficulty in selling all its production (see Chapter 6). In terms of the analysis carried out, the firm had built an optimum scale plant, but then not had sufficient financial resources to shift its demand curve to the required position. The financial problems of the firm are further indicated by the fact that the debt-equity ratio rose considerably from 1.5 in 1968 to 2.1 in 1969 and 3.4 in 1970.[30]

The difficulties of the company during the late 1960s were only one reason for the change of ownership at the end of 1971. Equally important was the new government policy, introduced in 1969, requiring firms to cover all their parts imports with exports by the end of a ten-year period (see above). The possibilities of exporting are obviously far greater for the wholly owned subsidiary, which is part of an integrated international operation, as was seen in the Chilean case. The multinational companies can concentrate the production of certain parts in a particular country in order that the subsidiary in that country can benefit from the government's legislation. Licensors may be unwilling to do this, and it has been widely predicted in Mexico that the new policy will make it particularly difficult for the local firms to continue production.[31] Despite the fact that, until 1970, Automex was one of the leading exporters among the Mexican automotive manufacturers, the need to increase these exports substantially has been mentioned as an important factor in the Chrysler takeover.

Another interesting case to analyze is that of the only other joint venture between Mexican and foreign capital, Vehículos Automotores Mexicanos. The firm was set up in 1946 as Willys Mexicana to import assembled Jeeps and distribute them in Mexico. In the late 1940s, the company began to have its vehicles assembled locally in the Armadora Automotriz (Nash) factory, and as demand for the company's cars continued to grow, it decided to build its own assembly plant in 1953. Between 1953 and 1964, the firm assembled cars of many different makes, including Austin, Datsun, Peugeot, and Rambler. Following the 1962 decree, the company set up a joint venture in which U.S. firms Kaiser Jeep and American Motors had a minority participation, and changed its name from Willys Mexicana to Vehículos Automotores Mexicanos.

Unlike Automex, the company has chosen not to build a large plant and has not filled its production quota. Until 1969, the plant had an estimated annual capacity of only just over 15,000 (working two shifts) and in 1970 it was increased to almost 20,000. As a result, the firm was able to enjoy relatively high levels of capacity utilization, reaching 74 percent in 1969 and 70 percent in 1971. Moreover, the decision not to utilize the company's production quota fully was a deliberate one in order to avoid running the company into sales difficulties. This enabled VAM to operate with very little sales financing, which was reflected in a very high ratio of net sales to credit to dealers. In the 1971-72 financial year, this was 34:1, much higher than the ratio found for Chrysler, the only other firm for which comparable data were available, 11:1 in the same year.

In analytical terms, this case is similar to that of Industria Automotriz Santa Fe in Argentina in that the company deliberately pursued a policy of small-scale production without massive install-ment financing. It differs, however, in that the financial constraint on VAM was not as stringent as that on IASF, since the Mexican government, through the Sociedad Mexicana de Crédito Industrial (SOMEX), was the majority shareholder in the company. It also differs from the Argentinian case because of the quota, which pre-vented the foreign firms from taking advantage of their large scale to drive the company out of the market. Despite this, VAM has been subject to a squeeze that reduced its pretax profits on capital plus reserves from 22.8 percent in 1964-65 to only 2.9 percent in 1970-71.

Before closing this section, it is worth mentioning briefly the case of FANASA, which bought the Borgward plant in West Germany and set it up in Mexico. The firm was 100 percent Mexican owned but signed a technical assistance contract with a Spanish firm in order to set up and operate the plant.[32] Despite official government encouragement, the firm was never able to get off the ground, al-though it started production in 1967. In 1969, the firm was taken over by the government, since it was in financial difficulties, and subsequently put into liquidation. Nothing came of the suggestion that all the majority Mexican-owned companies should be joined together to form one company capable of resisting the competition of the multinational corporations. Thus, by 1972, there were only two firms remaining in the Mexican automotive industry under local ownership, the majority-owned VAM and the wholly owned DINA. Significantly, both of these were government-controlled companies.

CONCLUSION

It has been shown in this chapter that there has been a tendency for production in the Latin American automotive industries considered to become increasingly concentrated in the hands of a limited number of firms, and that this has taken the specific form of denationalization, that is, the elimination or takeover of locally owned firms. The form and extent of the process have differed between countries, mainly as a result of the different legal and institutional framework within which it has taken place. Thus, in Argentina, developments have taken place virtually free from government intervention, whereas in Mexico, the quota system and government ownership of two of the local companies have played a determining role. In Chile, the form of integration within LAFTA through complementation agreements has given additional advantages to the multinational companies. Despite these differences, the underlying trend has been in the same direction in all three countries, and none has been able to resist the growing penetration of the international firms. Neither in Argentina nor in Mexico (with its much more favorable nationalistic policies) were suggestions for a merger of the major local companies, to combat the competitive strength of the foreign subsidiaries, taken up. The result in Argentina was the demise of all the companies concerned, and the same fate is a distinct possibility for the remaining Mexican companies.

NOTES

1. See, for example, J. Bain, Industrial Organization, 2nd ed. (New York: Wiley, 1968), pp. 81-92; and K. D. George, Industrial Organization: Competition, Growth, and Structural Change in Britain (London: Allen & Unwin, 1971), pp. 81-92. In addition, Bain mentions financial considerations promoting mergers and George discusses the growth motivation of managers, but both these may lead to diversification rather than concentration.

2. This is the sum of the squares of each firm's market share. See C. Rosenbluth, Concentration in Canadian Manufacturing Industry, National Bureau of Economic Research, General Series No. 61 (Princeton, N.J.: Princeton University Press, 1957), pp. 11-13.

3. See Jorge L. Remes Lenicov, "Algunos Resulutodos de la Política Desarollista (1958-64); El Caso de la Industria Automotriz," Económica 19, no. 3 (1973): 305-10.

4. See the statement of Herman Lacalle, undersecretary of economics at the Asociación de Industriales Metalúrgicos (ASIMET) seminar, Primer Seminario Nacional de la Industria Automotriz (Santiago: ASIMET, 1969), pp. 195-96.

5. See the statement of the minister of industry and commerce at the time of the 1962 decree: "Se esablecio, empero el sistema de quotas de producción, a fin de dar igual oportunidad a empresas con diferentes capacidades financieras, las poderosas, hubiesen absor-

bido desde un principio una parte muy apreciable del mercado."
Quoted in Jorge Orvananos Lascurain, "Aspectos de la Demanda y
Oferta Automotriz" (professional thesis, Instituto Tecnológico
Autonóme de México, 1967), Chap. 5.

6. C. M. Jiménez, "Contribución al Estudio Crítica Sobre
la Política de Radicación de Capitales en la República Argentina:
La Industria Automotriz" (Thesis, Universidad de Buenos Aires,
1964), Table 26.

7. F. G. Donner, The World-wide Industrial Enterprise:
Its Challenge and Promises (New York: McGraw-Hill, 1967), p. 66.

8. For a history of Siam, see T. C. Cochran and R. E. Reina,
Entrepreneurship in Argentine Culture: Torcuato di Tella and
S.I.A.M. (Philadelphia: University of Pennsylvania Press, 1962).

9. Siam de Tella, Memoria (Buenos Aires: 1961).

10. Company accounts.

11. Inverview with Guido di Tella.

12. J. F. McCloud, "Prologue," Documentos Referentes a la
Compra de Acciones de Siam di Tella Automotores (Industrias
Kaiser Argentina: n.d.).

13. Memoria, 1963.

14. Memoria, 1961.

15. See "The Argentine Motor Industry," Economist Intelligence
Unit, Motor Business, no. 38 (1964): 42-55.

16. Felix Gil Mitjans, "Un Modelo de Programación de la
Industria Automotriz Chilena" (professional thesis, Universidad
de Chile, 1969), Chap. 2.

17. Gamma Ingenieros, Estudio de la Industria Automotriz
Chilena, UNIDO (ID/WG 76/6), 1970, p. 78.

18. Interview with Sr. Patricio Salas (Nun y German).

19. Interview with Sr. Orlando Canalos (General Motors).

20. Asociación de Industriales Metalúrgicos (ASIMET), pp.
58-75. It seems probable in view of what has been said that this
item consists mainly of financing to suppliers rather than consumers.

21. Gil Mitjans, op. cit.

22. Importsur, Memoria, 1966.

23. See, for example, Instituto de Costos, op. cit., Chap. II 3a.
The point was also made to the author during interviews with company
executives in Chile.

24. Instituto de Costos, op. cit., Chap. II. 3a.

25. Industria Automotora del Pacífico, 13 Memoria (1968).
Automotores San Cristobal, 8th Memoria (October 1, 1968-
December 31, 1969). Problems concerning LAFTA exchanges were
also frequently referred to in interviews with executives of the
various companies undertaken by the author in January-March 1972.

26. Industrias Chilenas de Automotores, Estados Financieros July 1, 1966-June 30, 1967 and July 1, 1967-June 30, 1968.

27. Interview with Patricio Salas.

28. From annual reports of Automex and Chrysler.

29. A. G. Frank, J. D. Cockroft, and D. L. Johnson, Dependence and Underdevelopment: Latin America's Political Economy (New York: Doubleday, 1972).

30. Automex annual reports.

31. See Manuel Franco Rosas, "Problemas y Perspectivas de la Industria Automotriz en México (professional thesis, Universidad Nacional Autónoma de México, 1971), Chap. 3b.

32. M. Wionczek, G. Bueno, and J. E. Navarrette, "La Transferencia Internacional de Tecnología al Nivel de Empresa: El Caso de México," mimeographed (Mexico: Fondo de Cultura Económica, 1974), p. 85.

8

THE PATTERN
OF DEPENDENT
INDUSTRIALIZATION
IN THE AUTOMOTIVE
INDUSTRY

It is now possible to discuss the implications of the pattern of dependent industrial development that has been described in the last three chapters. Critical studies of the impact of multinational corporations on underdeveloped countries have tended to concentrate on the repatriation of profits from these countries. This, however, is only a part of the effect of penetration by international firms on the local economy. Equally important, in terms of the prospects for development, are the effects on the industrial structure, the forms of competition, and the consequences for cost and prices.

This chapter presents some evidence to suggest that there is a significant outflow of profits from the Latin American automotive industry. It concentrates mainly on the other effects that have tended to be neglected in the literature. The first part of the chapter extends the theoretical model of Chapter 4 to the situation where all locally owned firms have been eliminated and the industry is dominated by foreign subsidiaries. In the following sections, the main effects of this pattern of development will be analyzed in Argentina, Chile, and Mexico.

A MODEL OF THE DEPENDENT SECTOR
OF PRODUCTION

In Chapter 4 a model was presented in which significant cost differentials between foreign and nationally owned companies led to local firms becoming the marginal producers in the industry under consideration. Over time, a process of denationalization and concentration occurs, leading to the elimination of all locally owned firms. Once these firms have been driven out of the industry, the cost differential between firms is narrowed considerably and, at the same time, becomes a less important parameter in the competitive process, since all firms now have the backing of much larger parent corporations. These two factors are characteristic of monopolistic industries in Steindl's terminology.[1] In this chapter, we shall develop some of the implications of substituting a monopolistic structure of foreign-owned firms for a competitive structure (again in the Steindlian sense) composed of both foreign subsidiaries and national firms.

The main characteristic of the monopolistic type of industry (indeed, one might say its defining characteristic) is the fact that surplus capacity is not eliminated through price-cutting. The logic of this in the case of an industry dominated by foreign subsidiaries is easy to understand. The particular subsidiary of a multinational corporation in, say, Argentina represents a relatively small proportion of its total global sales and profits, and losses there cannot threaten the existence of the corporation as a whole. Having once made a commitment to a particular market, companies tend to be reluctant to abandon that market to their competitors, and since the parent company's existence cannot be threatened come what may, there is no mechanism that will force it to abandon the market.* This is not to say that companies cannot be forced out of a particular market by persistent price-cutting, but that the costs of doing so for the successful firm are likely to be so high as to act as a severe disincentive to such behavior.

Figure 8.1 illustrates this concept in a diagram similar to Figure 4.2. After the elimination of all locally owned firms, there is no longer a sharp discontinuity in the industry cost curve HL, although there may still be some differences in costs because of the different scales of operation of the various firms. Immediately after the elimination of all local firms, price AQ will be above the costs of the marginal firm AH as a result of the discontinuity in costs between local and foreign firms. It will still be possible for some firms to eliminate others by cutting prices from AQ to AR.

As in the case analyzed in Chapter 4, this will lead to the elimination of the firms whose output is represented by the segment AP on the horizontal axis and the expansion of those firms on PC to PM. There is little incentive to do this, however, since the additional profit from an expansion of output (area UELV minus

---

*If Ford had given away all the vehicles it produced in Argentina in that year, the rate of return of the parent company before tax would only have been reduced from 21.3 to 17.3 percent in 1969.

FIGURE 8.1

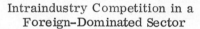

Intraindustry Competition in a
Foreign-Dominated Sector

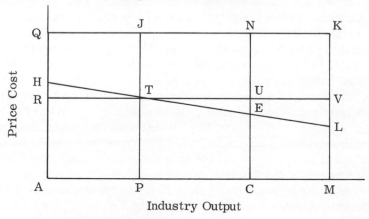

Source: Compiled by the author.

area JNUT) is small compared to the gain where there are local
firms in the industry (see Figure 4.2) and may even be negative.
Thus, in a monopolistic industry, supply is not likely to be adjusted
to demand through exits from the industry. It must therefore be
adjusted through changes in the capacity utilization of existing firms.

This rigidity is an important feature of a monopolistic market
structure dominated by foreign firms. Entry to and exit from the
industry are both extremely rare. Competition no longer operates
to reduce the number of firms to a level that would make it possible
for each firm to have an optimal scale of plant. Further rationalization of the industry in the peripheral country depends on developments
at the international level, such as mergers between two multinational
corporations or some kind of less formal cooperative agreement (for
example, the Renault-Peugeot linkup) rather than on developments
internal to that country itself.

Entry is also rendered difficult for both economic and institutional reasons. With increasing local content requirements, the
initial investment to start production increased considerably (see
Chapter 5), acting as a barrier to entry at least to local firms if
not to multinational corporations with their far greater financial
capacity. Moreover, the need to meet this content requirement
within a very short time span imposes additional costs. New investment requires government approval in most cases, and there may
be an increasing reluctance to grant this to latecomers, which are

in a weaker bargaining position in that they cannot accuse the government of discrimination if they themselves passed up the opportunity of entering the market initially.*

The rigidity of the market structure and its relative fragmentation, compared to the advanced countries where most companies were locally owned and there were few if any foreign subsidiaries at a similar stage in the industry's development, have meant uneconomic scales of production and high costs. This is an especially important factor in industries such as automotive manufacturing where economies of scale are so significant. With a given market size, a larger number of firms implies either a higher level of costs at a determined level of local integration or a lower level of local integration if a certain level of costs is taken as the objective. Market size, of course, need not be given. Thus, high costs lead to a high price for the product, which restricts the domestic market to certain income groups and makes it extremely difficult to achieve exports except under special arrangements.

Different economic (and social) structures will result in different rates and forms of capital accumulation. Monopolistic structures, it has been argued, are less favorable to accumulation than competitive structures.[2] At the macroeconomic level, this can be related to the effect of such structures on income distribution and the appropriation of the gains from technical progress and the effect that these in turn have on demand and hence on the incentive to invest. (See Chapter 10 for further details.) At the industry level, the emergence of excess capacity acts to dampen the rate of accumulation. Since capacity is no longer eliminated in the downswing through bankruptcies and so on, new investment in the upswing tends to be less as unused capacity can be brought back into production. In addition, the normal restraints on competition implicit in oligopolistic situations will tend to limit the extent to which firms will invest in order to expand their market shares. On the other hand, measures to increase capacity utilization through advertising, the extension of consumer credit, and so forth will be stimulated. Thus nonprice competition tends to assume particular significance in oligopolistic industries.

A further consequence of this model relates to the outflow of funds from the peripheral economy. The tendency over time is for the profit rates in the industry to increase relatively to the oppor-

---

*This is illustrated by the commitment Fiat had to make to the Brazilian government, to export a substantial portion of its output, in order to be able to enter the Brazilian automotive industry in 1973.

tunities for new investment. This phenomenon is a familiar argument
in Marxist writings on imperialism[3] and more recent writings on
capitalist development.[4] As we have seen, the oligopolistic market
structure tends to reduce the opportunities for new investment, either
through collusion in the form of cartels or through tacit understand-
ings. Profits continue to be generated, however, and these are in
excess of reinvestment requirements. The theories of imperialism
see the export of capital as an outlet for the investment of these
profits. Another alternative, from the point of view of the individual
firm, is diversification into other industries within the same country.
In the case of a peripheral economy, the two alternatives present
themselves as repatriation of profits or diversification locally.

It has been observed in the context of regional economics that
a large corporation is more likely to respond to investment opportunities in its traditional activity in new locations than to investment
opportunities in unrelated industries at existing locations.[5] This
point seems relevant in considering the possibilities of foreign
subsidiaries diversifying into new industries in underdeveloped
countries. On the whole, they will prefer to limit their investment
to those industries that are already familiar to the parent company;
indeed, in some cases, they may be prevented from diversifying
by host country policies (for example, the Mexican legislation
preventing the terminal firms in the automotive industry from investing in parts production). Diversification in underdeveloped countries
is also inhibited by the unequal income distribution and the interdependence of firm reactions, even in different industries, because
of the small size of the total market.[6]

Unfortunately, there are no available studies on the extent
of diversification by foreign subsidiaries in underdeveloped countries,
but a priori theorizing suggests that subsidiaries will be less diversified than their parents. Faced with these limitations, it will not be
long before a foreign firm finds itself with more profitable opportunities for investment elsewhere in the world, and starts to transfer
funds either indirectly through the parent company or directly to
other affiliates. Thus, even if in the initial years of development of
an industry there is a net inflow of funds to the country concerned,
this soon becomes negative once the scope for expansion has been
restricted.

It is worth noting here the comment of General Motors vice-
president T. A. Murphy.

> General Motors has relied on overseas capital markets
> to augment earnings retained for investment overseas.
> This has been our standard practice for the past 25 years.
> It has also been our policy to remit overseas earnings

promptly, retaining overseas only those resources necessary to maintaining and expanding the subsidiary as an effective competitor.[7]

The impact of foreign investment in terms of employment creation, both within the industry under consideration and on the economy as a whole, must also be examined. It is important to remember that capital accumulation has a dual effect on employment. It displaces labor through the incorporation of more advanced techniques of production, on the one hand, while absorbing labor through the expansion of the market, on the other. The balance struck between displacement and absorption depends on the competitive or monopolistic structures within which these mechansims operate. Competition tends to favor the expansion of the base of accumulation and the absorption of labor.[8] The rate of growth of employment depends on the rate of accumulation and the rate of growth of capital per man. As already seen, the rate of accumulation tends to be lower in the case of monopolistic structures, so that, unless technological advance embodied in the new investment was less, then the employment generation effects would be less. Monopoly tends to accentuate technological discontinuities, thus weakening the mechanisms for reabsorbing labor.[9] This is particularly true in peripheral economies where technology is exogeneously generated* and there is a substantial difference between the capital intensity of imported technology and indigenous technology. Therefore, it is to be expected that the employment effects of capital accumulation in an industry in a peripheral economy will be negative where it competes with existing industries and only limited when it replaces previously imported products.

CAPITAL FLOWS

One of the major implications to come out of the model described is that, as an industry develops over time, the accumulation of funds from profits tends to exceed the outlets for new investment. In the context of a metropolitan economy, this, it has been argued, is likely to lead to either foreign investment or diversification or both. In the case of a peripheral economy where the industry is dominated by foreign subsidiaries, the probable effect is an outflow

---

*At least if one thinks in terms of the national economy. It is, of course, endogenous if one thinks of the peripheral economy as integrated into the world economy.

of funds from the country. This is the equivalent at the industry level of what has become known as the drain of investable surplus from the underdeveloped countries at the macrolevel.

Unfortunately, it is not easy to obtain data on the total outflow of funds in profits, royalties, and overpricing of intermediate inputs either for entire economies or for particular industries. The figures that will be presented in this section, therefore, are incomplete and represent only rough orders of magnitude. In Argentina it has been estimated that between 1958 and 1964, that is, the period during which most of the foreign investment in the automotive industry was made, the inflow of $33 million into the industry was exceeded by the outflow of dividend payments that amounted to $52.3 million.[10] This is a truly remarkable figure if, as it suggests, foreign firms were able to recoup their investment in such a short period without even including royalty payments and overpricing of intermediates in the calculation.

In the second half of the 1960s, the balance between new inflows of foreign investment and outflows of dividends and technology payments was even less favorable to the Argentinian economy. The total amount of investment approved by the government between 1965 and 1970 came to U.S. $15.5 million, whereas data for the period 1968 to 1970 suggest that in each of these years profit remissions were at least U.S. $15 million. If technology payments are added to profit remissions, then the total outflow between 1968 and 1970 amounted to U.S. $83.9 million.[11] In the period 1971-72, it is estimated that a further U.S. $37.4 million was paid in royalty, technical assistance, dividend, and other payments.[12] There is, moreover, reason to believe that these figures underestimate the amounts actually transferred under the heading of technology payments.

According to this study, technology payments by eight firms in 1970 amounted to U.S. $10.7 million. A survey of contracts in the Registro Nacional de Contratos de Licencias y Transferencia de Tecnología indicated that royalty payments by the automotive industry came to U.S. $26 million, or 37 percent of the total royalties paid by Argentina, in 1970.[13] Of this total, more than U.S. $8 million was accounted for by the parts industry and at least U.S. $18 million by the seven terminal firms included. If the other three important automotive manufacturers are added, the total outflow could be more than U.S. $20 million, or twice the level indicated by the D.G.I. study. Data for 1973 indicate that the eight major foreign firms paid more than U.S. $18 million in royalties in that year, despite the introduction of measures by the government to restrict such payments.

It appears, therefore, that during the late 1960s and early 1970s, the annual payments of both dividends and royalties were at

least as great as the total amount of new foreign capital authorized
in the automotive industry during the six years from 1965 to 1970.
Moreover, these figures take no account of any overpricing of
intermediate inputs that may have occurred on imports by Argentinian
automotive manufacturers from their parent companies. In the early
years of the industry's development, the relatively low local content
of the vehicles produced gave considerable scope for such overpricing
with imports running at over U.S. $100 million a year.[14] Even in
the late 1960s and early 1970s, imports were between U.S. $50
million and U.S. $100 million a year, a high enough level to have
acted as a significant channel for profit remissions.[15] That this
is not simply a theoretical possibility is indicated by the decision
of the Argentinian supreme court that a part of deferred payments
made by the local Ford subsidiary to the parent company for imported
parts represented profit remissions.[16]

In Chile, dividend payments have not been an important form
of surplus transfer, since it is only locally owned companies that
have tended to pay dividends. Royalties have been more significant.
Estimates derived from the Ministry of Economics' Rol Industrial
suggest that, in 1968, the total amount paid by the automotive manufacturers in royalties came to around U.S. $650,000.[17]

More important than direct license and technical assistance
payments are the possibilities of overpricing mentioned in Chapter 7.
The Censo de Regalías made by the Corporación de Fomento (CORFO)
estimated that total payments from firms located in Chile to licensers
abroad in the transport equipment sector, the main component of
which is the automotive industry, came to $3,479,800 in 1968.[18]
An alternative estimate is to take the total imports of the terminal
firms of $23,940,000 in 1968 and assume that 20 percent of this
represented overpricing, so that the outflow under this heading
comes to $4,788,000, and add to it the previous estimate for royalty
payments, giving an approximate total outflow of U.S. $5,433,000.
Even if only 10 percent of the total value of imports was overpricing,
the total outflow would still be somewhat in excess of U.S. $3 million.
As was noted, all these calculations give only a rough order of
magnitude.

A comparative indication of this magnitude is obtained when
one finds that the total inflow of foreign capital into the transport
equipment sector over the period 1960-69 came to only $3,038,740,[19]
that is, less than our estimate of the outflow in a single year, 1968.*

---

*Between 1961 and 1966, no new inflow of foreign investment
into the automotive industry took place, all investment presumably
being reinvestment of profits by existing firms.

Over the three-year period 1967-69, during which all the above investment in the automotive industry was made, the outflow of payments for licenses and technical assistance alone came to almost $2 million, and had complete data been available for the period 1961-66, royalty payments would probably have exceeded the total inflow over the whole period.

Two general studies of foreign investment in Mexico have estimated the outflow of currency on capital account by industrial sector, taking the difference between new inflows of capital and remittances of profits, royalties, technical assistance, and other payments. Both studies present data on the transport equipment sector of which an important, but not the only, component is the terminal automotive industry. B. Sepulveda and A. Chumacero found that in 1967 new investment in the sector amounted to almost U.S. $25 million, while the capital outflow was U.S. $8,250,000, giving a favorable balance of U.S. $16,660,000.[20] By 1970, however, the situation had been dramatically reversed with new investment at U.S. $4,282,000 and remissions reaching U.S. $20,888,000, giving a net outflow of U.S. $16,600,000. The second study, by F. Fajnzylber and T. Martinez, gives a somewhat lower estimate of the outflow in 1970, the only year for which data are presented, of slightly over U.S. $10 million.[21] This clearly bears out the point that during the early phase of an industry's development there is a net inflow of capital as the initial investment is made, but subsequently investment falls off substantially or is financed by retained profits, while profit and other remissions increase, giving rise to a deficit on capital account.

As was seen earlier, the excess price charged for imported components should be added to the outflow of capital. If 10 percent of the total value of imported inputs represented overpricing (that is, if imported parts were overpriced by 11 percent), there would have been an outflow under this head in 1971 of about U.S. $17.1 million. This is greater than the total royalty and technical assistance payments made by the terminal automotive industry in the same year, which was estimated at U.S. $11.2 million (based on AMIA data on imports of parts).

MARKET STRUCTURE AND THE FORMS
OF COMPETITION

It has been argued that the domination of an industry by foreign subsidiaries tended to lead to a certain rigidity in its structure. This can be seen most clearly in the case of Argentina where the process of concentration and denationalization has been underway for the longest period of time. With the elimination of the last remaining national firm, Industria Automotriz Santa Fe, the number of firms in the industry has been stabilized, in marked contrast to the sharp fall from 21 in 1960 to 13 in 1965. Although it has not gone so far, and there are still two government-controlled firms in the industry, the same process can also be seen in Mexico, while prior to the election of Allende as president in 1970, Chile, too, was following the same path.

That competition will not continue to reduce the number of firms even further appears to be supported at least by developments in Argentina. This phenomenon, which is characteristic of the Latin American automotive industry, will be referred to as premature oligopolization, the main features of which are the importance of nonprice forms of competition, and few cases of either entries to or exits from the industry, while firms are still small relative to the optimum scale of plant, and the market is fragmented between a number of producers.

Argentina

This section seeks to show that competition in the Argentinian automotive industry has not taken the form of price-cutting, lower costs, and increased output, but rather the typical forms of nonprice competition characteristic of oligopolistic industries, such as advertising, consumer credit, model diversification, and so forth.

The pattern of competition in the automotive industry of developed countries, such as Britain and the United States, has been described as one of model-price competition. Companies direct their vehicles at particular segments of the market, and within these segments, price differentials are of no great significance. It seems probable that the same pattern of behavior has been carried over to the Argentinian market. One would expect, therefore, that in dividing the market up into segments, price differentials between competing models would be relatively small.

The segments identified in Table 8.1 correspond roughly with a division of the market according to engine capacity, the cutoff points being 1,100 cc, 1,500 cc, and 2,000 cc. The two segments described as U.S. compacts and U.S. standard are the cheapest and most expensive vehicles, respectively, produced in each line. Market segments are not, however, necessarily defined in technological terms, since what is relevant is which models the firms themselves and their customers see as competing. Thus, despite having a much smaller cc rating than other models, the Citroen Ami 8 has been included in the intermediate category since this

TABLE 8.1

Prices of Argentinian Cars by Market Segment, 1971
(pesos ley)

Small		Intermediate		European Compacts	
Fiat 600	12,440	Fiat 128	16,950	Fiat 1500	20,250
Citroen 2CV	11,500	Renault R6	15,600	Fiat 1600	20,250
Citroen 3CV	12,850	Renault R12	17,600	Peugeot 404	20,180
Renault R4L	11,900	Citroen Ami 8	14,950	Peugeot 504	23,305
Renault R4S	13,100	Dodge 1500	17,550		

U.S. Compacts		U.S. Standard	
Rambler Custom	24,590	Rambler Ambassador	35,900
Torino L	23,200	Torino GS	34,800
Ford Falcon	24,639	Ford Fairlane LTD	31,129
Chevrolet Special	20,740	Chevrolet SS Coupe	32,124
Dodge 4	21,234	Dodge GTX	32,764

Source: Fiat (unpublished data).

seems to be the sector of the market at which it is aimed in terms
of price and quality. That price is not the only consideration determining market segments can be seen from the fact that European
compacts are competitive in price, but since they are such different
products, they have been considered separately.

In Table 8.2, the coefficient of variation of prices has been
calculated for each of the market segments that has been identified
(based on Table 8.1). In no case does this coefficient come to over
10 percent, indicating little dispersion within each group, despite
the fact that the average price of the most expensive cars on the
market is almost three times that of the cheapest cars. This suggests
that firms follow a policy of aiming a model at a particular section
of the market and setting its price with reference to similar models,
that is, model-price competition.

Another indication of the lack of price competition in the automotive industry is obtained if one looks at the path of prices over
time. The data seem to indicate that prices for competing models
have tended to move more or less in step, increasing with increases
in the rate of taxation and increases in local costs and with devaluations. A detailed study of the years from 1960 to 1963 indicated
that, "the increases—even if not simultaneous—occurred on each
occasion within a period of two or three months for all firms, and
moreover by a similar amount in each case."22 What competition
there was on prices took the form of delaying price increases for
as long as possible, given the inflationary climate, in order to avoid
losing market shares. This pattern appears to have applied equally
to more recent years. It is worth noting here that most prices were
stabilized, in money terms, for a period of two or three years in
the late 1960s, despite a continued rise in the internal price level.

TABLE 8.2

Average Price and Dispersion by
Market Segment

	Small	Intermediate	European Compacts
Mean	12,358	16,530	20,996
Standard deviation	661	1,196	1,540
Coefficient of variation	5.35	7.24	7.33

	U.S. Compacts	U.S. Standard
Mean	22,881	33,343
Standard deviation	1,831	1,961
Coefficient of variation	8	5.88

As just seen, price competition has not been particularly significant in the Argentinian automotive industry. It seems, therefore, that what competition there may have been has taken other forms, which it is known are important in developed countries, such as advertising, the use of consumer credit, and model changes and diversity.

Table 8.3 gives the total advertising expenditure of the terminal firms in the Argentinian automotive industry. As can be seen, advertising has tended to increase, whether measured as a percentage of total sales (column 2) or as advertising per car (columns 3 and 4). It is to be expected that the Argentinian car market would show much lower levels of advertising than the more mature U.S. and U.K. markets. In fact, although the level is higher in the United States, the difference is small, while British firms spend a lower percentage on advertising than their Argentinian counterparts.

The average advertising expenditure by U.S. car manufacturers was about $40 per car in 1967, while the advertising expenditure of the Big Three, as a percentage of their worldwide sales, came to 0.9 percent for General Motors, 1.0 percent for Ford, and 1.3 percent for Chrysler.[23] (An almost equal amount of advertising per car in Argentina is translated into a lower ratio of advertising to sales because of the higher price of cars in that country.) Compared to Britain, where the ratio of advertising to sales in the automotive industry was only 0.5 percent in 1963,[24] advertising expenditures in Argentina were relatively heavy. Data for individual firms indicated advertising expenditures varying between 0.6 and 1.6 percent of sales, with a tendency for U.S. subsidiaries to show a higher level of advertising than the European firms.

It is not only the manufacturing firms that spend on advertising but also the dealers. A higher proportion of advertising expenditure by the former in Argentina might occur as a result of institutional arrangements that meant that dealers had to support a lesser part of the total expenditure than in developed countries. In fact, however, it appears that advertising by dealers is at least as great in relation to turnover as in the United States, being between 0.8 and 1.25 percent in Argentina compared to 0.88 percent in the United States in 1964.[25]

A second feature of competition within the industry has been the proliferation of models produced by the various firms. Taking the nine most important car producers, their range of models increased from 10 in 1960 to 48 in 1974, and the total number of models produced in Argentina increased from 22 in 1960, despite the reduction in the number of firms during the same period. As far as can be seen from the data, model diversity increased in a number of steps. The first was in 1962, as a result of Industrias

TABLE 8.3

Advertising in the Argentinian Automotive Industry, 1964–73

(millions of m$n)

	Advertising (1)	Advertising/Sales Percent (2)	Advertising per Car	
			m$n (3)	U.S. (4)
1964	750	0.65	4,505	29.9
1965	900	0.50	4,626	24.5
1966	1,300	0.64	7,244	29.3
1967	1,700	0.66	9,697	29.1
1968	2,200	0.79	12,156	34.7
1969	2,600	0.73	11,894	34.0
1970	3,350	0.93	15,255	38.1
1971	3,600	0.71	14,193	35.5
1972	6,500	0.81	24,200	29.1
1973	11,700	0.86	39,831	39.9

Source: ADEFA, Informe Estadistico, no. 588 (August 28, 1974), Table 4, and own investigation.

Kaiser Argentina and the Big Three from the United States starting production of large cars—Rambler, Falcon, Chevrolet, and Valiant.

A second significant increase occurred in 1966, again mainly as a result of IKA adding several variations of the Torino to its line and diversifying the production of Siam di Tella which it had taken over. In 1969, the number of models again increased, with Ford introducing the Fairlane line and General Motors introducing several new models, while, in the early 1970s, Chrysler led the U.S. firms into the medium-sized market with the Dodge 1500. The success of this model led Ford and General Motors to begin production of their Taunus and Opel medium-sized cars in 1974. Despite this increase in diversity, the average production of each model has increased from less than 2,000 in 1960 to 4,418 in 1974, although compared to the United States, where average production per model was 20,700 in 1967,[26] this figure is still extremely small.

Not surprisingly, the extent of model changes and model diversity is associated with its prevalence in the parent company. Thus, the firms that have most models and have changed them most often tend to be the subsidiaries of the U.S. companies and Fiat, known in Europe for its model policy, while Citroen and SAFRAR (Peugeot), like their parents, have had much less change and diversity.

Looking particularly at the large car section of the market, the models introduced in the early 1960s remained unchanged until the mid-1960s when General Motors, Chrysler, and Ford changed their models between 1965 and 1967 and IKA supplemented its range by introducing the Torino. Then, again in 1969 and 1970, Chrysler, General Motors, and IKA changed their models and Ford introduced the Fairlane. In other segments of the market, Fiat has had three basic model changes with the replacement of the 1100 by the 1500 in 1963, the 1500 by the 1600 in 1969, and the 1600 by the 125 in 1972.

Other firms have tended to introduce new models while keeping on the old ones for several years after, as did SAFRAR with the 404 in 1962 and the 504 in 1968 and IKA with the Renault 4 in 1963. As a result, model runs have tended to be extremely short in Argentina. Only one model has been reproduced in more than 100,000 units, namely, the Fiat 600, which reached 205,159 between 1960 and 1973. This was followed by a number of models with output of between 60,000 and 100,000. (See Table 8.4.) The problems of scale, owing to the small size of the market and the large number of producers, have been further aggravated by the diversity of models and the short life cycle of the majority of them.*

*See below, pp. 206-08, for a discussion of the effect of model diversity and model changes on costs of production.

TABLE 8.4

Total Output of Most Popular Argentinian Cars,
1959–73

Model	Total Output	Period
Fiat 600	205,159	1960–73
Peugeot 404	98,644	1962–73
Fiat 1500 Berlina	78,346	1963–69
Ford Falcon de Lujo	69,705	1967–73
Peugeot 504	61,561	1969–73
Fiat 128	60,970	1971–73

Source: ADEFA, Informe Estadistico, no. 577 (May 31, 1974):
3–6.

A further aspect of competition in the automotive industry
(previously discussed in a different context in Chapter 6) is the use
of installment finance. It was indicated that increasing use of hire
purchase arrangements came to be made as the market for cars
tightened. The use of consumer credit is by now widespread, and
the terms offered are generous with relatively small downpayments
and a long repayment period. As would be expected in an oligopolistic

TABLE 8.5

Examples of Credit Terms Offered to the
Consumer, 1971

	U.S. Compacts			
	IKA	Ford	General Motors	Chrysler
Cash (percent)	30 to 35	30 to 40	40	30
Interest (monthly) (percent)	1.50 to 1.70	1.30 to 1.52	1.45 to 1.65	1.52 to 1.84
Repayments (months)	9 to 36	12 to 40	12 to 36	12 to 30

	Intermediate		
	IKA	Fiat	Citroen
Cash (percent)	30 to 35	29 to 39	30
Interest (monthly) (percent)	1.50 to 1.60	1.46 to 1.87	1.50 to 1.70
Repayment (months)	9 to 36	12 to 36	9 to 36

Source: Industrias Kaiser Argentina (unpublished data).

situation, the credit terms offered by different firms do not vary
greatly (see Table 8.5). This is in marked contrast to the situation
in earlier years, when foreign subsidiaries made use of their preferential access to capital in order to compete with local firms by
offering more favorable credit terms (see Chapter 7).

Chile

Since 1966, vehicle prices in Chile have been subject to government control. Prices to the public are fixed by the Dirección de
Industria y Comercio (DIRINCO) of the ministry of economics using
one of two methods (this refers to the situation in 1970). For vehicles
that make up the entire local content requirement from Chilean parts,
the price is calculated by multiplying the FOB price of a complete
vehicle by a coefficient 5.4, determined by the Comisión Automotriz.
Vehicles that have a local content partly made up of parts imported
from other LAFTA countries have their prices calculated directly
on the basis of a study of costs made by the Cost Department of
DIRINCO.

Because of the very favorable demand conditions in Chile
throughout most of the 1960s, there has been no incentive for firms
to sell at below the official prices. In fact, prices have tended to
rise in real terms, and between 1964 and 1968 they increased by
20 percent.[27] Similarly, there was little incentive for firms to
resort to any other type of competitive behavior in order to improve
their market position. It was only in the last years of the period
that the situation changed significantly (see Chapter 6).

Table 8.6 shows the price of cars by market segments. The
market segments that can be identified in Chile are small cars (less
than 1,100 cc), medium (1,100 to 2,000 cc), and U.S. compacts
(over 2,000 cc). Unlike Argentina, cars in the intermediate category and larger U.S. models were not produced in Chile in 1970.
Table 8.7 (based on Table 8.6) shows that, apart from the case
of U.S. compacts, all of which are very similarly priced, there
is more price dispersion within each market segment in Chile than
there was in Argentina. This is not surprising, however, if one
remembers that prices are in fact controlled by the government
and, therefore, firms are not free to take account of the prices
being charged by other companies.

It has not been possible to obtain global figures for advertising
expenditure in the Chilean automotive industry. Data for individual
firms do not appear to be very different from the figures found for
Argentina. Thus, in 1970 Fiat's advertising expenditure was 0.83
percent of its total turnover and Citroen's was 0.92 percent. In

TABLE 8.6

Prices of Chilean Cars by Market Segment, July 1970

(escudos)

Small		Medium		U.S. Compacts	
Austin Mini	57,617	Datsun 1300	78,364	Chevrolet II Nova	118,198
Citroen AZAM	42,731	Fiat 1500	81,680	Dodge Dart 290	116,090
Citroen AZU	40,260	Peugeot 404	95,146	Ford Falcon	118,198
Fiat 600	48,198	Skoda Combi	74,595	Acadian	120,584
Renault 4L	51,879				

Source: Comisión Automotriz (unpublished data).

TABLE 8.7

Average Price and Dispersion by
Market Segment
(escudos)

	Small	Medium	U.S. Compacts
Mean	48,137	82,446	118,268
Standard deviation	6,985	8,948	1,836
Coefficient of variation	14.5%	10.85%	1.55%

terms of advertising per car produced, this came to $38.3 and $25.3, respectively. As the figures for Fiat indicate (see Table 8.8), however, high levels of advertising occurred during the late 1960s and early 1970s when demand conditions were unfavorable. Subsequently, the emergence of excess demand once more under the Unidad Popular led to a reduction in the level of advertising.

Similarly, the other forms of competition observed in Argentina were not very important in Chile throughout the greater part of the 1960s. Model diversification, for example, has been extremely limited. Almost all firms produce one or at most two basic models, usually one car and one commercial vehicle, as in the case of

TABLE 8.8

Fiat Advertising Expenditure, 1965-73
(escudos)

	Total Advertising	Percent of Sales	Advertising per Car (U.S. dollars)
1965	6,231	0.03	1.8
1966	15,444	0.04	2.1
1967	66,526	0.14	9.1
1968	619,116	0.50	18.9
1969	1,637,000	0.78	26.5
1970	2,911,000	0.83	38.3
1971	6,628,493	1.31	n.a.
1972	7,610,000	0.75	n.a.
1973	7,229,792	0.24	n.a.

*Converted at free market exchange rate.
Source: Company accounts.

Citroen and General Motors. In contrast to what was observed in Argentina, in Chile the reduction in the number of firms was accompanied by a reduction in the number of models produced from 37 in 1962 to 22 in 1970, to only 13 in 1971. Model changes have not been used as a competitive weapon in the industry, although changes have occurred quite frequently in response to changes in the models produced by the parent company or licensor, which it has been easy to reproduce in Chile since bodies and other parts are imported. This has made possible many variations that can be incorporated without altering any of the parts produced in Chile, which need to be amortized over a longer time period.

The growth of installment finance is a feature of the late 1960s and was absent for most of the period that is being considered. As was indicated in Chapter 6, credit to the consumer was relatively unimportant before 1968, being extended for less than a year with an average downpayment of 50 percent. Even in 1968, the disequilibrium between supply and demand meant relatively high downpayments.[28] It was only with the changing market conditions in 1969 and 1970 that credit to dealers and to the public assumed significant proportions. There is little uniformity in the terms that are offered to dealers, either in the length of time for which credit is extended or in the initial downpayment. (See Table 8.9.)

Mexico

In Mexico, as in Chile, price competition in the automotive industry has been limited by government control of prices. The prices of foreign makes are not allowed to exceed their prices in the country of origin by more than a certain percentage determined by the Secretaría de Industria y Comercio. The manufacturers have concentrated their attention on getting the price ceilings raised rather than attempting to cut prices below the official level. If they are to be believed, these ceilings are unreasonably low and they certainly would not wish to cut prices further. Moreover, even if this were not the case, they provide a convenient level for tacit price collusion. Government incentives in terms of additional quotas for price reductions have not proved sufficiently attractive for them to be used widely.

What is found again in Mexico appears to be model-price competition, although the different segments of the market are not as clearly separated as in the other cases considered. Table 8.10 gives the four main market segments identified by AMIA, the others not given being subcompacts, which includes only one model (Opel), and sports cars.

TABLE 8.9

Credit Terms to Dealers in Chile

	1968–69		October 1969		July 1970	
	Cash	Credit	Cash	Credit	Cash	Credit
Citroen	50	3 to 7	50	3	40	7
Fiat 600	55	7	45	10	60	6
Austin Mini	60	6	55	6	60	6
Renault	n.a.	n.a.	30	2	39	2
Fiat 1500	60	4	60	3	68	2
						(Fiat 125)
Peugeot	100*	—	100*	—	50	2
Datsun	50	6	50	2	n.a.	n.a.
Dart	30	6 to 8	n.a.	n.a.	40	6
Falcon	n.a.	n.a.	40	4	40	3
Chevrolet	100	—	100	—	100	—

*Advance payment made by dealer.

Note: Cash is given in percent, credit is given in months.

Sources: Instituto de Costos, Estudio Sobre la Industria Automotriz (Santiago, 1969), Table 73; and own investigation.

TABLE 8.10

Prices of Mexican Cars by Market Segment, 1971
(pesos)

Popular		Compact	
Renault R4L	23,800	Valiant Duster	45,363
Renault R8	28,986	Dodge Dart	48,087
Renault R10	31,047	Falcon Maverick	46,215
Datsun 1500	33,203	Rambler American	44,506
Volkswagen 1500	28,825		

Standard		DeLuxe	
Rambler Classic	54,585	Dodge Monaco	80,901
Chevrolet Chevelle	56,012	Ford Galaxie	81,363
Dodge Coronet	66,150	Chevrolet Impala	76,988

Note: Four-door versions when there is a choice of two- or four-door.

Source: Nacional Financiera (unpublished data).

TABLE 8.11

Average Price and Dispersion by
Market Segment
(pesos)

	Mean	Standard Deviation	Coefficient of Variation (percent)
Popular	29,172	3,492	11.97
Compact	46,043	1,531	3.33
Standard	58,916	6,306	10.7
Deluxe	79,751	2,404	3.01

Source: Secretaría de Industria y Comercio, Dirección General de Estadísticas, Annario Estadística de los Estados Unidos Mexicanos, 1960-61 and . . . 1968-69 (Mexico, 1962; 1971).

As Table 8.11 (based on Table 8.10) shows, two of the four groups considered have a very low degree of dispersion, tending to confirm the hypothesis that what is observed is model-price competition. In the case of popular cars, where the highest dispersion is observed, this can be explained by the fact that the group includes one car, the Renault 4, which is much smaller than the others and which would have been included in a different group in Argentina or Chile. If this is taken into account, then the degree of dispersion is roughly similar to that found in Argentina. Since prices have remained virtually frozen for several years, changes over time during the period since 1965 have been insignificant.

Advertising has been a significant feature of the Mexican automotive industry throughout the 1960s. Both in 1960 and in 1968, advertising expenditure amounted to slightly less than 1 percent of the value of the industry's total sales, a level that was only attained in Argentina at the end of the decade.[29] The total amount spent by the industry in 1968 came to 57,409,000 pesos, which represented an average expenditure per car of U.S. $31.2, slightly less than in Argentina. Data on individual companies seem to confirm these orders of magnitude. Thus, in 1970-71, VAM's advertising expenditure was 1.5 percent of its total turnover, while that of Automex was about 1 percent (figures based on author's investigations).

As with advertising, model diversity has been a feature of the Mexican automotive industry throughout the decade. It has already been indicated that when the Mexican automotive industry was essentially an assembly industry, a large number of different makes were available locally and an even greater number of different models. The number of firms was considerably reduced when manufacturing operations were begun, but each firm still produced a large number of different models, facilitated incidentally by the decision not to enforce local production of the major body stampings.

The number of different models of cars being produced in Mexico has fluctuated around 40 since 1965. This meant, in 1973, an average production of 4,950 units per model, almost the same as the corresponding figure for Argentina. The only model to be produced on a reasonably large scale in 1973 was the Volkswagen with an output of 62,914. Otherwise, the only models to have an output of more than 10,000 a year was the Datsun 1500 with 16,391 and the Chrysler Valiant Duster with 10,822. When comparing these figures with Argentina, one should bear in mind that small scale is likely to have less effect on costs in Mexico because of the higher import content.

The same considerations apply when one looks at model changes over time. In Argentina the high cost of dies for body stamping makes it necessary to maintain a basic model unchanged for a minimum of five years in order to amortize the investment, while in Mexico some firms make annual model changes. One must distinguish here between European and Japanese cars, which have a longer model life both in their country of origin and in Mexico, and the U.S. cars, which change annually. Of the former, Datsun, with a drastic model change in 1968, has used this as a weapon to increase market penetration, with considerable success, and DINA, in 1971, replaced the Renault 10 by the Renault 12. The producers of U.S. cars have a model year beginning slightly later than the U.S. model year in order to use U.S. parts and follow the U.S. model changes. As a result, the Volkswagen 113 sedan is the only car to have achieved a model run in excess of 100,000, with 291,941 being produced between 1965 and 1973.

As has already been indicated in Chapter 6, hire purchase facilities had come to be quite widely used in the sale of cars by the late 1960s. Generally speaking, the tendency has been for sales to the dealers to be made on a cash basis and for the dealers themselves to finance sales to the public from their own resources with the aid of financial institutions. Some firms do tend to provide assistance to their dealers and all tend to do so at the end of the model year. Renault only makes 30 percent of its sales to the dealers on a cash basis. Automex gave credit to dealers until about 1970, but the scheme has since been discontinued, while Ford sells to its dealers for cash, but intercedes with a local financial institution to provide credit for sales to the public.

TABLE 8.12

Distribution of Sales by Dealers According to
Length of Credit Granted, 1968
(percent)

Months	Small	Compact	Standard
0	48.0	42.8	41.9
0 to 12	21.9	25.6	26.7
12 to 24	29.6	30.8	30.5
24+	0.5	0.8	0.9

Source: J. Foncerrada Moreno and H. Vazquez Tercero,
Informe Económico (Mexico City: Asociacion Nacional de Distribuidores de Automóviles, 1969), p. 84.

As can be seen from Table 8.12, sales on credit vary from
52 to 58 percent of total sales, and over 30 percent of sales are
repayable over a period of more than a year. This does not indicate
the minimum downpayments involved, which tend to vary from firm
to firm. In the small car section of the market, deposits are low,
with Datsun requiring only 18 percent cash down and Volkswagen
introducing a similar plan with a cash payment of 21 percent in
1969. Renault, in the early 1970s, was selling for 20 to 25 percent
down. Thus, it appears that in at least one section of the market,
installment finance has reached substantial proportions. Significantly, this is a sector in which competition has been particularly
intense and where a supply shortage during the 1960s has been
rectified.

A Comparison of Competition in the
Three Countries

It is useful at this point to compare the forms of competition
that have been observed in each of the three countries, relating
them to the different demand and supply conditions in each case.
The most striking common characteristic of the industry in the
three countries is the lack of price competition and the tendency
of firms to follow the model-price competition pattern characteristic
of the developed countries, giving rise to well-defined market
segments in each country. As a result, the nonprice forms of competition characteristic of the developed countries have been transferred to Latin America to a greater or lesser extent depending on
market conditions in the host country concerned.

Here the most significant difference is that which marks Chile off from Argentina and Mexico. For most of the period, demand conditions were extremely favorable for the Chilean automotive industry, and as a result nonprice competition did not become significant until the end of the 1960s. Advertising expenditure did not acquire substantial proportions until 1968, while model diversity and model changes did not play the same role as in Argentina and Mexico. Similarly, hire purchase facilities were much less developed in Chile even at their peak. For example, the Renault 4, which was sold in Argentina for a minimum deposit of 30 percent and a maximum repayment period of 30 months, and in Mexico for a downpayment of 25 to 30 percent and a repayment period of 24 months, required 56 percent cash and the remainder in 12 monthly quotas in Chile. The Peugeot 404, which was sold for 45 percent cash in Argentina with a repayment period of up to 36 months, needed a 47.3 percent deposit with only a 12-month payback period in Chile.

MARKET FRAGMENTATION AND LOCAL COSTS

One of the features of what has been called here premature oligopolization in the Latin American automotive industry is that concentration has ceased to increase while firms are still below the optimal size from the point of view of economies of scale in production. The genesis of market fragmentation in the Latin American automotive industry and the failure of competition to rationalize market structures have already been analyzed. In this section, the consequences of the existing market structure for production costs in Argentina, Chile, and Mexico will be analyzed.

In this context the key concept is that of economies of scale.* It must be emphasized, however, that scale economies are not simply a technological relationship but also an economic one, since the cost curves from which they are derived assume certain factor prices. This implies that it is not possible to make universally valid statements about the minimum optimum scale of production, or the disadvantages of small-scale production, in a particular industry. Such statements are only meaningful when they refer to a particular economy at a given moment in time. It is not, therefore, possible to use the estimates of economies of scale referred to previously in discussing the automotive industry in the advanced

---

*See Appendix A for a discussion of the origins of economies of scale in production.

industrial countries (see Chapter 2 and Appendix A) when analyzing
the Latin American automotive industry. Rather, each case must
be considered on its own merit. This conclusion is reinforced when
it is remembered that costs in the automotive industry depend not
only on output but also on the number of models being produced,
the length of life of these models, and the level of local integration.

There are two aspects of the level of output that are important
from the point of view of economies of scale: the total market for
the industry as a whole and the level of output for each individual
firm.[30] The former determines the scale of production for certain
standardized components that are generally bought out, while the
latter determines the scale for engines and the main body parts that
give the vehicle its distinctive characteristics and are generally
produced by the terminal manufacturer itself, as well as for final
assembly. The need to distinguish between these two aspects of
output has been mentioned in the literature on the Latin American
automotive industry,[31] but little has been done by way of analyzing
the contribution made by each of these two factors to diseconomies
of scale in the industry. Indeed, the implicit assumption of much
of the work on regional integration is that it is the small size of
industry output that is responsible for the high cost of vehicles.[32]

In Argentina the total market for vehicles in 1971 was over
250,000 units, while the average output per firm was only 25,000.
Until 1970, the average output per firm was less than 20,000, a
figure that compared with several hundred thousands in the advanced
industrial countries. Since Argentina had achieved a high level of
local content during the 1960s, it is to be expected that such low
volumes of production would lead to high costs. In fact, Argentinian
car prices are about twice as high as those of the same car in its
country of origin.[33]

The Argentinian automotive industry has been the subject of
a detailed study of the factors that contribute to the high prices of
vehicles. This study, undertaken by the Comisión de Estudios
Económicos de la Industria Automotriz,[34] involved a minute breakdown of all the factors that contributed to the excess cost of Argentinian vehicles. It concluded that the average Argentinian car in
1967 cost 122 percent more than in the country of origin. Fifty-seven
percent, or almost half of this excess cost, could be accounted for
by the low scale of production in Argentina, and this could be further
broken down into 44 percent accounted for by differences in scale
economies in the terminal industry and 13 percent by differences in
the parts industry.[35]

One defect of the study is the fact that the excess cost attributable to a lack of scale economies was calculated using data from the
advanced industrial countries, and not from an examination of the

Argentinian automotive industry itself. There are two reasons for supposing that this has not led to large errors in the estimate of the cost penalty due to small-scale production. First, the study was able to account for all but 2 percent of the total excess cost, which suggests that the effect of economies of scale could not have been greatly underestimated or overestimated. Second, the effect of different factor prices is not likely to have distorted the results a great deal since the capital-labor ratio does not change much with increases of output at scales above 25,000 cars a year.[36]

It is by no means surprising that this study concludes that the greater part of the price inefficiency of the Argentinian automotive industry is accounted for by the low volumes of production in the terminal industry, and that only a secondary role is attributed to the parts industry. The relevant scale of production from the point of view of the terminal industry is that of the individual firm for virtually all purposes. A fully integrated plant producing 25,000 vehicles a year has excess costs of more than 100 percent for machining, stamping, foundry, and forge operations.[37] Thus, if it is assumed that the average plant in Argentina produced at this level, with an in-plant content of 45 percent of the total vehicle and an average excess cost of 100 percent for all operations, the contribution made to the increased price by a lack of economies of scale in the terminal sector would be almost exactly the same as that calculated by the Comisión de Estudios Económicos de la Industria Automotriz.

In terms of the earlier discussion, the relevance of the distinction between those costs that arise in the terminal sector and those that arise in the parts sector is that the former are clearly a consequence of the fragmentation of the market between a large number of firms. The fact that costs of production are so high among the terminal firms is due not to the small absolute size of the Argentinian market but to its division between ten firms. Nor can the entire contribution made by the lack of economies of scale in the auxiliary industry be attributed to the low volume of total production. The parts industry is also highly fragmented with a number of firms producing the same parts and components.[38] This is at least partly because of the desire of the terminal producers to set up "captive" suppliers.[39] Even where the number of suppliers is not excessive, the terminal producers may demand different specifications from their suppliers. Thus the fragmentation of the terminal industry contributes directly to the lack of economies of scale in the parts industry.

It can be concluded, therefore, that the most important factor accounting for the high prices of vehicles in Argentina is the loss of economies of scale as a result of the fragmentation of the market, while the small size of the total market has merely been a secondary factor.* This goes a long way to explain why Sweden, with a total production in 1971 of around 317,000 vehicles, has one of the most internationally competitive automotive industries in the world, while Argentina, with an output of only 60,000 less in the same year, has one of the highest cost industries. In Sweden there are only two firms, Volvo and Saab-Scania, whereas in Argentina there are ten.

Like that of Argentina, the Chilean automotive industry is also characterized by a high degree of market fragmentation between a large number of firms. Despite a considerable reduction in the number of firms and an increase in local production, average output was still less than 3,000 vehicles per firm in 1971. It has been seen previously in Chapter 7 how the Chilean government used local content requirements and price control to bring about increased levels of concentration in the industry. By the late 1960s, the limits of this policy had virtually been reached, with almost all of the remaining firms having well over the required local content or being able to increase it through imports from other LAFTA countries.[40]

The breakdown of costs given in Table 8.13 indicates that the main factor accounting for the high costs of vehicles in Chile, relative to the countries from which they originate, is the high duties paid on parts imported from third countries (that is, countries outside LAFTA). These consisted of a specific duty of $1.50 oro per kilo net of parts imported, an ad valorem duty of 17 percent, and an additional tax of 100 percent on the CIF value of all parts except the engine, for which the duty is only 5 percent. Thus, custom duties come to about twice the FOB price of parts imported and that imported parts have the highest ratio of Chilean price relative to the price in the country of origin.

If these duties are eliminated, Chilean vehicles have an excess cost of 152.1 percent. Of this, 56.6 percent arises in the parts industry and 51.6 percent in final assembly, the remainder being attributable to freight and insurance charges, the inefficiency of parts imported from other LAFTA countries relative to the country of origin, and any overpricing of imported parts that takes place. Some of the excess cost that arises both in parts production and in final assembly can be attributed to small scales of production as a

---

*The other important factors in explaining the high price of local vehicles were the high prices of certain raw materials, import duties, taxes, and distribution costs. The last mentioned could be a result of diseconomies of scale in distribution stemming from a large number of terminal firms each operating their own distribution systems.

TABLE 8.13

Structure of Costs in the Chilean
Automotive Industry, 1969

Item (1)	Percent Despiece (2)	Excess Cost Factor (3)	Inefficiency (4)	(2) × (4) (percent) (5)
Imported parts	40.9	Custom duties	2.00	81.8
		CIF costs	0.25	10.2
		Overpricing	0.22	9.0
LAFTA exchanges	13.7	Custom duties	0.19	2.6
		CIF costs	1.10	15.1
		Exchange loss	0.59	8.0
Local parts	40.4	Economies of scale	0.42	17.0
		Other	0.99	39.6
Production costs	5.0	Economies of scale	2.00	10.0
		Other	8.32	41.6
				233.9

Source: Own elaboration based on F. Gil Mitjans, "Un Modelo de Programación de la Industria Automotriz Chilena" (professional thesis, Universidad de Chile, 1969).

result of the fragmentation of the market between a large number of firms.

In the case of parts, it has been estimated that Chilean parts are 2.41 times as expensive as the FOB price of the same parts in the country of origin (see Table 8.13). It has also been shown that an increase in the scale of output from 1,000 to 8,000 cars a year would reduce the cost of parts to the assembler by about 17.5 percent[41] to a level just under twice the FOB price. Since the cost calculations have been made on the basis of existing technologies, whereas larger volumes of output would make possible the use of new technologies in some cases, 17.5 percent is an underestimate of the reduction in costs as a result of an increase in production to 8,000 cars a year. It should be noticed also that a large part of the remaining inefficiency (classified under other in the table) is due to the loss of economies of scale even at the higher level of production,[42] rather than to distortions such as the high price of raw materials. The relevance of the 17.5 percent figure is that it represents a scale of production that could have been achieved with a more rational productive structure during the late 1960s.

The highest level of inefficiency is found in production costs, that is, the costs of assembly, and the overheads of the terminal firm. This derives in part from the fact that the despiece value of vehicles has been taken as the base for comparison. This allows only 5 percent for the costs of final assembly, and so on, which, judging by most estimates, seems to be on the low side.[43] Other factors tending to contribute to the high excess cost of this section may be inefficient management, high profit rates, low capacity utilization, and, of course, economies of scale. It has already been argued that economies of scale are less significant in assembly than in the other processes involved in the production of vehicles, so that the cost disadvantage of small scale will be less in Chile where the engine and body are imported than in Argentina.

It is difficult to obtain estimates of assembly costs for volumes of output as low as 1,000 vehicles per year. Table 8.14 indicates that projecting backward, one may obtain an estimate of costs for final assembly of 1,000 units that would be somewhere in the region of twice what could be obtained at volumes of 10,000 units. Unfortunately, no other estimates are known that isolate assembly costs at low volumes of output against which this can be checked.

On the basis of these data, an increase in the average production by Chilean firms from 1,000 to 8,000 to 10,000 cars a year would only reduce the excess cost of Chilean vehicles by about 11 percent (27/234) and the excess cost excluding import duties by 18 percent (27/152). Obviously, increases to the level of production of 40,000+ per model, planned for 1980 under the Unidad Popular's program for the automotive industry, would lead to much greater cost reduction. This brings out the point that in Chile, unlike Argentina, the small size of the total market, as well as its fragmentation between a number of firms, are important factors accounting for the high level of local costs.

A more rational structure of production, although bringing about some reduction in costs, would still leave them considerably higher than in the country of origin, and the only hope of attaining efficient scales of production would be through regional integration as proposed, for example, within the Andean Pact. A more rational structure and regional integration would both make possible a further reduction in costs as a result of the elimination of some of the tariffs on imports of parts. Larger volumes of output per firm would make higher levels of local content economic, while the proposed regional integration of the industry within the Andean Pact would both give rise to further economies of scale and reduce the incidence of customs duties in the cost of the vehicle.[44]

In order to arrive from the cost figures given above to the price to the public, it is necessary to add the profit of the producer

TABLE 8.14

Index of Costs in the Assembly of Vehicles
(300,000 = 100)

3,500	300
5,000	245
10,000	215
25,000	185
50,000	155
100,000	122
200,000	103

Source: C. Sicard, Les Relations Cout-Volume dans l'Industrie Automobile, UNIDO (ID/WG 76/17), 1970.

and the dealer and also the sales tax. Taking the factory cost as 100, the profit of the producer was 7.7 and the dealer's (gross) profit 18.3, while the sales tax (9.4 percent of the price to the public) came to 13.1.[45] Thus, the final price to the public comes to 139.1, a markup of almost 40 percent on the cost of production. This does not seem to be significantly different from the markup normally found in the country of origin of the models produced,[46] so that the ratio of Chilean prices to prices in the country of origin is roughly equal to the ratio of Chilean costs to FOB costs in the country of origin. This, however, means higher absolute levels per car produced in Chile because of the higher level of cost.

A rationalization of production would reduce these costs, not only indirectly by reducing the base on which they are calculated but also directly by a corresponding rationalization of the distribution system. Thus, one can see that the high margins of dealers, relative to those in the country of origin in absolute terms, is a function partly of the high cost of local production, which means that stocks of vehicles and parts are more expensive to hold, and credit requirements greater, partly of the low average sales volumes. Thus, in the latter half of the 1960s, around 300 dealers made sales that varied between 10,000 and 20,000 vehicles. Data for 1968 indicate that some dealers managed to sell only one car (the Ford and Nun y German dealers in the province of Cautin and the Austin dealer in Valdivia).[47]

Insofar as there are economies of scale in the distribution of cars, then a reduction in the number of firms could reduce the dealer margin in Chile. It has been estimated[48] that distribution costs per unit fall from 130 with annual sales of cars of 100 a year

to 100 at a volume of 600 a year. Since some Chilean dealers sell
the vehicles of more than one firm, the total number of different
dealers is 240. Sales in 1969 were a little over 22,000, giving an
average per dealer of 92 units. A reduction in the number of dealers
to around 40 would reduce the total costs of distribution by more than
20 percent.*

The Mexican automotive industry also displays a considerable
degree of market fragmentation with an average output per firm of
only 17,570 in 1971. Prices of cars in Mexico are higher than in
the country of origin by between 30 and 65 percent, depending on the
segment of the market.[49] These represent lower levels of excess
cost than are found in most other Latin American countries.

Table 8.15 shows that in Mexico by far the most important
factor behind the high cost of local vehicles is the high cost of local
materials, which accounts for 36 percent of the total excess cost
of 42 percent. It has not been possible to calculate how far the
excess price of local parts is owing to a lack of scale economies
in the industry. One survey of a number of parts producers suggests
that it may be significant since 77 percent of the firms interviewed
mentioned the size of the market as one of the factors accounting
for the high price of their product.[50] This, however, does not
indicate the quantitative importance of small scale, especially since
all the firms studied mentioned the cost of locally produced inputs
as a factor making for high costs. Other factors also mentioned
were the cost of working capital, the cost of imported inputs, labor
costs, the costs of technology, and the incidence of taxes.

Since the major body parts, which are subject to large-scale
economies, are imported to Mexico, one would expect the excess
cost of local production to be less than in Argentina. There are
two studies available that attempt to measure the impact of scale
on costs in the Mexican automotive industry, taking account of the
particular local content requirements. The Wassink study[51] uses
the Maxcy and Silberston[52] data suitably adjusted to take account
of the less advanced industrial structure, lower wage rates, and
40 percent import content in Mexico, while that of Martinez[53] is
the increase in price of a Renault Dauphine (excluding the body) at
different levels of output. If one takes the average output per firm
of the late 1960s as around 12,500, then it appears that a large part
of the excess cost of Mexican production is due to the fragmentation
of the market. Orvananos has estimated, using Wassink's data,

---

*Owing to different factor prices in Chile, the shape of the
cost curve may, of course, be different from that estimated by
Pashigan.

TABLE 8.15

Direct Cost Structure in the Mexican
Automotive Industry, Late 1960s

Item	Local Costs (percent)	Country of Origin Costs (percent)	Inefficiency (percent)
Foreign materials	35.05	45.97	1.08
Local materials	51.70	36.71	1.99
Fuel, auxiliary materials	1.48	0.77	2.73
Electric energy	0.37	0.19	2.77
Wages and salaries	5.13	6.34	1.15
Other direct costs	2.12	6.05	0.50
Depreciation and amortization	4.15	3.97	1.48
Total	100	100	1.42

Source: Own elaboration based on R. Viscaino Velasco,
"La Industria Automotriz Mexicana: Análisis, Evaluación y Perspectivas" (professional thesis Escuela Superior de Economía, 1969).

that a reduction in the number of firms so that one company produced 120,000 vehicles would reduce costs by around 34 percent, or more than three quarters of the total excess.[54] If one takes Martinez's data, the cost reduction of an increase in output to 100,000 units would be of the order of 21 percent, that is, half of the total excess cost. (See Table 8.16.)

As in the case of Argentina, therefore, it can be concluded that the fragmentation of the Mexican automotive industry has been a much more important factor in explaining the high price of locally produced vehicles than the small absolute size of the market. This finding contradicts the usual argument that what is needed is regional integration in order to obtain larger markets.[55] While this is true for the countries of the Andean Pact, the main requirement for reducing costs in Argentina and Mexico is a rationalization of the structure of production.

This, however, will not come about, as some writers projecting from the experience of the new developed countries suppose, by the operation of the market mechanism.* The implications of

---

*Munk, discussing the large number of producers in Latin American countries, states that, "If the American experience is

TABLE 8.16

Economies of Scale in the Mexican
Automotive Industry
(Import = 100)

	A	B
8,000	153	n.a.
12,500	144	122
20,000	n.a.	117
25,000	130	n.a.
50,000	112	108
100,000	n.a.	101

Sources: Line A: D. Wassink, "Commercial Policy and
Development: A Study of the Automobile Industry in Developing
Countries" (Ph.D. thesis, Stanford University, 1968; Line B:
Constantino Martinez Tamayo, "La Mexicanización de la Industria
Automotriz: 'Caso Diesel Nacional, S. A.'" (professional thesis,
Universidad Nacional Autónoma de México, 1963).

continued market fragmentation are twofold. First, as was seen in
Chapter 6, the high prices that result in the domestic market confirm the demand for cars to a relatively limited high income group,
preventing the development of a mass market. Second, as will be
discussed, it makes it difficult to expand through penetration of
foreign markets.

In the discussion so far, attention has been concentrated on
two factors, the size of the overall market and the average firm
size. As was indicated previously, these are only two aspects of
the scale problem; it is also necessary to take account of the diversity of models and the frequency of model changes. An increase in
the number of models produced by a firm will certainly increase its
costs.* It results in shorter production runs for those parts that
are not common to all models, more detailed planning of product
flows within the plant, and larger inventories of parts and components.

---

used as a guide, such fragmentation is unlikely to persist."[56] This
overlooks the fact that the American experience cannot be used as
a guide to developments in dependent economies.

*It was with good reason that Henry Ford said, referring to
the Model T, "They can have any color they like as long as it's
black."

Pratten indicates that in Britain the costs of production of a firm producing three basic bodies and five basic engines would be more than 25 percent greater than that of a firm producing only one model, at a level of output of 100,000 vehicles a year.[57]

Some of these additional costs would not have to be borne by a subsidiary in an underdeveloped country since they include the initial research and development costs of developing a number of models. The cost penalty of model diversity will also reflect the level of local integration. The costs of producing a number of models are likely to be greater in Argentina, because the major body parts are stamped there, than in Mexico or Chile. Nevertheless, even in cases where there is only a limited local content, costs will increase as a result of diversity.[58] Thus, the form of competition observed in the last section, which led to a proliferation of models especially in Argentina and Mexico, is likely to have increased further the level of costs in those industries.

The length of life of models is a further important factor in determining production costs. Unlike model diversity, it has little effect on assembly costs, so that for plants with low levels of local content there is little incentive to keep models in production over a long time period.[59] The period over which a model is kept in production becomes much more significant at high levels of integration, especially when the major body stampings are produced locally. It has been estimated that extending a model's life from two to ten years reduces the cost of the body by about 30 percent at an output of 25,000 units a year.[60] Other estimates suggest an even greater saving in body costs as a result of freezing models over a number of years.[61] Savings can also be made in engine manufacture by spreading tooling costs over a longer time period. But because engines are changed less often than bodies and a lot of the machinery used can be adapted to produce different engines, these savings are likely to be less significant than those in stamping.

It is not surprising, therefore, that model changes tended to be less frequent in Argentina than in Chile or Mexico. Nevertheless, as was observed in the previous section, production runs have been relatively short in Argentina, and only one model had been produced in more than 100,000 units by 1970. In Mexico, an official study in 1960 that recommended that the government should develop an automotive manufacturing industry emphasized the need to freeze models for a minimum of five years in order to amortize tooling, since it considered that a total output of 100,000 over the period would be required for production to be economic.[62]

The conclusion of this section, therefore, must be that the nature of oligopolistic competition in the international automotive industry, which has led to a fragmentation of Latin American markets between a large number of producers, has been a major factor contributing to the high cost of cars, especially in Argentina and Mexico. These costs also have been raised by the forms of competition employed by the multinational corporations in these markets, which have emphasized model diversity and model changes rather than longer production runs and cost reductions.

THE UTILIZATION OF CAPACITY

It was indicated earlier that the main characteristic of a monopolistic industry, in the sense in which the term has been used here, is that excess capacity is not eliminated by some firms being driven out of the industry. It is to be expected, therefore, that those industries that are dominated by foreign subsidiaries will be characterized by a low level of capacity utilization. The concept of full capacity is a tricky one that is often difficult to measure accurately. In this context, it will be taken as the level of output at which costs begin to rise sharply.[63]

There are problems of measurement, however, where different machines or production processes within a plant have different output capacities.[64] There are also difficulties in determining the number of shifts on the basis of which capacity output should be calculated. For example, if demand conditions are such that only one shift is worked, a firm may not know whether it would be technically feasible to operate three daily shifts, and would certainly not have a very precise notion of the output that could be obtained with a three-shift schedule.

In what follows, estimates made by the terminal firms themselves have been used for the calculation of capacity utilization rates. These may tend to exaggerate the potential increase in output that could be obtained for the industry as a whole by operating at full capacity, since bottlenecks may appear in the parts industry if all firms expand output simultaneously.

During the early years of the development of the Argentinian automotive industry, in 1960 and 1961, the backlog of demand ensured that capacity was more or less fully utilized.[65] The rate of construction of new capacity far exceeded the growth of output, however, so that utilization fell to about 65 to 70 percent in 1962 and to 42 percent in the recession of 1963. Although the recovery brought about an increase in utilization, as did the elimination of some of the locally owned firms during the mid-1960s, only 61 percent of capacity was used in 1967, rising slightly to 63 percent in 1970 and about 70 percent in 1973.

Despite the fact that it has risen somewhat in the last few years, capacity utilization in the Argentinian automotive industry still has not regained the high levels of the early 1960s. It is significant that the automotive industry has one of the highest levels of excess capacity among Argentinian industries. An ECLA study of 15 industries in 1964 showed only four sectors with capacity utilization of less than the 53 percent that we estimated for the automotive industry in that year, and all were within 5 percent of that figure.[66] The level of utilization also compares unfavorably with that found in the same industry in the developed countries.[67]

It has been suggested by A. O. Hirschman[68] that excess capacity in import-substituting industries is a result of overoptimistic projections of market demand. Two reasons why this might occur are suggested. First, the higher price of the domestic article compared to the imported one tends to lower demand; second, import statistics tend to overestimate the market for the new domestic industry because they include some speciality products that the latter cannot supply. Neither of these arguments is applicable to the case of the Argentinian automotive industry since imports before the initiation of local production could provide no guide to market potential. The only direct information on what firms saw as the market potential in the early 1960s is a study by Industrias Kaiser Argentina,[69] which estimated the total market for vehicles in 1970 at between 135,000 and 159,000, depending on the assumptions made. Since production in 1970 reached almost 220,000 units, this seems to suggest that firms were unduly pessimistic rather than the reverse.

Nevertheless, even if firms did not overestimate the total market, it is quite possible that each firm overestimated its expected share of that market, and since investment decisions are taken on the basis of this, excess capacity may have been created. Even where firms are not unduly optimistic about their future market shares, they may deliberately "build ahead of demand." Steindl explains at some length how, under oligopolistic market conditions, indivisibilities of plant, and economies of scale, this tendency will appear.[70] Fajnzylber suggests that this is a typical form of operation for international firms that have the finance available to build a larger plant than is justified by the existing size of the market.[71]

As has already been seen, scale economies and indivisibilities are particularly important in the automotive industry, and although the size of plant found in Argentina is far below what would be considered the minimal optimum scale in developed countries, there is evidence to suggest that foreign corporations investing in Argentina tended to build plants with a capacity far in excess of the initial demand for their products. Both Ford and General Motors built plants with a capacity of over 30,000 a year, although they did not achieve an output of 30,000 until 1965 and 1969, respectively.

The result of this process was that considerable excess capacity was created once all the plants were completed. Since this occurred in 1963 and coincided with a downturn in the overall level of activity, the fall in utilization was spectacular. The elimination of some firms meant that total capacity fell somewhat around the mid-1960s so that utilization figures improved but were still relatively low in the early 1970s. The period during which capacity appears to have been reduced as a result of exits from the industry was short-lived and any further increase in capacity utilization would appear to have to come from increased output. This is rendered more difficult by the fact that firms with high utilization figures, such as Fiat, are continuously expanding their capacity so that total capacity also has been increasing.

The same pattern is also evident in the case of Mexico. Since 1965, capacity utilization has fluctuated between 40 and 60 percent, suggesting that utilization in Mexico is even lower than in Argentina. This refers only to assembly operations, however; if engine manufacture is considered, there is even greater excess capacity. Thus, in 1965, there were six engine plants in Mexico with a total capacity of 400,000 units, operating at only 25 percent of full capacity. Despite this, by 1967, the number of plants had increased to ten and the total capacity to more than 600,000 engines.[72]

A comparison with other Mexican industries also suggests that excess capacity in the automotive industry is extremely high. A survey of 92 manufacturing enterprises in 1968 indicated that the industry was one of those in which a number of firms with low levels of utilization were found.[73] Perhaps even more significant was the fact that only 7.6 percent of the firms had levels of utilization below 50 percent, and that the modal class was between 80 and 90 percent, whereas utilization in vehicle assembly was only 45 percent in that year.

In the Mexican automotive industry, as in the Argentinian, there is a market structure that prevents this vast excess capacity from being eliminated. Here, however, it is reinforced by the quota system, which prevents some firms from fully utilizing their capacity and from driving out competitors that have less favorable demand conditions. The phenomenon of building ahead of demand observed in Argentina can be seen here on an even greater scale.[74] This is particularly evident in the case of engine plants where both Ford and Volkswagen built plants in the mid-1960s with a capacity of 100,000 engine blocks and heads a year, working two shifts. By 1971, the firms still did not produce enough vehicles to justify more than one shift working.

The fact that the Chilean automotive industry is essentially an assembly operation makes the estimation of the extent of capacity utilization rather difficult. Generally speaking, at low levels of technology with little investment in machinery and equipment, the concept of capacity tends to become meaningless since operations are not machine paced and capacity can be easily increased by employing more labor. This is particularly true of the early years of the industry's development in Chile; however, it is possible to arrive at some estimate of capacity for the late 1960s and early 1970s. The Instituto de Costos' study[75] put capacity at 36,000 in 1969, giving a degree of utilization of over 60 percent, but it should be noted that a one-shift schedule is the rule. Capacity was increased somewhat in the early 1970s to 44,250 in 1973, according to ODEPLAN estimates. The fall in production in that year gave rise to a very low level of capacity utilization of less than 40 percent.

Excess capacity in the Chilean automotive industry has not been a consequence of foreign firms building up capacity ahead of demand. The leading foreign firms had plants with one-shift capacity of only 3,000 to 6,000 cars in the late 1960s.[76] The plans to build new plants in the early 1970s by Renault, Peugeot, and General Motors may have indicated the beginnings of such a phenomenon had other firms followed suit, but the Unidad Popular's policy of restructuring the industry prevented further developments. Excess capacity, rather, must be explained by problems of supply, references to which abound in the literature on the Chilean automotive industry.[77] This applies not only to the quality and quantity of local parts supplied to the terminal industry and the difficulty of increasing exchanges with other LAFTA countries but also to the availability of skilled labor. The firms themselves almost invariably cite difficulties in meeting local content requirements as a result of the inadequacy of local parts production as the main factor accounting for underutilization of capacity.

The low levels of capacity utilization in these industries involve an immense waste of resources. It appears paradoxical that in economies that are conventionally regarded as being short of capital, a significant part of the productive capacity that has been constructed is lying idle. In addition, underutilization of capacity is a further factor contributing to high costs in the industry. In Argentina it was estimated that full utilization of capacity in 1968 could have reduced car prices by 10 percent.[78] Relative to the cost penalties imposed by a lack of economies of scale, this is small, but it must be remembered that it is when excess capacity exceeds 40 percent that costs begin to rise sharply in the automotive industry. In Mexico it was estimated that costs were 7 percent higher than at full capacity with excess capacity of 40 and 16 percent higher if excess capacity was 60 percent.

THE POSSIBILITIES OF DEVELOPING EXPORTS

Foreign domination of the Latin American automotive industry has made it difficult to develop exports for two basic reasons. First, as just seen, one of the consequences of the presence of multinational corporations has been to raise local production costs through market fragmentation and capacity underutilization, which means that exports are not competitive in third markets. Second, foreign firms may impose export restrictions on their subsidiaries or on the licensees with which they have contractual agreements in order to prevent them competing with the parent company or another affiliate in third countries. This is particularly prevalent in the case of locally owned licensees, whereas with wholly owned subsidiaries, control may be exercised directly through ownership.[79]

There is considerable evidence of such contractual limitations on exports in the Latin American automotive industry, although the extent of participation by wholly owned subsidiaries limits the degree to which explicit restrictions are used. The most detailed survey has been carried out in Argentina where it was found that only 3.4 percent of the contracts studied in the terminal automotive industry and the parts industry explicitly permitted exports.[80] On the other hand, 31.7 percent of the contracts required the permission of the licensor for exports to be made, and 29.1 percent permitted exports of parts incorporated in Argentinian vehicles (but this was more of a restriction than an authorization since exports of completed vehicles are so limited). Another method of discriminating against exports found in a number of contracts was a higher royalty charge on exports than on products destined for the domestic market.

In Chile there has been no in-depth study of contractual arrangements in the automotive industry, but a general study of licensing contracts in Chilean industry found that of the six cases examined in the automotive industry, half explicitly restricted exports through absolute prohibition, limitation to certain areas, or by requiring the written permission of the licenser.[81]

In Mexico a similar pattern emerges. Out of 16 contracts between terminal automotive manufacturers and foreign firms, only 5 were free from any export restrictions. Of the remainder, three required the permission of the licenser for exports to be made, three permitted parts to be exported only if they were incorporated in terminated vehicles, three permitted exports only when made via the licenser, and two restricted exports to a certain area.

As Table 8.17 shows, Argentinian exports of completed vehicles were negligible up to 1971, and despite a rapid expansion between 1972 and 1974 reaching a value of U.S. $71 million, less than 5 percent of the vehicles produced in Argentina were sold abroad

TABLE 8.17

Exports by the Argentinian Automotive
Industry, 1965-74
(thousands of U.S. dollars)

| | Completed Units | | | |
	Number	Value	Parts	Total
1965	88	189	817	1,006
1966	35	113	3,648	3,761
1967	58	112	6,796	6,908
1968	76	216	6,396	6,612
1969	459	2,675	7,312	9,987
1970	884	3,444	7,405	10,849
1971	601	3,329	13,667	16,996
1972	3,493	17,791	21,014	38,806
1973	11,214	53,300	40,285	93,586
1974	15,132	71,131	60,207	131,339

Sources: Asosiación de Fabricas de Automotores (ADEFA),
"Informe Estadistico," no. 611 (February 5, 1975), no. 622 (May 7,
1975), Table 1; 1974 Industria Automotriz Argentina (Buenos Aires:
1975).

in that year. The rapid growth of vehicle exports in recent years
is directly attributable to government policy, which has attempted
to increase exports using both carrot and stick. The stick in this
case is Decree 680/73, which only permits firms to increase their
car sales in Argentina by 8 percent a year if certain export quotas
are met. Thus, in 1974, firms must make exports equal to 15
percent of their sales in 1973, and this percentage is increased
each year to reach 100 percent by 1978. Firms that fail to meet
the required level of exports will have their domestic sales reduced
accordingly. This decree applies only to cars and there is no such
requirement for commercial vehicles. As a result, in 1974, the
first year in which the decree was in force, exports of cars more
than doubled while those of commercial vehicles increased only
marginally.

The carrot, which has also played a part in export promotion,
is a whole series of incentives, subsidies, and drawbacks provided
by the government. The most important of these are a subsidy of
35 percent for cars and 40 percent for commercial vehicles on the
FOB value, established by Decree 3864/72, and the repayment of
taxes paid on earlier stages of production. This latter is estimated

at about 11 percent of the FOB price for cars and over 18 percent
for a heavy truck. Taken together with a number of other smaller
incentives, such as those for exporting tires, the repayment of
freight and insurance charges (Decree 2864/72), and the incentive
for exports to new markets (Decree 2863/72), the total payments
received by an exporting company can amount to almost 60 percent
of the export price for cars and 75 percent for heavy trucks. To
this must be added a number of financial incentives provided by
the Central Bank for pre- and postsales financing, which give a
further subsidy of more than 5 percent of the price of the vehicle.
Moreover, some exports made by the industry are financed by loans
from the Argentinian government, such as the much publicized
exports to Cuba.

Although these subsidies, together with substantial devaluations
in 1971 and 1972, made exports profitable in late 1972 and early
1973, internal cost increases, which were not compensated for by
devaluations, eroded this position. The oil crisis and the downturn
in demand for cars worldwide have also made it more difficult for
Argentina to find markets for its vehicles. There are signs that
commercial vehicle exports are already declining, while it is only
the need to export in order to maintain a share of the domestic
market that is keeping up car exports.

Until 1973, exports of parts were more important than those
of built-up vehicles, but the rapid growth of the latter has reversed
the situation. During the 1960s, exports of parts were almost
entirely to Chile under the LAFTA complementation agreement
between the two countries, but the expansion of these exports was
limited by the restrictions placed by the Argentinian legislation on
imports from Chile, which cannot exceed 6 percent of the FOB
value of production of each firm. The small size of the Chilean
market and that country's desire to expand its own parts industry
were also factors limiting the growth of exports. Since 1970,
so-called pure exports of parts, not under complementation agreements, have acquired a certain significance, and by 1974 accounted
for about two thirds of the value of exported parts in that year.
These have also benefited from government subsidies, although to
a lesser extent than completed vehicles, since the subsidy established
by Decree 3804/72 is only 20 percent for parts compared to 35 percent on cars and 40 percent on trucks.*

———————

*Exports of CKD packs that contain more than 50 percent of the
total parts can, however, be counted as complete vehicles for the
purpose of the subsidy.

TABLE 8.18

Exports of Parts from Chile, 1965-73
(thousands of U.S. dollars)

	To Argentina	Total
1965	32.1	32.1
1966	689.0	689.0
1967	1,370.7	1,370.7
1968	5,572.0	5,572.0
1969	8,531.2	9,243.5
1970	7,040.9	8,443.7
1971	3,902.2	4,477.7
1972	n.a.	4,121.1
1973	n.a.	3,131.6

Source: Comisión Automotriz (unpublished data).

Not surprisingly, considering the high price of locally produced
vehicles, even compared with Argentina, Chile does not export any
completed vehicles. The late 1960s did, however, see a significant
development of exports of parts, mainly to Argentina (see Table 8.18).
The main factor behind the growth of Chilean exports of parts has
been the government's policy of increasing local content requirements, which has led to local firms undertaking exchanges under
the special complementation arrangements discussed above in order
to avoid having to invest in Chile or develop Chilean suppliers.[82]
In the absence of such arrangements, Chilean parts exports would
have been negligible. In any case, the major Chilean exports are
low technology parts, such as springs, radiators, and wheels, in
contrast to the high technology parts that are imported.

Mexican exports of finished vehicles have grown spectacularly
from 11 units in 1970 to 20,141 in 1973 (see Table 8.19). An examination of the figures, however, reveals that this is almost entirely
due to one firm, Volkswagen, exporting one model, the Safari 181,
to the United States. This is a novelty model not produced elsewhere
and therefore represents something of a special case, although it
does indicate the possibility of certain countries specializing in the
production of particular models. Compared to Argentina there is
a greater emphasis on the export of parts from Mexico than of
assembled vehicles. Thus, 1973 was the first year during which
completed vehicles accounted for more than 10 percent of the
industry's exports.

TABLE 8.19

Exports by the Mexican Automotive Industry, 1967-73
(thousands of U.S. dollars)

	Completed Units Number	Value	Parts	Total
1967	31	82.1	9,040.0	9,122.1
1968	12	18.5	10,720.0	10,738.5
1969	33	511.1	20,880.0	21,391.1
1970	11	224.6	36,480.0	36,704.6
1971	244	1,565.0	50,240.0	51,805.0
1972	2,212	5,728.8	75,871.2	81,600.0
1973*	20,141	40,415.5	112,195.2	152,610.7

*Preliminary.

Source: AMIA on the basis of Anuario Estadística del Comercio Exterior; Informe Estadístico, no. 100 (April 15, 1974), p. 2.

216

As in the case of Argentina, the growth of exports is largely a consequence of government policy. As mentioned previously, since 1969, the terminal producers have been obliged to cover an increasing proportion of their import requirements with exports. The Decree of October 24, 1972, which at present regulates the industry, set the proportion of import requirements that must be covered by exports at 40 percent for 1974 and this is programmed to reach 100 percent by 1979. Exports have also been promoted through a tax drawback of 11 percent of the value of exports, which, although not on the massive scale found in Argentina, has provided an additional stimulus to growth since 1972.

Further factors have been the relatively low prices of parts in Mexico compared to other Latin American countries and the proximity to the U.S. market. Mexico, thus, has been able to make use of the inherent advantages that multinational corporations have in developing export markets. The most important parts being exported in 1973 were engines and parts for the engine and transmission, each accounting for more than U.S. $20 million in export earnings. This indicates the possibility for some countries favorably placed of specializing in particular parts for export. However, as has been seen, the government's policy already has contributed to further denationalization of the Mexican automotive industry.

CAPITAL ACCUMULATION AND EMPLOYMENT CREATION

As discussed in Chapter 5, the automotive industry in the countries under consideration passed through a rather short-lived period of heavy investment associated with increases in local content requirements imposed by the host country governments. Otherwise, as the model put forward in the first section of this chapter implies, the oligopolistic structure of the industry has tended to keep investment low. This, together with the tendency for capital intensity to increase considerably in the industry,* has meant that employment creation has been rather limited. Since automotive manufacturing has been an import-substituting industry in these countries, it has not had a major effect in displacing workers in other sectors. Thus, in the following discussion, attention will be focused on the extent to which additional employment has been created within the industry.

---

*See Chapter 5 on the increase in the capital-output ratio. This has been accompanied by an increase in the capital-labor ratio, which is the relevant variable in this context.

New sources of employment obviously have been created by the development of the automotive industry, but the extent to which this has occurred is often exaggerated. In Argentina, for example, the industry trade association, ADEFA, claims that over 1.75 million people are directly or indirectly related to the industry. However, the terminal and parts industries employed directly 112,800 people in 1973, only slightly more than 1 percent of the economically active population. The remainder were employed in sales, repair and maintenance, petroleum refining, service stations, insurance, road works, and transport services, none of which can be said to depend on a local industry for its existence.* It should be pointed out, moreover, that not all of these 112,800 jobs can be credited to the development of a local manufacturing industry since there already existed a well-developed parts industry, producing for the replacement market, before 1959. Unfortunately, it is impossible to estimate exactly what proportion of these jobs would have existed in the absence of a local terminal industry. Comparison of the 1964 National Economic Census with the Industrial Census of 1954 indicates a growth of employment in the automotive industry and related sectors from just under 90,000 to over 120,000.

Although the classification is different for the two years, the groups taken broadly cover the same area of vehicle and parts production and repair. The fact that over this ten-year period, in which a domestic automotive industry was effectively created, employment appears to have increased by only 33,000 suggests that industry sources' claims as to employment generation have been exaggerated.

In Chile, the automotive industry is relatively insignificant as a source of employment because of its small weight (in terms of value added) within the manufacturing sector. Thus, although employment in parts production and assembly increased more than tenfold between the 1957 and 1967 census, this merely reflects the low base from which the industry started in the earlier year. Thus, total employment in 1967 was only 7,063 compared to total employment in industry in the same year of 580,000. This total was divided roughly equally between the parts industry and the terminal industry. In 1968, employment in the terminal industry was estimated at 3,952, while five years later in 1973 it had increased to 4,550.

---

*It should be noted, however, that in the absence of a local industry the total number of vehicles in circulation might well have been considerably less, thus reducing the demand for gasoline, service stations, and so on. On the other hand, the greater average age of the vehicle stock under such conditions might increase the demand for repair and maintenance.

The limited employment in the auxiliary industry is an indication of the latter's underdevelopment and the fact that a large proportion of the parts used by the terminals still comes from abroad.

Estimates of employment in the terminal automotive industry in Mexico are available from both the industry trade association, AMIA, and the Ministry of Industry and Commerce (SIC). The estimates made by the latter are considerably lower than those of the firms themselves. For example, in 1965, SIC census data gave a figure of only 13,838, compared to the 19,308 claimed by AMIA, and, in 1969, the corresponding figures were 21,937 and 29,091. If one takes the AMIA estimates, employment in the terminal industry increased more than fourfold between 1960 and 1970, mainly between 1963 and 1966. If employment in parts production is put at around 10,000 in 1960, this has grown even more spectacularly to reach 56,309 in 1970.[83] Again, however, most of the growth took place before 1966 when employment in the auxiliary industry was already about 52,000.[84]

Thus, one can estimate that total employment in the parts and terminal industries together increased more than four times between 1960 and 1966 and by only some 16 percent between 1966 and 1970. As has already been indicated, official government statistics suggest that employment creation in the industry was substantially less. Thus, according to the 1960 census, total employment in the production of vehicles and parts (including tires) was 18,488; by the time of the 1965 census it had reached only 40,018, which was substantially less than the figures of over 74,000 given by industry sources for the following year. It appears to be the case, therefore, that, although the development of the automotive industry generated considerable additional employment in the first half of the 1960s, this has been overestimated in unofficial statistics, and in the second half of the decade, there has been relatively little further growth. As a result, the automotive industry in 1970 employed less than 0.5 percent of the economically active population, even on the basis of the AMIA figures.[85]

CONCLUSION

This chapter has indicated that a number of features that were earlier identified as being characteristic of the Latin American automotive industry can be explained, at least in part, by the operations of the multinational corporations in that industry. The manner of operations was discussed, and it was found that, to a greater or lesser degree, the tendency was for the same forms of nonprice competition to be used as are current in the developed countries. This, together with the market fragmentation that has resulted from the nature of international competition in the automotive industry analyzed in Chapter 2, has led to high costs of production, high prices, low capacity utilization, an inability to develop exports, and only limited employment creation. Chapter 9 discusses how government policy has contributed to, or failed to avoid, these problems.

NOTES

1. Josef Steindl, Maturity and Stagnation in American Capitalism (Oxford: Blackwell, 1952).

2. P. Sylos-Labini, Oligopoly and Technical Progress (Cambridge, Mass.: Harvard University Press, 1962), pp. 103-31.

3. See, for example, R. Hilferding, El Capital Financiero, trans. V. Romano Garcia (Madrid: Editorial Tecnos, 1963); V. I. Lenin, Imperialism, the Highest Stage of Capitalism (Moscow: Progress Publishers, 1968); and N. Bukharin, Imperialism and World Economy (London: Merlin Press, 1972).

4. For example, Steindl, op. cit., and P. Baran and P. Sweezy, Monopoly Capital, An Essay on the American Economic and Social Order (London: Penguin, 1968).

5. B. Chinitz, "Contrasts in Agglomeration: New York and Pittsburgh," AER Papers and Proceedings 51 (1961), pp. 279-89.

6. See M. Merhav, Technological Dependence, Monopoly and Growth (Oxford: Pergamon Press, 1969), pp. 96-102, for an elaboration of these and other points.

7. U.S., Congress, Senate, Subcommittee on International Trade of the Committee on Finance, statement of General Motors Corporation, 1973.

8. P. Salama, Le Proces de Sous Développement (Paris: Maspero, 1972), pp. 95-108.

9. Sylos-Labini, op. cit., pp. 132-42.

10. E. Cimillo, E. Gastiazoro, and E. Lifschitz, "Acumulación y Centralización del Capital en la Industria Argentina" (Paper presented to the Congreso de Economía Política, Buenos Aires, November 1971), p. 16.

11. S. M. MacDonell and M. R. Lascano, La Industria Automotriz, Aspectos Económicos y Fiscales (Dirección General Impositiva, Departemento de Estudios, División Planes, June 1974), Table 40.

12. Ibid., Table 8.

13. B. C. Raddavero, "Análisis de la Transferencia de la Tecnología Externa a la Industria Argentina: El Caso de la Industria Automotriz," Económica 18 (1972): 367-88.

14. Consejo Nacional de Desarrollo (CONADE), Sector Industria y Minería, Diagnósticos Global y de Siderurgia y Métales, Fundición Ferrossa, Bienes de Capital, Industria Automotriz, Celulosa y Papel, Industria Textil, Industria Petroquímica (Buenos Aires, 1967).

15. MacDonell and Lascano, op. cit., Table 40.

16. La Opinion (May 22, 1974).

17. This is surprisingly much higher than the estimate arrived at by E. Acevedo and H. Vergara, but they used Banco Central data. E. Acevedo and H. Vergana, "Algunos Antecedentes Sobre Concentracion, Participacion Extranjera y Transferencia Tecnologica en la Industria Manufacturera en Chile" (Professional thesis, Universidad de Chile 1970).

18. Corporación de Fomento (CORFO), Censo de Regalías, in United Nations, Division of Public Finance and Financial Institutions, Arrangements for the Transfer of Operative Technology to Developing Countries: Case Study of Chile (ST/ECA/151/A), 1971, p. 64.

19. CORFO, División de Planificación Industrial, Las Inversiones Extranjeras en la Industria Chilena, 1960-69, Publicación No. 57-a/71, 1971.

20. B. Sepulveda and A. Chumacero, La Inversión Extranjera en México (Mexico City: Fondo de Cultura Económica, 1973), pp. 104-05.

21. Fernando Fajnzylber and Trinidad Martinez Tarrago, "Las Empresas Transnacionales, Expansión a Nivel Mundial y Proyección en la Industria Mexicana" (versión preliminar), mimeographed (Mexico: Centro de Investigacion y Docencia Economica, 1975), p. 517.

22. Industrias Kaiser Argentina (IKA), La Industria Automotriz Argentina (1963), p. 109.

23. L. J. White, The Automobile Industry Since 1945 (Cambridge, Mass.: Harvard University Press, 1971), pp. 222-27.

24. C. Pratten, Economies of Scale in Manufacturing Industry (Cambridge: Cambridge University Press, 1971).

25. Asociación de Concesionarios de Automotores de la República Argentina (ACARA), El Concesionario de Automotores en la Argentina. Examen de Su Situación Jurídica, Impositiva y Económico-Financiero (Mar del Plata, 1965), p. 136.

26. White, op. cit., Table 12.4.

27. Instituto de Costos, Estudio Sobre la Industria Automotriz (Santiago, 1969), Table 81. The deflator used was the consumer price index.

28. F. Cordova, L. Muxica, and G. Wagner, "Algunos Aspectos del Crédito al Consumo," Cuadernos de Economía 5 (1968): 30-50.

29. Departamento General de Estadisticas, Secretaría de Industria y Comercio.

30. This corresponds to the distinction between the optimum size of firm and optimum size of industry made by E. A. G. Robinson, The Structure of Competitive Industry, new ed. (Cambridge: Cambridge University Press, 1958), pp. 10-33, 118-26.

31. See, for example, B. Munk, "The Welfare Costs of Content Protection: The Automotive Industry in Latin America," Journal of Political Economy 77 (1969): 85-98.

32. See, for instance, J. Behrman, The Role of International Companies in Latin American Integration: Autos and Petrochemicals (Lexington, Mass.: D. C. Heath, 1972).

33. Economic Commission for Latin America (ECLA), Perspectivas y Modalidades de Integración Regional de la Industria Automotriz en America Latina, ECLA/DI/DRAFT/92, División de Desarrollo Industrial (1973), Table I.23.

34. Comisión de Estudios Económicos de la Industria Automotriz, La Industria Automotriz Argentina: Informe Económico 1969 (Buenos Aires: Asociación de Fabricas de Automotores [ADEFA], 1969).

35. A study carried out a year later came to similar conclusions. Local cars had an excess cost of 102 percent, of which 48 percent was accounted for by a lack of scale economies. Dirección Nacional de Estudios Industriales, Situación Actual y Perspectivas del Mercado de Automóviles en la Republica Argentina (Buenos Aires, 1969), pp. 41-42.

36. ECLA, op. cit., Table II.7. It is often thought that at larger volumes of output, production becomes more capital intensive as capital is substituted for labor. In the automotive industry, however, economies of scale are so important that the savings on capital costs equal or even exceed the savings on labor as output increases.

37. Ibid., pp. 128-50.

38. Comisión de Estudios Económicos de la Industria Automotriz, op. cit.

39. J. Baranson, Automotive Industries in Developing Countries, World Bank Staff Occasion Paper No. 8, 1969, p. 47.

40. On this point, see A. Aguilera Jorquera, "La Industria Automotriz Chilena y su Participación en el Sector Industrial" (professional thesis, Universidad de Chile, 1970), Chap. 8.

41. J. de Coyeneche Valdovinos, Economies of Scale in the Chilean Motor-Vehicle Industry, UNIDO (ID/WG. 76/4), 1970, p. 17.

42. ECLA estimates that parts have an excess cost due to a lack of economies of scale of 85 percent at an output of 10,000 vehicles a year. ECLA, Perspectivas, op. cit., Table II.33.